To: Brian
Welecome to visit my
Hometown
Rauf Naqishbendi

The Garden
of the Poets

Rauf Naqishbendi

PublishAmerica
Baltimore

First printing

PublishAmerica has allowed this work to remain exactly as the author intended, verbatim, without editorial input.

ISBN: 1-60703-704-1
PUBLISHED BY PUBLISHAMERICA, LLLP
www.publishamerica.com
Baltimore

Printed in the United States of America

The Garden
of the Poets

Chapter One

People called it *The Garden Of The Poets*, for many modern Kurdish Poets had lived in this place at one time or another. It was a community of people who embraced beauty and art. It was my hometown. Its name was Halabja.

The town's population was about eight thousand people. It was built partly on flat ground, and then sloped gradually, which after a few miles turned into the mountains on three sides. Halabja was a gorgeous town filled with wonderful people. In spring, the town was blossomed into Mother Nature's bride, dressed up like a young Kurdish bride in her colorful costume. The ground became carpeted with rich green for as far as the eye could see. Up in the mountains, the green of this plush carpet was mixed with the white of scattered snow. We were dazzled by the color. As the snow melted, we could see the sun reflecting on the silver runoff streams. Wildflowers decorated the green grass, offering up a colorful image relaxing to the eyes and soothing to the soul. Cattle stood, dotting the landscape of flowers and grass, enjoying their share of this wonderful season. In this gifted place, birds by the thousands flew everywhere, adding another dimension of joy and entertainment to Mother Nature's canvas of wonder and beauty.

When spring arrived, people went out for picnics. They took their food into the wild to enjoy their meal in the fresh air, fragranced with flowers and tress. The women in their colorful traditional dress added another layer of beauty to nature. People danced. They were optimistic with the arrival of spring and expected that wonderful changes were on the horizon.

Summer was the season of farming. In spite of the dry heat turning the green grass gray, the party went on wherever spring water and trees met.

When autumn came, the falling yellow leaves gave romantic notions. The weather cooled and the sunlight began to fade, signaling the time to store food for the long harsh winter. At this time the tribes were leaving the mountains seeking warmer places for themselves and their cattle. It was the end of harvest and this meant the end of the wonderful seasonal fruits and vegetables. Everything seemed to taste different at this time, as if nature had imbued our food with a delectable flavor of seasonal spices. We savored each taste of the watermelons, pomegranates and tomatoes as they were the last of the harvest. Their flavor would be remembered until the birth of the next harvest.

Winter lavished snow on the town and its surrounding area. A blanket of snow swept across the mountains, hills and valleys. The cold season had its own charm and beauty. Winter created a culture of a common sense of security and togetherness, a strong bond that was a hallmark of Kurdish culture.

While it was snowing outside, conversations around the fireplaces inside the big houses were heating up, giving the Kurdish culture its richness and a mirror of its history. If it weren't for the cold snowy winters and mountainous terrain, perhaps the Kurdish nation, like so many other nations in Mesopotamia, would have been liquidated long time ago.

City of Sulaymanya was seventy-five kilometers from Halabja. The land on the side of Halabja that was not protected by the mountains led to a fertile region called Sharazor. Farmland extended for thousands of square kilometers in Sharazor, producing a variety of products including grains, cotton, rice, tobacco and vegetables. Several of towns and dozens of villages were scattered throughout the land of Sharazor.

Halabja had two main streets, each about a mile in length. The streets intersected in the middle of town, forming an X. Most of the town's business took place around that intersection. There was a shopping center called Kaysary, built in an old architectural style, shaped like a triangle with three main entrances. The Kaysary was walled in brick and roofed in wood cemented with mud. It contained over fifty stores, the bulk of which were fabric stores and tailor shops. At each end of the center there was a café serving tea and other drinks.

Across from the Kaysary was a street stretching for about two hundred yards. There was a wholesaler for general merchandise and stores of different kinds. My father kept a store located near the middle of this short street. Imam's restaurant was a few doors down from my father's store. Imam's, which seated about fifty people, was the favorite restaurant in Halabja at the time. Imam himself was the cook and he served good food and kept the restaurant clean. There was a gas station at the end of the street.

On each corner of the *X* intersection there was a large café. My Uncle Kazem had a store about fifty yards from the intersection. He sold blankets and other merchandise. He was also the main distributor of soft drinks such as Coca-Cola, Pepsi, Fanta and 7up. His store was twice as large as my dad's. He used some of this space to set up an area where up to six people could be seated. Friends and relatives would go to his store to have tea and talk. It was like a little club where one could enjoy a variety of conversations.

Right before the intersection, one of the main streets met a side street that curved around and ended at the other main street. My grandfather's fabric shop was located on the opposite side of the curved street alongside some other stores. There were also several Kebab house on that street as well as two bakeries and two fresh produce stores.

The curving street was wide toward the middle and ladies form the surrounding villages would bring yogurt there to sell. They would use the proceeds to buy necessities. These ladies had no method of transportation other than walking. Therefore, they had to walk for at about an hour into town from their remote villages with a tower of yogurt pots on top of their heads. They would load up to a dozen pots, arranged from largest to smallest, and carry them on their heads over rough muddy roads through the down pours of spring rain and the blistering heat of the summer sun.

When I was a boy I wondered if these poor women got headaches from carrying mountainous stacks of yogurt pots on their heads. I was amazed that they could walk for so long with these towers on their heads without dropping any. My father told me that they had been trained to carry those pots and so it was easy for them. But it still looked hard to me and I remained sympathetic to the yogurt ladies.

In the spring villagers brought goat cheese and wild vegetables to sell. In the summer villagers from as far away as two hours walking distance brought other products, primarily fruit, such as apples, pears, figs and berries in baskets made of wooden sticks. The villagers loaded the baskets onto donkeys and led them for hours through mountains and valleys. The baskets came in two sizes: small ones to be sold to families, and large ones to be sold to wholesalers.

Near the end of my father's store there was an open area the villagers used to park their donkeys. Leaving the animals here solved two problems. It was an annoyance to the town people to have the streets crowded with donkeys and the animals needed to rest. To avoid causing problems, the villagers parked their donkeys in the designated area for a small fee.

The government offices were located at the upper end of town. There one could find the mayor's office, the police station, office of records, the army center, the courthouse, a post office, the secret police, a jail, the utilities management office and an army recruitment office. The courthouse was presided over by a judge. In order to present a case, a written brief was required. In front of the government headquarters there were clerks of the court. These clerks wrote the brief in a format acceptable by the court. All such documents had to be written in Arabic as it was Iraq's official language at the time. The clerks charged a fee for their services. Sometimes the clerks gave people instructions as to their legal rights and on how to proceed in court. Clerks who were knowledgeable would even give specific legal advice. Both plaintiff and defendant had to go before the judge and present their case. There were no lawyers or public defenders and the judge's decision was final.

In civil cases and in minor criminal cases people could simply forgive each other and make peace without getting entangled in court proceedings. This practice is very much reflected in Islam, which calls for forgiveness and denounces seeking revenge and acting in anger. As a result of this belief, most people forgave one another and didn't bother with the court proceedings. It has been an old Kurdish tradition for elders of the community to get involved helping in reconciling personal disputes. Even if people went before the judge, each side could forgive the other and the case would be closed.

Near the main entrance of the courthouse there was a small jail that housed about half a dozen people. The people housed there had been found guilty of minor crimes. People involved in more serious criminal cases were taken to Sulaymanya. The government headquarters had a large tall metal gate that was locked at the end of business hours.

There was a park, near uptown, filled with trees and spring water forming a water stream crossing through the park. The park was a place for picnics where friends and families went to entertain themselves. The park was called Mer Park.

On the other side of the government headquarters was the only hospital in town. The hospital had a pharmacy, one doctor and about six nurses. The hospital had beds for fifteen people. There was a small kitchen staffed by a single chef. The hospital chef was my mother's cousin. As a young boy, whenever I got close to the hospital, I would stop to see him because he always gave me a tasty treat of fresh milk and fried meat. When he saw me standing at the door, after greeting he would say, "My dear Rauf, can I give you a glass of fresh warm milk?"

"Yes, please. I'd like that," I would reply.

I drank the milk greedily and expected him to follow it up with a piece of fried leg of lamb or the like.

"Oh, that was so good," I would say, hoping to prompt the next course.

"Would you like me to sauté a tender piece of leg of lamb for you? You can have that with fresh bakery bread," he'd suggest.

I wondered why he bothered to ask. He knew I'd eat anything he made. He was a good cook.

"Yes, please," I replied eagerly.

He'd cook the meat and make the sandwich, which I devoured in no time.

As soon as I finished I'd say, "That was good Mr. Khalid. Thank you. I have to go now."

"You're welcome, Rauf. I'll see you later," he would say.

I guess he was too hospitable to say, I'll see you next time you want a little snack.

My father didn't think it was right that I made a habit of accepting food from Mr. Khalid. He told me it was wrong to eat food meant for other people. I decided to ignore him because Mr. Khalid's food was so good. I thought my dad would forget about it if I didn't mention it to him again.

The hospital grounds were well landscaped. The green lawn was enhanced with trees and plants. People sat on the benches to rest or while waiting for someone. The ambulance could be seen taking emergency cases on the seventy-five kilometer trip to Sulaymania where there were better facilities and equipment to perform surgery.

There were no modern dentists in town until the 1970's. But there were traditional dentists. The only treatment they offered was tooth extraction. The best local tooth-puller was a man named Helmi. He was a tall with gray hair and spectacles. Helmi loved poetry and had a good sense of humor. He had a reputation as a kind, intelligent man. His store was small, with only enough room for a desk and a few chairs. A huge mirror hung on one wall. I remember hearing an amusing story about Helmi.

A poor man from a village came to see him.

"What is bothering you, my friend?" asked Helmi.

"This tooth is bothering me," the villager said, pointing to the tooth, "I want you to pull it."

Touching the customer's tooth, Helmi asked, "Is this the one?"

"Yes, sir, that is the one. How did you know?"said the surprised villager, who had forgotten pointing to the tooth, was impressed.

"What do you expect? I am dentist, not a shoemaker. This tooth is eroded. It's already loose."

"I don't know what I would do without your help," the man said.

"Now be patient with me," Helmi said as he brought out his tools and strapped the villager to the chair.

"Sure. I have a lot of tolerance for pain. Don't worry."

"This is going to be an easy job. You don't need tolerance for it's not going to be as painful as you think."

The customer looked relieved. "Are you sure?" he asked.

"Yes, I am sure. I am only going to pull out your tooth, not your ear. I have such a light touch, I tell you I could even pull an elephant's tooth without causing much pain," assured Helmi.

"Okay, if you can pull an elephant's tooth, then mine should be easy. Did you really work on an elephant's mouth?"

"No. But if you bring one here, I'll prove what I said."

"How in the world am I supposed to find an elephant?"

"Look, forget about the elephant. There's no elephant here. But you are here and you need your tooth pulled. Let us get it done."

"I guess you're right."

"Now, close your eyes and pretend you hear nothing," said Helmi.

"Why? Does it make a noise when you pull a tooth?" asked the villager.

"No, I was only joking. Have you ever had a tooth pulled before?"

"No, sir. This is my first time."

"Don't worry, you'll be back again," said Helmi. "Now close your eyes and let me do the work."

Helmi pulled the tooth with one quick motion and gave the man a piece of cotton to stop the bleeding.

After a few minutes, the villager, stood and gave Helmi a half a dinar.

"You don't have the exact amount?" asked Helmi.

"No, that is all I have," the man answered.

"Have a seat while I go and try to find someone who will break your half dinar."

Helmi went to his neighbor's store and asked if he would give him change for the half dinar, but he said he could not.

In a short time, Helmi returned to his store and told the waiting customer, "My friend, I could not get change. I went to several stores, and still I could not get change for your half dinar."

"I am not paying you half a dinar for pulling one tooth. I know you only charge two-third of half a dinar for that. Aren't you going to give me my change?" asked concerned customer.

Looked customer on eyes "listen, my friend, I know you are a good man, and, as every one will tell you, I am very fair. Let us make a deal."

"What deal? Tell me." asked the customer anxiously.

"I pull one tooth for two thirds of a half dinar, and now I owe you one third of a half dinar. That means if I pull another tooth for the remaining money, you will get a fifty percent discount. I confess, this is the first time I have given such a break to anyone. Don't expect me to pull a tooth for this price if when you come back next time. This is a one time offer."

"I like this deal!" said the customer happily.

"Do you have any preference as to which tooth I pull or do you want me to pull out one of my choice?"

The customer thought he had been offered a great deal; he couldn't wait to get it.

"Please, be my guest."

So Helmi pulled out a perfectly good tooth. When he was done, he said, "You're a winner, my friend. You got a good price, the best deal."

The man went around town proudly telling any one who would listen how smart he was for getting a tooth pulled at half price.

Halabja did its best to provide schools for its children. There were four elementary schools for boys and one for girls, one junior high for boys and one for girls, and one high school for both boys and girls. There was a public library and a bookstore. The public library had approximately 5,000 books. Some of these books were novels and some were about subjects such as history, science and literature. Nearly all of those books, except for a few hundred in Kurdish, were in Arabic. The Kurdish holdings were mostly collections of poetry, biographies about Kurdish poets and books about Kurdish culture. The reading room seated about twenty people. The people of Halabja kept the room very clean and organized as a sign of their respect for the library.

My father sold everything from groceries and herbs to modern medicine in his small store. His store was particularly known as a place to get medicine. For many years his store was the only one in town that sold medicine to the general public and so my father dealt with almost everyone in town. We had free healthcare. But the availability of healthcare was very limited in Halabja, as it was in all of Iraq. The care that was available at the local hospital was free; however, if one wanted to get good medical attention, they had to see the doctor at the doctor's private office and pay a fee. It was a common practice in Iraq for doctors to see patients after hours. There was no such thing as health insurance, or any other kind of insurance, as all majors industries and services were state owned.

Old herbal medicines were still popular when I was a boy and people used them for almost all diseases. There really wasn't much of an alternative with only one hospital, one doctor, and a handful nurses to accommodate the medical needs of the entire town and all the surrounding small towns and villages. The nurses did their best to treat the simple ailments and in many cases functioned like doctors. But still, the state of healthcare was pretty dismal. My father's *pharmacy* was important to the town. He sold simple medicines such as penicillin and painkillers. He had an entire shelf full of painkillers including Morphine. There were no restrictions on purchasing medicines. They were sold to whoever asked for them without question. Still, there was basically no problem with people using drugs to experience a high.

Summer was harvest time. The main crop was Tobacco and the farmers sold their tobacco to the government. During the winter, most of the farmers were short on money. My dad sold them the goods they needed on credit. When summer came, they sold the harvest and cleared their debts. My father, like most merchants in town, had a large book filled with almost a hundred accounts. He didn't charge interest on these accounts. The idea of charging interest is unacceptable in Islam because it allows a person to take advantage of someone in need or due to their unfortunate circumstances. In Islam, one is expected to help those who are less fortunate. Nevertheless, there were still people who found loopholes around the teachings of Islam. Some merchants took advantage of the tobacco farmers by getting them to sign contracts allowing the merchants *options* on the farmer's crop at harvest time. The options were worth thirty to fifty dollars each and the merchants paid the farmers half of that amount. The farmers used that money to buy goods during the year. When the harvest came, the farmers had in effect sold their crop at price defined by the options, which was far below the full market value. Thus, as always, the rich got richer and the poor lost out.

Most people were good about paying back their debts. However, there were some who default on a loan. My father was careful about his accounts; in a small community you knew who had a reputation as not creditworthy. Still, a few of his customers did default; he took them to court to remedy.

My grandfather, on the other hand, was not so careful about giving credit. He sold fabric and had many customers. His ledger was three times larger than my father's. He recoded transactions himself, and he perhaps was the only one who could read his hand writing. He allowed people dress nice and overload themselves with debt. As a result, he made more and more trips to court every year to recover the debt.

My father had many customers who were government employees. These customers were sought after by all the town merchants because they got paid monthly. Their salary was high relative to average income of most people in the area. But even with a steady and good income, some of the government employees would hit the bottom of their budget in the middle of the month. Some of them ran out of money because they were compulsive gamblers, or they spent beyond their means. But whatever the cause, they all wanted cash to get by and make it to the next paycheck.

My dad would lend them money which they paid back once they received their pay at the end of the month. Being under the constant scrutiny of the local merchants was the price these big spenders paid for their excesses.

The town had a mosque on nearly every corner. Almost every one in town was a Muslim. But there were a dozen or so Christians; and there had once been a community of Jewish people in town whom migrated to Israel. Even after their migration, the district where the Jews had lived was still referred to as *The Jewish District*. My family lived in this area for a few years. The houses were made of mud with a wooden roof cemented with mud. What was surprising about these homes was that each one had a huge basement and in some instances the basement was connected to other basements. This feature was not to be found anywhere else in town.

By and large, the Jewish population had been merchants. They had a reputation as hard workers and enjoyed a comfortable level of prosperity in comparison to the general population. Overall the Jews had been treated well in our town. Once in a while, an individual might harass someone for being Jewish, but this type of behavior was not accepted by the town. So the problem of persecution was almost nonsexist for the Jews in Halalbja and for that matter in entire Kurdistan. A story with regard to Jews which I heard from my father's uncle, still resonates in my mind. He knew most of the high-ranking people of the city and when he told this story he referred to the people involved by name. Over the years, their names have slipped from my memory, but the events of the tale remain clear.

A prominent landlord in the city assigned one of his servants to handle all his dealings with a Jewish merchant. The landlord didn't want to be bothered with everyday bills, so he sent his servant out to get his household's need. Sometimes the merchant let the landlord borrow cash. For every transaction the merchant gave the servant a receipt and he recorded it in his ledger. He also made another receipts to be signed by the servant which he kept.

The landlord asked for his bill periodically. The merchant didn't charge interest; instead, he inflated the bill by padding it with extra items.

Abruptly, the landlord became very unfriendly due to his family problems and didn't want to be bothered with anything, including paying the merchant. So the merchant didn't get paid but the landlord kept piling up his account.

The merchant realized his disadvantage of taking the landlord to court for the landlord knew the government officials, including the judge.

In a meanwhile, a new judge was appointed to the city. The new judge and the landlord became something of enemies. The judge detested the landlord due to their family differences and the landlord's excessive family pride. The merchant saw this as his golden opportunity and so he took advantage of it. He filed a complaint in court and presented all the landlord's receipts, which contained the amounts, dates and the servant's signatures. A few days later, unfortunately for the merchant, the new judge passed away.

The landlord had grown furious over the court proceedings and seeking revenge. He called the merchant to come to his house with all the receipts. When the merchant arrived, the landlord told his guards to led him to his room. The landlord pointed to a chair. Once the merchant had seated himself, the landlord began to hurl curses at him, denouncing him for filing a complaint against him in court.

The landlord, who was a proud and egotistical man, was very offended by being taken to court by the merchant. He found it insulting to be brought in front of the judge by a lowly merchant. He told the merchant that he was going to punish him for daring to insult him. The landlord forced the merchant to eat all the receipts.

A month later, the landlord needed cash and so he sent his servant to see the merchant. He instructed the servant to ask for a particular amount and to have the merchant write up a contract for them both to sign. The merchant was afraid to refuse the landlord but he was also afraid to do as he had been told. So he took the money and a piece of bread and went to see the landlord. When he arrived, the landlord asked, "Did you bring the cash I need?"

The merchant replied that he had.

"Did you bring two copies of the contract to sign?"

"No, sir" said the merchant.

"Why not?"

The merchant replies, "Sir, I have brought this piece of bread. Perhaps we can write the contract on it, for it is easier to eat bread than to be forced to eat a paper contract."

The landlord paused for a moment and then made his decision.

Calling to his clerk and said, "Give this man all the money I previously owed him."

Even though Kurds were tolerant toward Jews, they, as Muslims, would not marry Jews. Both Muslims and Jews had the same restrictions against mixed marriages. Each would expect the other to convert to their religion before marriage would be possible. The few Christians in town were also treated with respect. I never saw anyone commit an act of violence against the Christians or mistreat them in any way. We were a community that survived tragedies and atrocities by opening our arms in compassion to each other. That was the blessing that helped us to survive the difficult days.

The Muslim population, which made up most of the town, was not fanatical group. In fact, it was an unspoken and unwritten law in Halabja that when someone was seen doing something inconsistent with the Muslim faith, as long as it was harmless to the general public, it should be ignored. Usually, the inconsistent acts people engaged in were not so extreme as to be an insult. For instance, just having a drink of alcohol was not upsetting to the town like it would be if a person engaged in acts of public drunkenness. In this little town, while the people were Muslim, they didn't take God's law into their own hands and act like God. They didn't fight violators. For example, my father, who was a good Muslim, didn't decline to do business with alcoholics or avoid people who drank. That's just how it was in Halabja.

There was one liquor store in town. It was run by a man of Christian Assyrian descent named Agy. My father sold fuel alcohol which people used to burn in lamps. He bought the alcohol in large containers and then divided it into smaller bottles for resale. To do this, he needed many empty bottles. So he would send me to Agy's to buy empty liquor bottles. (My father didn't think it was a sin to deal with someone who sold alcohol even though Islam condemned selling it.) No matter what time of day it was when I went to Agy's, he and his beautiful wife Khorsheda, God bless her heart, were both drunk. They drank but without harming anyone. Agy was a good man and his wife, who was of Assyrian descent also, was a little loud. But she was also beautiful and a lovely person. I still love them both to this day. In the democratic little town of Halabja, these harmless but different people were able to live, be tolerated and run a business.

Assyrians are a minority in Kurdistan. But the Assyrians have a long history of standing side-by-side with their Kurdish brothers in our fight for freedom and national recognition. Our fates are intertwined and the

Kurdish leaders have kept this in mind when working for our independence. Kurds and Assyrians have common ground and common objectives. In Halabja, people understood things like this.

There was no curfew for selling alcohol. A person could go to Agy's at three o'clock in the morning and as long as he had money, Agy would sell him what he wanted. But drinking in public was rare as it would be seen as an insulting action. Nevertheless, there were still certain alcoholic drinks that were popular. The favorite was a drink called Araq, which tasted like Greek Ozo and was quite strong. Another popular drink was the Iraqi made beer, Fareda. It was an excellent beer with a wheat flavor and high alcohol content, much higher than beer in the United States. Just a few of those beers could knock a person right off his feet or have him dancing naked. The beer was even stronger sometimes than others because the alcohol content was not regulated. I remember reading about President Jimmy Carter's brother Billy taking a trip to Libya. The headline in the *New York Post* read, "There is No Beer for Billy." When I saw this I thought, if he went to Iraq, he could drink plenty of good strong beer. Some people also enjoyed imported drinks such as Johnny Walker, Black Label, but those types of liquor were very expensive. Iraq also produced several types of wine. The most popular was Hadba. There were some people who made their own wine and, on rare occasion, aged it for years.

In some Christian communities near Arbel, they brewed their own version of Araq and sold it at a discount price. But the Araq was poor quality. It was an established Iraqi law that only Christians could own liquor store for Islam religion forbids Moslems from selling liquors. But it was the Muslims who did most of the drinking, thus Moslems drunk and Christians made business.

Information and entertainment from the outside world could be hard to come by in Halabja. We didn't have a local radio station. In fact, there were only two radio stations in the entire country. One broadcast in Arabic and the other in Kurdish. Their transmissions always followed the same pattern. Both stations opened in the morning by reciting the Qur'an for almost half an hour followed by preaching for another half hour. At the top of the hour was world news, followed by discussion and music. In early 1960's we did get another source of news and amusement when the

18

Iranian government opened a Kurdish radio station. The station broadcast Kurdish music, poetry and a radio play.

The main sources of entertainment, particularly in wintertime, were the gatherings that took place at night in peoples' homes. People came together to visit and perhaps share a meal. There was no T. V. in Halalbja until my first year of high school, so these gatherings centered on story telling, singing and playing games.

In old Kurdish tradition people in the villages usually gathered at the landlord's house. Some landlords were very rich, owning hundreds of villages, and their homes were very large. These landlords entertained themselves by inviting people to their homes. Everyone would gather in the giant living room, and the landlords would run the event to their liking. Often the landlord would invite a storyteller. Some of these storytellers were traveling professionals who spent most of their time on the road. The best of these had good diction and acted out the story as much as possible, generating excitement among their audience. The stories they told had been passed from generation to generation. Sometimes a singer accompanied the storytellers, adding to the entertainment. In return for providing this amusement, people gave them money and valuables.

The gatherings at the landlord's house themselves sometimes became stories. My father told me one such story that came from Kurdistan of Iran.

There was a landlord who used to invite people to his home in the wintertime. He would tell stories about his life experience. All of his stories were greatly exaggerated. His guard, who always stood at his side during these events, would lean into the landlord's ear when he told his exaggerated tales and say, "Master, that can't be true." Finally, the landlord grew annoyed with this. In anger he told his guard, "You better not contradict me anymore. Every time I tell a story, you tell me I am lying. From now on, just be quiet and count the number of times I lie.

For each lie you count, I will give one Qaran."

The guard was very happy with this arrangement and eager to be quiet and count lies. One day the landlord told a story of a freezing winter day. He looked at the crowd gathered in his living room and said, "It was such a cold winter's day that I saw a cat jumping from roof to roof freeze in midair between two houses. I saw it with my own eyes."

The guard leaned in close to the landlord's ear and said, "Master, am I only going to get one Qaran for this one, too?"

While we didn't have a local newspaper, people in town did read the official government paper. It was published in Arabic and had no criticism about the government. The paper only reported the news as the officials told, the rest of the paper had little or no substance. There were all kinds of Arabic magazines, most of which were published in Beirut. Only educated people could read Arabic and the magazines were too expensive for an average person. So my town was not much of a market for these magazines. But the new government legislation and policies still needed to be communicated to the general public. This was done by word of mouth. A merchant named Ra' of Abas, who had a store in the center of the town's business district, was also our town crier. It was his responsibility to bring news to the people. Usually a policeman would bring Ra' of Abas the regulations he was to announce. The crier then went to the circle where the two main streets intersected and read the announcement in a loud voice. He would repeat the announcement several times. About three hours later, he would return and repeat the same process. His most common announcement, which he delivered twice a month, was to remind people that if they didn't pay their utility bills, their water and electricity supply would be cut off.

In the center of the business district, there was a place where *hamals*, or *carriers*, gathered to look for work. The *hamals* unloaded the trucks that came to town. The only equipment a *hamal* had for this heavy labor was his strong back. Some of these men were unbelievably strong, carrying very heavy loads for over fifty feet. The *hamals* also delivered heavy goods to people's homes. The only other transport available in town was carriages pulled by donkeys. In the city of Sulaymanya one could rent beautiful, European style horse drawn carriages for taxi service. These carriages looked like those seen on the streets of London or Paris prior to the automobile.

There were many cafés in the town. In most of them one could find backgammon sets, dominos and decks of cards. There were two cafes near the circle where offered bingo game. Some cafes in town didn't allow any gambling, but most did. There were no official age restrictions. As long as a person had money to play, that person was allowed to play. But that didn't mean that the adults didn't look out for underage gamblers. When people noticed that a kid was hitting the cafes, the word quickly spread back to the parents. Once the parents found out, the father usually came down and yanked the kid out of the café. I know how this went because when I was in junior high school, I started gambling. Word got back to my parents and my father came down and caught me. After that, I stopped gambling, not because I felt bad about doing it, but because I knew that if I didn't stop, I'd just get caught again.

Gambling wasn't popular just for the chance of winning money. It was also enjoyed just as a social activity. Friends went to the café to have tea, custard, or baklava and played cards, backgammon or dominos. The loser had to treat the winner and his friends.

More serious gambling took place at Hussein Kafrosh's place. His café was right on the circle, three stores down from my father's store. Hussein Kafrosh was a tall, quiet blond man with green eyes. He was a bit overweight as suspected for he sat on his ass and gamble all day. He had two people working in his café. He only served breakfast, and that was just yogurt and tea. The rest of his income came from serving tea and gambling fees. It was the custom for the gamblers to set out a bucket and put money in it to pay the café. The gamblers paid their dues even if the owner wasn't watching over them. But still Kafrosh gambled with the players from the time his café opened in the morning until every one left at the end of the day. Heavy gamblers from other towns and cities came there along with local gamblers. They played twenty-one, ramie and other games. Surprisingly, the gambling in town didn't cause a lot of fighting or other crime related problems. Even though gambling was officially illegal, the police didn't bother to enforce the law.

The only time the police got involved with the gambling in town was during the holidays when children commonly got gifts of money from relatives. At those times, older teenagers would go to the playground and set up a gambling table. They would play dice games with the children and take their money. The police would come and take away the teenagers' dice and tell them to leave. The teens would leave only to come back once the police were gone. This cat-and-mouse game was ongoing.

Most of the businesses in the shopping center closed between 5:00 and 6:00 in the evening. There were security guards on duty all night. But the town didn't close completely at this hour. The biggest gambling place in town was the government employee only club. It served food and alcoholic beverages until midnight and people gambled there until early morning.

While there were few compulsive gamblers, and many others who gambles but overall those who gambled were a very small portion of town's population. Gambling is forbidden in Islam, not just for the monetary considerations, but also for the social disturbances and family problems it can cause, and, most importantly, for the separation it creates between the gambler and God. When gambling, a person's heart and mind is taken up in the excitement. This leaves no room for any thought of God. Islam demands that a person to mind God at all times. So most people who went to the cafes went not to gamble but to play and have fun. So, people went to café to meet friends, and there were people who affiliated with political organizations went to share information and debate current affairs. Some people came to hold intellectual discussions about literature, poetry and other subjects. The cafes were an important part of the social life in Halabja.

A daily auction was held in the circle. Of the few auctioneers in Halabja, the most successful was a tall, slim, bald man named Hama. His loud voice which commanded people's attention and his flair for exaggeration generated interest in the merchandise. Hama could quickly draw a large crowd. He always began his pitch by telling the crowd his merchandise was the best quality. He would go on to explain how special it was. He kept at this until people showed interest; then he would take bids. If the last bid was less than his price, he would withdraw the item and save it for another occasion. People liked to shop at the auction because it was possible to get good deals. The merchandise came from people who either needed to raise cash or just wanted to sell an unneeded items.

In Halabja, as in all small towns, every one knew each other. People were connected either through friendship, family or business. There was a sense of community that was built on strong family ties. Family members were very protective of one another. If a member of a family did something inappropriate, the entire family was affected by the shame and embarrassment. Individuals felt responsible for protecting the reputations of their families. On the other hand, when one member of a family did well, it enhanced the standing of the whole family.

Bonds of friendship were important to people in Halabja. Friendship is deeply rooted in the Kurdish mind and heart. There is a Kurdish proverb that says, "A thousand friends is too few, one enemy is too many." Kurds believed in friendship and almost everyone made an effort to show acts of hospitality to others. Sometimes these actions came from the heart and sometimes they were more a matter of custom. It was the tradition for new neighbors to be invited to meals at the surrounding homes. This helped the family to feel welcome and to get settled in their new home. Neighbors, family and friends visited often. People only felt lonely by choice. A Kurdish proverb says that a man's heaven is his house and so it was right to share your heaven with others. In Kurdish culture people believe in being positive toward others. There is another proverb that applies, "If you can't be a rose, then don't be a thorn," implying, if you can't help, then at least make sure you are not an obstacle. These values are an important part of Kurdish people's life.

It was a common practice for merchants to invite their regular customers home and establish relationships. My father went to Sulaymanya regularly to buy merchandise from wholesalers. The wholesalers often invited my father for dinner and offered to let him stay overnight in their homes. The home was the center of family entertainment and the gatherings allowed people to share more than food. These times together kept the friendships fresh and alive. Kurds embraced this tradition because it was natural to our culture. Kurds lived for thousands of years in a difficult mountainous area and our survival had always depended upon banding together to overcome difficulties. We were wise enough to see the wisdom of these beliefs.

The winter months in Kurdistan were long and desperate. In many areas, particularly in remote regions, the roads were poor and travel was not possible for long periods of time. People had little choice but to get along with their neighbors and to help each other. During times of family tragedy or need, the community came together to comfort and help. When someone passed away, even members of the community who had not been close to the deceased came to the funeral to offer support and pay their respects. During the funeral, men gathered in the mosque and women gathered in the home of the bereaved. The women, all dressed in black, would stay for up to three days and mourn with the family. They would cry and wail in sympathy and for their own losses. This was the traditional way even though Islam is against crying for the dead, as showing such strong emotion might be a protest against God's will. The men would gather in the mosques to pray in honor of the deceased for three days after the funeral. During these days, all the family members and friends came to have dinner with the bereaved family.

Good Muslims did charity in the name of the one who had died. They believed their giving would help the dead person to reach heaven. It is a beautiful act even if only for the help it brings to those in need. This is a good way to honor someone's life. I remember my parents sacrificing lambs several times every year and sending the meat to people who could not afford it. This charity was done on the behalf of family members who had died.

People also committed themselves to charity as a way to get out of trouble. These acts of charity were done along with their prayers to God to help them out of a difficult time. Sometimes people would give more charity if they wanted a prayer or dream to come true. In a sense, people were bribing God, hoping to increase their chances of getting what they wanted. However, there were many people whose charity was really from the heart. Some people would commit themselves to charity to be forgiven for past sins. They knew it was not possible to turn back the clock, yet it was realized that time is neutral and anytime in life is goodtime to do good and makeup for past sins.

One tradition of Kurdish culture that I have always admired is that no matter what type of life a person led, once that person died, everyone spoke well of them. Islam requires that people speak well of the dead because once someone has died, that person is in God's hands and God will be the one to judge.

In retrospect, Halabja might seem to have had a rather lax environment and one might expect bad behaviors to flourish there. This remote town had limited resources, no law enforcement and basically no mental health care services. But we didn't have a big problem with drug use or alcohol consumption. When a person did develop problems like this, family members would try to help. But once they had exhausted all the ways they could think of to help, they would resign themselves to the situation. They would say to themselves, "I am not God. I have done all I can do for this person. Now it is in God's hands." I found comfort in this approach.

I knew of only one person in town with a drug problem. A tailor whose store was next to the most popular mosque in town smoked opium. He puffed on his *nargila* all day long. But even though drug use is prohibited as a sin in Islam, the Muslims who passed his store didn't curse him or bother him in anyway. They didn't feel it was their place to interfere since he didn't try to force his habit on others and he continued to work and support himself. He refused to drop the habit but didn't harm others, so people just left him alone. All in all, the environment in Halabja seemed to bring out the better side of people, not the worst side.

During my time growing up in Halabja, I am sure no one had a freezer; I don't think more than a couple people had a refrigerator. Butchers had to sell the meat from the goats, lambs or cows they killed the same day. It would not be fit for sale after the end of the day. Most fruits and vegetables were sold as soon as possible after being picked. At the time, if we had really thought about there being another choice, we might have thought that it would be an improvement to have the conveniences brought by freezers or other modern innovations. But now that I have left that place and time, I miss the fresh, organic food that was always free of pesticides and chemical fertilizers.

There was a post office in town, but the houses and businesses were not numbered, streets were not named and very few businesses were named. This made delivering the mail a challenge. We only had one mailman in town and he knew almost everyone. If he had something to deliver and he didn't recognize the name, he would ask around until he found someone who did. Sometimes he was careful and he left it to thers to clear up the confusion. Nearly all the mail was almost entirely letters in those days.

Childhood was short. By the age of six or seven, children were expected to work like adults, specially in a farmland. Even when a child had a chance to play, there weren't many toys. For the generations before mine, there were basically no toys at all except homemade dolls for little girls. The toys that were available to my generation were very expensive and most people could not afford them. By the time I was six years old, I was expected to help my father in his store. My father prayed five times a day. The first daily prayer started at dawn right before sunrise, the second at noon, the third in the middle of the afternoon, the fourth right after sunset and the fifth a couple of hours after sunset. Starting at noon, I sat in my father's store and ran the business for him. He took a two-hour lunch during the spring and summer, when the days were long, and a one-hour lunch during the autumn and winter, when the days were short. He went home for lunch and took a short nap before returning. About an hour after he came back to the store, he went to the mosque for the third prayers. My father did his best to pray with the group led by a mullah at the mosque. In the Islamic belief, people can double or triple their credit with God this way.

When I was sitting in the store for my father, the same thing was going on in the neighboring stores. So when our fathers were gone to prayer, all of the sons would get together and play Dama, a game very similar to chess. The pieces were made of empty wooden thread spools, each cut into two pieces.

Children who lived in the villages began working on the farm when they were six or seven. Farming was so demanded that in order to survive, every member of the family had to work from seeding time until end of harvest time.

Friday is a Muslim holiday. People took special advantage of this break during the colorful beauty of spring. On Fridays, schools and most government offices were closed. Neighbors, family and friends would go picnicking in places with tress and spring water. They cooked food, sang and did their traditional Kurdish Dances. The women would wear colorful clothes and put on their jewelry to better display their beauty. The Kurdish dances were breathtaking and the women were amazing. Some of the dancers made enticing moves, brushing up against those watching. A traditional Kurdish dress is usually made from a single piece covering the whole body, but it leaves a "V" from the neck down the chest. The people danced together, putting their arms around each other in a circle, alternating between men and women. Often, there would be a singer standing in the middle of the circle singing along with the dance and swaying to the rhythm.

On special occasions such as weddings, professional singers were brought in and the crowd tipped them. When a person tipped a singer, the singer would then add a flattering description of the person into the song. Women especially enjoyed weddings and picnics. These were their major social events. During weddings, the women danced in a big crowd, making the most of the chance to interact with others. But at Kurdish gatherings, unlike other Muslim cultures, men and women would also sit together and interact. Social events were a time for everyone, men and women, to socialize together.

Halabja was hot in the summer. We would take our vacation in the cool mountain town of Byra. It was a small town with about thousand population, and we stayed with relatives who lived there. When coming to Byra, one sees two mountains flanking a valley. People built their houses on the mountain side and had their market place down in the valley. The walls of the houses were made of stone cemented with mud and the roofs were made of wood, also cemented with mud. Sometimes these houses were built one on top of the other and they had a gravel or stone trail leading to them.

The mountains in this area were covered in fruit trees and walnut trees. These trees were the main source of income for people in the region. Spring water was everywhere and people used it for drinking and irrigation. The town of Byra was visited by thousands of people each summer that came to enjoy its beautiful mountain scenery and cool summer climate. It could have been developed into a wonderful resort town.

Byra lies near the border of Iran and Iraq. A little stream of water was all that separated the two countries. Every once in a while, I would see a few Iranian soldiers on the other side of the stream armed with small rifles. This spot on the border attracted a lot of smugglers from both sides. After the Islamic Revolution in Iran, it was illegal to import alcoholic beverages. But there was still a demand for those products. Almost all the alcohol going into Iran after the Islamic Revolution was smuggled in from Kurdistan.

The people who lived in Byra and the surrounding area were called Hawrami and their region called Hawraman. They spoke a different Kurdish dialect than we did in my hometown. We didn't know how to speak their dialect, but they knew how to speak ours. The Hawrami people were, and still are, the most self-sufficient people in all of Kurdistan. They made shoes and marketed them all over. The bottoms of the shoes were made from cloth and the uppers were made from manually woven cotton. These shoes were the most comfortable shoes to wear during summer and the Hawrami were able to sell them at a higher price than imported shoes. They also made pillows from feathers and blankets and socks. In a section of Hawrami called Hajeji, the people made dishes and utensils from wood. Most of Hawraman is a rocky mountains, people had transformed the rocky terrain into land capable of growing fruit trees and vegetables. They dug countless rocks out of the hills and filled the holes with earth from the base of the mountain.

As is typical of the Kurds, Hawrami loved to sing and to dance, maybe even more than other Kurds. They loved their poetry and made it into songs. They sang happy songs in times of joy and sad songs in times of sorrow. One could tell the mood of a Hawrami by the song they sung. Most of their songs came from the poetry of the legendary Kurdish poet Mawlawe. His poetry was in the Hawrami dialect, which is closest to the Med language spoken 2,500 years ago. The Med civilization was once the most powerful in the world. The Hawrami dialect is very similar to the language of the Avesta, the holy book of Zoroastrians. Mawlawe a prominent Kurdish poet who honored this dialect is one of the popular Kurdish poet in particular amongst Hawramis.

Mawlawe was a God-loving, faithful man and was a follower of my great-grandfather. Most of his poetry was found in the letters he wrote. Some of these letters were written as correspondence with others and some were written to honor those who had passed away. But if one who was unfamiliar with the subject matter of his poems, the poem seemed to be about romance. He had written many romantic poems in his youth. Mawlawe's poetry was unique. It is typical for a poet writing about his lover's beauty to show how beautiful she is by comparing her to something in nature that is admired for its beauty, such as a rose. Mawlawe reversed this comparison. His poetry would prove the rose's beauty be comparing it to his lover. Some of his most beautiful poetry was written to express his grief at the death of his wife.

Mawlawe suffered in his old age. He never recovered from the death of his wife and he later lost his sight. After he had become blind, he went to visit some friends in a different village. A man was leading him on a horse. Mawlawe warned the man to watch out for an overhanging tree some miles down the path. He told the guide to let him know when he needed to duck so he would not be knocked from the horse. But by the time they reached the tree, the man had forgotten he should warn Mawlawe. The man led the horse right under the branches, causing Mawlawe to smack into them. The impact knocked him from the horse onto the ground. The hard earth broke Mawlawe's back. Thus, he was still grieving his wife's death, he was blind, and now his back was broken. He wrote poems during his last day talking to God: "God, you took away everything you gave me one by one; all I owe you is your judgment when judgment day comes." Mawlawe is highly regarded by the Hawramis as both a poet and a spiritual figure. Furthermore, he is highly regarded by poetry lovers in general, many of whom think he was the best poet of his time, and perhaps thereafter.

The Hawrami people were proud of their heritage and they loved to speak their dialect. In most towns and cities, there was a café or restaurant that catered to the Hawramis, a place where they could go and speak their dialect. Even in Baghdad there was a place called the Hawrami Café.

When I went to Byra in the summers, I stayed with my father's cousin or my step grandmother. My father's cousin's two-story house was built on top of a stream that ran through the middle of town. The stream continued until it ran through a narrow valley. In this valley was the shrine of my Great Grandfather Najmadeen. His shrine was visited by many of the followers of Naqishbendi and others. I have been told that my grandfather's great Grandfather Osman had inherited the leadership of the Naqishbendi sect form the original leader and founder Shaykh Mawlana Naqishbendi.

In four generations, my forefathers attracted more than a million followers from all over the Islamic world. The Naqishbendi leaders were well respected by the kings of the Middle East and even by the Shah of Iran. The main principle of the Naqishbendi was that it was important to be a good Muslim and that in order to be a good Muslim, one must be well educated and help educated others. The Naqishbendi belief is that faith must be the product of a profound education. They believe that if a person's faith results from their education about God, then their faith and times of prayer will bring them enjoyment. People who have this type of faith feel happy because they understand God's unconditional love. When a person feels God's unconditional love, he or she will want to devote himself to sharing love with others by believing in a common good and helping others.

The Naqishbendi's belief is that people should act out of love instead of fear of going to hell or wanting reward to get to heaven. Followers of the Naqishbendi value peace of mind and establish a solid foundation of harmony and peace among the people around them. They curse violence and believe that it is an act of evil to commit violence in any form for any reason. Even when the Naqishbendi were insulted and offended, they didn't look to confront the persons responsible or to seek revenge. In stead, they would pray for their enemies.

Many followers donated money and land to the Naqishbendi leaders whom they called Shaykh meant elder. The Naqishbendi used only what they needed to live and run God's business and gave the rest to help others. The leaders were considered holy and people went to them for help in prayer. They asked the Shaykh to pray for them when they got married or to be healed from disease. Some went just to visit and experience the holy presence. The Naqishbendi shrine was a place people went to be comforted and supported spiritually and emotionally. The Naqishbendi turned no one away. They paid attention to all who came and prayed for everyone, whether rich or poor. Inclusion is a main characteristic of Naqishbendi; exclusionism had no place in this sect of Islam.

The place where the Shaykh welcomed his followers was called a *Khanaqa*. It was a place for poets and writers and the Naqishbendi always welcomed them. In the Khanaqa, no one was turned away. At any given time, hundreds of people were sheltered and fed there. There was more than one Khanaqa. My great grandfather managed a Khanaqa and so did each of his brothers. The Naqishbendi were honest and peace-loving people. There are no records of violence or theft by the Naqishbendi Shaykhs. They remained well-respected and loved by many. However, there were atheists and members of the Communist Party and left wing Marxists who thought religion as impediment to economic and social progress. They used propaganda to alienate people from the Naqishbendis. When the Communist Party started growing in Iraq in 1958, the Naqishbendi didn't feel safe. Some left and went to settle in Iran.

My grandfather Shaykh Mohammed died young, when my father was still a small child. So, of course, I never knew him. I didn't know much about him until I was in my senior year in high school. I was visiting my Uncle Kazem and he showed me my grandfather's diary. It contained beautiful poetry and drawings. He had been very intellectual and artistic. His handwriting is among the best I've ever seen. His art was so beautiful, like something to be seen in a museum.

Unfortunately, my father was only a few years old when both his parent passed away. He was so young he didn't remember what they looked like. My father's uncle, Shaykh Zaynadeen, decided to provide for my father and raise him. Shaykh Zaynadeen lived in Sulaymanya. In Kurdish tradition, there is no such thing as adoption. I'd never heard of any such thing, particularly if one parent was still alive. However, in situation where a child was left an orphan, the closest family member

31

would take custody of the child. Shaykh Zaynadeen took my father and raised him with his own children. Uncle Zaynadeen was married to a sweetheart of a woman named Halaw. While my father lived with them, Halaw gave birth to two babies who both died. Uncle Zaynadeen and Aunt Halaw were sad and fearful that if Aunt Halaw had another child, he or she might not survive. My Aunt and Uncle made a commitment to God hoping that would make theirs prayers for a healthy baby come true. They promised God that if the next baby were a healthy girl, they would arrange for her to be my father's wife. They felt bad for my father; he was an orphan with no one to arrange these matters for him. Without someone to do that, it could be difficult to ever have a good wife. The custom of arranged marriages, which is still practiced today, is important in a culture that does not allow dating. It is a very serious matter that a lady remains a virgin until she is married, and if the ladies are virgins, then the men must be chaste also. The cultural tradition of chastity before marriage is imposed on both sexes. Usually marriages are arranged with the children's happiness in mind. Only rarely does it become a situation were the family forces an unwelcome marriage upon their child.

My father didn't have the exact same opportunities as my uncle's children. This difference in treatment was not a mark against my Uncle and Aunt; it was simply that in Kurdish tradition, my father was an orphan they had taken in, not an adopted son. They gave my father a good home a good start in life. My uncle sent my father all the way through six years of grade school, which was a respectable education at that time in Iraq. Most people were illiterate and very few completed high school. Two of my uncle's children, on the other hand, graduated from college. Two of the other three became teachers. One of my Uncle's sons graduated from the military academy and became an officer in the Iraqi army. He eventually became a powerful general and retired after the Iraq-Iran war. He then became an entrepreneur.

My father went out on his own at an early age and was drafted into army. Military service was mandatory then for young men who were not in college, college graduates or working as teachers. (Later that rule would be changed and nearly everyone had to serve for a minimum of two years.) My dad served in the army for seven years longer than he was supposed to. He did so for he had no home to go back to or simply no better alternative.

During his last year of service, he received a letter from his Uncle Ezat who lived in Halabja. My father's uncle invited him to join him in Halabja and offered to help him start a life there. My father was excited at the prospect and he left the military. The idea of living in Halabja was very appealing to my father. Not only did he have his Uncle Ezat living there, but he also had his brother Kazim, two other uncles, an aunt and dozens of cousins there as well. My father arrived in Halabja with little money, but uncle Ezat was an upper middle-class man and he was able to house my father and help him start his small grocery store. Later, my father married Uncle Ezat's daughter.

My father's fluency in Arabic and basic English skills gave him an edge in his business. This knowledge made it possible for him to sell medicine because he could read the Arabic instructions as how to use it and he could read the medicine names in English. Meanwhile, Uncle Zaynadeen's family kept close ties with my father and still considered him one of their families. I often went to visit in Sulaymanya and would spend my whole three-month summer vacation with Uncle Zaynadeen and his family.

Sulaymanya was a big city and it had many things we didn't have in Halabja such as cinemas, big shopping malls, soccer fields, musical bands, publishers and big restaurants. During my summers in Sulaymanya, I worked with my cousin Fasel, Uncle Zaynadeen's youngest son, in Yosef Abaka's bicycle shop. Fasel, who was about five years older than me. When we were at work, part of our job was to fix bikes and to keep the shop clean. We also rented bikes by the hour. Most of our customers were young kids and teenagers. If we knew the customers, we let them take the bikes on their word. But when strangers rented the bikes, we required that they leave us their birth certificates. One day just before noon, a stranger came asking to rent a bicycle. Yosef took care of him and took his birth certificate. Evening came and it was about time to close the shop. The stranger had not returned. Yosef checked the birth certificate to see if he knew the man's family. Of course it was a fake certificate with a made-up name—Akhli Pakhli. Yosef was angry. He looked at us and said,

"What a bastard. How can I find *Akhli Pakhli?*"

Across from Yosef's shop was his father Abaka's shop. I called him uncle *Aba* as it is a Kurdish custom to refer to older men as *Uncle* and to older women as *Aunt*. Uncle Abaka was a tall man with light skin who dressed in a robe crossed in the middle and tied with a belt made of fine, sheer cloth. He made candies and his shop was very small, filled with the heavy pots and other equipment needed to make candy. Uncle Aba's son Jabar worked with us at the bike shop. Occasionally, at the end of our day at the bicycle shop, we went to help at the candy shop. By that time of day, the candy was made and ready to be packaged. The foot long candies were shaped like a stick. Jabar and I used scissors to cut the candy to the right length so they could be packed in layers in wooden boxes. After each layer was made, we floured it and placed a small thin paper over it to separate it from the next layer. If a section of candy was too long to fit in the box, we trimmed it and kept the trimming for ourselves. It didn't take us long to learn that if we cut the pieces long intentionally, there would be some extra left for us. Sometimes the candy was crooked at the end as a result of our deliberate over sizing. This method left a good chunk for us. Uncle Abaka knew that we were doing this, but he didn't make us stop. We thought of those bits of candy as our wages and I guess Uncle Abaka was generous enough to think it was an acceptable, unspoken arrangement. After the candy was packaged, Uncle Abaka sold it to other retailers or sold from his own shop, and we left with chunks of delicious candy lasted few days.

A few stores down from Yosef's bike shop was Mullah Najmadeen's school. At that time, there weren't many schools. People would send their children to Mosques to be taught by mullahs. The mullahs taught the children to read and write. Mullah Najmadeen had such a school and he made a big contribution to hundreds of children's education. He was also a well-known Kurdish nationalist who was very open about his views regarding a free Kurdistan. During this time, the desire for an independent Kurdistan was flourishing out in the open light of day and nearly every educated Kurd in Sulaymanya was involved in the movement.

I recall hearing Mullah Najmadeen's voice as he read to the students when I passed by the school. After school was out for the day, he sat down to have a few drinks. He was just as open about his drinking as he was about his political views. But this didn't change how well respected he was in the city. He spent most of his life educating the children of Sulaymanya. When he died, people wanted to honor the request in his will that people should come to his funeral drunk, in honor of his love for drinking, and shower his grave with alcoholic beverages. At the time of his death, it was not possible to fulfill his request because of the political unrest. Years later, however, thousands of people came to his grave to pay their respects. Those who drank brought their drinks with them and at the end sprayed his grave with Araq and whiskey.

Mullah Kaniskani was another drinking mullah. During his religious services, he preached about how to be a good Muslim, which of course included abstaining form alcohol and narcotics. But everyone knew he had been drinking since he was a teenager. It made me wonder why he had chosen to be a mullah when Islam is so strongly against drinking, I think some people just do damn things or chose wrong path in their lives. What was really surprising was that his reputation for drinking didn't effect his reputation as a mullah. People went to the mosque to listen to him preach and tried to follow his teachings even though they knew he drank alcohol.

There were many odd stories about Mullah Kaniskani. Many times he would be drunk in the middle of his preaching or prayers. He would begin to dance during the religious gatherings, yet people would go back to him. I was once told a story about a time when Mullah Kaniskani was a guest at a home in Kirkuk. The man of the house told his wife what a good man Mullah Kaniskani was and how good his sermon had been. She responded by saying she had heard he was an alcoholic. The husband got mad and said, "How dare you make up such an accusation against Mullah Kaniskani!"

The wife was silent but she decided to prove to her husband that what she said was true. When the mullah asked her for a glass of water, she filled his glass with Araq. He drank it and thanked her. In front of her husband, the wife told the mullah that it had not been water in the glass, it had been Araq. Then mullah replied, "I swear to God, it was water! Please bring me another just like it."

My summers in Sulaymanya were good times for me. When I worked for Yosef, he paid me wages on a daily basis. I gave the money to aunt Halaw and she saved it for me. She didn't let me spend any of my money. If I needed spending money, she gave me some of her own. When it was time for me to return to Halabja, she would give me all the money I had earned. It was enough for me to buy some school clothes and supplies for the year.

I enjoyed every day of my summers in Sulaymanya. I had a great time when I was with Fasel working at the bike shop. Jabar, Yosef's younger brother, was my best friend and we hung out, he was around my age. We took time to play soccer and ride bicycles. We made fun of customers and ate candy. I got along well with all my relatives there. Uncle Zaynadeen's son Qtbadeen was a math teacher in elementary school and he had three beautiful daughters. We had fun playing cards. Uncle Zaynadeen had had two grown daughters, Nasreen and Parween. Parween liked to tease me. She told me how lucky I was to get to be in the company of her nephews.

I went back to Halabja when it was time for school to start. I knew most of the kids at the Halabja elementary school and the teachers were all family friends, my father's customers or family members. That is the way life is in a small town—everyone knows or related to everyone, and one can't do wrong and hide it. This pressure helped to keep people, including the school kids, in line. Rumors fly all the time. Who had gotten in trouble or been caught doing something wrong was a favorite topic for conversations, especially at women's gatherings.

My mother didn't go to school at all. In her time there weren't schools for girls so she missed her education. But, like most Kurdish women, she loved poetry. She loved to have someone read to her from the Qur'an, recite poetry or read a good story. She knew the words to many songs and she taught me how to sing. She sat with me and taught me the words and the rhythm. She taught me the words to the first piece of poetry I memorized. On many occasions I went before the entire school and recited it. When she taught me poetry she also taught me how to recite it properly. She explained that no matter how good the poem was, it wouldn't sound good if it wasn't recited as it should be. She showed me how significant diction was and taught me much about the art of speech.

My mother told me the traditional stories and expected me to memorize them. As with any parent, her aim was to teach me how to be good and to help others. While these values are a basic part of Islam or for that matter any other religion, they are also deeply rooted in the Kurdish culture which is by far much older than Islam. She loved the old Kurdish proverbs, the lessons they taught and the stories behind them. She told me everyone she knew, and thanks to parents like her, this great literature has survived and passed from one generation to the next.

When I was in the third grade, the teacher instructed us to find a good proverb and learn the story behind it. I came home and told my mother about the assignment.

"Mom, the teacher wants us to find a story and a proverb," I said.

"What story, son?" she asked.

"My teacher said a proverb with a good moral and a story to go with it."

"I'll give you one, but later I want you to tell it back to me so I can be sure you've learned it. Okay?"

"Okay, Mom."

"Then I want you to polish the story and see if you can make it even better. Deal?"

I agreed.

"This story is about doing good and not asking for anything in return. Our forefathers said, 'Do good and throw it on a river. Let it flow with the water.'"

The story she told me went like this:

There was a husband and a wife who lived in a little town. They had no children and the man was wealthy. He owned a lot of property. He kept all of his wealth for himself. He shared with no one. His wife was a descent lady who would like to help others but she couldn't because her husband would get very angry.

One summer night the couple was sitting on the roof of their house, barbequing chicken. The appetizing smell of the chicken filled the air. A poor man followed the aroma and knocked at their door.

"What do you want?" asked the husband.

"I am hungry, please feed me," said the poor man.

"Get out of here or I will come down and thrash you"

"I am really hungry and have nothing…for God's sake, give me some food, anything!"

"This is the last time I am going to warn you before I come down!" yelled the husband.

At this outburst, the poor man left.

A few years later, the rich man lost all his wealth. His wife left him and remarried. He was left alone and broke.

Years later the woman was sitting with her new husband on the deck of their house barbequing chicken. They were about to eat when they heard a knock at the door. A voice called out, "I am a poor man. Can you please feed me? I am hungry and have nothing."

"Honey, take my plate to that poor, hungry man," said her new husband.

"But what will you eat?" asked the wife.

"Don't worry about me, sweetheart, just take it to him."

The wife took her husband's food to the poor man and gave it to him. When she returned to her husband, she felt in tears.

"Why are you crying?" asked her husband.

"How can I not cry?" After a pause—then she continued "That man was my former husband. At one time he was wealthy and had everything. Now he is begging for food," she aid.

"We will feed him for the time being," said the husband.

Then the wife told her husband about the night she and her former husband had been having supper, and her former husband had driven away a hungry man in exactly the same situation.

"Yes, dear. You know that night you were sitting with your husband having that barbecue? That poor, hungry man who knocked on the door begging for food was me."

"Mom, that is a sad story," I said.

Yes, it is sad. When you are rich, remember no matter how much anyone has, God can take it away in the blink of an eye."

I asked her who had told her the story.

"Your grandfather told it to me when I was a little girl," said my mother. "Here is another story he told me:

There was a wealthy landlord in a village. He was expecting a visitor who meant a lot to him. The landlord sent a few of his servants to the main road in the village to look out for the visitor.

He told his men, "Go to the main entrance road to the village and as soon as you see Chief Hamza, run back to me so that I can go to personally receive him."

"How will we recognize Chief Hamza?" asked one of the landlord's men named Auob.

"He has a big mustache," said the landlord.

The Landlord's men went and stood on the road. About an hour later, Auob ran back to the landlord's house, short of breath.

"What is happening, Auob?" asked the landlord.

"Master, Chief Hamza is here," said Auob.

The landlord got on his horse and rode out to receive the chief. He got to the road leading to the village. The only man there was an old man with a big mustache. "Where is Chief Hamza?" asked the landlord.

"There he is, Sir. The man with the big mustache," Auob said, pointing to the old man.

"No, that isn't him," said the landlord.

"Master, you said the man with the big mustache would be Chief Hamza."

"No, Auob, *not every man with a big mustache is Chief Hamza*," said the landlord.

"The moral of the story is not to see things as black and white," said Mom.

"What do you mean by that?" I asked.

"Let us say that people in this town are good. That is a general statement—sure, people in our town are good people, but there are some who are not so good," said Mom. "Just like the proverb says, *'not every one with a big mustache is Chief Hamza.'* The same goes for thinking everyone in town is a good person."

"Mom, who wrote these stories?" I asked.

"I don't know. I can't even read. I only know what I have been told. I would guess that many of these stories have never been written down."

"That can be a job for me when I grow up. I can write these stories down and let people read them," I said.

"That would be a good job for you," said Mom.

Once when I was in the Fifth grade, my teacher told us to bring a good math puzzle to school. I went home and asked my father for he used to be my math helper.

"Dad, my teacher wants me to bring a good math puzzle to school. He wants us to bring a good story about mathematics. Do you know any?"

"It's true I am not a mathematician, son. But I do know a good math puzzle. By now you should know fractions and division, is that right?"

"Yes, of course, Dad."

"So what is one third of 18?" asked dad.

"You know I know that; it's six," I said.

"So, can you divide six into seventeen without a remainder?"

"You need one more to make it eighteen to divide. My teacher said seventeen is good for nothing and is a poor figure to divide," I said.

"Why is that?" asked Dad.

"Teacher said it's a prime number and can't be divided by anything other than itself and one. The teacher hates these numbers and calls them selfish and good for nothing," I said.

"Now, here is your puzzle. It's said to be a true story," said Dad.

"Good. So this is a story and not math?" he continued.

"It's both. During Kalepha Ali's time... You know who that is?" asked Dad.

"He was the son-in-law of the prophet Muhammad, and he was to be the head of the Islamic Empire, and he was killed." I said.

"That is right." He said.

They say that a man died and left 17 camels behind. He declared in his will that his older son would inherit one half, his younger son would inherit one third and his daughter would inherit one ninth. Since 17 can't be divided by any number but itself and one, the family wrestled with the problem of dividing the camels and they didn't know how to arrive at ½,

1/3, and 1/9 of 17. They decided to take the matter to Kalepha Ali. They went to him and told him about the will.

Ali said, "There is a problem with this but we can resolve it. You can't tale 17 and divide it into 2, 3, and 9 because you end up with a fraction and that means you need to kill one or two camels to arrive at the answer." That wasn't what they wanted to do and they all said they didn't want to chop up their camels. Then Ali told them, "Very well, if we had 18 camels, we could execute the will without killing any camels. Now, you have 17 camels and I'll give you one of my own. Then you will have 18 camels. The older son can take ½ of the 18 camels and that is 9 camels. Then the younger son can take 1/3 of the 18 camels and that yields 6 camels. Finally, the daughter can take 1/9 of 18 camels and that yields 2 camels. Let us add the shares up, 9 + 6+2 = 17 and I take my own camel back," said Ali.

Thus everyone was happy.

"That is a good math trick, Dad. My teacher will like it," I said.

When I grew older my mother would ask me to read her poetry. Throughout my primary school years, I often read her stories in my Kurdish language textbook.

When I was growing up in Halabja, there were very few college graduates in town. But there were many teachers. Due to the teacher shortage, the government had allowed mullahs to apply to be teachers in the regular schools. Many did and were employed. The teachers in Halabja enjoyed a relatively easy life with three months of holiday in the summer. They earned enough to place them in the upper middle class. They also earned a good pension and received government assistance with housing. Good teachers could also tutor outside their school time for a relatively handsome fee. My father's cousin Qtbadeen was a teacher in Sulaymanya. He had a nice house and lived very comfortably. Qtbadeen had grown up with my father and my father advised me that I should study so that I would secure my future prosperity. He repeated more than once I must study hard so that I could be like Qtbadeen. As time passed people began to demand more from their lives. Still, few people in my hometown made it into the college of medicine and engineering. But my parents raised their expectations and hoped that I would be a doctor or an engineer.

In grammar school, our lessons included Arabic as well as Kurdish language. The mullahs who had become teachers could only teach Arabic and religion classes. We students were less enthusiastic about these two subjects. Many students would make fun of the mullahs. Most of the mullahs gave up their traditional dress for three-piece modern European suits, and some acquired desire to drink alcoholic beverages.

My Arabic class was taught by Mullah Qader. Even though he wore the traditional clothes, he displayed a good sense of humor in class. But since we were just kids, a lot of his jokes flew over our heads. I can still remember some of the things he said. They struck me as odd back then, but now I get the joke.

One day a student asked the mullah, "Teacher, how old are you?"

"Fifty-one," he answered.

"How old were you fifteen years ago?" asked another student.

"Fifty-one," answered Mullah Qader.

"That doesn't sound right, Teacher," said the student.

"Oh yes, it sounds right. You have to stick to your story and don't change it."

One of the older students asked the mullah, "Are you as strong as you were when you were fourteen?"

"Oh yes," answered the mullah.

"How can that be?" asked the student.

"I'll tell you how. In my village there was a big rock. When I was fourteen I couldn't move it. I tried when I was twenty and I couldn't move it. Now I'm fifty-one and I still can't move it."

Once he told us this story:

"In my village there was a son and a father who worked on a farm. They dig a deep well in their property—I tell you kids, you better be careful and don't play around wells. If you fall down a well you might never make it out—One day the son went to draw water from the well. He slipped and fell in. The father looked down at the bottom of the well. He yelled, "Son, don't go anywhere. Stay right where you are until I get back with a rope."

Just as much as we resented our Arabic class, we admired our Kurdish language class. The authors we studied were intelligent and brilliant. Studying them made us feel proud of our heritage. The Kurdish teachers knew that Kurds enjoy stories and that is what they gave us. The Kurdish culture is rich in proverbs and behind every one is a story. These stories are fascinating and Kurdish people loved to hear them. However, the stories behind many of the proverbs have gotten lost over the years. Sadly, very few have survived. I remember in grade school we were taught to be good for what goes around will come around. We were also told that for every despot there is another despot. The moral of this proverb came from an old Kurdish story passed from one generation to another. The story went like this:

Once upon a time, there were two bandits who would attack people on the road and strip them of their valuables. One day a traveling merchant came by carrying his merchandise on the backs of two donkeys. The merchant left the road to rest by a spring. While he was resting, the bandits approached him. They took the merchants money and valuables and tied him up. They told him they were going to kill him. The merchant begged, "Please, don't kill me. You will gain nothing from my death and you have already taken all I own."

The bandits were unmoved by the man's pleas for his life. They told the merchant to shut up because they were going to kill him no matter what he said. The poor merchant said his prayers to God, "dear God, I've done no wrong to these people and I have given them everything they wanted. Now they want to end my life for no reason." Immediately after his prayer, two partridges passed nearby tree. The merchant noticed the partridges and said to them, "You partridges know that I have done no wrong to these two men. I want you to be my witnesses before God that these bandits are ending my life for no reason." The bandits killed the merchant and left his dead body lying in the dirt.

Years later those two same bandit came to be guests of a landlord who was a prominent figure in his village. One of the dishes being served at dinner was fried partridge, a Kurdish favorite. The dinner was presented and the landlord sat with   the bandits, his family, friends and other guests. The bandits exchanged a sly smile when they saw the partridges.

The landlord noticed their suspicious glances and decided to keep an eye on them. The two bandit, unaware of the landlord's scrutiny, looked at each other and smiled again.

The landlord found their smiles disturbing and he asked them outright, "What are those smiles about, are you making fun of our meal?" The robbers were shocked by his question and replied lamely, "It's a great meal Sir."

"No."

The landlord insisted, "there is something hidden in your smiles."

"No, Sir. We meant no disrespect to you," one of the bandit replied.

"I don't care if it was about me or somebody else. There was something hidden in your smiles and you must tell me the truth or I'll order you to be hanged."

One of the bandits replied, "We should not try to hide anything from you, Sir. One day we robbed a businessman as he rested near a spring. We took all his money and we killed him. Just as we were about to execute him, the merchant looked up and saw two partridges. He asked them to be his witnesses for judgment day. The partridges here reminded us of him."

"Don't you think he was foolish to do that?" asked the other bandit with a smile.

The landlord, putting his head down, was silent for a moment. When he raised his head, he was furious. "You think the merchant was stupid for begging those birds to be his witnesses? He was not stupid. He tried to make his case to God, since he knew that God is aware of everything. Did it come to your mind that these two partridges might be the same two that the merchant asked to be his witnesses?

Now they are testifying for us. You two have confessed that you are murderers of an innocent, hardworking man. God knows how many others you have murdered, but I will stop you from killing. You will get a handsome payback for what you have done."

The landlord had the bandits executed. Just before they were killed he told them, "For every despot, there is another despot."

We heard many such stories as this in our Kurdish language class in grammar school. These stories excited us and seemed connected to our lives with our families and friends. The Arabic language classes, on the other hand, had no relevance to our lives and were dull and difficult. They were about Arabs and their culture which was a world different than ours.

My first year of grammar school was two years after the Republic of Iraq was declared by General Abdul Karem Qasim in 1958, end of British colonialism. At school, we would often line up with the other members of our class and make a rectangular formation around the flag of the newly formed Iraqi Republic. We would make our pledge to the flag and after that, students were allowed to come forward and recite poetry or sing a song.

I was often called upon to recite poetry or sing song at school assemblies. During our assemblies school announcements were rendered. It was also a time to check students' hygiene. Every time we gathered, a teacher would check each student's hands, fingernails and hair. If anyone had dirty nails or hair, or if they needed a haircut, they would be grounded and sometimes sent home. When the weather was favorable the school gatherings took place in the schoolyard, otherwise they were held in the hallway.

The principal's name was Farag. Like the rest of the teachers, he dressed in a three-piece suit, but his was often an unattractive polyester one. He was bald, thin and had fair skin. He had lost nearly all the hair on his head except for a few stragglers on the sides. He was easily irritated and not well tempered, and known for having high standards and expectations for both students and teachers. Basically, Farag was every kid's nightmare. Teachers had the power to be as strict as they wanted to be. Parents liked the idea of having the teachers straighten their kids out if they should start to go wrong.

One day at a school gathering, I was called up to sing. Afterward, as usual, everyone clapped in appreciation. Right before I entered class, Mr. Farag called me to his office. He sat behind his desk. I looked at him with a big smile on my face. I thought he had called me to his office because he might have been impressed with my song. I was thinking that my mother would be happy when I told her that the principal had complimented me. Mr. Farag was silent for a moment and then his face took on a sour look. I realized I was in trouble. To my dismay, he remained silent and his face got even sourer. That scared the hell out of me. All of a sudden he shouted, "Do you know why I called you to my office?"

"No, Sir," I replied.

He shifted in his chair and raise his finger at me. "I want you to get a haircut. Tomorrow when you come back to school, you should be clean cut—your hair is too long! Now, go back to class and do not forget."

"Yes, Sir," I said and went back to class.

I had meant to do what Mr. Farag told me to do, but after school I got distracted playing soccer with my friends. I didn't get home until late. That night I remembered but it was too late to do anything about it. I was terrified to go back to school and face Mr. Farag.

The next day at school gathering I didn't volunteer to recite poetry or sing a song. I was trying to stay out of Mr. Farag's sight. To my dismay, one of my teachers, Jamal, asked me to sing a song. That was it for my attempt to hide.

As I approached my class after the gathering, I saw Mr. Farag standing outside my class. I knew he was waiting for me. I walked between two taller kids trying to be invisible. I put my head down as we walked past Mr. Farag.

I felt a hand grip me. "You're a little rat trying to hide. Where do you think you are? In a jungle where there are no barbershops? There are dozens of them in this town. I told you yesterday to get your haircut and you didn't. This is a blatant disobedience. Now, I want you to go home and shave your head before coming back to school."

I left school and walked away as quickly as I could. It was just after eight o'clock in the morning. I stopped at the first barbershop. I encountered, Taher's Barbershop. Taher was a muscular man about six feet tall with a big mustache and a scary face. He had just opened his shop for business. I went in and he asked, "Do you want your hair cut?"

I told him that I wanted a bit more than a haircut. I needed to have my head shaved. I told him I had no money with me and asked if my father could pay him later.

Taher, who knew me by name, said, "Rauf, this is no good."

"No, Sir. Really, my dad will pay you."

"Not that kid. I meant how can I shave your head, for heaven's sake? Your dad will get upset," said Taher confusedly.

"You don't understand. I have to get my head shaved." I replied.

"Why not just a haircut? Do really want me to cut this beautiful hair? What a crazy kid." He flipped both hands open upward appeared overwhelmed with the situation.

"Please, just do it quick. Mr. Farag told me that I must shave my head and get back to school."

"In that case, it's all right. Probably shaving your head isn't such a bad thing,"

"I just want Mr. Farag off my case."

"It's not so bad to shave your head. Many people do that. Shaving your head will not turn you into monkey or something. In fact, it will make your head lighter, easier to carry," said Mr. Taher.

I was getting impatient with Mr. Taher. But I didn't think I should show it because I was afraid he might not shave my head, or, worse still, he might decide he should send me to my dad. I just couldn't risk having return to school and raise hell with Mr. Farag. I knew when I went home I'd have a lot of explaining to do as it was.

But I didn't exactly feel relieved when Mr. Taher began to sharpen his scary looking razor. He kept stropping it against a piece of leather, over and over again, until the blade gleamed in the sunlight. I had never had a blade like that used on me and the sight of it terrified me. My mind reeled. Thoughts whizzed through my head, chills traveled through my spine.

"Why in the world does he need such a sharp knife? He's not going to sacrifice me. I wonder for a moment if he really was a barber or a butcher."

Another panicked thought formed in my mind, "Maybe he's going to shave my eyebrows, too!"

My fear really started getting to me. I blurted out, "Mr. Taher, only shave my head. No eyebrows or anything like that."

"What do you think kid? Do you think I'm stupid? What made you think something like that? I've never shaved anybody's *eyebrows.*"

I was still too nervous even to be embarrassed. "Thank you," I replied meekly.

First, he used his machine to cut all my hair short. Then he soaped my hair and rubbed my hair with his hands. I looked in the mirror and saw my head completely white with soap all the way down to my eyebrows. Then he started shaving with that deadly razor. He asked me casually, "Rauf, how many of you boys are in your house?"

"If I survive this shaving there will be three of us," I answered.

He laughed. "Hey, Rauf, don't worry. After I shave your head, your hair will grow back much stronger and better looking. I promise you will look like a handsome star."

While he was talking he had his sharp razor in his hands and it looked like he was going to make Rauf-kebab and barbecue me. I closed my eyes and didn't open them until the shaving was done. To add to my misery, he would stop shaving every now and then and make small talk that was totally incomprehensible to me. I was far too busy being frightened. It was all I could do to keep from screaming, "Shut up and finish the bloody job, for God's sake!" My eyes were still closed when I finally heard him say he was done. Relief washed over me. He wiped his hand and got a little towel to dry my head. The towel smelled sour and that made me think that this idiot might use the same towel for all of his customers. It smelled like he washed it once a week.

He brought a mirror and held it in back so I could see myself. When I looked in the mirror, I had a small identity crisis. I couldn't believe that I had this to look forward to when I get old. Who could stand to look this bad? I said to myself, "No wonder people don't want to get old. Look what happened to me."

As I was getting ready to go, Taher gave me a worried look. Then the idiot laughed at me and I left him. I knew that his laugh at the sight of my baldhead was only the first in many more to follow. My head felt unnaturally light. I could feel the wind blowing across it like never before. It occurred to me that now I knew why everyone hated getting drafted into the military so much. They shaved your head. I run to school as hard as I could pelt. I didn't want to be seen. I got back to school during Mullah Qader's Arabic class. As soon as I walked through the door, all the kids in the class laughed as loud as they could. Then a kid sitting behind me rapped me on the head with his knuckles. It wasn't just humiliating, it actually hurt. Mullah Qader called for order in the class, but that hadn't been in before. There certainly wasn't going to be any now. The kids were wound up and each wanted to have a shot at making fun of me. I thought for a moment that it would be good if I could wear Mullah Qader's turban. Maybe that would at least stop the kids from knocking on my head. But then I realized I would look like Mullah Qader, and who would want to look like that fool Mullah? While I was distracted with these wild thoughts, Mullah Qader, showing what a royal pain he really was, called on me to answer the question he had posed. I hadn't heard a word he had said so I just answered, "No.'

This started all the idiots in class laughing again. He called on a different student, and, by the grace of God, I was saved from their laughter for a moment. Soon Mullah Qader starting writing on the board, and the usual bombardment of chalk began. But today Mullah Qader wasn't the only target; some of that chalk was aimed at me. Those morons didn't stop throwing chalk at me until my hair started to fully grow back. That was a long time in coming, a life in itself.

My reception at home wasn't much better. When I walked in the door, my mother just about screamed.

"What the hell happened to you?"

"Mr. Farag told me to shave my head, Mom."

"Mr. Farag? That damn Mr. Farag, he's made you into a small version of himself." She said angrily as she was stirring at me furiously.

When my father came home, he was outraged that I had done something like this without going to him first. But finally all he said was, "Well, all you really did was do what stupid Mr. Farag told you to do." I promised him I would never do anything so serious again without asking him first.

A few days later I was walking home after school and I saw some older kids hanging out. I paid no attention to them and just kept walking. Suddenly, I felt something soft hit my head. Liquid was running down my neck. I touched my head and looked at my hand. I had been hit by a rotten tomato and the juice was oozing down my neck. Not only did I have to put up with kids knocking me on the head, but now they were throwing rotten vegetables at me, too!

My hometown was small but within its limited population there were many good men and women. We also had our share of characters and strange people. I remember one woman in particular who was a real character. Her life made quite a good story.

Her name was Qata and people called her Qata Chata, which means Qata the bandit. She was quite plain, and like most women in small towns of that day, she didn't use cosmetics. As a matter of fact, her face was a bit hairy and she dressed in men's clothing. She carried a knife at her waist and she wore a hat with a turban wrapped around it.

She had a little grocery store. Her store had very little merchandize, mostly candies, nuts and tobacco. She lived in her small store. I knew she was a woman even though she dressed in men's clothes. I wondered why she had never married. I thought she was very strange and I was curious about her. Finally my mom told me:

"Qata is as tough as they come. She is a better fighter than any man in the area. She could take on a whole clan by herself and win."

"You mean she can fight men?" I asked.

"Oh, yes. Wait until you hear her story."

"Years ago, Qata was going to be married. She loved the man she was to marry and just before their wedding, he was mistakenly shot by the police. Qata was devastated and she vowed to get revenge against those who had killed her husband to be."

"They killed him by mistake?"

"I had never heard of such a thing before." I said.

"Yes. People sometimes make mistakes that are so serious that can cause the loss of someone's life. Qata armed herself and began attacking government posts by night, hiding in caves by day. She seemed to be everywhere and yet no one could find her anywhere. She killed several policemen and started stealing government equipments.

Eventually, the Iranian police agreed to cooperate with the Iraqi police so they could bring Qata to justice. This made Qata furious. She fought both the Iranian and the Iraqi government. This went on for months until the police on both sides of the border were worried and shaken. Finally, both governments were worn down by the loss of men and equipment. It was too costly for a battle against one woman. The Iraqi King Fasel sent one of his officers to meet with Shaykh Aladen, my father's uncle, who was the elder and leader of the Naqishbendi. The officer asked for the Shaykh's help to stop Qata. The Shaykh told him that he could bring Qata back to being a good citizen if she were given a pardon for her crimes along with some monetary assistance to restart her life. The king agreed to this arrangement. Shaykh got word to Qata to invite her to his place. Qata could not say no to the leader of the Naqishbendi, so she came to his place. She went even though she feared he might turn her in to the government. Qata came to the Shaykh's house and he told her that if she would stop fighting the government they would pardon her. Moreover, she would receive a salary from the government to support herself. Qata agreed and the government kept its word. They gave her some money to put her life together. Since then she has been a very good person and repentant.

"Qata loved her fiancé. She remained faithful to his memory and never married."

There are many stories about heroic Kurdish women. Kurdish history is full of the names of women who have played heroic roles in their community and even on a national level. More than once in modern times, women have been some of the most powerful figures in Kurdistan.

That is how life was in Halabja before things changed. After the revolution came in 1961, the things that I had taken for granted would never be the same again. But I didn't know this yet.

Chapter Two

Although Halabja was a small town in a remote part of the world, I had always seen it as the most important place in the world. I had felt that the mountains that surrounded us combined with the walls of our home were more than enough to keep us safe from any harm. Despite the history of the Kurds, as a child, I didn't yet understand how the decision and actions of unknown leaders and soldiers could have a direct impact on my little life in my small town. Sadly, my little town was about to become an important location in the fighting of the Kurdish revolution. These bloody events would teach me a hard lesson about what it means to be caught in the middle of a power and armed struggle.

In 1948, a popular Kurdish leader named Mustafa Barzani led an uprising in Iraqi Kurdistan aimed at gaining Kurdish national recognition within Iraq. It didn't take long for the Iraqi army to corner him at the intersecting borders of Iraq, Iran and Turkey. With the army of all three neighboring countries attacking, Barzani managed to escape. He and his followers took refuge U.S. S. R.

An army general named Abdul Karem Qasim made a bloody coup on July 14, 1958, killing the King of Iraq and ended the British colonialism in Iraq. Qasim didn't affiliate with any political party and had no allies, but he leaned toward the communist party. He tried to build a friendship with the Kurds. Once Qasim had consolidated a base of power, he took a big risk and invited Barzani to return to Iraq. Barzani accepted Qasim's invitation to return to Iraq and came home to a hero's welcome. Barzani was a tribesman and a former mullah. He was probably wise but not an intellectual, a good fighter but not diplomatic. Qasim, on the other hand, came from a military background but acted and talked like a madman. Iraq is predominately an agrarian country with vast petroleum resources. The Communist Party wanted land reform so Qasim decided to achieve just that. The Iraqi farmers including Kurdish farmers found this change to be a relief. Now they would farm the land for themselves instead of for wealthy landlords.

In the meanwhile, the Kurdish Democratic Party (KDP) was trying to grow. They were focused on achieving an autonomous Kurdish region within Iraq.

Qasim had his own pet project. His main concern was building a dam in Darbandikhan, which was less than an hour's drive from Halabja. The landlords made a lot of noise in response to this plan and revolted. A dam at Darbandikhan would cover most of the farmland in the area and the only beneficiaries from it would be the Arabs in the south. The landlords and their people took up arms against the government to stop construction of the dam. The KDP seized this opportunity, they worked with the landlords and took charge of the situation. Landlords who feared land reform joined the KDP which grew in popularity and number. The controversy over the dam and land reform became the base for the Kurdish protest demanding an autonomous Kurdish region.

The KDP lacked charismatic leader so they approached Barzani. Their offer was well timed as Barzani's relationship with Baghdad was deteriorating because of the problems in Kurdistan. He was more than willing to accept the role of leader for the KDP. This is how the Kurdish revolution born 1961 under the leadership of tribesman, Mustafa Barzani.

Toward 1962 a Kurdish socialist party named Kazhek formed. My mother's cousin Harseny was one of the founders and a leader of this newly formed political party. From the onset, this political party was very popular with the most intellectual among the Kurds, particularly with those in Sulaymanya. The Kazhek's fundamental belief in a long term was a sovereign state unifying Kurds from Iraq, Iran, Syria and Turkey. Their immediate goal was an independent Iraqi Kurdistan. The party operated under rules of extreme secrecy. Members of the Kazhek penetrated deeply into the KDP. In fact, they gained so much influence within the party that when the division erupted between Talabani and Barzani, it was the Kazhek who ran the show. My mother's cousin Harseny is a good example of this power. People didn't know he was a founding member of the Kazhek and yet he was the second most powerful voice in the KDP after Barzani for years.

The KDP was in charge of the uprising against the government. In a show of strength, the KDP gathered a group of approximately a thousand to two thousand men and brought them to Halabja. Each man was armed with a rifle and had bullets draped over their vest. There must have been at least one hundred trucks and Land Rovers carrying revolutionaries. They lined up in two rows and marched through the street from one end of town to the other. It took a half an hour for the whole procession to pass by. Scores of people congregated on both sides of the street to watch this power display. People applauded them and shouted slogans like "Long live the Kurds!" or, "Long live Barzani!" For the Kurds, this marked the beginning of an age of freedom and liberty. We believed the time was right to regain our national identity and be a free nation.

Qasim was preparing to squelch the uprising. He made a deal with the Soviet Union to equip the army with modern arms. After that, we would see MiG jet fighters on a daily basis around Halabja. However, people thought nothing of them; they thought they could shoot them down with their hunting rifles.

The government continued to support the Communist Party. The Party began to insult religion in general and Islam in particular. We had lived all our lives without any religious confrontation in Kurdistan and now the communists were trying to instigate a war among us. It was during this period, when so many insults were committed against the Naqishbendi, that many members of my father's family decided to leave everything behind and immigrate to Iran. The communists initiated a hate campaign of anti-religion propaganda. They took up the slogan that religion was the opiate of the masses. They publicly insulted religion and denied the existence of God.

The situation polarized. The Kurdish Revolution, headed by the KDP, was able to take over most villages and small towns. In these small towns, the KDP outnumbered the local police force. There were many cases where the KDP made deals with the police allowing them to join the revolution and retain their rank within the KDP forces. The police forces in most small towns and villages gave themselves over to the revolution and brought enough arms and equipment to allow the revolutionaries to continue their fight against the government.

A police chief in Pengewin, a town near the Iranian border, dragged his feet and didn't want to give away his town. His name was Abdul Wahab Atroshy. He was in love with a schoolteacher in Sulaymanya. Their marriage was arranged. The KDP could not get to Atroshy so they put pressure on his fiancée's family. She finally agreed to write to Atroshy saying she would not marry him until he gave up his town. Atroshy at last cut a deal to join the revolution, giving up his town that included a communications system, weapons and government money.

In 1962, the treasurer of Halabja, a man named Abdul Razaq, made a deal with the KDP. In exchange for the money from Halabja's treasury, the KDP agreed to arrange for political asylum for Razaq and his family in Iran. They also gave him a portion of 75,000 dinar ($225,000) he brought to the KDP. Deals such as this were made in towns all over Iraqi Kurdistan.

Chapter Three

It was an early on a Friday morning, 1962, the Muslims holy day, and some people were still eating their breakfasts. I was nine years old at the time and it was my custom to get daily allowance from my grandfather at his shop. I was enjoying the beautiful spring morning. The town circle was alive with people from the villagers displaying their produce and selling yogurt.

I had been going to get my daily allowance every mornings from my grandfather since I was four years old. It always made me impatient when I had to wait for him to take care of his customers. He would often tell me to come back later. I thought this was a big pain and didn't understand why he didn't just stop his business for a minute to give me my allowance.

Fridays were busy at my grandfather's shop. This day was no exception. While waiting impatiently for my grandfather to wrap up his business, I noticed my friend Hama. My grandfather's neighbor Ala Dom was unloading fresh tomatoes and figs he had bought from a villager. The villager and his donkey were waiting by the store until Ala Dom had unloaded the produce from the villager's basket. We were watching the villager have a nervous breakdown as Ala Dom was taking out one tomato at a time. We were laughing hysterically and we kept saying, "Come on, faster, Ala Dom! If you go at this speed you will never unload that little basket!"

Ala Dom heard us. He turned around with a tomato in each hand and gave us a dirty look, for a moment I thought he would through the tomatoes on my face. "Hey, what are you laughing at?" said Ala Dom abrasively.

"We are just joking. We are not laughing at anything," I said.

"Hama, let me see what my grandpa is up to."

I went and glanced in my grandpa's store. I saw the customers were still there and I heard my grandfather ordering tea for them. I figured that meant it would be another hour of waiting before they left. When I went back, Hama was still sitting on a pavement, watching Ala Dom. I sat down with Hama and saw the poor villager still waiting for Ala Dom to finish unloading the basket so he could get his basket back and leave the town.

"Let's ride this guy's donkey. He will still be here waiting when we get back," said Hama.

The villager looked at us because Hama was so loud. "You little devils better leave my donkey alone," said the villager.

We went back to laughing at them. They seemed to be annoyed with our laughter. In the middle of this, an old man with a beard and gray hair came along. He could scarcely walk but he had three or four baskets loaded on his donkey full of roosters and chickens. A man stopped the old man to buy a chicken from him. The old man lifted up one of the baskets and dropped it on the ground. Roosters and chickens scattered all over. Feathers billowed in the air. Hama and I ran around and saved some of the birds and the old man got the rest. He thanked us and went about his business. We went back to our spot and Ala Dom was still holding the poor villager's basket hostage. We could tell that the villager was fed up. To make matters worse, Ala Dom had started telling some one a long story. Hama asked the villager, "Are you staying in town tonight?"

The villager was mad as hell and told us to mind our own damn business. We laughed again.

All in a sudden we heard three loud explosions in sequence. I thought it must have been a bomb. We saw everyone in the street running, stampeding to get out of the area. We could hear women crying as they were holding their children, trying to escape the scene. Hama and I ran to the end of the block and then split off in different directions heading home. I was frightened and bolted for home.

As soon as I saw my mother, I asked her, "Mom, did you hear the bomb?"

"What bomb? Must have been a balloon or something."

"No, Mom, I swear it was a bomb. I heard three of them," I said.

My mother looked at me suspiciously and asked, "Where have you been?" Her look accused me of being somewhere I should not have been.

"Mom, I was with Hama at grandpa's store—"

She interrupted me, "Then what?"

I got really mad and said loudly, "Then what? That's when the bombs exploded!"

"Okay, we will find out about this. Keep cool."

I was just about to step out when Merriam, our neighbor, came in. Merriam was the kind of person one can read like an open book. She looked worried and shaken.

"Merriam, have a seat and tell me what is going on," said my mother.

"My brother Rasol just came home and told me that a gunman killed soldiers in Swara's Café," said Merriam.

"Oh my God, Rauf! I pray your grandpa is okay," said my mother as she turned to me. "He should be okay," I said.

"How do you know he is okay? Swara's Café is across the street from my father's store. That is why I am worried," said my mother.

"I'll go check on him right now," I said.

I ran out the door. My mother kept calling for me to stop. She called me several times but I pretended deaf kept going as fast as my feet would carry me. As I was running toward the scene of the shooting, everyone else was running the other direction. I ran until I came to his store. I noticed that all the stores were closed down. All of a sudden, I found myself surrounded by several armed soldiers.

On the opposite side of the street, I saw an ambulance. I assumed it was carrying the soldiers the gunmen had killed. I saw two soldiers lifting up a body right in front of the café where people sat on two long wooden benches. The café's doors were open and so were the doors at Baba's produce store next to the cafe. I saw a couple of soldiers inside. I saw blood everywhere. That gave me a chill and I started to get scared. It seemed like soldiers were taking over every corner downtown. The only people out on the streets were soldiers with machineguns. Soldiers were running in disoriented circles as if from confusion. They moved toward me and formed a circle around me. They closed the circle and moved in closer to me. They started talking as loud as they could and had their fingers on the triggers of their guns. I could not understand a word they said because they spoke in Arabic. If I could have spoken enough Arabic, I would have asked them why they had to shout all the time. I was getting a headache from all the noise. Finally, they broke the circle around me and I understood the word "GO." I left.

I was frightened as I ran back home. I realized I was probably very lucky for the soldiers could have easily killed me. As I ran, I saw neighbors congregated in groups talking about what had happened. When I got home, I was out of breath. My mother looked worried. She was sitting in the front yard with two neighbor women, Haba and Aysha.

My mother asked me, "Didn't you hear me calling you? Why didn't you stop?"

"No, Mom, I went to check on grandpa, all right?"

"No it isn't alright when you don't listen. You know there was a shooting and you could easily have gotten killed."

"Sorry, Mom, I won't do it again." My usual promise whenever I caught doing what I wasn't suppose to do.

"Did you see your grandpa?" she asked.

"No, the store was locked. I'm sure he's gone home."

"Good, that makes me feel better," said my mother.

The two neighbor women were looking at me as if I was nuts. I went to sit down on a chair a little away from them, but I could still hear them. You could have heard Aysha from the end of the street. She was a royal pain in the neck. She spoke with a rhythm and she sounded like she was talking through her nose. Her voice was so annoying it would have even gotten into Mother Teresa's nerve. She complained about everything but her real talent was picking at things to find faults with. She was damn good at it and no person or topic was safe from her faultfinding. We had just had a shooting in town, but it didn't stop her from complaining about the local shoe seller Haji Amen.

"I bought these shoes, I paid a fortune for them. The damn things don't even fit!"

"So just return them to him and get a bigger shoe," said my mother.

But Aysa was just warming up. "You don't know. I told this arrogant Haji Amen that the shoe was too small. He told me the shoes are leather so they will stretch.

He said wear the shoe and by the time you get home, they will be okay. Now the shoes are not okay and my feet have gotten red like tomatoes."

"Now you've worn the shoes and can't return them. He sometimes gets difficult," said my mother.

Listening to this nonsense made me angry. I thought these women care more about some stupid shoes than a killing in town. They couldn't seem to help themselves. Aysha was trying to be quiet, but she just couldn't help but warm up to her hell raising about shoes. Soon I grew tired of listening to those crazy women talk. As I was getting up, my father entered the house. He told me not to go far. I should stay close to the house. Finally, word spread that *peshmargas* had assassinated one army officer and a soldier as they were eating their breakfast at the café. That made almost everyone in town happy, for it was seen as a victory for the revolution. A week later, we found out the assassin was a man named Jaza Shal from Sulaymanya. He was a young man in his early twenties who walked with a limp. He had committed several more assassinations in Sulaymanya.

The assassinations in Halabja that day marked the beginning of violence in our town which went on for decades.

Chapter Four

Peshmargas commenced attacking government posts everywhere they could. It finally got to the point that the government couldn't send ammunition from Sulaymania to Halabja without military convoy. When the government troops made a move, the *peshmargas* were already entrenched and attacked the army from different directions. The army's casualties would mount quickly, and they were only left with the option of retreat.

The *peshmargas* couldn't take over Halabja and there was no deal to be made. It was too a big of a town for them to manage, yet they were willing to risk it if they could gain control. They decided to cut off the town from its main supplier, Sulaymanya. In Halabja there was still a police station and the town was officially under the government's control. It was important to the government to keep Halabja because it was the biggest town near Iranian border. The government tried to hold the pieces of Iraqi Kurdistan together and Halabja was one of their priorities. Summer 1963, the Iraqi army prepared convoys of artillery, tanks and other heavy war machines as well as their MiG jets. The convoy started from Sulaymanya destined to Halabja. The *peshmargas* fought all the way along the road from Sulaymanya to Halabja. As the army's casualties piled up each time, they had to retreat back to the city. At last an army convoy made it to Halabja.

Then the government started establishing secret agents and recruiting locals in Halabja to report those who were against the government so they could be punished. Those recruited soon started turning in innocent people and fabricating false information about them. Imprisonment started on a large scale causing public resentment toward authorities. People could easily find themselves in prison just for criticizing the government or saying anything in favor of the revolution.

One day after school, early in the spring of 1962, I went to my father's store. As I got to the store I saw a policeman and a secret agent standing by my father and talking to him. My father looked lost and sad. I moved close to my father. Arief, the storeowner next door was outside watching. Dad gave me the keys to the store and told Arief to help me close. Then my father left with the agent and the policeman.

I couldn't make anything out of what is going on. I asked Arief, "Do you know where my father went?"

Arief looked very upset, "Let's close the store then we'll talk."

Arief and I took all the merchandise outside into the store. As we were closing other storeowners came and talked to Arief to see what had happened. Arief told them my father had been arrested. As each one of them went away, one could see they all were very upset with what they heard. We took everything back inside and Arief locked the store.

"Rauf, wait until I cover the stuff outside of my store." I waited as he got a huge piece of cloth and covered the table where he had his merchandise on display. He covered the table and double-checked everything.

"Rauf, I'm ready. I'll come with you to have a talk with your mother," said Arief.

We walked home; Arief's house was on our block and we were neighbors.

As we walked Arief turned toward me after he looked back to make sure no one was behind us, then in a low voice "I tell you where the policeman and the government agent took your dad, but you should not say anything to the other kids about this."

"Okay," I said.

"Your dad is arrested and he will probably be taken to the prison," said Arief.

"Prison? Why? My father has not stolen anything from anyone! He hasn't fought anyone! How can he be taken to prison?"

"No, it's not that, Rauf."

He looked behind him again; it seemed like he didn't want anyone overhear him.

"Now when people are taken to prison it isn't for stealing or fighting. Everyday people are taken to prison because of what they say or for no reason other than angering the wrong people," said Arief.

"Then do you know? How long my dad will be in prison?" I asked.

"God knows, I hope will not be for too long. But they can keep him there for as long as they want."

We were about home when Arief turned to me, "Again, I want you say nothing to other people about your father's arrest because anything we say may complicate his situation, do you understand that?"

"Yes." I assented.

We went to our house and he at knocked the door. My mother came forward, welcomed Arief and offered him a place to sit. Our shoes were muddy; we both took our shoes off and went to the living room and sat.

Then Arief started, "Mahboob Khan…less than an hour ago Shaykh Gareeb was arrested. A policeman and Hamay Hajy took him to the police station. I helped

Rauf to close the store. Here are the keys." He handed Mom the store keys.

My mother started crying right away. Through tears, "But why him, for heaven sake? What had he done wrong?"

"I am sorry, Mahboob Khan, but it could be any one of us, they seem to be taking people at random and there are no justifications for the arrest. You need to know we're dealing with the devil," said Arief.

After a few more minutes of talking with my mother Arief said, "If you need help, please don't hesitate, I will be at your disposal."

My mother thanked him and Arief left. My mother still crying and frustrated and didn't know what to do. She prepared my lunch, and left to see her father. "I will be back. I want you to stay here until I return,"

She left and didn't come back for another hour.

As soon as she left my sister Ronak started crying. She was about a year and a half old and my brother Abdul about five years old. My brother and I used every trick we knew to calm her down until she finally stopped crying.

When my mother got home, she held my sister and sat by the heater. A few minutes later she put her down and got a cigarette. My mother used to occasional smoking but when she was frustrated she smoked a few more.

After my mother relented, I left the house and went to my grandpa's house so that I could see my uncles Sarwat and Aram.

When I came back in the late afternoon, my mother had prepared dinner.

"Mom is there any news about my father?"

"Not much, he is in prison. While you were gone I fixed him dinner and went with your grandpa to see him in prison."

"Mom, what is Dad doing in prison?"

"Not much *to* do, what can one do there?"

"Did anyone say when he would be released?" I asked.

"Hamay Haji told your grandfather that he would manage to have your father released if we gave him one hundred Dinar," she said.

"One hundred Dinar is a lot of money. That is more than what dad makes in five months," I said.

"I know, but he said that is not all going to him. Most of that money goes to the head of the secret police in town. They split it amongst themselves. I hope and pray they will all get ill and that it won't be enough to cover their medical expense," she said.

"Where do we get one hundred Dinar?"

"All we have is my jewelry and I have no choice but to sell it for cash tomorrow," she said. Then started crying, "God, please don't accept this, this is not right. All I have is my jewelry and yet I have to give it away to these thieves. That was all I had for security and that will be gone tomorrow."

It got late and my mother asked me to get ready for bed.

I went to bed, worried about my father. I had a bad feeling that they might kill him or keep him in prison for years. I didn't know what prison looked like but all I knew it was not a good place to be. What bothered me was that only bad people went to prison. Robbers, thieves and other violent people might be housed with my father and they might harm him. I kept tossing in bed and thought of all kinds of horrible things. I got really frightened they might kill my dad leaving my brother, my sister, mom and I without Dad and have no one to provide for us. That was the horror I went through that night before I finally got to sleep.

In the mornings, my father used to get up early to do his prayer. Afterward he got fresh bakery bread and yogurt. Sometimes Dad didn't get bread and mom woke me up early to get bread, and she had some walnuts and tea for breakfast. That morning Grandpa came early with a pot of yogurt and fresh bakery bread. He sat with us and we all had our breakfast.

At last my mother sold her jewelry, the agent paid and my father was released.

Chapter Five

In 1963 the Ba'th regime come to power. This was a pan-Arab political organization with an extreme nationalistic principles undermining the well-being of minorities in the entire Arab world, in particular the Kurds. Early in 1963 Baghdad had appointed General sadiq, a member of the Ba'th party, to head the Iraqi military in Sulaymanya. sadiq believed that the head of the Kurdish revolution was in Sulaymanya. He had said that if he could get the head of the snake, the rest of the body would die. He was determined to employ every cruelty and terror to control the city.

Early that summer, he declared a curfew in Sulaymanya. His troops were attempting in hunting down the revolutionaries. There weren't any armed *peshmargas* in the city, but there were members of the KDP. The government didn't know who they were as it was still an underground organization.

Soldiers come down and scattered everywhere in the city. They started shooting young men in the street or shot them in front of their families. They arrested more then 200 people and buried them alive with bulldozers. It was some time later on that their bodies were discovered and taken to a new graveyard specifically devoted to them in Sulaymanya. It was named the Mortar Graveyard and is still called by that name.

This episode of brutality terrified many people who feared for their lives. They left the city and joined the revolution. sadiq also imprisoned hundreds of artists, writers, athletes and prominent members of the community. They were all housed in stables and were treated like less than animals. They stayed there for months under the cruelest circumstances. Some were starved to death and others were transferred to the death camps in the south, Abu Graybe and were never heard from again. One of the people they arrested was Rafek Chalak, who was a popular theater actor, writer, singer a radio personality. He wrote songs while in jail describing their conditions and yet expressing his support for revolution and the *peshmargas* who aimed at freedom and liberty.

sadiq's atrocities fueled the struggle and encouraged attacks against the Ba'th government and their political party. A wave of assassinations started against Ba'th agents and soldiers. No day went by without Ba'th casualties.

Syria, which was also ruled by the Ba'th regime, collaborated with the Iraqi government to crush the Kurdish revolution. At the same time Turkey and Iran closed their border to Kurds. We were surrounded by three governments all aimed at crushing the Kurdish revolution and that to silence the Kurdish demand for freedom. The Syrian and Iraqi armies both engaged in fighting, but the Kurdish *peshmargas* gave them a lesson they didn't expect.

The *peshmargas* intensified their attack on government posts everywhere they could. In Halabja, *peshmargas* ran the town at night. They tried to break the link between the army headquarters in Sulaymanya and the town of Halabja. They were employed along the road between Halabja and Sulaymanya to attack army convoys and to stop them from reaching Halabja. They managed to isolate Halabja from the city for months.

Soon things got worse for Halabja. At night *peshmargas* entered the town and controlled all the roads leading to the town. They were in every street. They went on the roofs of the tall buildings and the towers of the mosques setting up their machineguns, which were the heaviest weapons they possessed at the time. They'd fire away at the government posts including the government's headquarter. They kept on until dawn when they retreated. This went on for a long time. By now the *peshmargas* had control over all the surrounding towns all the way to the Iranian border which was about twenty-five miles away from Halabja.

People in Halabja were terrified that General sadiq and his troops would do the same thing in Halabja as they did in Sulaymanya. Once sadiq's troop arrived, people decided to go and welcome sadiq and his troops to the town hoping it would soften his heart and keep him from doing harm to them.

I was about ten years old then. I and many other kids and adults had brought containers of water and ice in cups. Soldiers coming into the town one after another got full cups of water and some smiled and others gave me dirty looks. I was scared, in particular at the beginning I couldn't trust them. I was afraid they might open fire on the crowd for they had already shown their potential for mass murder. Along the main road in Halabja people from both sides of the road stood to show that we welcomed the Iraqi army. That was a show aimed at saving our lives. In reality we all despised them. There were some elders in town who didn't agree with what we did and they told us that if sadiq didn't do anything at the time, he would do it later. We stayed on the main road and witnessed hundreds of army trucks pulling artilleries, dozens of tanks and thousands soldiers enter the town.

The next day we woke up to the sound of tanks shelling nearby villages. We ran to the roofs of the houses and watched the bombing. We saw the bombs hitting these villages; we could see people running amongst the smoke of the explosions. A few days later we heard that many people from the bombed villages were killed and many others were wounded. The bombing also devastated farmers by killing their cattle, which for many was the main source of their income.

General sadiq was determined to uproot the revolution and cleanse the area from *peshmargas* and their supporters. He moved his armed forces close to the Iranian border. The army's firepower was supported by advanced artillery and Russian-made tanks which easily overmatched the primitive weapons of the *peshmargas*. There was minimal resistance and the army took over. In most areas the army stayed for a short time, and upon their departure *peshmargas* regained control.

sadiq's forces came back to Halabja and recruited hundreds of locals to fight the *peshmargas*. The lowlifes in town took up the jobs and he named them *Frsan Al Salahadeen*, The Horsemen Of Salahadeen, referring to Salahadeen Al Ayobe who was Moslems leader during the Crusades war. Salahadeen was a member of a prominent Kurdish family in Syria, Ayob. People didn't want to waste name Salahadeen instead they called them the sons of donkeys, *Jash*. General sadiq armed and housed them. They built barracks all over town and placed these *Jashs* there to be on patrol and hinder *peshmargas* entry to town.

A couple months after sadiq's massacres and mass imprisonment my father went to Sulaymanya in a business trip, and took me along with him. There was a wholesaler in a city owned by two brothers, Karem and Muhmood, my dad used to do business with. The two brothers were partners in their business, I don't know if they inherited the business from their father or built it on their own. They also lived together, they were always together at home and outside in place of their business. The two brothers had married a pair of sisters. Muhmood was the older and Karem was the younger brother. They had another brother named Kader who lived with his family nearby. My father told me they had an older brother Adeb who died in a car crash on the highway between Baghdad and Sulaymanya. That family tragedy brought Muhmood and Karem together and since then they lived together and partnered in their business.

Muhmood and Karem used to be my father's favorite vendors. My dad told me these two brothers were models of honesty and they had good hearts. Through time my father established friendship with them and they became good friends.

When my father and I went to the city, we went to them as usual. They invited us for dinner and offered us to stay there overnight and to have dinner with them. We went to their house for dinner; it was a nice place not far from uncle Zaynadeen's house. Both Karem and Muhmood and their families shared the house, and they were a good society.

We had dinner in their living room, a sizable room carpeted with Persian rugs, and there were pictures of the family on one wall. They had enlarged photos of all four brothers together and individually. It was relatively a modern house made of stones, bricks and cement. We sat for dinner with everyone in the family; they made us what called Kfta Shorba. It's made of rice stuffed with ground lamb, raisin, and nuts and flavored with herbs. It was the best Kfta I ever had.

After dinner, Karem conversed with my dad about his brother,

Muhmood. I really didn't know what had happened to him; I just knew that Muhmood wasn't there. They talked about general sadiq's days of curfew. My father hadn't been in Sulaymanya since. He seemed to be interested to know more about the curfew and the people's experience. They talked about that for a long time; Karem was doing most of the talking. Dad mostly listened and once in a while he asked a question or made a comment.

There were five kids in the house and the youngest one was about two years older than I was, his name was Dara, Muhmood's son. We started to play a game, but I kept my ears open and listened to my father and Karem's conversation. I wanted to hear, so I stopped playing with Dara and sat next to my dad. Karem looked pale and sad or he may have been in pain. He was sitting nervously on a mattress with a couple pillows behind him, every few minutes shifting his body and gently rubbing his face. Then Karem mentioned something he had placed in their backyard. I wasn't sure, but I thought he said it was a body. That frightened me and it had me follow their conversation intently so that I could figure out the story.

About this time, Karem's wife showed me my room where there were two beds, one for me and the other for my father. She told me I could go to my room whenever I felt like sleeping. It was after nine o'clock and felt like going to bed but yet I was frightened and wanted to be sure of what I heard before I went to sleep. I noticed the two ladies in the house were dressed in black, which was a sign that they were mourning a family member.

Then my dad and Karem switched their conversation to politics. They talked about revolution, its leaders and the prospects for peace. They went on for another half an hour before saying goodnight.

Once me and my dad got to our room, I asked my father what was it in the backyard Karem talking about. He paused for a minute, then he said, "There are things you may not want to know, you don't need to know everything."

"I'll promise not to talk about it to anyone, if you want," I pleaded.

My dad got changed to go bed and he lay down. He rubbed his face a couple of times, looked at me and said in a very low voice so that he wouldn't disturb anyone, "When sadiq's troops committed their massacre in Sulaymanya, several soldiers came to this house. They searched everywhere, and that night Qader, Karem's other brother was visiting them, and all three brothers were together."

He continued: "Then soldiers took Muhmood and wanted to kill him. Karem offered himself to be killed instead of his brother Muhmood. The soldiers beat Karem until he fell down unconscious and bleeding, then they killed his brother Muhmood and Qader. Karem has not recovered from that beating which resulted in a brain concussion and back problems," said my father.

"Why didn't he go to the hospital?" I asked.

"It was a curfew and it went for a long time. People were not free to go from one place to another. Karem decided to bury his brothers' bodies in the backyard, and that was the only option. Karem loved his brothers and he feels guilty for being a survivor. Even though his brothers are dead, he still wants them to spend another month with them.

Next month he will transfer their bodies to the graveyard. Karem's family is not alone in their tragedy, what they did to Karem's family was done to many people in the city."

My dad added, "Karem is a good and God-loving man. He takes care of his brother's family and he treats Muhmood and Qader's children like his own. I pray God that Karem will be healed because he is going through a lot of pain, and he is supporting two of his children and three of his brothers' kids."

He pause, then resumed "that is all about it, and now It's bedtime son, try get some sleep."

I was unlikely to sleep well after what I'd heard. I must admit nothing in my life has broken my heart as much as the sad story of this family. I always felt scared in graveyards even during the daylight. That night it seemed that I was out on a dark night visiting the graveyard, and thought of Karem's backyard as a graveyard, which it was. I felt badly for everyone in Karem's family. I kept tossing on the bed and was so disturbed that I couldn't go sleep for a long time. That night and the tragedy of this family is something that will always stay with me.

My mother's relatives told stories of curfews and imprisonments. I didn't know the exact details of what general sadiq and the Ba'th Party had done in Sulaymanya until years later. I also talked to one of the prominent individuals from Sulaymanya, named Bayazed, who was very much involved with the community and was very well respected in the city.

Bayazed was a slim person dressed in suit and a white shirt with no tie. His hair was receding and very much gray above his skinny face. He was well traveled and a good sense of humor and calm voice. He enjoyed drinking red wine but no more than a couple of glasses. Talking to Bayazed was quite interesting. He knew my father from his childhood and he told me that for years he did business with my grandfather.

I opened my conversation regarding days of General sadiq, "Bayazed, were you in Sulaymanya during General sadiq's massacre and mass imprisonment?"

"Yes I was," he replied.

"Can I bother you to tell me of those days?"

"I'll tell you what I can," he replied. "I never forgot those days and it's always detailed in my mind, even if it's painful when I talk about it."

"I surely know that, yet painful memories such as these need to be told so that they will not be forgotten. No one has written about those days and it will need to be told and remembered," I said.

"Let me rewind my memory and tell you what happened." he said. Then he started telling me his story.

Chapter Six

I was at home that day of June 1963. At about five o'clock in a morning I woke up to the sound of a megaphone on an army vehicle that was going around the city and making an announcement—telling people to stay home and not to leave their houses. They made the announcement in both Arabic and Kurdish and they toured every district in the city. We did what we were instructed to do.

I was looking out from the windows, which were overlooking the street. I saw trucks unloading soldiers in the intersection of the two streets by my house. I saw the soldiers carrying *kalashnikovs* and their fingers were on their triggers. When I saw soldiers coming toward our house, I hid myself in the closet. When the soldiers inspected my house, they went from room to room and checked everything.

I remained in the closet, and my heart was beating so fast, I thought I might have a heart attack. They came to the room and I was lucky they didn't bother opening the closet. I heard two soldiers examining the room and I tried to hold my breath so that they didn't get a feeling that someone was hiding in the room. They stayed in that room for a minute or two. Every second of that felt like years, and I thought when I got out of the closet I would be looking twenty years older. I was shaking and overwhelmed with fear of being caught. The soldiers left the room. I must say that I was lucky—they searched the closet in every other room but God helped me and they missed the closet where I was hiding. If they had caught me hiding, I am sure they would have gunned me down or at minimum brutally beaten.

My legs shook so badly they couldn't hold me—I thought that I was going to collapse. I heard the door to the room open and as I fell down, hitting my head against the closet door, I heard a voice. "Bayazed, come on out. The soldiers have gone." My wife Zaynab opened the closet door and I fell out onto the floor.

"What did you do to yourself?" asked Zaynab.

"I don't know, just get me some ice and something to wrap around my forehead."

"Lift up your head, let me see," she gasped at the sight. "Your forehead is swelling very badly. Listen dear, the soldiers may come back again. If they catch you hiding, they might kill you."

"So what am I supposed to do?" I asked.

"Go ahead, sit in one of our rooms and take the *Qur'an* with you. If soldiers come back, start reading it out loud. These soldiers are Muslims; if they hear you reading the *Qur'an*, they may leave you alone."

"That makes sense." The pain in my forehead was throbbing. "But these are not Muslims. If they were, they wouldn't be so cruel to us."

"At least you can remind them that they are Muslims as you read the *Qur'an*, that is the only thing I can think of, what else?"

"I will do what you said, but frankly that is not going to work, lady," I said.

As I finished my sentence, came in another crew of soldiers. I had a copy of the *Qur'an* on a shelf so I pulled it out, sat on a *barmal*,* and started reading. I heard the soldiers again searching from room to room. A soldier came to my room and had his finger on the trigger of his *kalashnikov*. I didn't make a fuss and kept reading the Qur'an but he kicked me in the middle of my back and pulled me up by the collar of my shirt, the Qur'an dropped on the floor. When I stood up he hit me with the butt of his *Kalashnikov* several times until I fell down on the floor. He cursed me in Arabic—curses too disgusting and offensive to repeat.

"Get up now, bastard, and follow me outside!" the soldier shouted in Arabic.

---

* A prayer mat

I got up and went outside. He followed me with his *Kalashnikov* pointed at my head. He asked me to walk to an army truck parked a couple houses down from ours. When I got close to the truck I saw several soldiers and at least a dozen civilians all sitting on their knees in a back of the truck. At his order I got in and kneeled like the others with my hands behind my neck.

Three soldiers in the back of the truck stood pointing their *kalashnikovs* at us. My head felt like it was splitting in the middle and the pain in my shoulders and back were excruciating. The army truck started moving. I didn't know where they would take us.

The soldiers in the truck told us to put our heads down and they spit on us and kicked us and hit us with their *kalashnikovs*. All I could see was other people's feet and after the truck made a couple of turns I didn't know what direction we were heading and where we were. I had a feeling that this was it for my life, and to be honest I didn't care if I was shot dead as much as being sent to their torture camps.

After we'd driven for about ten minutes the truck stopped and we were all told to keep our hands behind our necks and keep our heads down. A soldier inside shouted in Arabic for us to get out one by one. As we came down there were two soldiers—one on each side of the truck—kicking us in the butt and hitting us on the back of the head with the butt of their *kalashnikovs*. I got kicked and thank God I missed the hit on the head.

I knew we were at *Hamya*, the army base. We housed in a stable as spacious as a movie theater and was very crowded. It must have smelled bad before, but now with the throng of people swarming around made it even worse. It was hot in the month of June. There were no places to sit but the floor. The floor was moist and covered with animal waste. I saw some curtains hanging down—they must have been used to partition the stable. I was squeamish with the smell and I felt like I was going to spew.

I surveyed around and spotted few people I knew. I went and sat next to Dr. Omed and Dr. Kamal. Dr. Omed was optometrist who studied medicine in East Germany. He was dressed in his suit just as if he was at his office. He was in his early thirties, around my age. He had a full head of hair, brown eyes, was of average height and in good physical shape. Dr.

Kamal was general practitioner who I had dealt with several times when I had needed care.

I had a sharp Swiss Army knife. I'd always loved Swiss knives. I was lucky that I wasn't inspected by the soldiers—they would have taken it from me. I took the knife out and cut a big piece from the curtain and laid it beneath me. Then I glanced at the window and saw it was a screen. I walked near the window and cut the screen from the top to the bottom. I really don't know why I did that, probably from frustration.

"What are you doing, Bayazed?" asked Dr. Omed.

"I just cut whatever my knife could cut, what else am I to do?" I said.

"I don't know how long we'll be here, but eventually we will find something to keep us busy," said Dr. Omed.

"I really don't know why they brought us here, or where would we go from here," said Dr. Kamal.

I looked at him. "My God, why are we here? It is simple, Doctor. We are here because we Kurds declared an armed revolutionary struggle to achieve freedom for our people. We want to master our own destiny, but these thugs are doing everything to deprive us from freedom."

"That's right, for every blessing there is a price—that blessing is freedom, and our suffering is a part of the price," said Dr. Kamal.

"You said that right," I said.

Dr. Omed looked around the stable. "This is so inhumane. It's beyond the sense of any decent person in the world for people to be treated the way we are being treated."

"Don't expect anything better. We are dealing with this Arab extremist Ba'th party and they are violent and have no respect for human life. They are as bad as the Turks. You know what the Turks did to the Armenians and Assyrians. They committed genocide against them and killed almost a million of them. Why kill them? Because they were Christians, or simply they were different than Turks There are thousands like us in Turkish jails because they were caught speaking Kurdish or reading Kurdish poetry or demanding freedom and decency. I am afraid we are facing a similar situation here," said Dr. Kamal.

"I am thirsty and hungry," I said.

"Forget about being hungry. If you think this is a restaurant then you'll need to wait for the menu," laughed Dr. Omed.

"Who do you think we are? presidential guests? We are not even in prison. We are in the stables, we are taking those poor animals' places," joked Dr. Kamal.

"How about a cocktail before your meal, Mr. Bayazed?" said Dr. Omed. We all laughed.

"Let's laugh while we can, gentlemen. God knows what will happen to us. The next thing might be a daily session of torture," I said.

Dr. Kamal lowered his voice. "keep in mind we are dealing with Ba'th party and General Sadiq. This general after his troop attacked in their way from Sulaymania to Darbandy, he entered village Chnira. He ordered his solders to enter the village and invite all their adults. They came back with about twenty married couples, the queued men in one line and behind them their wives. Sadeq ordered his solders to gun them down. Solders open fired and killed everyone of them. These are the kinds of people we're dealing with. sick people, sick in a head. Let's not expect mercy from him."

The crowd started growing as the day went by. They kept bringing more and more people to the stables. By the time I got there, there were about a hundred of us. By the end of the day it grew to several hundreds. The whole stable was left to the prisoners. The combination of people's odor, the animal waste and the human waste was making everyone sick. The situation got more disgusting, with all those people in the stables. There was no bathroom, people had use to the corner. After a couple day, the place got so crowded that we barely have enough room to lay down on the ground. When I tried to lay on the ground my nose stuck to some animal droppings and my stomach roiled. The first night no one could sleep. There was no more humor and little conversation going on as we enter our second day. I sat near the same people as on the first day. We all sat and gazing at each other sullenly. No one had enough strength to talk. We thought we would be starved to death, that we would all be dead in that stable or transported to the torture camp in south.

By the third day we were all thirsty, hungry and exhausted from sleep depravation. I looked around and everyone in that stable looked like the living dead. All of a sudden, Dr. Kamal tapped me on a shoulder. "Look at the window, Bayazed, that sergeant is staring at you."

"Me?" I asked.

"Yes, yes you, look at the window."

I looked toward the window and observed a man waving to me, a tall muscular sergeant, shave headed, and dark skin. I recognized him as Yasen Al Chalabi, one of my customers. I went through the crowd as fast as I could and got to the window. I had high hopes that I might be saved. "I am sorry to see you here, Mr. Bayazed. Just let me know what I can do for you," said Al Chalabi as he got closer to the window. He spoke quietly, not wanting to be overheard.

"You see my friend, we all are hungry and we need to eat," I told him.

"Wait right there, I will be back in a few minutes," he said, and left.

I stayed by the window and observed everyone's eyes on me. A man I didn't know said, "Good, you found one of your friends. We need to have more like him." A few minutes later Chalabi returned carrying a bag. He looked nervous.

"Here, take these loaves of bread. Sorry, that's all I could get," said Chalabi.

"Thanks, my friend," I said.

I took the bread from him; he walked away from the window quickly so that he wouldn't be seen interacting with us. There were about five loaves of bread. I cut every loaf into pieces. I took one piece for myself and handed the rest to others. It wasn't much of anything, and everyone was still hungry. A few of us had had a piece of bread while the rest had none. For this I felt guilty. I was disappointed that Chalabi didn't offer any help to get me out but I thought it was probably beyond his doing.

Just a couple hours later, soldiers came with huge containers of soup and everyone got a very small piece of bread, small enough to put it in your mouth all at once. They called it soup; it looked gruesome and filthy. It was just water and a little green vegetable in it. It tasted horrible. Even as hungry as we were, we had to force ourselves to eat it. They gave each one of us no more than half a cup. We were told that was the meal for the day, and if we all behaved, we would have the privilege of a daily meal just like that.

Then I went back and sat where I was sitting as before next to Dr. Omed and Dr. Kamal. Chalak the writer, singer and actor had moved close to us.

"Now I know why you cut the window screen. You had a plan," said Dr. Kamal.

"What plan?"

"Your friend gave you all that bread. The only way you could have smuggled that in was through the cut in a window you made with your Swiss knife." said Dr. Kamal.

"Did you get a piece Doctor?" I asked.

"Not really. That is okay. Well, now tell us how do you mange to befriend Mr. Chalabi?"

"I got to know Chalabi three weeks ago. He came to my store. He introduced himself. We shook hands and introduced himself."

He said: "'I need to buy two black veils for my relatives in the south. I am going home and I want to take it with me as a gift to my mother and my sister. But I have no money. When I receive my next paycheck I will be back to pay you.'"

"At the time I had to think about it for a minute. You know these people—when they get time off and return south they can't allow themselves to return empty-handed. So I knew how dear that was to him. I said to myself if I told him no, he could easily get me into trouble, and two veils are not worth it. I'd bribe him with that to avoid trouble. Then I was concerned he might make it more frequent, and worst of it to bring his friends, then I could be in trouble."

"Sure, Mr. Chalabi,' I told him, 'don't worry about it, my friend. While I am sure you'd come back with the money, I'll give it to you.' So I got two veils and wrapped them up for him. He told me as he left, 'Thank you, you are a good man. May God be with you.'"

"Since then I haven't seen him until today. I must tell you I am thankful for that deal. I don't know how much he can do for us, but maybe he can help a little."

The next day Chalabi came back with several loaves of bread. As he'd done on the previous day, he passed the bread through the cut in the window screen. I received the bread, took my own share and gave the rest to the others. Before I left the window I saw Esa, a janitor who I knew. I had known him and his father for as long as I could remember. His father was a construction worker and was a friend of my father. The tiny bald-headed man wasn't difficult to spot. I stared at him and as he came close to the window he recognized me. He pretended to be busy cleaning and he looked around to make sure no one would see him.

"Mr. Esa," I whispered.

"Yes, Mr. Bayazed. Make it brief and very quiet. I need to go soon," said Esa.

"Can you get a little closer so that I can talk to you, sir?" I said.

He looked all around him again to make sure no one was watching him. Then he stepped toward the window.

"Esa, we need your help," I said.

"Sure just tell me. I'll do anything I can do for you," he said. He had a garbage container in one hand and a broom in the other.

"We need you to take letters to our families so that they know where we are." He whispered, "sure, just write your letters and I will be back to pick them up."

"But Esa, we have no pencils or paper," I replied in a low voice.

"I will get you some. Give me about an hour, and make sure you are by the window."

When he talked he had his head down, pretending that he was cleaning the ground in fear that someone might see him and report him to the military. He was undoubtedly afraid he'd end up locked inside with us.

"Esa, is there still a curfew?"

"Yes," he whispered.

"Where will you find paper, pencils and envelopes?" I asked.

"Don't worry, there is a stationary store on the army base," whispered Esa.

"Thanks, Esa, I owe you big time for this."

"Look, you will owe me nothing man, these days we need to help each other."

Esa left and I stood by the window talking to two high school teachers who were brothers, Sarhang and Nasem. They were both my teachers in high school. Sarhang was a math teacher and Nasem was an English teacher.

"How are you doing, teachers?" I asked.

"Not too good, we are here," said Sarhang.

"Where were you arrested?" I asked.

"We were both in one of our teachers friend's house, Awan, the night before curfew. We played cards until dawn in Awan's house. The next day soldiers came to Awan's house and we got arrested," said Sarhang.

"Then your families don't know you are here," I said.

"That's right. I wish I could send my family a note so that they'd know we are here," said Sarhang.

"Just wait for about an hour. Hopefully we can get some stationary and you can write to them."

Sarhang nodded. "That would be really good, are you sure you can manage that, Mr. Bayazed?"

"I think I can, but no promises."

"You know there are many people in need. Due to the curfew, many people haven't had any way to earn money to buy food and fuel," said Sarhang.

"I think we all are in trouble. Let us give charity so that God will help us out from this misery," I said.

"Where would you get the money? Do you have any money on you?" asked Nasem.

"No, but our families could. We'll write to our families and have each one of them help a needy family, deal?" I said.

While I was talking with Sarhang and Nasem, Esa came back with a stack of envelopes and couple paper pads and two pens, all hidden in his garbage container. He passed them through the cut in the window very quietly while holding the container and the broom, and I took it from him.

"Can you take our letters before you leave today?" I asked Esa.

"Yes, but please make it a small pile so that I won't be noticed, or give me half today and I'll take the rest tomorrow."

"Mr. Esa please, once I hand you the letters, take them to my wife. But if you find someone's name on the envelope that you know, get it to that person if you can."

"I will," whispered Esa.

"See you later, and God be with you," I said.

"God be with you too," replied Esa as he left, pretending that he was cleaning.

I told people to write their letters. We didn't have enough envelopes and we didn't want the stack to be too big. Two people needed to write on one sheet, and we placed five sheets in one envelope. As I gave them the paper, I asked people to contribute charity to those families who are in need, and everyone liked the idea.

"You are right Mr. Bayazed. We always help the poor and those in need in the city. We have always taken care of our needy. I never see homeless people in our city, and you never hear stories of starvation because we always take care of those who can't make it in their own. But you're right, at some point we all need to reconcile with God, and helping the needy is the best reconciliation," said Nasem. He really got on my nerves. "Nasem no more of these lectures, just do it, okay?"

Everyone was eager to write to their families. I wrote my letter to my wife and I asked her to help three families and told her that I was in a stable with many others. That is all that I wrote. As I was writing my letter, Chalak was looking at me. He put his hands on my shoulder and said with a laugh, "Mr. Bayazed, don't press so hard with the pen, you'll leave no ink in it."

I stayed near the window, talking to Nasem and Chalak. About two hours later all of the letters were written. They brought me the letters and I piled them up and pressed down the pile so that it wouldn't look too bulky.

Some time passed before I spotted Esa. He had his garbage container in one hand and the broom in the other. When he got close, I handed him the letters. He placed them in his garbage container.

The following day, I waited by the window. I was staring at the window and saw Esa as he passed by. I ran to the window and Esa spotted me. He came near the window and with his garbage bag and broom in his hands he pretended he was cleaning up.

"I delivered all your mail. I will be stopping by again before I leave for the day," he put his head down and whispered in a way I could hardly hear him. While he was whispering he scanned to make sure that no one was watching.

After the first week they started taking some of us out every day. Those who were taken didn't come back to the stable.

One day they came and took both Dr. Omed and Dr. Kamal. I didn't see Chalabi for two weeks. In the third week, I saw him by the window.

"I missed you, Chalabi. Where have you been?"

"Take these loaves of bread first," he said and passed them through the cut in the window screen. I took the bread and thanked him.

"Do you know were they have been taking people to?" I asked.

"The people who were taken...all of them will be sent to the jail in Abu Ghreb. I need to go and I will see you tomorrow," he said.

I went and sat next to Chalak, and Nasem and Sarhang came over as well.

"What did Chalabi tell you? Anything new?" asked Chalak.

"Yes, he told me something disturbing."

"What is it so disturbing? Let us know, Mr. Bayazed."

"I asked him about the people taken from here. I was wondering what happened to them. He said they have been taken to the prison in Abu Ghreb." When I told them that news, they all turned pale and I could feel their blood was boiling, such was the shock to their hearts and minds.

"Oh no, my brother, this is like being taken to the death row," said Chalak.

When Chalabi had mentioned the name Abu Ghreb, I was terrified. Abu Ghreb was a torture camp. We heard all kinds of horror stories about how they tortured people with electric shocks, hot irons, and simply beat people to death. Whenever a person was taken to Abu Ghreb, their family started to mourn.

A man nearby saw us talking and got closer, sitting between Chalak and me. Close to seventy years old, he was short and skinny with a long beard and mustache. He wore a goatskin vest and woven wool clothes like those made in Hawraman.

"Mister, what is your name?" I asked.

"My name is Abala."

"Where are you from? You're dressed like you are from Hawraman."

"Yes, I am from Hawraman," said Abala.

"What brought you here? I guess it must've been bad luck," said Chalak.

"My son was in the hospital and had surgery on part of his stomach," Abala looked to us. "You know what they call it?"

"Appendix," I said.

"Yes, so I went along with him to the hospital here in the city".

"Uncle Abala, did they come to the hospital too?" asked Nasem.

"Oh yes, they came and arrested everyone, that is why I am here. One soldier even kicked me. I told him it was shameful, that in our village nobody is disrespectful to the sick people or older people like that, but he kicked me again. They were violent even with the elderly and sick."

Dr. Farhang was sitting in a corner and I waved him closer. He stepped toward me and I asked him to sit down. "You know Dr. Farhang, I was just saying that according to

Sergeant Chalabi, people who are taken from here get transferred to Abu Ghreb."

"That is not good," said Dr. Farhang. "Abu Ghreb is well known as a torture camp. Hardly anyone gets out there alive."

"So to these government animals, the stables aren't good enough punishment?" said Chalak.

"You said that right, they want us to die with torture like thousands of others," said Nasem.

"You mean they will kill us? I have done no wrong," said Abala.

"No, Uncle. Just keep praying. Not only you, but none of the people in this place have committed any crimes. Just because you've done no wrong—that is not enough to be somewhere else," I said.

"So why they don't let us go? I am already out of tobacco," said Abala.

"Just stay here man, we will know later," said Chalak.

Abala got upset. He left and sat in a corner.

"Poor guy, he is right, but I don't know what he's thinking," said Sarhang.

I kept seeing more and more people taken away, never to be seen again. What didn't come into my mind was that those people might have been released. So far I'd seen no one to be released.

The next time Chalabi came back, as usual he brought me bread and he rushed to leave so that no one would see him.

"Mr. Chalabi, please don't run off yet. Let me ask you a question," I whispered.

"Yes, come on, hurry up because there are a few more soldiers around. Take the bread first," he said.

I took the bread from him and passed it to Nasem who was standing behind me and listening to our conversation. I turned back to Chalabi.

"Do you know what happened to all those who have been taken from here?"

"You know that everyone who has been taken in the past month—I didn't want to upset you—they were all tortured for days before being taken to prison in the south."

"Thanks, Mr. Chalabi, as usual."

He left, and Nasem passed me half a loaf of bread.

"Nasem, did you hear what Chalabi said?" I asked.

"I heard some but you were whispering."

As usual I was approached by the crowd as everyone wanted to know the news. Our window to the outside world was Esa and Chalabi. Esa was very brief and he always wanted to say what he had to say in half a minute or less. Chalabi was not comfortable but at least he gave himself the time to say few sentences.

We went around to see if we could identify those who were missing. We prepared a list and wrote letters to their families to inform them.

I spend close to three months in those stables. Every day seemed like a year and all I lived on were my sections of bread. The food they gave us was making everyone sick. Later in the afternoon they let us to go to the bathroom. The stables smelled very much like a bathroom without water. They gave us a cup of dirty water daily, and it wasn't enough. I don't know where it came from.

We were all dirty and smelled like dead animals. Every one of us looked like a wild being, like those pictures of people from the Stone Age. Our hair and beards grew long and greasy. Our nails were disgusting.

Fleas swarmed by the millions in that place and lice were nesting in our hair. Roaches crawled everywhere. I was constantly itching and I kept scratching myself to the point that I dug holes all over my body. I was bleeding all over. The fleas were big and you could feel them crawling on your body. There were ticks all over and they stuck to the skin. Sleeping on the bare stable ground, we all suffered from sleep deprivation as well as backache.

Once they let us go, I ended up sick in the bed for three months. After a year or so some of those who were transferred to the jail in Arabia came back with terrible stories of torture and beating. Hundreds never made it back, and their families, up to this day, do not know what happened to their loved ones.

I must tell you what happened to us was beyond the imagination of any decent human being. My experiences and those of others in that stable are unforgettable and unforgivable. I believe we need our independent Kurdistan and anyone who wants to compromise for less, let them consider the cruelty of these Arab, Turkish and Iranian governments toward us. We suffered so much that I personally could never say we should reconcile with these regimes and their people.

Chapter Seven

Years later I saw Kamaran, son of Shaykh Zyad. Shaykh Zyad was a prominent figure and a well-respected man in Sulaymanya. My friend Kamaran, a civil engineer was involved with the Kurdish revolution from its onset. He had always been an activist and pursued good humanitarian initiatives to help people back home. He had a good memory and he knew almost everything one needed to know about Kurdish revolution, Kurdish leaders and people in Sulaymanya. Kamaran told me of his experience during General sadiq's suppression of the city:

It was during June recess, my last year in junior high school. I studied all the subjects, which involved heavy reading in history, geography, Arabic and English. All students in my class were sent home. They let us have four weeks to study for the final exam. I used to get up at about five o'clock in the morning to study. I found that I was a bit behind, in order to catch up, I decided to get up an hour earlier.

At this time my brother Delaware was coming back home from Baghdad, where he attended the Institute of Arts and Crafts as a freshman. Delaware was a good artist and liked to write. My Father had been in prison for two months—someone had reported him to the Iraqi intelligence claiming he was one of the leaders of the underground Kurdish Democratic Party—coordinating links between the *peshmargas* and the merchant community. My sister had also been arrested—accused of being the head of the Kurdish women's organization supporting the *peshmargas*. We were all concerned my father would be taken to the death squad in the south. People taken to prison in a city often ended up in the south and were never heard from again.

It was early in June 1963. I got up at four o'clock as I'd intended. I felt sort of tired and lazy so I reset the alarm for an hour later.

Right before my alarm clock rang, I heard a voice. It was obvious the voice was coming from a megaphone. The way the voice was moving, I could tell that it must have been broadcast from a vehicle. It informed people that there would be a curfew and warned people not to leave their homes. It asked people to leave their doors unlocked. It stated that any violation would have severe consequences.

It was too early in the morning and I didn't want to wake up my mother and my brother. I started reading my history book when all of a sudden I heard a noise in the street. It sounded like it was coming from the next block. I thought that maybe the neighbors hadn't heard the announcement and were outside. In my room there was a small window high up, the window was screened and had a view of a part of the street in certain angle. The window was high and I couldn't reach it without something to stand on. Very quietly I went to the kitchen and got a chair.

I saw soldiers on each side of the street carrying *kalashnikov*. I ducked my head down so that I wouldn't be seen and I kept watching for almost a half an hour. In the beginning all I saw were soldiers along each side of the street and an army vehicle passing by.

When they were just three houses down from our house, the soldiers moved to one side of the street. They looked like they were staring at the window. I got down off the chair and put it back in the kitchen before returning to my room and lying in bed. I was shaking and expected that the soldiers would knock at the door any minute and arrest me for spying. I heard movements on the street. I thought that definitely the two soldiers knew I'd watched them from the window and would be there at any minute. Concerned my brother Delaware or I would get arrested, my mother had told me almost every day to be quiet and do nothing obvious.

I stayed in bed for almost fifteen minutes. The soldier's boots moved down the street. I returned to the kitchen, brought back the chair, and closed my door. I looked through the window and saw the soldiers still on the side of the street. A young boy, who must have been about eleven years old, approached carrying a pot balanced on his head. It could have been a pot of yogurt, I am not sure. The soldiers approached and spoke to him. One of the soldiers pulled the boy by the collar of his shirt with one hand—the other hand pointing a *kalashnikov*. Still the young boy had the pot of the yogurt on his head. I was wondering what these soldiers were saying to him. I thought they might be telling the boy to put down his pot of yogurt so they could have themselves a yogurt party. Both soldiers pulled the boy toward the fence of the neighbor's house. The fence was made of stone, and the soldier had the boy stand with both hands on it, with his back to them. I saw the soldiers move to the other side of the street and all of a sudden the sound of bullets rang out and the boy was down on the ground. My chin hit the edge of the window and I fell down, shaking and terrified.

The next thing I remember was opening my eyes, lying flat on my back as my mother rubbed my face with a cold towel and my brother Delaware stood over me.

"What have you done to yourself son?" asked my mother.

"I don't know mom."

"Are you in pain, Kamaran?" she asked.

"Yes, mom, a lot of pain."

"Can you tell me where?"

"On my chin and the back of my head," I said and sat up.

"It's all swollen, mom," said Delaware.

"Let me give you a quick exam. Stop me if it hurts."

"All right Dr. Mam,"

She applied pressure with the tip of her finger gently around my neck and head.

"Thank God…at least you don't seem to have a concussion," she said, feeling my jaw to see if I had any fractured bones. "I think you will be okay. Once this curfew is over, you need to see a doctor. You should get some sleep son, just go back to bed."

"Can you tell us how you made such a mess of yourself?" asked Delaware.

"I saw a little boy—he must have been around eleven years old. The soldiers had him put his hands against the fence, and they gunned him down dead."

"What happened after that?" asked Delaware.

"All I remember is being woken up by you and mom."

"You said they shot a boy by the fence, what fence?"

"Mr. Adeb's house, they killed the boy right there."

Delaware looked at me closely. "You must be crazy, you want me to believe that? Did you just make up that story?"

My mother listened, astonished, without saying anything. Later on when the curfew was over I took them to see Mr. Adeb's wall and they saw for themselves the blood all over the wall and the sidewalk.

It got close to noon. I was sitting with my mother and Delaware was telling us about living in Baghdad and a weird roommate of his. Two soldiers entered the house with machineguns. They told my brother and me to freeze, and one of the soldiers pointed his gun at us while the others searched room to room. My mother was crying. I stood frozen and my blood started boiling. The soldiers looked absolutely evil and scary—with their dark complexions and shaved heads, one easily could tell they were from the deep south. I looked right into the eyes of one of the soldiers and saw nothing but evil. I could see he was enjoying his power over my brother and me.

As the machinegun was pointed at us, and soldiers finger was on the trigger, I was afraid that the gun might accidentally fire. The soldier searched the house and found nothing. He returned and shouted in Arabic for our identification.

I reached into my pocket, got out my ID, and handed it to him. He looked my ID and kept it in his hand as Delaware reached his pocket. Delaware handed him his ID. At this moment we saw a captain entered the house. He ordered the solder to hand him Delaware's Id. He did. The captain looked at the ID. He went on looking Delaware and then me and he did that twice. He looked at Delaware's ID one more time then he turned to him. "Is this your ID," he asked Delaware.

"Yes sir, this is my student ID," said Delaware.

"You attend the Art Institute in Baghdad," said the captain.

"Yes, sir," answered Delaware.

"Do you know Jasem?"

"Yes, sir," answered Delaware.

The captain turned to the two solders and ordered them to leave the house and stay in front of the house, and let no other solders in.

"You probably don't know this, but you are my brother's roommate. You know Jasem?"

"Yes, he is my roommate," answered Delaware.

"He told me your name and said you are one of his best friends. My name is Kanan," said the captain.

He took his finger off the trigger, hung his AK-47 on his shoulder, and asked the other soldier to go and stand in front of the house.

The soldier left and I saw him waiting at the front of the house.

Delaware and I stood with a breath of relief. I thought to myself he is a Godsend.

"This is very serious," he said. "I must tell you both that we are told to feel free to kill or imprison any male over the age of ten. My advice to you are to hide anywhere on the roof of the house or anywhere else that you could not be found by other soldiers. You will see soldiers coming to your house more than once every day for as long as this situation continues. I didn't take you but eventually some other soldier will. I will leave you and you know what to do. Remember that I can't help you if you get caught. I am not supposed to have a close association with anyone in the city." He took his *kalashnikov* back, with his finger on the trigger, and left.

All that time my poor mother was standing across from us in silent tears. I knew she was afraid for us. She was shaking like a tree in a storm.

Delaware and I sat and mom came over to sit with us, still shaking and crying.

"Your dad has been in prison for two months and I haven't heard a word from him since his arrest. I am not even sure if he is alive, and the same goes for your sister. This is evil, I have never heard of any women to be imprisoned. This is all new for me. I can't take more than my load of misery. I don't want lose either one of you too, so be careful."

"I know that mom. I wish I was in Baghdad—I could have been much safer. I don't know what to do."

"Just do what the soldier told you," said mom.

91

"Let's go to the side of the house and hide there," I said to Delaware.

"Remember son, if you get caught trying to hide, they will arrest you and they'll probably think that you are up to no good."

"If we get caught, we'll pretend that we are playing," said Delaware.

The side of the house had a stone fence separating our house from our neighbor Mr. Bahjat. There were trees covering the walls of the house and near the fence we had a little room that we used for storage.

Delaware turned to me. "We'll hide by the wall. Let's get a soccer ball. As soon as the soldiers come near us, we'll throw the ball, pretending to play catch. If we have to, we'll quietly throw the ball into Mr. Bahjat's yard and jump over the wall."

"Sounds like a good plan. Let's get covered with the tree branches and leaves so

that they can't spot us."

"Hold on, you've got a white shirt, you can easily be spotted. Go find a green shirt or at least something other than red and white."

We both went and found a couple old green shirts and some darker pants to wear, and then climbed into the trees right above the wall, covered by branches. From where I was hiding I could see the street and monitor the soldiers' movement.

"My God, Delaware, look," I said when I saw a half-dozen soldiers enter our house.

"Keep quiet and get ready to jump over," said Delaware.

I saw the soldiers coming into the backyard. Fearing the soldiers would spot us, we both climbed down the wall to Mr. Bahjat's house. I held the soccer ball in my hands.

"Be quiet," whispered Delaware. "I hear soldiers."

"I know that," I said.

I heard noise and crying in Mr. Bahjat's house. I saw Mr. Bahjat getting beaten by a couple of soldiers. They were shouting and cursing him. Suddenly a voice spoke "What are you doing here?"

I threw the ball to Delaware. "You see we are playing," I said.

"No you are not. You both come with me," said the soldier, his *kalashnikov* pointed at us. When we got to the street, I saw Mr. Bahjat being led toward an army truck.

"Go to the truck," said the soldier.

"Yes sir," we said.

Once we got to the truck, I saw the soldier Kanan standing in front of it.

Kanan gave us an angry look, and whispered something to the officer—I assume he was in charge. I saw the truck had about four people kneeling inside it, their hands up in the air. Mr. Bahjat was among them.

I heard the officer yelling at Kanan. They moved apart before the officer called Kanan back. After they exchanged a few more words, I heard the officer tell Kanan, "It's all right."

Then Kanan came up to us as we were standing in a front of the truck and said,

"You both come with me." We followed him and went back towards our house.

"You two were lucky. Did you hear my boss shouting at me because I didn't want you arrested? I begged him to save you. Now go home and remember. Next time I may not be here for you."

We went home and we did exactly the same thing for a few days of the curfew—hiding by the tree near the fence. I don't know how, but we managed not to be seen.

After the curfew was eased, I had to take my final exam. It was my final junior high school year, and we had a nationwide test. All of the students from all of the schools came to Sulaymanya high school. Hundreds of us were there. During all five days of testing army officers read the questions because our teachers had been arrested. Tanks and artillery were parked in front of the school.

Just as we do now, we had women and men in the KDP of all professions and genders: a woman's organization, a teacher's organization, a labor organization, and so on. Members of these organizations were instrumental in collecting funds for the *peshmargas*, informing the KDP about any government movements and being solid internal supporters of the revolution. My father, in fact, for heading the merchant's organization, was arrested and sent to prison in 1963. It wasn't like a normal prison; there was sleep deprivation, starvation, and both psychological and physical torture.

I knew the prominent members of the KDP in the city through their association with my dad, and my mother knew them too. I loved my dad and fears were consuming me that he would be tortured or killed. What frightened me more, however, was that if he was transferred to the prison in the south he'd almost certainly be killed.

My father was one of hundreds imprisoned whose families were waiting anxiously to hear anything about their status. No one expected any good news—everyone had a bad feeling that the prisoners would be taken to the south and the prospect was dreadful.

On June 16, 1963, I was home with my mother and both my brothers. We had just had breakfast with my father's favorite cousin, Shaykh Nouri—dad used to invite him to our house and sometimes he'd stay for a month at a time, particularly during the winter when he wasn't busy.

Shaykh Nouri was a landlord with a sizable farmland in a nearby village. It seemed he knew almost every rock on the ground around Sulaymanya. He was a poet, and a brave man with a great sense of humor. He was short and strong with a full brown hair, hazel eyes, and a mysterious, inscrutable look—in that sense he wasn't your average Kurd, as most people's faces were like open books.

He'd come to visit us right when the curfew partially lifted and didn't know that my dad and sister were both in prison. We were all surprised by his visit because Sulaymanya wasn't a good place to be.

The day wore on towards noon, the weather got hot and we went to sit out on the deck. We had some nice *dow** and my mother made us tea. As we were sitting and talking, we heard a voice from a megaphone.

"Please let us be quiet and see what are they announcing," said my mother. You could tell she was angry from her voice and she looked bothered.

The announcement said that on June 18th, the day before the military would transfer all of the prisoners to the south, we would have a chance to see them. Visits were to be pre-arranged by making appointment.

"That may be the last chance we can see your dad, son," said my mother with tears rolling down her cheeks.

---

* Yogurt mixed with water

Nouri took a deep breath and lit a cigarette, frowning. "Don't be so afraid, and be patient. God willing, nothing bad will happen."

"Anything is possible but I wish I could be more optimistic," mom said quietly.

Someone knocked the door. I opened it and greeted Nezam, who sat down with us. Mom served him a glass of *dow* and gave him a cup of tea. I had known Nezam and his family since I was born. One of the old members of the Kurdish Democratic Party, he was very intelligent and politically active. He was a handsome man of fifty, with big brown eyes, a long mustache, wide shoulders, and a muscular build.

Nezam repeated the gist of the announcement to make sure we knew about it.

"We all heard that, that was just a few moments ago," said Shaykh Nouri. I knew that Nezam had something else to add and waited impatiently as I got up from my chair and stood right in front of him.

"Sit down Kamaran, I need to tell you something. I want your mom and Shaykh Nouri to hear what I am about to say," he said, talking in a rush as if he had not a moment to spare. He reached to his pocket and produced a sealed letter, he held it up with his right hand. "I hand you this letter, it needs to be taken to the head of the *peshmarga* battalion in Glazarda. The day the army convoy moves the prisoners, the *peshmarga* forces are to attack the convoy and rescue all of the prisoners. Kamaran, you are to take the letter. This letter needs to be handed to *peshmarga* at Glazarda by tomorrow before noon." He turned to my mother. "Is that is okay with you?"

My mother wanted to reply but I interrupted her. "Yes I will do it. Just give me the letter."

My mother looked confused and stood up. She put her hands on my shoulders and looked me right in the eyes. "Son, I already have your dad and your sister in a prison. I can't lose you. Although I know you think this is a good idea, just too many scary things are going on."

"Mom, listen, you know hundreds of people have been taken to the prisons in south—there has been no word from any of them. I am afraid dad might not make it back."

"I know, son, but what if the *peshmargas* attack and the prisoners get killed in the crossfire? This is very dangerous endeavor."

"Well, you're right," Shaykh Nouri said to my mother, "but that's still the only choice we have. Even if those people get killed, it's better than dying under the most inhumane torture. But I tell you if the *peshmargas* attack, the soldiers will give themselves up. Soldiers can't fight *peshmargas*, and we all know that. Don't you worry, I will go along with Kamaran to deliver the letter, and I'll do my best to assure his safe return"

"I don't know what to say, I am just worried and uneasy about it. But should you persist to pursue please be careful," said mom.

Nezam handed the letter to Nouri and said goodbye. We were ready to deliver it. Shaykh Nouri thought we should wait until it got dark and then make our way out of the city.

There was a curfew after sunset and the army fired their machineguns at anything that moved. The outskirts of the city were tangled called "death trap" with army barricades in every direction. The army had mines, barbed wire which was not visible, and dogs around these barricades. Along the wire they hung metal cans so that anyone touching them would make noise and subsequently the dogs bark to inform soldiers.

We had to walk too many city streets in order to get there, and that meant risking being gunned down at almost every intersection. For safety we went to Shaykh Nouri's friend's house in the Jewish district near the end of the city. We waited there until sunset and walked the unlit streets towards the edge of the city.

The street ended with a triangular section of land. In a middle of that triangle was a lamppost. The army watch post stood at the roof of an elementary school overlooked the lit triangle, and soldiers could see everything.

At the far end of the street were two main sewage ditches, each about four meters deep, which met and formed an open channel. The trenches of each ditch, flowing with shallow sewage, were shielded from the army post.

Just like most evenings, there was machinegun fire in the city. I was terribly frightened and felt that I was going to get shot. At the time I was about fourteen years old—the age boys want to look strong and not seem like cowards—and I pretended I was brave and more than ready for the job even though I was scared like never before.

We got to the end of the street, near the final lamppost.

"Let's stop for a minute and sit down, please," Shaykh Nouri said, quietly.

"Listen, Kamaran, I am going to pass that trail and make my way to the other side. If I get shot and killed, you'll need to find your way home. As soon as I go down reach under the lam post, I give you a signal with my head turning to you, you start coming, I will go into the ditch and disappear, you come after me. As soon as you reach the post near the ditch, wave and pretend that there are others behind you. Right after you wave, get in the ditch and lie flat. If anything happens to me go immediately back to my friend's house and then go to your home tomorrow."

I nodded, and Shaykh Nouri left. The army picket was set up on top of a school, very close to where I was. I could hear soldiers talking amongst themselves, when one of them matched a cigarette, I could see his face lit like being in front of a light bulb.

Once Nouri disappeared into the ditch, I followed. When I arrived at the end I waved, just as Shaykh Nouri had told me, trying to fool the soldiers into thinking that there were more people behind me. If the army thought people were crossing in a group, they would save their bullets until most of the group tried to cross, and then gun them all down so to maximize their victims.

When I got to that little trail all my fears were gone and felt brave. I could hear the soldiers talking amongst themselves and I imagined they hadn't even noticed me.

Arriving on the other side and I threw myself in the ditch. Just as I was bending down to lie flat, they opened fire at me with bullets whizzing over my head. I crawled out to the edge, laying flat on my chest, smelling terribly of sewage. I saw Shaykh Nouri lying flat on the ground.

"Kamaran, you know why they shot at you?" he asked me as he raised his head above the side of the ditch. "They got mad when they didn't see a group of people following us."

We crawled away from the city on the side of the ditch for more than two hours in a farmland of dell and beans. I smelled disgusting, and I kept pulling dell weeds and rub it on my face so that I wouldn't smell the odor from the sewage. We kept crawling until we arrived at a water spring. The spring was fairly big and the water was at least a meter deep. I threw myself into the water and washed my clothes but I still smelled bad.

"Kamaran I think you made a big mess out of the water. I think you've had enough," said Shaykh Nouri as he sat by the water and smoked.

I looked behind me at the full moon and saw something behind Shaykh Nouri.

"Shaykh," I whispered, "look at all those soldiers behind us. They are staring at us and they're all dressed in uniforms."

He looked around, and after a short pause "those are sunflower plants,".

I looked behind him again, and they were indeed sunflower plants, hundreds of them, but in the dark they resembled soldiers in uniform.

As we walked toward *Zergwez*, we passed an okra farm. Where the leaves were thinned out, I could see a man with something in his hand. I thought he might be a soldier who would kill us. The man got closer to us and turned out to be a farmer with a donkey and a big stick.

"*Salaam* to you," said the farmer (*salaam* is an Islamic word for greeting, it means "peace").

"And to you," I said.

"Mistr, is it safe for me to go to the city?" he asked Shaykh Nouri.

"What is your load?"

"I have a load of green beans to sell," said the man.

"Just go and get close to the city and wait until sunrise. If you find any traffic, go into the city. Otherwise something's wrong, especially if you hear gunfire.

Farmers are usually allowed to travel to the city from just before sunrise until four P.M. If you cross the edge of the city afterward you will be fired at."

The man waved and left with his donkey.

When we arrived at *Zergwez*, we encountered a few *peshmargas*. They told us that we needed to go to Glazarda which is two hours away.

We kept walking until we got to Glazarda. When we arrived, we saw a few *peshmargas*. They told us that we needed to walk to Zergwez, about two hours away. Our path took us up a trail on Baranan Mountain. As we walked the curving bare trail, completely out in the open amongst dry weeds, airplanes showed up and bombed everywhere around us. We threw ourselves under a huge rock and hid until the planes were gone. I don't know what in the world they were bombing—the mountain held nothing and utterly naked.

We arrived at Glazarda and were told that Tareq, the head of the *peshmarga* battalion, was not there. I asked one of Tareq's deputies to take the letter and told him that hundreds of civilians in Sulaymanya would be taken to the prison in the south on June 19th. At that time it was June 17th at about two-thirty pm. Tareq's deputy understood the importance of the message. My letter was sent with one of the *peshmargas* to Qaradagh, which was hours away. That night Tareq got the letter and the *peshmargas* prepared to attack the army convoy.

I stayed in Zergwez and the next day saw the army convoy leave Sulaymanya through Arbat, which was about twenty kilometers from the city. The army had changed their plans and the *peshmargas* were planning to ambush the convoy one day late. I cried like a child, disappointed knowing that I might never see my father again.

Finally I returned home.

My father was kept in prison for eighteen months of savage treatment and torture. They freed him—they had no proof to support their claims. After he returned home I told him what I did to block the convoy and rescue them. "Yes, son, you did well, but I am glad it didn't happen. While we were transferred from the city to the south our hands were cuffed and the soldiers stood in front of us with machineguns. They told us that if *peshmargas* attacked, we would be shot. If the *peshmargas* had attacked, I wouldn't be here."

Chapter Eight

Summer 1963, shortly after General sadiq arrived Halabja, he had recruited enough locals to support him and fight for him. He thought that the town was safe and he felt comfortable enough to leave. He left some army soldiers and heavy artillery behind. Locals he recruited were people with bad reputations and thought of as uneducated low-lifes who had betrayed their people and their country.

These *Jash* didn't take the job out of loyalty to the Ba'th government. They received a small stipend and were housed in small barracks, packed like sardines. *Jash* were isolated, and nobody wanted to be associated with them. They had only each other. People in Halabja loved to hear any bad news about them and prayed for their demise. Most of the people in town thought that these Jashs had betrayed their people by siding with the enemy.

Peshmargas used to enter the town almost every night. We knew their entry as usually initiated with few gunshots. It followed by dogs howling and barking all around. Soon after they went on the roofs of the taller buildings and fire on the *Jash* and the police stations. They often came in close to the *Jash* barracks and we could hear them cursing the *Jash* or calling them by name and trying to get them to show themselves so they could gun them down.

After General Sadiq left, the army convoys from Sulaymanya continued to bring fuel and supplies to the town. The most critical was the flour for the bakeries, which was subsidized by government and sold at an affordable price.

Soon *peshmargas* started attacking the army convoys, and their attacks intensified as time passed. Around November 1963, *peshmargas* attacked in force during the day, entered the town and looked street by street for *Jash,* police, and soldiers. At the time I was in the store with my father. We heard shotguns and machineguns firing all over midtown. People ran in every direction. My father closing the store very slowly. I kept telling my dad to hurry. He had put some of his merchandise outside for display and was taking it in slowly, one thing at a time as if business was normal. Soon couple *peshmargas* stopped and told my dad to hurry up. Only then did Dad rush all the items into the store.

The *peshmargas* told us to walk close to the walls and not to go near the middle of the street. We managed to get home safely but saw *peshmargas* running from one place to another trying to deploy all over town in an organized manner. One of them stayed at each corner of the street and pointed the new arrivals in the right direction. It was a cold day and several feet of snow had fallen. A cold wind blew. I wore a hat, gloves and a long wool-lined overcoat. The street was slippery and if one didn't watch out they could have easily fallen down and broken their head.

The *peshmargas* wore no overcoats or anything warm. All they had on were khaki pants, a jacket and long woolen knee-socks. They wore turbans on their head wrapped around thin hats and most had a wool or goatskin vest. Every one of them had rows of bullets hanging around their waists and necks. Some carried Kalashinkov's and about a half dozen bullet cases; others had rifles and a few were equipped with heavy machineguns.

I went home with my father and sat next to the kerosene heater. At the time we lived in a house on the same street as my father's store only few minutes walk. At the end of the street was Ahmed Beg's house and the front yard of his house was a gas station. Gasoline and heating oil were in containers piled up behind a fence in his front yard.

Our house had four bedrooms. Two we lived in, one we used for storage, and one occupied by a man named Saber who worked repairing and shining shoes. Living with him was his wife Shahla and his mother Pary. Shahla was about thirty years old, a little over five feet tall with very dark hair, olive skin, big brown eyes, and a dark mole below her nose and one in the middle of her cheek. My mother told me Shahla couldn't have children, but to me she looked healthy and strong. Once in a while she'd clean people's houses to earn some money.

Saber's mother Pary must have been in her late fifties. She was fair-skinned and her hair was still partly gray. She looked beautiful for her age. She loved her son Saber, her only child. She told me that her husband has been a peaceful man and had passed away in his sleep twenty years ago at a very young age. Since then she had been living with her son and didn't look to get married again.

Pary was one of the kindest people I have ever met, in part because she was afraid of doing wrong before God. My mother told me that you'd never hear her say a bad word about others. They were all nice, polite people. Every time my mother made a special meal she made sure that she made enough of it so that they could have some. They were poor and had a hard time getting by.

My mother was pregnant. I was ten years old, my sister Ronak about two, and my brother Abdul seven. The larger of our two bedrooms was the master bedroom and also it was used as a living room and dining room. We slept on a mattress on the floor which was moved during the day. In both rooms we had Persian rugs. In the larger room we had a huge Persian carpet that covered most of the floor. A chest of drawers for clothes, and another china cabinet containing dishes and silverware. Both the chest of drawers and the china cabinet were plain and without any particular design. There was a small open area near the entrance door that we used as a kitchen. The front of the house was cemented, and led to the street behind the house was our neighbor's front yard.

My father and I sat by the kerosene heater until we were warmed. Late that afternoon, while my mother was cooking dinner we heard artillery fire and *peshmargas* in the street. As the night progressed the gunfire intensified, we could hear it going toward the *Jash* barracks at the end of the town.

We didn't think much of it that night, and assumed it was just like many nights before and that the *peshmargas* would leave at the end of the night. The next day was sunny day and freezing. We heard *peshmargas* shooting everywhere on the street. My father told me that there would be no school. I thought that was comforting, as I'd have no homework, but after a few hours I got bored and then worried as I didn't know what to do in the house all day. There was absolutely nothing to do. I couldn't go outside, and I couldn't see my friends. After school at this time of year we'd have snowball fights from street to street until sunset before returning home for dinner and homework. I got very frustrated, but I told myself that it would only be for a day, even if I thought one day was one too many to spend stuck at home. When asked my father if I could go to the neighbor's house a couple blocks away he outraged and told me that I must be out of my mind to go out in this besieged town with gunfire everywhere.

All we had was a radio, but the radio didn't have any programs for children. I decided to hunt birds. I had bought some brand new metal spring traps that we used to trap small pigeons. The cement front yard was enclosed by a cemented-stone wall about six feet tall. The birds needed to feel safe enough to come into the front yard, but people weren't inclined to go out in that weather anyway. I set out the traps and left them in the front yard. Once I caught a couple, I had my mother clean, salted and fried them. These little birds were delicious, but there were barely any meat on them.

I placed a trap in the yard and watched from the window. The weather was so cold that the glass fogged and I couldn't see through it. I brought two blankets and covered myself with them and stayed in the hall, which was all stone, but felt like ice. I placed one blanket underneath me and used the other to cover myself. I had to stay silent and motionless so that birds came. God, it was cold. After ten minutes of sitting there the blankets froze. I felt like I was covered with an ice blanket. I went back into the room and tried wiping the window from outside and wiped it from the inside, but a minute later it got foggy again. After every attempt failed I stayed in the room and simply went out very slowly and quietly every once in a while to see if any birds were trapped. After about five minutes I went out and saw more than a dozen birds in the yard. I was sure that it would only be a matter of minutes before both traps went off. I stayed out in the hall quiet and motionless. I saw a couple birds come and eat the little pieces of bread near the trap; I got excited and as another three more gradually moved towards the trap, I knew two of them would be our lunch. All of a sudden, my sister came out and screamed, "Rauf! Where is my little doll?" Every bird flew away.

I got really mad and I told my sister, "See what you did? I have to start all over, are you happy now?"

"I want my doll," she said.

"I will get your doll but I want you not to do again what you just did."

"Just get them for me," she demanded.

I knew I couldn't win and for that matter I knew she didn't understand what I told her, so to get her off my back I went in the room I found her doll.

"You got your toys, now I want you to know you just cost me two birds. I want you not to go out there again." I didn't think she heard what I said, but I knew that she was a little sister and little sisters were meant to be a royal pain.

I resumed the business of hunting. I came out having wrapped myself in a blanket and I saw several birds in the yard, but none were around the trap. I kept watching and eventually I saw birds heading toward the trap. Soon I saw half a dozen of them get close. A couple were about to go for the bread when the noise of machinegun fire scattered them. If it's not one thing then it's another.

I kept trying all day and all I got were three, which wasn't enough for any one of us. There was no refrigerator, and even if there had been it wouldn't have done us much good because we only had electricity every other day. Since the revolution started they had rationed electricity. When we had food left over my mother put it in covered dishes.

Usually she covered them with big pot and placed a heavy rock on the top so that cats wouldn't get to it. She always kept it outside because it was cooler.

Kurdistan is mostly mountainous and since the winters are harsh, people try to make sure they have enough in storage to get by until the following year. During the summer there were a lot of tomatoes, and my dad bought a lot of them. My mother washed these and squeezed them by hand before putting them on a tray to thicken in the sun. After that she salted and put them in a ceramics container stored for the wintertime. She also sliced tomatoes in a half, placed them in the sun until they dried out, and packed them so we had sun-dried tomatoes for the rest of the year. She also dried okra and eggplant. All fruits and vegetables were seasonal.

Villagers made pomegranate juice and dried raisins and my father bought enough at the end of the summer to last until next season. My mom used the pomegranate juice to cook rice with. My father bought large bags of flour so that mom could make fresh bread, but most of the time we got bread from the bakery.

Since we couldn't go outside, we couldn't get meat or vegetables. We had to live on what we had in the house. Many people couldn't afford to stock up the food they needed like we did.

The first day went by, with us all shut in the house. All we heard was uninterrupted sound of machineguns and artillery firing away. A second day, MiGs flew low over the town, and their supersonic sound shook the town. They were dropping bombs everywhere with no real targets, they were just trying to scare citizens and *peshmargas* by scattering bombs. Those planes attacked the city in perfect safety, there were no anti-aircraft weapons. People were defenseless.

On the third day, it felt like three months had passed. Time just doesn't pass fast enough when one is bored. My father got worried in particular about my grandpa and his family. It was late evening, and the room was freezing. We dressed warmly even though we were sitting inside because all we had to warm up the room was a small heater. We had our radio on and my father as usual was listening to the BBC. The broadcast was in Arabic. When they broadcast the news, my father hoped they would mention something about the Kurdish revolution. Most Kurds listened to the Israeli broadcast in Arabic and this one mentioned battles between the Kurds and the Iraqi government more than any other radio station.

My father muted the radio as heavy machinegun shelling started. We could hear people running outside, and we knew it was the *peshmargas*. I was looking at my father and could tell that something was bothering him. We had just had our dinner and mom was pouring tea. My father took a sip and broke the silence, "I know my uncle doesn't have enough flour. I wish this had happened a day later." By his uncle, he meant his father-in-law and indeed he was his uncle and my mother was his cosine.

"How do you know that?" asked mom as she rinsed teacups.

Dad paused for a moment and looked at my mother. "I saw him in the morning, the same day *the peshmargas* attacked and he told me that in the afternoon he was going to buy a bag of flour. He asked me if I needed a bag and I told him I'd just bought one yesterday.". "I am very concerned," continued dad "I am sure that by tomorrow they'll run out of flour. They have enough rice but rice without bread will be consumed quickly, and all of sudden they'll run out of rice, too."

Mom took a deep breath and said, "I wish I could deliver half of our full bag of flour to them now so that they don't go hungry."

"If things don't clear by tomorrow, then we'll need to do something."

"I don't know how you'd get anything to them. I take back what I said. Even if we get them two days of flour to make their bread, then how about after that, and what about us?"

"We should take one day at a time. You need not think like that," said Dad.

"I pray to God that this curfew will end soon so that we don't have to do that," said mom.

My father raised the volume of the radio. Things got quieter. I was playing by myself, trying to arrange chips and play dama. Machineguns and rifles were firing. It was the loudest since it started. It kept on going, we were all frightened. I'd had a nightmare that soon government troops and *peshmargas* might start killing each other in front of our house. I'd also been afraid of government troops getting to town and killing everyone. Saber knocked on the door and my dad opened it.

"You hear the heavy machinegun and artillery shelling? Must be some serious fighting nearby," he said.

"Come on in and close the door, the room is already cold," said my Dad.

Saber closed the door and took his shoes off.

"Would you like to go get your mom and your wife and have a cup of tea? Indeed that was all we can offer," said my father.

He walked to his room and brought his wife and his mother back with him. They all took off their shoes and sat down on the mattress. It is a custom for people to take their shoes off because people pray at home and sit on the floor.

We all sat still while the bullets rang out around all over town.

Saber turned to my father and said, "Shaykh, things are getting worse with the passing of every day."

Dad lit up a cigarette. "Things are already bad. Let us hope things don't get to be worse."

My mother served everyone tea. I was still playing dama by myself and got distracted trying to listen to them while still hearing the shooting.

"Do you have enough flour and food left to feed your family?" Dad asked Sabre.

"I don't know. Maybe for a few more days, we didn't have much to start with. I hope this chaos will end soon." He passed and said, "Shaykh, what if the *peshmargas* take over the town?"

"I very much doubt that and hope it will not happen because the *peshmargas* have no resources to manage the town. They have no way to defend people against government attacks. Remember the *peshmargas* don't need to take over Halabja, all they want is to bring about instability to force the government to bow to their demands."

My dad usually went to sleep around nine, but that night they stayed up past eleven and all they talked about were the prospects of the Kurdish revolution and about the current battle in Halabja. Beneath the sound of machineguns, no one could sleep anyway. My mother and Shahla, Sabre's wife, were busy talking about anything but the current situation in the town. Eventually they said good night and left.

My mother turned off the lamp and I went to my room with my brother and sister. A few times artillery shells shook the house so violently that I thought it had hit next door. I was restless and uncomfortable, hoping for this thing to be over so that I could have snowball fights with my friends. I tried to force myself to sleep but every time I was just about to fall asleep I was woken up by gunfire.

The next day we woke up and had our breakfast. It was only bread and tea. I told myself that it was all we could manage, like it or not. There was nothing else.

On the fourth day, I got my two traps out. I cleaned and dried them with a dirty towel. My mother gave me a bag of dried bread.

"Mom, I don't think the birds will want this dried crispy bread, they want something soft. If we don't like it then birds want' like it either," I said.

"No, son, just try it and if it doesn't work, then I will give you fresh bread. Birds eat a lot of junk that we don't. Believe me birds eat anything." I whined: "but I only need a little piece of bread."

"No, you don't understand. Listen, Rauf this is not a normal time. We need to conserve what little we have to last as long as we can. We are running out of everything and God knows when this curfew will end. Do you understand?"

"Okay, mom, I'll try. I am planning to get about twenty pigeons. That would be enough for us and I probably could give about three pigeons to Saber's family," Mom nodded. "You should make sure your brother and sister don't scare off the birds today."

I put the traps down and went to my sister, who was playing with a couple of dolls. They were dolls my mom had made for her, dolls with real hair glued on and dressed the dolls in traditional Kurdish cloth. They really looked weird, and I used to make fun of them, but to my sister they looked real.

"Ronak, you are not to make any noise and you are not to go outside. Do you understand?"

The little stinker started crying and ran to Mom. "Mom, Rauf is yelling at me."

My mother held my sister and kissed her.

Then my brother Abdul popped up and said, "I will help you and we can catch one hundred of them."

"How would you get a hundred birds? You don't know what you are talking about. If we get one hundred birds, there will be none left for tomorrow."

"That is not true, there are millions of these little creatures, so don't be stingy with your catch," said Mom.

I put both traps and placed them on the front yard. I was watching from my room's window. Again the window was too foggy, so I stepped out and stayed in front of my door. Almost twenty birds came, and ate only the bread around the traps, leaving the piece I'd set on traps. My brother and I watched. My brother was saying, "here we go, Rauf. Those two birds in the front are going to get it."

A big machinegun went off and it was so loud that the birds flew away. I got really mad. "Why don't these idiots wait until we get the birds before they fire?"

I decided to leave bread on the traps alone. I couldn't afford wasting bread by scattering it around the trap. A another group of birds came.

"Isn't this group the same we saw last time? They sure look like them," I asked my brother.

"You don't know that, how can you tell one bird from another, they all look alike," said mom.

"I can tell. I swear to God they are the same, I know every one of these birds," said Abdul.

Instead of one, three birds went on one trap, fighting for the same piece of bread, and at the other trap there was two of them. Both traps snapped simultaneously and I got three birds at once. I ran to the trap and put them on a dish to take to my mom.

"Wow. This is good, Rauf. You'll do better than you thought if you keep going like that," she said.

I learned that I didn't need to put any bread around the trap, I only put it on the trap and that way I wasted no bread. I wanted to tell my mother, but I waited to see if it really worked. I tried again and it did work. I caught another two. Then I went to Mom as she was making bread. She was in the front yard and it was all smoky the firewood must have been still wet. I showed her the other two birds and told her about my discovery.

She seemed happy. "See, you can find out these things when you try them. I told you it's going to work and you didn't believe me. Now you know," Meanwhile my sister was sitting next to my mother and she thought she was helping. Her eyes were red and teary from the smoke. My mom took her back to the room. "You stay inside, it's cold out and you might get sick from smoke," mom told her.

"Okay mom," said Ronak.

"No mom, I said. "it's not okay, let her stay with you so that I can get more birds."

"Just keep her entertained," said mom.

"I knew she was going to mess things up for me, so I enlisted Abdul. "Abdul, keep Ronak busy so that she won't intervene with my hunting."

He looked disappointed. "Okay, but you have to give me some birds to eat."

"You get three but you keep Ronak busy and don't let her outside," I said and continued to hunt.

By the end of the day I had about a dozen birds. Mom cleaned them all up and fried them and shared them for dinner. These birds were really small, all dozen of them together weren't much, but trapping them had also helped the day go by unnoticed.

The town was still smothered by the fighting and it was obvious that fear was running high. As we were eating I asked my father, "Dad, this government is really bad, why can't they stop fighting?"

My sister wasn't paying attention and thought we are talking about birds.

"Dad, I helped Rauf to catch all the birds, you like that?"

My dad leaned toward her and gave her a kiss because he thought she was cute.

"You don't know what we talk about, you think like a bird," I said.

"Rauf, God has his own way to work things out. Don't worry. The government is doing bad things and God will punish them."

"Dad, I've heard that a lot, but how will that happen?"

"A day will come when God will destroy the world. Then we will all rise from the dead and God will judge everyone. He knows everything we've done and it'll be easy for him to judge."

"Then all the soldiers and *Jashes* will be judged?" I asked.

"I hope God will get impatient with this government and will give them justice now. What good does it do me to wait for judgment day? That will be after we die," said my mother.

"Son, think of God and whatever he does as right. God is patient. Thank him for not rushing. Always thank him no matter what. I know you've had enough, so have I. But remember, God does not think in our terms, and we should never judge God. We should be God's silent servants and take his will with grace. Our only job is to be thankful to him and obey him."

"But dad, the government is bad and the sooner they go the better for everyone," I said.

"Son, God only brings good things to people. Don't blame God for evil. There are times God lets people reap the fruit of their doings in life, but there are times when justice takes time. Be comforted that God lets no one get away with doing evil. Sooner or later God will catch up with them and that is his promise."

It got cloudy and dark and my dad stood up. He put on an old thick overcoat he'd been wearing for years.

"I'm going to take some flour to your dad's family." he told mom.

"I am afraid you'll get shot," she said. "The soldiers on top of the Mayor's office can spot anyone crossing the street and they can shoot you down, and the *Jash*'s barracks are overlooking the street where my dad's house is so be sure to walk close to the walls so that they wouldn't be able to see you."

"I am aware of it. Just keep praying." said dad.

"I am pregnant and I don't want anything bad happen to you."

My dad got an empty bag and filled it up with half of our full bag of flour. He slung the bag on his back, asked mom to pray for him, and left.

Just as he stepped out we heard one of the *peshmargas* on the street questioning him, but we were not worried about that.

Mom was in the late stage of pregnancy and had a hard time moving around. I played with a deck of cards while my mother was silent and worried, lay down next to my sister. Soon we heard a series of a machinegun shots so close that I thought it was targeted at the circle where my father had to cross.

After that we heard even more gunshots. My mom held Ronak and asked her to be quiet. Ronak was tired, and thankfully she soon fell asleep. I got quiet and pretended that everything was all right, for my mother's sake. She was very quiet and said nothing. Sometimes two people so close to each other can only comfort each other with silence. We were both tortured by the same thought, but neither wanted to say anything. I had my cards in my hands and was twisting them around but my hands froze as a dreadful feeling overwhelmed me. What if that machinegun burst had been aimed at my dad? I stared at the walls with my frozen hands on the deck of cards.

I turned to look at my mother during another burst of gunfire. I saw tears running from her eyes like an April shower as she cried silently.

"Mom, are you okay?"

"I can't believe we have to go through all this. I don't want anything to happen to your dad."

There wasn't anything that I could say to comfort her. I was terrified to think we might go out the next day to see my father's body lying dead in the street, and have to leave it there until the curfew is over. I went to the bathroom and looked at the sky it was cloudy and so dark that visibility was almost zero. When I returned mom had not moved.

"I am really worried. your dad's been gone for a long time, he should have been back by now."

I sat near her. "It's been about an hour, that isn't long."

"But it's less than a half an hour back and forth from here to my dad's house."

"It's so dark outside that you can't see anything." I said trying to comfort her.

There were two lampposts on each side of the road leading to the circle. *Peshmargas* used to shoot the light bulbs on both sides every night they came to town so that it would make it difficult for police, soldiers and *jashs* to spot them. That made me feel better knowing dad would have the cover of darkness.

It must have been about eight PM when Saber and his family knocked on the door. Mom told them that dad had taken half bag of flour to grandpa's house. Saber was shocked and couldn't believe anyone would try something like that, but he was also bothered that my father didn't let him know what he was up to. If he'd known, he would have escorted my father. I didn't know how that could have helped.

The gunfire slowed down somewhat but still there were sporadic shots. Sabre and his wife came into the room and sat with us, trying to carry on a conversation with Mom to keep her distracted.

We heard the door open and I looked up to see my father. He came back in, took his shoes off, and sat as close to the heater as he could. I saw the relief of my mother and also of Saber and his wife. Dad sat, still wearing his huge overcoat and told Sabre, "It's really cold out there."

"Did they shoot at you?" asked Sabre.

"Not really…I don't think so. I think I was lucky that it was so dark. It's pitch black out there and it saved me from being fired at," said dad.

"How are my father and everyone? Are they all okay?" asked mom.

"Yes they are all okay right now. They had only one more day of flour and aunt Halaw was relived when I brought them some."

"You're back home safe and we are all glad, but your uncle's family will be worried about you now," said Sabre.

"What can you do? If it's not one thing, it's another. You just can't win."

"I don't know how long half a bag of flour will last ten people, probably two or three days at most," said mom.

That night after my father came home I was happy and very tired. I went to bed and fell asleep right away.

The next day there was bread and tea for breakfast again.

"We're running short of kerosene and we may only have enough for a few days," said my mother.

"What about the wood?" asked my father.

"Well, if I use the wood just to make bread, it'll be used up in a week," said my mother.

"This is bad. I didn't know we were so low on wood and kerosene."

"I'll go to see if Amed Bag has any kerosene," said my father. Ahmed Bag's shop was just a couple houses away on the other side of the street.

"Well, let us pray that this ends soon or most people in town will die from starvation," said my mother.

"It doesn't look like it will be over soon, so we may have to tighten our belts."

After breakfast dad went out and shortly came back. He told my mother that Ahmed Bag had no more kerosene. His lot was empty.

I started getting depressed, I was used to having no spare time in my days. After school we'd play soccer and when it snowed we had snowball fights with the kids in the neighborhood. So often we went to my grandpa's house and joined up with my Uncle Sarwat and my other friends in their neighborhood, in particular Jamal and Aram.

Aram was about two years older than I was; he was just like my older brother. We became best friends. He was the most intelligent kid I knew in town. He used to read a lot; probably he learned that from his father who also loved to read. He was so quiet that nobody knew about him. He liked writing, and wrote well, even if he often threw away what he wrote. Aram's father worked for the government. He was a clerk and took care of property records and things like that.

When I went to Grandpa's, I saw my Uncle Sarwat and my aunt Lotfi. I also saw my older uncles Shawkat and Omar and my older aunts Kalthom and Sargool. It was great, there were so many of us that there was always something going on. I used to stay over at grandpa's house for dinner and often spent the night.

Now I was confined to our house with little to eat and nothing to do. I was frustrated and disenchanted with this revolution for its cruelty toward kids. I was thinking of my friend Aram. I wished I could write as well as he could. I hoped he would write something about these dark days when we were confined to our houses. Aram used to show me some of his writing. Often he used to write things like memos; he'd read it to me and afterward would throw it away.

One week passed before things got worse. While the *peshmargas* were in town, government troops were making attempts to reach the town. Up to that moment every government foray had ended with casualties and retreat. We didn't see many people but occsionally one of the neighbors came and told us the news. A few times my dad heard *peshmargas* outside and he cautiously went and talked to them to get the news. Meanwhile the MiG jet fighters visited us almost every day and bombed whatever they could. Their sonic booms shook the foundations of the town.

The second week was much the same and yet worse. While before we had electricity about four nights a week, the government pulled the plug and shutting down the power. We had a dim little lamp working on kerosene.

Late at night when I went to my room, my brother and my sister were both asleep in the living room. My room was dark and freezing and I was bumping around trying to get to bed. My mother came in with a flashlight in her hand." What are you trying to do? It's too dark to find your bed."

"But Mom, you said that from now on we need to conserve our kerosene and the flashlight."

"It's okay when you first go to bed. Take the flashlight with you and once you get to bed, put it beside you in case if you wake up in the middle of night and want to go to the bathroom. But we have to make the best use of everything we have, so don't play with flashlight and make sure that you turn it off before you go to sleep."

"The flashlight can only last for so long. It's not going to last forever," I said.

"I know that sweetheart, but we can only make sure we don't waste what we have. It's cold, so use this extra blanket so that you don't get sick." She put another blanket over me. "I want you to make sure you wear your socks and leave your sweater on to keep warm. I don't want you get sick. We can't afford sickness on a top of everything else that we're dealing with."

It felt like I was lying under a snow bank. When the room was warmer the glass would get foggy but now it was crystal clear and I could see a layer of ice on the windows. I had my sweater and overcoat on. I took my gloves from my overcoat pocket and put them on as well. I sat on my bed to let it warm up and very gradually I climbed in. I had my head covered with a blanket and I wrapped myself up and covered my face.

Our neighbor Saber had no kerosene left and was almost out of food. My mom let them fill their heater with kerosene and reminded them that she was left with very little kerosene herself.

My mother used to bake bread daily but she said that from now on she'd bake every other day. When she baked her bread, she shared with Saber's family.

I told my mother, when mom and dad where both sitting together, "mom you know that we could have enough if you didn't give any to Saber's family."

"Don't say anything like that. We can't be eating while someone next to us is hungry. You know that we would never have anything for ourselves if we didn't share with others. The only reason God gives to us is because we share whatever we have with those who are not so privileged."

"You mean when I grow up, I should give everything away? I asked.

My father answered "Son, let me tell you this once and remember it for the rest of your life: there is something called balance, by that I mean how you balance between your needs and the needs of others. Your needs come first and other's second. We are believers and therefore we believe that once life ends here we enter eternal life and that means everlasting life. How wonderful or miserable that life will be depends on how we acts in this life. So to be judged as a good person by God, you sometimes have to sacrifice in life and give to needy people from your own needs, not from your wealth. The person who said it best was Kalipha Ali, he prophet Muhammad's son-in-law. He said, 'Work for your life as if you live forever and do for your eternal life as if you die tomorrow.'"

Things got tight and not much food was left. We were all worried that the situation would continue for a long time. My mother rationed our bread and didn't let us have much of it with every meal, and she cooked rice less than she used to.

To make the situation even more difficult, the weather was getting even colder. My parents used to express concern for those who barely had any food at all and wondered how so many poor people in town were weathering those harsh days. It was harsh for us too, but at least we had some food. But at the start of the third week I was always hungry. My mother was worried about my grandpa's family and she thought that they must've run out of food.

The most difficult time was when I went to bed. My room was freezing; I felt like ice, and I was still hungry. I woke up to see a thicker layer of ice on the window. It was so cold at night I was frightened to even think about going to bed. After the first two weeks we sat in the room with no heater until dinnertime and then mom turned the heater on for only a half an hour.

We didn't have a bath in our house, it was too expensive. Like almost everyone in town we used to go to the public bath once a week. There were several public baths in the town, some were big with room for up to twenty or thirty people. During that time I dream of going to the public baths, if only warmth. Public baths were partitioned into two rooms, one room for people to bathe and the other part for people to dry themselves and get dressed. There was an attendant who brought people towels and on request he'd scrub people's backs. Once people were done with their bath they usually sit and have hot tea or hot milk. The bath was really hot, and one would sweat after they got out, so they sat for a while before drying themselves.

While people waited to dry out or dressed, they embark on different topics. They talked about things in town, about politics or business.

In three weeks I'd had no bath. I wished I were in the public bath, where it was nice and warm. I felt like I might never feel warm again. By the fourth week my parents were terrified. We'd almost run out of food and there was no more kerosene left. We had no heat and there wasn't any rice left. My mother's condition got worsen. She felt tired and exhausted all the time.

Still the fighting went on. The battle intensified on the road between Halabja and Sulaymanya as the army tried to break through the *peshmarga* line and reach Halabja.

It was toward the end of the fourth week that hell really broke loose. The army advanced, supported by MiGs, artillery, more than twenty tanks, and thousands of soldiers. *Peshmargas* couldn't fight the heavy war machinery with their simple rifles and machineguns. The *peshmargas* fought a heroic battle on the road and many of them got killed as they tried to stop the army from entering the town.

Early morning it was snowing heavily. We woke up to the sound of shouting in the street. We heard the tanks moving toward uptown. The shouting grew louder and we all sat in the main room, waiting to see what would happen next. Meanwhile we heard the sound of machineguns. I don't know what their targets were the *peshmargas* had already left.

We were all frightened and my mother was shaking. She had a hard time getting into a comfortable position, as she was pregnant and getting close to giving birth.

We heard shouting and yelling like someone was fighting on the street. There was shouting in every direction, some of it in Arabic and some in

Kurdish. Then the noise got closer and it sounded like someone was shouting and cursing by the house door. My father was nervous and kept pacing the room.

We smelled smoke and thought it was coming from outside, but as it got stronger and thicker and we saw a thick cloud of smoke coming from the roof on the back end of the house.

"We need to get out of here, I think our house is burning!" cried my mother as she held my sister.

"We need to hurry up," said my father. I could see he was frightened.

"Okay, let's go," I said. Our eyes were watering from the smoke.

"Please keep calm and watch your step. It's slippery outside," my father said to my mom.

My mother gripped my sister and held her close. "Rauf you hold your brother's hand and follow me, and Gareeb, watch the kids."

"You all get out now and I will be out in just a minute," said my father.

We all got out. It took no time for the fire to spread throughout the roof of the house and begin to burn downward. As we got out, several soldiers and *Jash* surrounded us. We were waiting for my father and worried that he didn't come out. I was afraid that he might burn in the house. Soon he made his way out carrying a Persian rug on his shoulder.

Dad was approached by couple soldiers and a few *Jash*. One of the soldiers hit him with the back of his *kalashinkov* and another soldier joined him, hitting him until he dropped the rug and lay on the ground covered in blood. Then one of the soldiers took away the Persian rug. I heard one of the *Jash* curse the soldier in Kurdish—he wanted it for himself.

By this time the whole house was on fire. I saw Saber, Shahla and Pary were running to get out of their house, Saber was holding his mother's hand. I felt she must be sick for she could barely walk. They were surrounded by *Jash* and soldiers but then let go.

We walked away from the fire. My father was bleeding and my mother nine months pregnant, could barely walk. It was snowing and in our hurry we had all forgot our overcoats. My brother and I were both in pajamas and sandals and my sister and mother had thin clothes with no overcoats.

We were freezing. My feet were quickly red like blood. I could barely walk, my hands and feet felt like ice. As we walked, we saw more and more soldiers, and *Jash* all over the street. We could see houses burning and hear children screaming. It was terrifying.

We were only walking for a minute before we all started coughing. The smoke was thick and we were all quickly dizzy from it. My father said, "let's go to grandpa's house."

As we headed towards grandpa's house, we passed by our store and saw *Jash* and soldiers were using their *kalashinkovs* as keys shooting the locks of the shops to open. Almost all the stores had been opened, and soldiers were looting them, loading goods into their trucks. Kaysary, the main shopping center it's gate was open and we saw soldiers coming in and out as they stole fabrics and all kinds of other things.

My father was still bleeding and one could see he was in shock. My mother kept coughing and she was getting short of breath and crying. My sister and brother Abdul were frightened and crying. I was crying and shaking from the cold and my parents looked helpless. I knew my mom was tired and she probably would have liked to sit somewhere to rest for a minute, but not in that cold. We saw other families whose houses were burnt, all walking in the street like us, trying to find home somewhere else with their relatives or friends. I saw children crying, many with shorts and pyjamas and some in bare feet.

During that walk my father was quiet and he didn't complain or curse anyone, all he did was wipe his face as the blood poured out. My mother was crying quietly all the way.

On the other side of the circle we saw a tank with soldiers around it, sitting and laughing. They'd looted everywhere they liked. I wanted to go to them and tell them what bastards they were for causing us such hardships. I told that to my dad.

He told me, "son you can talk about these kinds of things to someone with a conscience, but these soldiers don't have any." These soldiers laughed at their victims but called themselves Muslim. We were Muslims too, but they must've been reading a different version of the Qur'an.

We kept walking, but it was unforgettably painful. In every corner of the town we could see destruction and fire. Smoke formed a thick cloud over the town.

We continued on walking toward grandpa's house through empty neighborhoods where soldiers were searching houses. Trucks loaded with soldiers drove through the street. My grand pa's house was toward the middle of one of the two main streets; in the front of their house was a very wide circle, branching to two streets, one toward midtown and the other toward uptown. We got near grandpa's house and saw a tank right in the middle of the open area.

Mom was walking slower and slower and with more difficulty. It was early morning when we got to grandpa's house and saw their door was broken. I found out later that the soldiers couldn't wait for someone to open the door and they broke into the house. It was a sigh of relief when we arrived at grandpa's house, but still I feared that soldiers may come and burn down grandpa's house, leaving us with no place to go. The fear of worst to happen terrified me.

"What is going on Gareeb?" asked grandpa.

"They burned our house while we were inside. We had to run out as quick as we could, and for now we will be here until I don't know when." My aunts and my uncles gathered around us.

"Why are you bleeding, Gareeb?" asked grandpa.

"Let me get you a towel to clean up the blood or you'll get an infection. Now is not a good time to be sick," said Halaw and she fetched my dad a big towel.

"Your clothes are all bloody and muddy, I'll get your uncle's clothes. Just get changed and clean yourself up," said Halaw.

"You seen they ruined the entrance door to our house." said grandpa to my father "soldiers came in and started searching. Thank God a minute later a young officer came and called the soldiers outside. He saved us."

Having been in the cold for so long, the skin on our hands was cracked and bleeding. We all sat in grandpa's living room. Everyone was frightened, in particular my uncles Shawkat and Omar. They must have been about eighteen years old.

"Kids, you all need to sit down and rest. Here is a blanket for each one of you. Make sure you wrap yourself well to keep warm," said Halaw giving each one of us a blanket.

"You need to take care of yourself. Look, you need to spit out that black mucus and clear your lungs, that must be from the smoke," said Halaw to my mother who was coughing violently.

"I don't feel good and I am sore everywhere. My chest is tight and I'm having a hard time breathing," said Mom to Halaw. My aunt Sargool came and sat next to her.

Aunt Sargool she was about sixteen years old at the time. She was attending junior high school.

"Just rest for now and hopefully soon you'll get better," she said to mom.

"Well, I am angry, these people dragged me to walk in this frozen weather."

"Let us hope that things settle and we can get you to see a doctor," said grandpa.

"I don't know if things will ever get better. I have a feeling that I might not make it through this pregnancy," said mom.

I sat and covered myself with the blanket. I still felt chilled and now and then my teeth would chatter. My sister Ronak was crying. My aunt Lotfi sat next to us. She was just a year older than me, a beautiful little girl with fair skin, light brown hair and hazel eyes. She was always very kind and sentimental.

Mom was kept shifting from one side to another, unable to get comfortable and complaining of pain. Everything sad and tragic had all seemed to happen in a matter of a few hours and we felt every minute of it.

A meager lunch consisted of a small bowl of rice was served for each one of us. It was sticky and there was hardly any oil. At Grandpa's house they always ate well but then it was different. Grandpa looked at us when they put out lunch and said, "kids, you know there is not much to eat, but these days will be behind us soon. We ran out of food, and I was lucky to purchase a small bag of rice but for ten times the market price."

As soon as we'd eaten lunch, Shaykh Ahmed, one of my dad's family's friends and a follower of my great-grandfather, knocked on the door. Shaykh Ahmed was older than my father, and was dressed very much like a mullah. He had short beard and no mustache, was thin, and talked slowly.

"Come on Shaykh, please have a seat," said my grandpa. We all welcomed Shaykh Ahmed and he sat. He looked sad and frustrated.

"Forgive me, I wish I could serve you a cup of tea, but we are running out of almost everything," said grandpa in a humble tone.

"Haji, you are not alone. In fact we have nothing left. I hoped that they would let stores open so that I could get something to eat."

"I'll be walking around to see if any stores are open," said grandpa.

"I have some sugar and tea and oil in the store, if they haven't looted it," said my father.

"Shaykh Gareeb, I am sorry for what happened, I saw that your house burnt down," said Shaykh Ahmed.

"Yes, I can do nothing about it. I am not alone in this—I know it has happened to many people. Still I am thankful to God. I am sure he will take care of us."

"Yes, I know that, you are right, and having me here validates what you just said," said Shaykh Ahmed.

My father turned to the Shaykh. "I am upset but not angry, I take nothing for granted and I am thankful my family and I are all alive. I know now we are homeless and have nothing, but God has his own way of working things out for the better. I am sure he will give me strength and opportunity to rebuild what has been ruined."

Shaykh Ahmed said to my father. "Shaykh, you and your family will not be homeless. You have my house, I have two sets of rooms, one with three bedrooms and a kitchen and another one with two bedrooms and a kitchen. You have seen it and you know what I am talking about. Both are vacant and you can live in the one with three rooms. I urge you not to worry about paying rent until such a time that you feel comfortable financially Again."

"That is good but I need to pay you rent," said my father.

"Shaykh, I am a follower of you grandfather—he is dear to me. You need not to pay me rent for I'd have nothing if it wasn't for him. Treat it just like your own. We are friends and money is nothing in days like these."

"Thank you. Your offer could not have come at a better time," said my father.

"I am glad that you didn't turn down my offer. You'll have a place to live if it is still there by the time we get home."

"See what our lives come down to, one doesn't know what might happen from one minute to another," said my dad.

"Shaykh, I want you not to be concerned with furniture. Whatever my family has we will share. We may as well get going whenever you are all ready," said Shaykh Ahmed.

My dad went to the other room where my mother was lying down and I followed him. "Mahboob are you feeling better?" he asked her.

"A little better."

"Can you walk?" He continued, "Shaykh Ahmed will let us to stay in the unit with the three rooms you remember the place the teacher Jalal used to live in?"

"But we have no furniture, how that can help?" asked my mom.

"Shaykh Ahmed told me that he would share some of his furniture with us, and my brother Kazem lives around the corner from there, we'll borrow something from him."

"That's good," said my mother, sitting up.

"Listen Mahboob, if you can't walk, it's all right for you and Ronak to stay here, I don't want you go unless you feel up to it," said Halaw.

"I think I can make it," said mom.

We left grandpa's house and went to Shaykh Ahmed's house, retracing the same road that had taken us to grandpa's.

We got near the main intersection and saw people trying to piece together their lives, at least until the next atrocities. My father saw that the lock on our store was broken, and the store was open just like any other store in the midtown.

"I need to fix the lock on our store and relock it, so you can go with Shaykh Ahmed and I'll catch up with you when I'm done," dad said to us.

"Dad, can I stay with you?" I asked. He nodded.

Haji Hama Sharef, who had the store next door, saw my father. He greeted him and said, "can you see what these thugs have done, Shaykh?"

"Yes I see it and I fell it."

"I have an extra lock you can use, Shaykh." said Haji Hama.

"Thank you. God be your savior, Haji."

Dad took the lock from him and went in the store to get his tools. He started working to fix it. While we were there people came and wanted to buy things from him. He sold some sugar, oil, tea, and pain medicine. Dad went and crossed the circle by the main street and came back with a small bag of rice. He took a bag of rice, a container of cooking oil, sugar, tea, a teapot, cups and saucers, and some other little things. I helped him carry everything and we left for Shaykh Ahmed's house.

On the way to the Shaykh's house I asked, "dad, did they steal a lot from our store?"

"Rauf, the skin of your hands is all cracked and before it starts bleeding again you need to apply some Vaseline, and have everybody else do the same."

We arrived at Shaykh Ahmed's house. His house was a few minutes' walk away from our old place. Our old place was just half a block away from Shaykh's house

Fifteen minutes after our arrival at Shaykh Ahmed's house my Uncle Kazem, and his son Jama and his wife showed up. I saw our new place, three naked empty rooms, as cold as ice. The front had a cement patio. Next to it was another set of two bedrooms and a little landing and Shaykh Ahmed's residence. The bathroom was outside, a few feet away from the unit. The water faucets were near the bathroom.

Later Shaykh Ahmed brought us a mattresses and a few blankets. My Uncle Kazem had gone to his store and bought us about a dozen blankets, two mattresses and pillows. One of Shaykh Ahmed's neighbors gave us a little heater and another one brought us a couple of mattresses, and a few more blankets. Uncle Kazem and his wife went home and returned carried basic necessities such as dishes and lamps. As soon they put the mattresses on the floor, mom laid down. She looked exhausted and was breathing heavily. Dad went and got a container of kerosene. As the army arrived they brought kerosene so at least they did one good thing.

Dad got the floor covered with blankets. He arranged things very quickly there wasn't much to arrange. We put two mattresses in one room for my brother, sister and me. Mom brought in the heaters to warm up the room and started cooking dinner.

In the late afternoon, the snow stopped. What a long day—how much can happen in one day? I thought. I'd never imagined it even in my most terrific nightmare.

It didn't take long before we saw Saber's family coming to Shaykh Ahmed's house. We knew that these poor people had no place to go. Shaykh Ahmed came in, he and Saber's family greeted each other. "Saber I assume your place has burned down."

"Yes sir, that is right."

"So, do you have a place to live?" asked Shaykh Ahmed.

"No sir," said Saber with a sad voice.

"What you been doing the whole day in this freezing weather, Saber?" asked Shaykh Ahmed.

"I don't know. We were all freezing and I had to drag my poor mother here and there to kill the time. We had nowhere to go, and we didn't know exactly where Shaykh Gareeb was. We have no money. I didn't know what to do. We went to Haji Ezat's house and they told us that he'd come here. So came back to see if we could stay with Shaykh Gareeb."

I saw that Saber, his wife, and his poor old mother all had the skin on their hands cracked from the freezing cold."Well Saber, I'm glad you found us. You can live with us and share whatever God blessed us with," said dad.

"I have better idea. You may stay in the two-bedroom unit and don't worry about rent until you get yourself together," said Shaykh Ahmed.

"Thank you Shaykh, I'll never forget this," said Saber his face full of relief.

"So now you are Shaykh Gareeb's neighbors again. Please wait, I should return in a few minutes."

"Saber, just sit down and let your mom and your wife warm up. When the Shaykhcomes back, we can talk about furniture because you can't live in those bare rooms. We may have to share our furniture," said dad.

"Where did you get this furniture?" asked Saber.

"Shaykh Ahmed, my brother, and couple of neighbors brought them."

"Shaykh Gareeb, people just gave you enough things to meet your basic needs. You keep it, it's not right for me to take your necessities," said Saber.

"Don't worry Saber, this is not a time for luxuries. We are fighting for our survival, and having basic necessities is more than enough. Anyhow, just wait."

About a half an hour later Shaykh Ahmed came back and along with him were a couple of his neighbors carrying two mattresses, a little stove, food, some blankets a few dishes. Saber's family left to go to their new place. It seemed that Shaykh Ahmed must have gone around the neighborhood asking his neighbors to chip in.

It got to be late in the afternoon when mom started cooking dinner and the rest of us sat in a circle near the heater. My dad was obviously in pain. He wrapped his head with bandages. Every once in a while he'd touch his head where the soldiers had injured him, and he was massaging his shoulder.

"Dad, are you in pain?" I asked.

"Yes, I have a sharp headache and back pain."

"Dad why does God let these soldiers do so many bad things? God knows it's wrong," I thought out loud.

"Son, we fight for freedom and that is a godly thing and we know we are right.

Our enemies are tyrants and we know that. Do you agree?"

"Yes," I said.

"But simply because we are right, doesn't mean that we'll win. Fight for your rights but don't expect to win just because you are right. God willing you'll live long and life will teach you that at times even though you are right, you might still lose the battle. Does that makes sense?"

"Dad when you're right, you should win. God should be on your side," I replied.

"Just because you are right doesn't mean you win. Imagine the nearest people to God are the Prophet Mohammed and Jesus Christ. The Arabs tortured Mohammed and they laid him during summertime on his naked back in Arabian desert and God let them to torture him. The same Jesus Christ was also God's beloved one, yet he was crucified. That doesn't mean God abandoned his beloved ones, not at all. But why God makes these things happen, the only answer I can give you, is that God has a purpose in everything."

"Dad, what is God's purpose in all this suffering?" I asked.

"Son, don't ask God's purpose, we will never know for God doesn't think in our terms. If God was to think in our terms then he would have been a human being and we need no human being as God. As far as my pain is concerned, be comforted that I will get better. What I want you to know is that I am not angry at the soldiers who hurt me. All I pray is that God would bring wrongdoers to justice so that there will be a just answer to this chaos."

"But Dad, these soldiers are all bad."

"You know son if you have a dog you can breed it to be vicious and tear people apart, or you can have the same dog bred to be a loving creature, a friend. So it's not a dog who is vicious but the master who manipulates the dog. These soldiers obey the orders of their masters exactly as dog. It's the masters not the soldiers who need to be chained."

Mom came in and ended our conversation. "Let's lay *sfra**" and have dinner," She laid *sfra* and we had Spanish rice and no bread. We started eating dinner but things looked strange and we were all tired. Dad looked ill. One could read the pain in his face. Mom looked pale. I could see she was in pain.

That night I went sleep but I was still chilled to the bone. Our new place wasn't warm enough. I was totally exhausted from walking in that frozen cold with sandals and no warm clothes. I prayed never to see another day like that one.

In the morning fresh bakery bread, yogurt and hot tea was for breakfast. After breakfast dad left for the store as usual, and soon after my mother started crying. "Mom what's wrong?" I asked.

"I think I am in labor."

"What is that, Mom?" I asked.

"That means I will have the baby. I know that you have no overcoat and your shoes are still wet. I don't want you be out in this freezing cold, but I have no choice but to send you to go and get Selma the maman****." She continued. "You need to be back soon."

"You mean you want her now?" I asked.

---

* Set the table

** A Kurdish midwife

"Yes, now," she said. Still crying and in pain.

I left her to find Selma.

Selma lived at the other end of town. Her small house was on the street behind grandpa's. I didn't know of anyone living with Selma. She was a short lady with a round face. She used to dress in her traditional clothes with a little hat tied down with a nice black cloth, a few gold coins hanging on her hat. She was very dominant and had a strong personality. She was a widow in mid-fifties. I don't know what had happened to her husband. She was short and looked much younger than her age. She loved my mother and had helped her when my sister, my brother, and I were born. She was just like one of our relatives who used to visit us regularly.

I had no overcoat. I'd left it in our old house and it must have been turned to ashes, just like my shoes. I'd borrowed my uncle's shoes but they were a little big for me and were wet inside. It was cold, the street was muddy, and snow was piled up everywhere. I stopped by my father's store and saw dad was sitting with a couple of his customers. I quickly let him know that mom was about to have the baby and ran on.

I could see army trucks on the street passing by. I saw burned houses and shops that still reeked from the fires. I saw people going through the rubble to find whatever they could salvage, but I didn't know what they were trying to save. The burnt-out messes had turned to mud and were mixed with ashes and charred material.

I arrived at Selma's house. She was busy shoveling snow and piling it on the side of her house. Once she saw me she came and gave me a big hug and started crying. It wasn't an easy time and wasn't difficult for people to cry as almost everyone had been touched. I related to her that mom needed her urgent care immediately.

She threw down the shovel and got her veil.

"I will be with your mom shortly. Do you want come with me?"

"No, it's all right. I'll go back later," I said.

On my way back I saw Aram's father and he already knew everything that had happened. He looked sad and broken, the curve in his back had gotten more obvious and it must've been hurting him. His beard was long and he looked like he'd aged ten years in the past month.

"So Mr. Aziz, how is Aram?" I asked.

"Aram is sick. He had a bad cold and a cough and he feels very weak," Aziz said.

"Is it bad?" I asked.

"Rauf, I really don't know, but I am sure he will be okay."

"I want to see Aram, but I need to go home because my mom is sick. I will come later to visit Aram. Goodbye Mr. Aziz." I said.

"Goodbye Rauf," he said.

I headed home and the cold was seeping right in my bones. I was concerned for Aram because when his father told me that he would be fine. I saw the worry in his face.

The streets in the town were all muddy. It used to get muddy after the rain, but this time as the snow melted it brought even more mud from the ruined buildings to the street. Midtown still smelled from the fires, people were cleaning up. I saw a few storeowners standing by their burned-down stores looking angry and sad as they stared into the rubble. It was late in the morning when I passed my dad's store, but it was already locked. I thought dad must have gone home. Selma was sitting beside mom and dad was in the other room. Mom was in pain, but was breathing heavily and yelling every once in a while.

Selma looked me and said, "Rauf, go to the other room. Your mom may have ababy any time."

Dad came out in the room holding Ronak's hand.

"I hate to leave your mom, but you kids need to be clothed. Abdul and Rauf, put on your shoes and come with me," said dad.

"Where are we going?" I asked.

"You all need clothes. Let's go and find something warm for you. Let us make it quick and came back to your mom," said dad.

"That sounds good dad, let's go," I said.

I felt happy about that. I had been worried that I would have to be confined in our home for I didn't have any warm clothes to wear but still I didn't want to ask dad because I thought that he may not have any money.

We all went with dad and he took us to store. He got all of us nice warm overcoats, shoes, gloves, and hats. After I got my new shoes, I put my Uncle Sarwat's shoes in a bag and brought them home so that he could have them back.

When we got home, it was past lunchtime. Dad cooked Kokoo because we didn't have enough eggs. Kokoo is made from eggs and flour. Dad wasn't a good cook. All he knew was how to make eggs and tea. It was delicious, probably because we were still cold from going from one store to another. We devoured it all.

After lunch Dad left and went back to store. I started thinking about school. My textbooks, notebooks and everything else turned to the ashes in the fire of our house. What would I tell my teachers? I would get bad grades. I thought that the fire had burned it, but indeed now I had to deal with the aftermath of destruction.

Then I started feeling better. I had my overcoat, hat and gloves. I thought I was ready to deal with things again. I checked on my mom. She was still not doing well and there was no baby yet. I told myself she'd be all right with Selma, so I went out to Dad's store so that I could see the kids in the neighborhood.

"What are you doing here Rauf?" asked my father.

"I came here to help you."

"No you don't. There are no kids around, do you see that?"

"Yes dad,"

"You go home...it's not safe to be here, and it's freezing."

"Okay, dad," I said and left to go home.

That day after dinner my dad sat with me, my brother and my sister and told us,

"Children I want to let you know that although bad things have happened to us and to so many other people in this town, we are all right. Regardless of what happened, we all are still here."

"Dad, what about all my school things?" I asked.

"I will get you all you need, don't worry about that. Children, I want you to be comforted. I want you to be comforted that we all are alive and I will take care of you. It won't be long before we get back to normal." He got up and stood in the doorway of the room where mom was.

We were all tired. My sister and brother soon ate their dinner and went right to sleep, but I couldn't help worrying about mom and I stayed up. About eight PM my dad came and told me that mom had given a birth to a little boy. I could hear the baby crying. I went and saw mom. She gave me a kiss and I went back to my room. I started thinking about this little brother and how I would take care of him when he grew older. I went to sleep with that thought, and everything else that had been bothering me throughout the day was erased.

The next day was Friday schools were closed. Businesses were supposed to be open and dad went back to work. I realized dad was going through a difficult time and had no money. Later I found out that grandpa had lend him enough to jumpstart his business going and to take care of our needs.

On Saturday we woke up and went to school. School started as usual and I went to my classes. The routine was the same as usual on the surface but it felt different. Even the brats in the class were quiet. The teachers were not as motivated as they used to be. Things were quieter than ever before. I searched for Aram with no avail. I knew something was wrong with Aram and I decided to go and visit him after school.

Chapter Nine

Our history exam had been scheduled for the day when the curfew was declared. When I got to school the teacher unexpectedly gave us the exam. All the students in my class thought this teacher Saleh was nuts. We hadn't have any time to study. Saleh knew that but still went ahead with it. Average tall, he was a half-bald, very unattractive man. I felt sorry for his wife. He was as hairy as a monkey. He was a communist, which didn't surprise me at all, and he was very bad tempered. Saleh wasn't generous about his grading and he wasn't the kind of a teacher to give a passing grade just for showing up for the exam. I had done little for my exam, and I had to rely on my memory. There was a question about China, asking why the Chinese were doing so well now relative to their past. I didn't know a darn thing about China and had only quickly glanced at that chapter. Honestly I hadn't seen anything in that chapter to suggest that the Chinese were doing better, but I knew that our idiot teacher was a communist and that the Communist Party ruled China. The exam was made up of four questions. I answered the three questions I knew, but last question about China I didn't know what to do with it.

I didn't know what to put down but I knew it was worth one fourth of my grade. I wrote down whatever I could make up. I stated that China's advancement is attributed to the ruling communist party. It motivated people to work hard and subsequently develop their country. The Communist Party I wrote was a good Party and I think that God loves them.

At the next session he brought back our test papers and I'd gotten the highest mark. Saleh pointed to me in class and said, "only one student had the right answer and that was Rauf. He is smart. There was not a clear answer on your book, but he was smart enough to conclude the answer on his own." He read my answer and said, "what a good answer. This is a great thinker and his thinking is in line with the reality of China."

When he said that, all my classmates looked at me, and I thought that from now on I could conclude my own answers and forget all about my textbook after all, this way worked better. I thought about pulling the same scam in my religion class.

Later I told my father, "that I had received the highest grade in my history class." I handed him my paper, and he saw I had scored ninety out of one hundred, equivalent to an A. He didn't even bother to look my paper. All that mattered to him was my grade and he trusted the rest.

"This is good. Keep it up," he said.

"But Dad, I wrote this thing about China and my teacher liked it."

"Let me have your paper back," he said.

I watched him shaking his head as he read my paper.

"Where did you learn this garbage about China?" he asked with a smile.

"Nowhere, Dad, I made it up."

"But you know this is a lie. For this kind of a lie you should have been given a failing grade. China is not advanced. It's the poorest country and most overpopulated country in the world. They don't even have enough to eat."

"Dad I know that," I replied.

"Then why write an answer that's wrong?".

"But dad, the question he gave has no answer in my textbook."

"Then you made it up," he said.

"Yes, Dad, and I knew Saleh was a Communist. I knew he'd like that kind of answer and that he'd give me a good grade."

"Getting good grades is okay, but I don't want ever hear you say that God loves Communists. Communism is evil. When things are wrong you have a responsibility to say so, not to tell lies just to get ahead. Son, when you do wrong or when you say wrong things even if it turns out well at the time, it will come back to haunt you later. You will pay for it, so just do right everyday without fearing adverse consequences. Once an old Kurdish man said, 'If you have no master, let your conscience be your master.'"

"I am sorry. I will not do that again."

"Good. I hope we have an understanding."

That made me feel bad. I shouldn't have told Dad to read my answer. I told myself I could easily have avoided that long lecture.

Jash and soldiers rounded up the members of families of anyone who had joined the revolution. My friend Ahmed's brother Nouri was a member of the KDP's regional committee. His father Haji Hamay Nanawa was and old man in his sixties, with one blind eye and other health problems. As I returned from school just a few weeks after the army's breakthrough, I saw Haji Hama Nanawa was followed by a soldier and a *Jash*. They'd made him take his shoes and socks off walking in the freezing cold and snow, the soldier repeatedly hit him with the stock of his *kalashinkov*. The old man lost his balance with every hit and I saw him fall a couple of times. It was disheartening to watch that as I did until they disappeared from my sight.

I went home and I didn't tell my mother what I had seen. For she was still sick. She had caught a bad cold and the new baby kept crying. Selma still was there and she cooked some rice and dried okra with sun-dried tomatoes. My father came back and we sat to have our lunch. Selma took the baby from my mother and said, "you'd better eat your lunch. You are getting weak, Mahboob."

My mother started crying, "I don't think this baby will make it, he hasn't eaten anything so far and hasn't slept. He just cries and I don't know what to do."

"Let's take him to the doctor," agreed my father.

My father was drinking tea, and as soon as he was done he put on his overcoat and shoes. "Rauf, I want you go and watch the store. I'll be back once we're done with the doctor."

Selma wrapped the baby in a heavy blanket and held it near her chest.

I went to store and sat there until my dad returned. When dad returned, I asked him, "Dad, what did the doctor said about the baby?" I asked.

"Hell, what do they know? He thinks the baby will be okay and if its not, to visit him next week."

"Dad, I am going to Grandpa's house," I said.

"Make sure you come back on time. You need to do your homework," he said.

"Yes dad, I will," I said.

I left the store and went to Grandpa's house. When I arrived saw my uncle and Aram sitting at the front door. They had on their overcoats, hats, and gloves.

"I have been looking for you at school and they told me you were not feeling well," I said to Aram.

He started coughing, and once the coughing stopped, he said, "yes I have been really sick with a bad cold." After a short time Aram left and my uncle and I went into the house. My step-grandmother Halaw was sitting along with my aunts and my older uncle.

"Aram is sick. He was really coughing badly."

Halaw nodded "During the curfew they ran out of heating fuel and their house was without heat for more than three weeks. Aram has developed asthma."

I thought for a moment and asked, "what is asthma?"

"It's a respiratory disease that makes people short of breath," she said.

"Is it serious?"

"Their doctor told them that it's in an early stage and he may heal. If not he may have to live with it." She talked about the newborn baby briefly.

"Too much has happened in a short period of time," said Halaw, she continued.

"It's incredible. I have never seen anything like it. Now it's your newborn baby brother. Poor little thing."

"Yes, I wish he would stop crying. How can he cry for so long?"

"Rauf, this what happens when one is in pain, especially a little thing like that. All he knows is crying. Babies tell you if they are wet, hungry, or in pain through their crying. I think the baby got sick because your mom didn't have proper nutrition for the last month of her pregnancy. I'm worried that your mom isn't getting any sleep. She stays up with him all night and day,"

"Mom, let Rauf stay here with us until the baby gets better," said my Uncle Sarwat.

"Sure he can, but he needs to let his parents know," she said.

"No, I'll go home, its not fair to leave Mom all alone," I said to them.

I stayed with my Uncle Sarwat out on the streets, walking around for a long time. Snow was piled up in front of every house. When we used to walk on days like that, we would always encounter some brats who would throw snowballs at us, provoking some kind of snowball fight, and we'd chase each other from street to street. Now things were quiet and it seemed like even the brats of the town were hibernating.

We returned to Grandma's house and sat by the heater to get warm. Halaw was outside cooking in the kitchen. She was using the wood to cook and the smoke made her eyes water. She came toward us and asked if we were hungry. She had cooked beans and rice with lamb. I said "yes," I was famished after all that strolling in streets during such a frigid day.

"Then you should eat dinner now so you can get home before dark," she said as she handed me the meal. I cleaned my plate in no time and was ready to head home.

"Can I have some too, Mom?" said Sarwat.

"No you may not, you wait until we all sit and have our dinner. Rauf has to go home soon but you can wait," said Halaw.

I retraced same places as I did the day our house was burnt down and my memories were still fresh. I wished I lived in the big city with different routes to every place so I could've chosen another way to go. I was sick of revisiting the same road and reminded of what happened a few days ago when our house had burnt and we had walked to Grandpa's house. Just a few days ago I had seen so much misery along this street, and I was now continually reminded of those scenes. It used to be safe no matter whether it was day or night, now I had to be home before dark or I'd be shot at. With Halaw telling me the whole story about Aram, I didn't know how many people I should think and worry about.

When I got home I could hear the baby crying his lungs out. Selma was in our room with the baby and had left Mom to get some sleep. I went near the baby and told him, "You little angel, let me kiss you. See this kiss will heal you."

I found it to be disheartening, a little creature had just opened his eyes to this world, yet his world is a painful ordeal which through his crying informing us of his agony and his helplessness. I wondered about my mother I didn't know what fabric she was made of. It has been a long trial of her ailing pregnancy and now the condition of her baby which deprived her from her peace of mind. She was completely drained out of her vigor and energy. I don't think she had more than two hours of sleep at once since the baby was born. To make the matter worse holding this crying baby in her bosom and listening to his crying and feeling pain for it and often joining the baby in his crying. Yet she didn't give up and neither did she complain about the baby, instead she directed her frustration toward whatever the illness baby was suffering from. She was fighting hard to make sure her baby will survive, and she still loved that baby perhaps more than anything else in her universe. She selflessly undermined her fatigue and her ruinous wellbeing in a horizon should the baby to continue in same the manner, instead she was entangled in sorrow feelings for the helpless baby in her own helplessness. It's a mystery, a little soul such as this baby to cause her so much of discomfort, keep her up day and night and yet she loved him, adored him and called him "my angel", and never even for a silent moment in her private time wanting him to go and to tell enough is enough. I thought could it be a matter of motherhood's duty or love, not perhaps but for sure both. I was sure men could never handle a situation like that as gracefully as women do. Sure God has created men and women to be different, profound differences so necessary for humankind's survival and wellbeing.

Then my little sister sat next to him and she gave him a kiss and said in her little baby talk, "You baby need to sleep, okay?"

The baby kept on crying. Then my father came back home. As soon as he got in he went to check on my mother and saw her asleep.

"Kids, keep quiet let your mom sleep," he said to us.

All of a sudden the baby stopped crying. He must have been exhausted after crying so long. Selma placed the baby in the bassinet.

Selma stayed up with my mother day and night, and she looked like hell. Her eyes were all swollen and sleepy from sleep deprivation. She looked at my father and said, "I am going to get your dinner, then try get some sleep."

"Is dinner made?" said my father.

"Yes," said Selma.

"Go ahead, you need to get some sleep. I'll feed the kids. Go now, because if the baby wakes up there will be no peace."

Selma quietly opened the door to my mother's room and went inside. My father went and set *sfra* and gave my brother and my sister their dinner. I told Dad I'd eaten at Grandpa's house and he sat to eat.

Another day went by, and thank God, my mother started feeling a little better. The baby continued crying and wasn't eating. Mom held the baby and tried everything to calm him down. I overheard her saying, "please God this baby doesn't deserve this punishment. Please help him God, I want this baby to live. Please, God."

A week had passed since the baby was born, I came back from school and headed home. As I entered the house I heard my mother crying and went into the living room and saw her holding the baby. She looked at me and said, "my little baby boy is dead. God, what else? Please, enough is enough." Then she paused and said, "God, forgive me. This is just too much to handle."

She still held the baby close to her chest as he was alive. Selma held my mother tight as if my mother would break into pieces if she let her go, and both crying.

"God, you took away my baby. I got this little sweetheart at the worst time in my life. So many bad things have happened, yet I thought I would keep this baby. I prayed that he would be a reminder that at the same time bad things happen, good things also happen. My God, you took this baby away. I loved him so much, poor baby had to suffer so much."

She kissed the baby, and then kissed him again and again, then she put him down. She bent down, gave him kisses while her tears were dripping on his face which she wiped, and said, "let me give you my last kiss, sweet angel. May God be with you. One day we will be together again in God's kingdom. I want you to know my little angel that I loved you so much and

I wish you were with me but as you go, I will be left to wonder why it happened?"

I went to Dad's store to let my father know. I arrived at the store dad was rearranging one of the shelves.

"Dad, the little baby is dead," I said.

"Rauf, go let your grandpa and your Uncle Kazem know," he said calmly after he'd taken a deep breath. I felt that he'd known the baby would not make it and that he'd had time to prepare himself.

First I let my Uncle Kazem know, I went there and my uncle still was in the store, although he was usually gone by that time. He had a couple of customers in his store. As I got there they were about to leave. I waited until they left.

"Rauf how are you doing? Are you up to no good?" he joked.

"I am okay, Uncle I just came here to let you know my baby brother is dead, and now I have to go tell Grandpa."

When I went away, I heard him saying, "one thing after another. It seems the end isn't near."

I walked to my grandpa's store. Sarwat and my older Uncle Shawkat were there rolling long bolts of fabric onto a holder. My Uncle Shawkat was surprised and said, "what are you doing here? Shouldn't you be sitting in for your dad at the store?"

"No Uncle, I came here to let you know that my brother is dead," I said. My Uncle Sarwat got totally disoriented fell into a chair. The roll of fabric fell from his hand.

"Which brother?" he asked.

"My newborn brother," I said.

"You scared the hell out of me, I thought for a moment you were talking about Abdul," he said.

"Sarwat, run home and let my parents know," said Shawkat.

Sarwat was upset and left without saying anything.

I think that Uncle Shawkat was more worried about the timing of my newborn brother's death. With the devastation to the town, the shock of the additional tragedy was especially hard.

I cried all the way back home. I was upset and confused about every thing that happened to us and the town. When I got back home, Mom was crying and Selma was beside her. I went to Mom and gave her a hug.

She kissed me and said, "Your dad took the baby to the mosque."

I went to the mosque. I saw my dad had just finished washing the baby. I didn't know why it was my father who did that, usually they had a designated person in the mosque to wash the dead bodies. He was ready to dress him for his resting place. He placed him gently in a white cloth and he took a last look. His tears fell on the face of the baby. He gave him a kiss and said, "let this be the last kiss son. More will follow when we meet again. God be with you, son. I love you," He wrapped him in a Barmal.

Even though the baby was sick since his birth, Dad loved him and felt bad for this little baby who had to suffer so much. No doubt it tore at my dad's heart.

We went to the graveyard, all men. Usually women stayed home. We walked a muddy dirt road for almost fifteen minutes to the graveyard. I was freezing even though I wore gloves, a hat and an overcoat. It was windy and everywhere was covered with snow. As usual there was a mullah to recite the Qur'an. I wished the mullah could say things in Kurdish, I couldn't understand why everything needed to be in Arabic which very few understood. I knew they talked to dead people, so what difference would it make whether you said it in Kurdish or Arabic or for that matter in a dog's language? They should still understand if they heard. A little baby couldn't even understand Kurdish and they were telling him things in Arabic. I told myself he would not understand even a word of what the mullah was saying.

We stayed around the graveyard until they buried the baby and the mullah was done with reciting from the Qur'an. People as usual stayed and talked to each other. I stayed with my dad and my grandpa. All I heard that day were people's sad stories about the recent atrocities. Everyone had their own story to tell. When it was so cold that everyone wanted to leave and get back home.

At home my mother was waiting for us, her eyes blood red and her face all swollen. She looked like a wrecked ship, or a lost soul without a destination. Selma was still there and wanted to go home, but my father asked her to stay with mom for at least another day. Selma wore the same dress as when she first came to our house. She looked forlorn and one could tell that if she didn't get a good rest she would fall down where she stood.

My grandfather and my uncle and at least a dozen more people had come back home with us. I went to see my mother. She was holding my sister, but as soon as she saw me she took me into her arms. She kissed me on both cheeks and told me how much she loved me. Then my mother came out and everyone expressed their sympathy to her and individually said their prayers for her. Then my grandpa held her. She rested her head on his shoulder and cried for a minute before letting go.

My father had an uncle named Shaykh Sayfadeen. He was tall and slim with a very short grey beard and a thin moustache. He owned a grocery store and was one of the nicest people one could meet. He was a very quiet person afraid that if he committed a sin he'd alienate himself from God. Perhaps I should say it just came naturally to him to be good in speech, action and manner. He didn't judge other people or say things that weren't Godly. He had three sons: Akram, Farok, and Abdula. Akram was about four years older than I was but Farok and Abdula were around my age. Akram was tall and sort of weird looking, but was very pleasant and loved to laugh. Farok was a bit hyper and had very exciting personality while Abdula was very cool and quite.

My father liked his uncle Sayfadeen; we used to invite him and his family over every once in a while for lunch or dinner. His wife Naheda was a good lady. She was very quiet, well mannered and well tempered. Their family worked hard and as their business was doing well, not to say rich, but financially comfortable. Uncle Sayfadeen grew up in a small village across the Serwan River about twenty or thirty miles away from Halabja. He could read and write and all his schooling, like most of people of his generation, was through the mosque. I used to go and sit in uncle Sayfadeen's store when he was away and hang out with his sons. We loved to tease other kids and make fun of them.

Two weeks had passed since the army entered our town. Rubble was everywhere and the town didn't look anything like it used to be. It was worn out by the killing and destruction. I got my allowance from my grandpa and my father and went with my Uncle Sarwat. We knocked the door, and I asked Aram to come with us to see Farok at Uncle Sayfadeen's store. We let in Aram's house and went straight to Aram's room.

"It's not fun when Uncle Sayfadeen is there. He gets frustrated every time we laugh and he thinks that we're making fun of others," said Sarwat.

"Yes, but we wait until he goes for his prayer," I said.

"Okay, let's go," said Sarwat.

"I already spent my allowance," said Aram.

"I still have my allowance," said Sarwat.

"With my money and Sarwat's we have enough money to buy things for all three of us," I said.

Before we parted I asked Aram, "Aram, have you written anything recently?"

"Yes, I did one little essay. It is in that box." He pointed it out to me. It was a metal box with a small lock. I asked to see it, but he said I should wait.

"Why is that?" I asked him.

"I am not through with it when I am done you will see it." Said Aram.

"Is it going to be a book?"

"No, I told you before, I don't want to write a book. I will write this as an essay. Once I am done it'll be a few pages. I may have to burn it at the end. You know that I don't want to be caught with anything that might send me and my father to prison." Said Aram.

Aram was still coughing and didn't seem that he had gotten any better. He put on his overcoat and all three of us went out, heading towards Uncle Sayfadeen's store. When we arrived, Akram, Farok and Abdula were all sitting and they told us that Uncle Sayfadeen was staying home today, he had caught cold. They had a mukaly* full of sparking mesquite. Sarwat and I bought candies and peanuts and shared with everyone.

"Mr. Akram, can we sit and eat our candies here?" I asked.

He looked at all of us "Yes you may, as long as you're not brats and make fun of the customers. You know people were complaining about you and your friends."

"We won't do that, I promise," I said.

---

* A stove

"Then you may sit," said Akram.

We sat and he moved the warm mukaly close to us. We had a good time eating candies and peanuts. People passing by were looking at us as though we were trying to pull a scam on Akram or as if we may have been a bunch of nuts. Everyone in the neighborhood knew us as brats, but I really didn't care what the others thought.

A lady came in wanting to buy a pack of cigarettes from Akram. In a very nasty tone she shook her finger and pointed, looking at Akram, "How much is it?"

"Sixty flis," he replied.

"I bought it for half that!" said the lady.

"Sister if you find it for half that price, I'll give you money and you can go buy me some," he replied.

"I bought it in midtown and I have no time to go that far!" she shouted, her voice high and grating.

"I have no problem walking to midtown for that kind of price," said Farok.

"Never mind, I'll buy it from you," said the woman. She seemed to have a cold.

The woman took her wallet and kept counting her change, and we were giggling and wondering how long it would take her. Finally she got her pack of cigarette and left. As she left we were all relieved and laughed, and she turned around and said, "You little brats, I wish you were from a different town."

A minute later we saw her coming back.

"What a pain. Here she comes again," said Akram.

"Give me another pack of cigarettes," said the woman. She acted like she was rushing to get somewhere. Akram handed her a pack of cigarettes. She took her wallet out and slowly started counting her change.

"It will take an hour to count all these pennies?" I asked.

"Can I help you count your money?" laughed Sarwat.

"No, I don't need your help. Go help yourself," said the woman.

My Uncle Sarwat said, "Let's go. We've spent enough time here today."

The woman was still counting her change and it seemed to take forever. She looked at my uncle and said, "Get the hell out of here. You made me confused and I can't even count."

"When we come back tomorrow you'll still be here counting your change," I said.

"You little brat, you distracted me again. I have to start all over," the lady said.

"Just go home."

We left Uncle Sayfadeen's store, looking back to make sure the lady was not behind us, laughing and continuing to make fun of her.

It was a sunny day. People shoveled snow and piled it up in front of their houses. One could see little hills of snow in front of everyone's house. As we were walking we saw a man was spanking a five-year-old kid. We got closer, and my Uncle Sarwat had enough nerve to intervene. He got closer to the man and asked, "Why are you beating this kid?"

The man stopped spanking the kid. "Because he doesn't listen to me, and he constantly gets into trouble."

"Bad kid, you need to listen to your father, you little brat. Beat him up some more so he will listen from now on. How dare you not listen to your dad?" said Sarwat.

The man spanked the kid again and as we left them, we all laughed, saying,

"Beat him up some more, the little brat."

We were going back toward my grandpa's house, making snowballs and targeting icicles on the house roofs. We were watching each other to see who was a good shot.

When we suddenly were hit by snowballs. Three came at us at once. It stunned me for a moment. We turned around and saw three kids we knew from the neighborhood. We each made a couple big of snowballs each held one and put the extra one in our pockets, and run to get these kids who tried to hide. Two of them scattered and hid leaving Rafat, who was always at work to get us. We started working on him. He kept throwing snowballs at us until we got close to him and got him cornered. My Uncle Sarwat caught him and held him standing with his back to us. We all reached for more snow and shoved it under his shirt and filled both his back and front with snow.

He was screaming, "Come on guys, I am freezing!" We let him go and he ran home, which was fairly close. I yelled after him "Rafat, you idiot, remember what did you do to me the other day!" I yelled after him. I was happy I finally gave him back what he deserved.

We went back to grandpa's house, and Halaw was sitting next to the heater with my aunts and my mother. Our faces and our hands were as red as blood. We took our shoes off and sat around the mukaly to warm ourselves up.

Halaw scolded us. "Why do you have to freeze yourselves like that? Don't you know you might get sick?"

"No, we are all right, really, we are not freezing," I said with my hands extended over the mukaly.

"What do you mean you are not freezing? Go look the mirror your faces and hands are all red like blood," Halaw said as she was folding clothes.

"Mom, don't worry about us. In a few minutes we will be all warm again. We could even go out and play some more," said Sarwat.

"No you're not going out again. Just move a bit let me warm up this towel," said Halaw. She held the towel over Mukaly to warm it up. After she warmed it up, she turned to Aram, "Here, use this towel to warm up your face."

"Thanks," said Aram.

He took the towel and wrapped it around his face and neck. Aram grew short of breath and had started coughing. Halaw was very kind to him. She got up and went to the kitchen and came back with huge pot full of fresh warm popcorn and we ate it like we were starved.

It was a couple of weeks since the army arrived, and still more news was circulating as more harm was revealed. There was a well-known local poet named Harek. He was well known in the town and everyone had heard his poetry. The town was proud of him and expected one day he would be added to the list of great Kurdish poets, and keep the name of our town in the history of Kurdish literature, and another rose in the garden of the poets.

One night we were having dinner, my father mentioned him. "Harek has been devastated, he has lost thirty years of his work. His house was burnt and he couldn't rescue his writings. It's hit him so badly that he is about to go insane."

The poet was with his family in his house when the soldiers set their house on fire, just as they'd done to us. He died from a heart attack just a few months later. A decade after that one of his friends collected some of his poetry from different people and had it published, but it wasn't anything close to the life work of this vanished poet.

I knew my best friend Aram got asthma and that there were many other people who got sick. Hundreds of children who'd developed respiratory and other illnesses as a result of the cold and malnutrition. The news from that horrible curfew kept surfacing for months.

A couple weeks after the attack, the *peshmargas* resumed attacks on government posts and army convoys between Halabja and Sulaymanya. There was a curfew every night just after sunset. Kurdish publications were banned. People were afraid to keep any Kurdish publications at home regardless of the nature of the publication. The only place one could get a hold of Kurdish publications was the public library, but people were reluctant to go there for fear of being reported to authorities. The government continued to round up people who had family members in the KDP. During the daytime government MiGs often bombed anything that moved around the town. It was at this time that the revolutionaries started their radio station. The government had devices to jam the stations so that people couldn't receive their broadcasts, but everyone still listened to the radio at night. All they broadcast was the news of fighting throughout Kurdistan and some revolutionary slogans.

We were living in the new place and still barely had any furniture. Like any other family we were fearful and felt no peace of mind. After what we had experienced, we recognized the government's potential for atrocities. The government was looked upon as an unnecessary evil and the source of wrongdoing, irrelevant to justice and civil society. Everyone was praying for the government to change. People used to talk about the days before revolution, how safe the town was, and how people could go anywhere at anytime.

Almost every night after dark we had to listen to the fighting. Late at night we could hear machineguns and artillery. The road between Halabja and Sulaymanya was still closed and there were checkpoints everywhere.

One could not travel anywhere without being stopped at checkpoints to be harassed by soldiers.

We were often without electricity. When power generators run out of fuel, we would have no electricity at all until the army convoy and oil supply arrived. The same was true with bakeries. Most of the time they were shut down and that was a burden to almost everyone. The price of flour skyrocketed and the quality was horrible. This went on for a long time, until the summer of the 1964.

Chapter Ten

In the summer 1964, I was eleven years old. We had moved to a new place near my grandpa's house. It was a house with two sets of three bedrooms and a huge well-landscaped yard. My father had just started doing better and he had paid off his debt. That summer my parents decided that me, my brother, Aziz my cousin and my Uncle Sarwat should all be circumcised. They delayed this stupid thing until we were so old because of what had been going on in the town. Circumcisions were an important event as it was in old traditional Jewish religion. People were invited over and food was cooked. The circumcision took place at home. There were people who had experience with circumcisions, but they were not medically trained doctors and there were no anesthetics or anything such as that.

I remember it well. It was one day in summer when we were all at home. My brother Abdul, my cousin Aziz, my Uncle Sarwat and I were waiting for a man named sadiq to come and circumcise us. We were all scared. We got a deck of cards and a dama board so that we could play afterwards; we even went as far as buying a soccer ball. I knew sadiq. He was a tall guy as neat and as clean as one could be. He had a long face and huge ears, dressed immaculately clean and handsome.

sadiq arrived. They took me first and sent the rest to the other room. When sadiq started he said, "You know what I am here to do?"

"Yes, I know," I replied, of course terrified.

"If a male does not get the flesh of his foreskin circumcised, his soul must be cut off from his people. He has broken the covenant. That was God's word in Old Testament, and you will not be allowed into heaven unless you are circumcised.

That will pave your way to heaven. Aren't you excited?"

"No, I'm terrified," I replied.

I thought that line he gave me from bible was all he knew from the bible, and only because it fitted his business. I was staring at the toolbox he had with him. "Don't you know that without circumcision you will never see heaven?" he asked.

"I know its not going to be heaven once you're done," I said.

"Did someone scare you? Do not worry, its going to be fine," said sadiq with a calm demeanor.

"You are a big boy; I'll do nothing to hurt you. There's just a little skin that needs to be removed. You can handle that, can't you?"

I said nothing; I knew he was trying to buffalo me.

My father and both my uncles Omar and Shawkat were present at the time. I was dressed in a long cotton robe with nothing underneath it. It felt strange. sadiq reached for his toolbox. He got out this sharp metal, which resembled a knife.

"Now you need to sit down straight and don't move," said sadiq.

I sat on the chair. It felt like I was sitting on an electric chair ready to be executed.

He started his job by pulling the foreskin as hard as he could and tying it with some thick thread until he got the biggest scream out of me. It hurt like hell. I almost ran away.

"Please be seated and don't move so that we can get this over with. It will take less than a minute."

He tried to take my attention away so that I didn't watch what he did. "Look how those birds got up on the roof," he said as he pointed his finger to the roof while looking at the foreskin with the knife in his other hand. I was angry at him and wished that I could cut his finger to give him a dose of his own medicine.

I asked him to hurry up and cut so it'd be over with.

"Now please close your eyes," said sadiq.

I closed my eyes and he got his knife and sharpened it against a piece of leather several time. That got me angry, I asked myself why didn't this idiot do that before he tied my foreskin. Meanwhile I was hurting like never before. I opened my eyes and saw the knife, it shone like the gold of the sun, and looked razor sharp. He wiped it twice with alcohol to sterilize it and then held the foreskin and cut it right behind the tied thread. I didn't scream but it was like an electric shock going through my whole body. I told myself after that hell, I'd better be going to heaven. I had my turn in hell and knew what it felt like.

I felt the blood around my legs, and I was so much in pain that I could barely see or think.

"Okay now, let me hold your hand, and please as you walk keep your legs apart from each other so that they will not touch your wound," said my father.

I walked to the other room and laid flat on my back. I could not use a blanket because it could have touched my wound.

I knew everyone else would join me right away. Before the circumcision took place, my Uncle Shawkat had told us it was going to be a piece of cake but that for one hour we'd have to be in bed and after that we could even go out and play soccer. That is what my Uncle Shawkat said but my friends told me it was going to hurt like hell. When I told my uncle what my friends had said, he got mad and told us we believed our stupid friends rather than believing him. He told us this story:

Once upon time there was a wise old man with a donkey. One day one of his neighbors came and asked him to borrow the donkey. The wise man said his donkey wasn't there. The man was about to leave when the donkey started braying. The neighbor came back to the wise man and told him, "It's a shame you lied to me, you said the donkey isn't here, but it's braying loudly". The wise man replied, "my God, this is a disgrace. You believe the braying of a donkey rather than believing in me."

My Uncle Shawkat said, "just like the story I told you, you believe in these friends who are braying like donkeys, and you believe the braying of donkeys rather than me."

We were sort of persuaded by this explanation, because he was very serious when he talked to us. That is why we got a deck of cards ready and other games so that we could play right after the circumcision was done.

After everyone was done, all four of us sounded like an opera of braying donkeys. I thought about this idiot sadiq relating heaven to circumcision. I really didn't understand what God had to do with circumcision or why only circumcised people should go to heaven. I thought if it is so, then there are many countries in this world where circumcision is unpracticed. Muslims and Jews should go there and render a national circumcision day. They could circumcise everybody so that these nations would be nations of donkeys, all braying at once, and stepping toward Heaven's Gate.

The following day my Uncle Shawkat was with us he was happy to see us all stuck home since we didn't have to be his preoccupation. "Mr. Shawkat, what is this thing about only people who are circumcised go to Heaven. Is this is right?" asked my Uncle Sarwat.

"Yes it's true, they have this clinic during judgment day. Men need to be sorted out. Men will go to this clinic to be examined by angel doctors, and those who are not circumcised will be kicked in the ass and sent to hell without judgment, but those who are circumcised will get a fair trial.

"You mean even people who have done good all their lives will go to hell, just because they didn't cut off that little piece of skin?" I asked.

Shawkat nodded. "Yes, that is right. This mean you can't go to heaven if you are not circumcised, no matter how good you are, forget all about it. What is more important to God is circumcision, and that is all written in the Old Testament and Q'uran."

"You are making fun of us, I don't think what you said is right." I said.

"If you think I am wrong, let us call back sadiq, and have that foreskin stitched back so that you will look like you were never circumcised."

"He threw out that foreskin," said my cousin Aziz.

"Shut up all of you, he can't do that. Its required by law that sadiq keeps the foreskin he cuts for one month, just in case some one wants it to be reattached so they can go hell. You know it hurts more to reattach the foreskin than to cut it off. So if you want to do that I swear to heaven that I will go and get sadiq now," said uncle Shawkat.

"I wish I never saw him, and now if you want to bring him back, forget all about it. No one wants to face him again, and one day if I have my own way I will do to him what he did to us," I said.

Uncle Shawkat laughed.

"You think it's funny that we can do nothing but lay in bed?" said Uncle Sarwat.

My Uncle Shawkat told us it would hurt only for an hour. That wasn't so. Not for an hour, but for a month we were not ourselves. For the first two weeks whenever we got up and tried to walk we were in pain and had to pay for every move we made.

They had us wear a cotton robe. As soon as we woke we had to pull the robe up with our hand so that it wouldn't touch the wound. In the street everyone knew we were circumcised, and there were many jerks making nasty comments, like "whoever did the job didn't do it right...they should not have only cut the foreskin but the whole thing." What bothered us most were the women who laughed when they saw us. Some were more polite and only smiled as they tried to control their laughter. There were also some nasty little girls and teenagers in the neighborhood who giggled and pointed, as if it was really funny thing that had happened to us. Part of it had to do with there being four of us. Usually one didn't see four circumcised children together at the same time and the same place. My cousin Aziz was just stupid, he couldn't control himself. Right after the first week he tried to ride a bicycle. He fell onto the bicycle and couldn't move for two more weeks.

It was difficult for us during the daytime since we had to stay home, but after a few days friends came over to play cards and other games. At night we fell asleep earlier than usual. All the while there was still fighting and gunshots at night.

That was it for my summer. It was the second summer that I couldn't spend in Sulaymanya. We used to go to Byra and enjoy the mountain and pleasant weather. Byra then was under the control of the *peshmargas* as was everywhere surrounding Halabja up to the Iranian border. These areas were targeted by MiGs which would shoot at anything moving, destroying villages, cattle, scores of innocent people were killed and wounded. Sometimes we used to go up on the roof of the house and watch the MiGs as they bombed nearby villages. We could see explosions and fires. The rebels in town were still there and slowly people were rebuilding. Imprisonments and threats from the government continued as did the shooting at nigh. There was not much of anything going on after sunset; everyone was locked behind their doors. *Peshmargas* attacked the town almost every night, often penetrating the *Jash's* barricades and entering town. We often had curfews which lasted as long as a week. This went on until 1966.

Chapter Eleven

Nineteen sixty six brought an ugly dimension to the Kurdish revolution. Until then the Kurds were united under one leader, Mustafa Barzani, the head of the Kurdish Democratic Party. The secretary of the KDP was Ibrahem Ahmed. Barzani's background was that of an old Mullah and he had no formal education. He was considered a hero by Kurds throughout Kurdistan and was well respected. He was a good fighter and wise, but not a brilliant diplomat. Smart, but not intellectual, he was more a tribesman than a politician. As far as I can remember, Barzani never made a speech. He rarely went out in public places to speak and rarely wrote anything to his people. On the other hand, Ibrahem Ahmad was well educated a former judge who had studied law and was one of the most brilliant Kurdish writers. Another leader of the KDP was Jalal Talabani, a writer and eloquent speaker often gave lectures and speeches. Both Jalal and Ibrahim were popular among intellectuals and writers.

Jalal and Ibrahim persuaded many members of the KDP that Barzani didn't deserve the leadership that he didn't understand law and treated the revolutionaries like his tribe. They insisted that Barzani had created chaos in the Kurdish Democratic Party and should be expelled. Barzani certainly wasn't a politician and had little or no respect for the KDP and its high-ranking personnel.

Finally the friction between Barzani and Jalal Talabani intensified and the Talabani decided to split from the KDP. He and his followers made an agreement with the Iraqi government. They left Barzani and entered the towns and cities under Iraqi government protection. That was the beginning of fighting amongst Kurds, bloody fighting that lasted years and cost thousands of lives.

We witnessed Kurds fighting and killing each other. Talabani's armed men increased in Halabja. Talabani and the Iraqi government unified in fighting Barzani.

We used to watch both sides as they engaged in battle. It was so close to Halabja and we used to watch live battles between Barzani and the government troops aided by Jalal Talabani. It was like a live movie played in Halabja and its surroundings.

I remember in 1967 when the government's troops attacked Barzani's men. The Iranian government recruited thousands of Iranian Kurds, named Qalkhani, to fight alongside Barzani's troops against the Iraqi regime and their allied Talabani forces. The army, with Talabani's aid attacked Barzani and butchered his troops. A t Talabani man made an announcement that they'd had a victory over Barzani and invited people to the mosque to see that victory with their own eyes. I went with a couple kids from my neighborhood to the mosque to see what was going on.

As we walked to the mosque and the officer kept repeating the announcements over and over. On my way I saw groups of armed Talabani men driving around the town in jeeps, and saw people going toward the mosque. Shwan and Dara were with me, kids in my neighborhood who were around my age. Shwan asked me, "What in the world are these guys doing, driving around the town and wasting gas?"

All they were doing was lifting up their machineguns and chanting, "Death to Barzani!"

"It looks they've had a victory," said Dara.

Soon we saw jeeps loaded with government soldiers. They had set their machineguns on the top of their jeeps and were driving around the town, doing the same thing as Talabani's men. We got close to the mosque and saw a tank and several army jeeps on the street near the entrance. Shwan said, "I think we should go home."

"Why do you say that? Let's see what's happened now that we're already here," said Dara.

"What if someone kills a soldier and we get right in the middle of it?" worried Shwan.

"Come on, we're almost there, let's go see what's happening. Dara is right," I said.

Shwan agreed. "That is right. Don't be afraid, nothing will happen. Look at all those people out there, we will be just one of them."

"Okay, but if something happens I don't want to be a part of the crowd that's shot at," said Dara.

We got close to the mosque and saw two trucks stopped nearby. A couple of soldiers went to the truck. We got close, holding each other's hands as we walked. We got right next to the truck. It smelled so bad, I closed my nose with my hand.

I looked at the two trucks. Both were full of dead bodies piled on a top of one other like cement bags, dead bloodies men with their clothes on. The bottom of the truck was running with blood.

I saw Aram and he came over. I said good-bye to Shwan and Dara as they wanted to leave, and I stayed and waited with Aram. Aram was pale and hoped he would not get an asthma attack. He looked short of breath. He looked at me and said in a low voice, "let's get out of this butcher shop."

That's what I was hoping for—just to get out of that disgusting place, away from that disgusting smell. I'd already had my share of seeing things that I regretted.

"Let's go towards your house," said Aram.

"Sure, anywhere but here. Thanks, Aram."

We walked and saw Talabani's men unloading dead bodies. The soldiers told us that there were more trucks coming. We waited for a couple minutes and saw army vehicles all around the main circle.

"Let's go back past the mosque and avoid this crowd of ignorant soldiers," said Aram.

"Do you realize we'd have to go back and see the same disgusting things we just saw?" I asked.

"I know, but I don't feel safe going through the circle with this crowd of ignorant soldiers."

We walked back to the mosque and saw more people leaving than entering. The two loaded trucks had left, and another came with more bodies. We went past the mosque and saw the guy in the mosque washing dead bodies. He already had three of them wrapped in cloth. Next to him more than a hundred bodies were piled up. We both held our nose to avoid the smell and saw another person undressing the dead bodies. There were three caskets, and a bunch of a people by the entrance to the mosque waiting to take them to the graveyard.

The cost of the funeral and everything else was paid by the people in town. They had a bucket for donations in. As we passed by, I spotted my father and Grandpa with at least another ten people lifting one of the caskets and heading toward the graveyard as an act of charity.

We passed the mosque, very upset. Once we got out and crossed the main street, we sat on the stairs of a nearby bakery.

"That smell was terrible, wasn't it?" said Aram.

"Yes it was. I'll never forget it," I said.

"The officer who made the announcements and invited people to the mosque must have some nerve," said Aram.

"You know, I didn't know what victory he was taking about. Dara, Shwan, and I couldn't wait to go and see what they were talking about. Imagine that," I said.

"The officer's voice was so loud that I thought he would tear apart the megaphone," said Aram.

"This is the most stupid thing anyone can imagine. They call this a victory? Who is victorious and who is vanquished?" wondered aloud.

"If this is to be called a victory by anyone other than this government, you know who that would be?"

"Who?" I asked.

"The Turks, they are even worse than the Arabs to us. Turks kill Kurds just for speaking Kurdish, and they kill Kurds just for being Kurds."

"We Kurds have never done anything bad to the people who are aiming at our annihilation," said Aram.

"I think Arabs, Turks, and Persians have just decided to make us the losers," I said. "Who is left to help us?" Aram asked.

"I don't know. I'm just tired of everything happening around us, Aram."

"Who isn't?"

"I wish we could have written our experiences and recorded these days for history."

Aram nodded "Most of the time at night, I write about my days, and then I need to trash whatever I write. If the authorities catch me writing, my dad will be jailed.

You know there is no freedom. You can't write in Kurdish in Iraq, Iran or Turkey. You talk about history, we know little of our history because we haven't been free for more than a thousand years. Where history comes from if a nation to be forbidden from writing or speaking in its own language"

"I believe that is why we are revolting against the government," I said.

"Yes, it was nice when we were united. At least we knew who we fought, but now you see this bloodshed. You see Kurds are killing Kurds and that is so stupid and evil. I am really sick after seeing all those dead bodies. I don't know how I can keep this massacre out of my mind. God help me," said Aram.

"I feel the same way. I just can never understand how people can be so cruel and kill like that. We saw hundreds of dead bodies loaded on trucks. No one deserves that." I said.

"There is no more fighting for Kurds rights, Mustafa Barzani is Shah of Iran and CIA's agent, and Talabani is an agent of Iraqi government. These two leaders are selfish and sick. All this killing is to cater to these two leaders' insatiable greed for money and power. They don't mind people get slaughtered as long as they maintain their leadership. I tell you Kurds will never be free for as long as Barzani or Talabani or their extended families' are our leaders." said Aram.

We sat silently for a while until Shwan came and stood right before us." It must have been really heavy fighting with all those dead. We saw so many that were killed. I heard there are more trucks on their way with even more bodies."

"Those are the bodies they found. God knows how many are left on the battlefield. No one ever knows for sure," said Aram.

"Those dead people must have families and relatives. How do their families know they have been killed?" Said Shwan.

"They don't," I said.

"Leave it alone, Shwan. Some of those people's families will never believe their beloved ones are dead. They may wait their entire life for their return," said Aram.

"Can you imagine not being sure someone is dead, yet you wait all your life, hoping one day that person will return?" I said.

"That is exactly what happen to the families of these dead people we just saw," said Shwan.

We were really paying attention to each other, and we were serious, unlike before when we used to make jokes, teasing each other or acting smart. As we were talking, we saw three army jeeps driving fast like ambulances, one after another, leaving behind clouds of dust. A truck carrying soldiers came and they all climbed down, talking in Arabic and laughing. It seemed that they were having a good time. We went to the street and looked to see where these jeeps were heading. They drove quickly out of sight.

We went back and sat down again. We watched these happy soldiers, and every once in a while one of them would look over at us. The street was relatively quiet and there were not many people.

"You see these lowlifes, these are the scumbags of the world, and I wish someone would tell me what is so funny in this town to laugh at. It is becoming a funeral town with more dead bodies than it can handle," said Aram.

Shwan looked away from them "I was wondering, if all of those dead bodies were soldiers instead of Kurds, would they still laugh this hard and be as happy?"

Aram appeared too upset, "I am not feeling well. I need to go," he said finally.

We all left to walk Aram home.

I was really worried about Aram, and didn't want him to go off alone and get sick in the middle of his walk. We walked in a complete circle to bypass the mosque all the way uptown and then back toward Aram's home. As we walked, we saw army vehicles coming back and forth and few people around in the street. We saw people walking with sad faces, and disgusted with the bloodshed that hunted the town.

Aram looked weak, and didn't even feel like talking. As we were walking he turned to me with his haggard looking, "Rauf, I am tired of being sick all the time. I have a feeling that I may be out of my misery not before long."

It was the most painful sentence or expression to hear and not with any right answer on hand. I paused for a few moment and said "No, Aram you'll be okay, don't think like that,"

We took Aram home and started walking back.

"I'll dread remembering this day, Shwan." I said.

"Rauf, I have been very close to Aram and our families has been friends for Years. He is a good kid. I didn't know he was that ill, I really feel bad for him."

Said Shwan.

"I don't know what to tell you. I can tell you this town is being ripped apart and no one is without problems. Bad things just don't seem to end, they just keep coming. Just look at what they dumped into the town today."

We walked. It was nice evening with a nice weather for that time of the year. It was near sunset, people were still in the street but everyone seemed to be in mourning. Once Shwan and I got close to home we split up.

When I arrived at home my mother was cooking and Ronak was following her.

Mom looked concerned. "You look pale, are you all right?"

"Yes mom, I'm okay, but I've seen too much for one day to make me sick."

"Yes, your dad came back and said he would be gone for a while. He may not be back until late in the evening." said mom.

"Yes mom, I saw dad…with the rest of the people taking the caskets to the graveyard."

"I cooked Spanish rice and lamb for dinner. do you want to eat now?" She fixed me a plate. I ate it all and went for seconds.

"Leave some for your dad," said mom.

I went to my room to study for my final, but I couldn't focus on anything. I went back to mom.

"Mom, I am tired. I want to go bed," I said.

"It's too early," said mom.

"Yes I know, I want to get up early to study."

"Okay, get some sleep," said mom.

I went to bed early before dark, it was hot summer and we slept up the roof of our house. There was a full moon. I covered my head with the blanket even though it was warm.

I thought of poor Aram, how strong he used to be and how sick he was then. Barely a day passed without him getting sick and now he was questioning his own mortality. How quickly things could change. Illness could rob people of optimism.

That was 1966, the year when Kurds started killing each other. The Kurdish Democratic Party that had initiated the armed movement against the Iraqi regime was now fighting side by side with the Iraqi army against Barzani. Barzani got strong enough to capture back almost all of Kurdistan with the exception of the big towns and cities. He did that with the support of arms and money from the CIA, and from the Shah of Iran who was at odds with the Iraqi regime over a territorial dispute.

Through 1967 attacks on Halabja by Barzani's followers were practically a daily occurrence. This time they used short-range missiles capable of hitting government posts. They were very inaccurate and most of the time missed the targets. Barzani's men fired their missiles at night as they were silenced during daytime fearing Iraqi MiGs, artilleries, and tanks.

After Talabani sided with the Iraqi government, Talabani's armed men defended the army and the town. For the most part the fighting was on the outskirts of town but every now and then Barzani's armed men were able to penetrate into the town.

During this time people restrained themselves from moving around at night for fear of getting caught in the crossfire. Even though a few cafés opened at night, people dispersed and the cafés closed up when there were gunshots.

Halabja remains as a battleground relentlessly without any hope or promise for peace. We all knew the continuation of war would bring us more impending tragedies. We were sure of that, unfortunately that was true as we go forward.

Chapter Twelve

In 1968 the Ba'th regime came back into power. It was the winter of 1968 during the very last days of Ramadan. During Ramadan Muslims fast from sunrise to sunset. Two days remained of Ramadan, and after that there would be a holy day. It was a sunny day, snow was covering the town and there was a blanket of snow as far as the eye could see.

It was a sunny day and the snow was melting away into little streams of water. We saw the dripping of water from days before had formed icicles on the roofs. The icicles were all different sizes and shapes. Some were formed like chandeliers and others like little trees. We loved the icicles and would jump up to bring them down and sometimes we ate them.

My Uncle Sarwat, Aram and I were all tossing snowballs and breaking the icicles on the roofs of the houses. Some icicles were so long that they came halfway to the ground. We came across a group of icicles about two feet long that looked like a crowd of people. In the middle of these icicles was a flat area, it looked like a courtyard and a little shape in the middle resembled a culprit getting executed. The icicle looked like a disastrous court drama.

Aram pointed to it. "Look at this; can you believe how frightening it looks?" Sarwat was about to hit it, but Aram held his hand, "No, Sarwat, please leave it alone. It's beautiful. Don't mess it up."

"You're right Aram, it looks interesting," said Sarwat.

I kept looking at the scene of the icicles and couldn't get it off my mind, it looked so real. I thought that God might be trying talk to us through those icicles.

"Let's not mess it up and come back to look at it tomorrow. If tomorrow is sunny like today, there will be more water drips and there will be an additional formation of icicles. Perhaps it will even look more fascinating," said Aram.

We walked on. "Wouldn't be nice if we had a color camera? We could've made a tableaux out of that icicle drama." said Aram.

I wasn't really paying much attention to the conversation between Aram and Sarwat, I kept dwelling on the image. It had looked so real I thought that it might be a warning, like a prophesy hinting impending events.

"You dumb? What's the matter, is your brain frozen or are you retarded?" laughed Aram.

"Shut up Aram. I was still thinking about the icicles," I said.

We were growing cold playing with snowballs and staying out in the snow. My feet felt like some ice inside my shoes.

Late in the evening, I went back to Grandpa's house. My mother, sister and brother were there. They had the charcoal stove lit and it had almost turned to ashes. They were roasting potatoes and walnuts for the children. As it was Ramadan, the adults were fasting. It was still light out and Mom asked my brother, sister and me to get ready to leave.

"No Mom, I'll stay at grandpa' house tonight," I said.

"Do you have your books with you?" she asked.

"Yes, I brought everything with me today since I have homework to do."

"Okay, make sure you get to school on time and have all your homework done," said my mother as she left.

"I am going home too, Rauf," said Aram.

"Aram you're welcome to have dinner with us, do you want to stay for supper?" asked Halaw.

"Thanks, but I have to go home and have dinner with my family. My brother and his wife are here," said Aram.

Aram's brother was about twenty-one years old and he'd just gotten married. He had about six more months until he'd graduate from institution of education in Sulaymanya to become a teacher.

"In that case Aram, we'll see you later," said Halaw.

Aram left.

Halaw looked at me worried. "Look at your hand…it's peeling. Oh my God, what have you done?"

"We were throwing snowballs," I said.

"Look at your socks, they're all wet. Come on, take them off, I'll get a pair of Sarwat's socks."

"Come here, Sarwat. Let me see your hands." she said.

He took off his gloves and his hands looked worse than mine.

"Mom, it's nothing. I don't feel sick or anything. My hands are just numb."

"I'll bring in the *mukaly* full of charcoal so you can warm yourselves up."

She brought back the *mukaly* and we sat next to it. Halaw went out and cooked rice and fried chicken for dinner. I was hungry and impatiently waiting for that.

It got dark and the call for the evening prayer was made. Once the call for prayer was made then those who are fasting could eat, and almost everyone had a glass of water or a cup of tea handy to enjoy right after the prayer call. Grandma placed the *sfra* and brought the food. She put out plates and silverware and we all waited for grandpa to get home so that we could eat.

Just about half an hour after the prayer call, just as Grandpa entered the house, a huge bomb hit so close by that it shook the house, I thought it had hit the roof. Grandpa rushed in and was shaking, he almost lost his balance. I'd never heard anything with such a big frightening noise in my life. As the bomb exploded we heard crying and then machinegun fire started nearby, and suddenly the crying stopped.

"God, it must have hit nearby. I pray it hasn't hit someone's house," said Grandpa.

"Why can't they stop fighting at least on Ramadan? We have only two more days to go before the holy holiday," Halaw said.

Everyone was quiet, shaky and pale. My younger aunt Ronak was crying and holding her mother as tightly as she could. We waited silently for about ten minutes before Halaw went to the kitchen and brought the food in. We all sat for dinner, everyone nervous and terrified. Halaw was praying that would be the last one and with harm to no one, and we were all fearful there would be more to follow. We knew that the bomb had fallen on one of our neighbors. Aram's family in particular was my feared target.

"I wish that I could go out and see where the bomb hit," I told Grandpa.

He looked at me like I was out of my mind. "You want to go out and see what? We will know all about it tomorrow…if we make it."

Dinner was good but I didn't taste much of anything. As I was eating I kept thinking that there might be more bombing and that if one hit Grandpa's house we would all be killed. Machineguns and small artillery fire rattled away. Even though it was Ramadan and the adults hadn't eaten all day, our appetites were pretty well gone.

After dinner we were all talking about what might have happened. We all knew it must have been army artillery. We thought that Barzani's men must have entered the town and been spotted in the neighborhood and attacked by the army. My Uncle Omar and Shawkat were speculating where the bomb might hit. We feared that Barzani's men might still be walking around in the neighborhood and that would give the army an excuse for even more bombing.

That night I tried to sleep, but I couldn't relax. I was frightened and hid myself under the blanket. I thought of the explosion and wished that one day this war would be over so that we didn't have to be bothered with killing, and go to sleep without horrible fear.

We woke up in the morning with the shooting still going on and we assumed that there would be no school. It wasn't until late morning that the shooting stopped and we walked out.

Sarwat and I went to Aram's neighborhood. I saw a crowd of people with shovels going through rubble, and many other people standing in front of their houses and conversing. "No, please God, I hope Aram's family is okay," I prayed.

"Let's go see what is happening," said my Uncle Sarwat.

We went to Aram's house but a guy with a shovel asked us not get too close. Rafat joined us, Aram's next door neighbor. His house had been damaged too, and he had tears in his eyes. "Last night the bomb landed on Aram's house. They were all in the house along with Aram's brother and his brother's new wife. His father was at the mosque praying, and when he came home he found his entire family had been vanished."

"You mean the only survivor is Aram's father?" I asked.

"Yes, he would've been among them if he hadn't been in the mosque praying."

As he told us what had happened, he was crying more and more.

"You mean Aram is dead?" I said with a loud and angry voice.

"Yes, I am not making this up," said Rafat.

My uncle and I both started crying and went home. We told the story to grandma. She said that, she'd heard. She looked stung. She sat and asked us to sit down.

"I wish Aram had eaten with us last night, but who knows what God has planned for any one of us," said Grandma as tears poured down her face. She continued, "But I must say even if Aram had stayed with us for dinner, it wouldn't have done any good. He'd still have had to see his loved ones killed. This is difficult to accept and it's unfair."

Halaw said to me "I know Aram was your friend, and he loved you so much just as you loved him, and I treated him just like my child. But remember he is gone. You have to pray for his father now so that God can give him the strength to weather this calamity."

"I know mom" said Sarwat "This is not going to be easy on Aram's father, left alone at his age, not only alone but with the massacre of his family."

"Aram is gone. I can't believe that I will not see him again," I said.

"Listen Rauf, you have to accept it. You have been good to him when he was alive and he is gone. You need to know that we all go, one way or another. But how Aram and his family left this world is not natural. Evil did that to them. I know it's sad. My heart goes out to Aram and his family, but you have to accept what happened. I am sure Aram is in heaven with God."

"Mom, we'll go out for a bit and we'll be back soon," said Sarwat.

"Listen, both of you, don't go too far. Stay near the house and don't go hanging around Aram's house. Do you hear me?" said Halaw.

"Yes, mom, we heard you," said Sarwat.

My uncle and I went back to the ruins of Aram's house. People were still going through the rubble and they didn't let us get too close. We saw a casket full of human body parts, and they were still searching for the remainder of the bodies.

We were really shocked and were both crying, and you could see the people who were searching for the body parts in the rubble all had tears in their eyes. The neighborhood ladies were in front of their houses crying silently and wiping their tears with handkerchiefs. People came and looked at the ruin were all shocked at the scene.

"Yesterday we were playing with Aram in the same area, and now he'd been cut into pieces and people are looking for parts of his body," I told my Uncle Sarwat with tears in my eyes.

"This is too much, no one knows who will be next," said my Uncle Sarwat. I could barely talk and my voice was fading away as I was crying so much.

"Let's go to where we saw icicles with Aram yesterday," I said.

"Let's go there so that we can remember him," said Sarwat.

Then Rafat and Essa another kid in the neighbor came by.

"Where are you going?" asked Essa.

"We're just going for a walk," I said.

They joined us and we walked to the place we'd seen the icicles. We spotted the same icicles we'd found with Aram were still there. Essa and Rafat were trailing a little ways behind us.

"We looked at it yesterday it looked like a court drama with a tragic execution. Now it is different," I said.

"Yesterday it looked like a crowd of people, now it looks like somebody hit the crowd with something. The court we saw yesterday now looks like a smashed house. Look at those icicles, they all look like human beings with their bodies cut up." said Sarwat.

"My God, Sarwat this looks like Aram's house after what happened." I said.

Rafat and Essa approached and Essa asked, "what are you looking at?" My uncle told them about the icicles and how their shape had changed.

Essa said, "You're right Sarwat, I can't believe it. This looks just like what happened."

We continued looking at the icicles. I looked at Rafat and Essa and told them, "Please don't mess up these icicles because that was what Aram asked us. He told us that they might form different shapes and wanted to see what they'd show. Sarwat and Aram and I were supposed come back and look at it again." The words went through their minds and saw them both in a state of shock.

"It's too bad we're all here without Aram. Hell to this world," said Essa.

We stayed around and kept looking at the icicles and talking about Aram and his family. "Let's go check other icicles and see if we can find another one like this," said Essa.

"Yes, let's see if any other icicles foretelling future events." Said Sarwat.

We searched for icicles with stories to tell. Essa had a long, skinny stick in his hand, which he threw at any icicles that he didn't like. Near the mosque where there was a concrete pole covered with layers of ice on it where forming what looked like a little town. It was melting very slowly as the sun shone on it.

"This is probably says something about another town meltdown," said Rafat.

Essa pointed with his stick. "Show me what looks like houses," said Essa.

"Can I have your stick, Essa?" asked Rafat.

"Are you blind?" he said as he pointed with the stick, "Don't these spots look like houses?" He traced the stick in a circle. "Doesn't this look like a town? Look at these little gaps between these spots, between the little houses. Don't they look like town streets?"

"I think you are right," said my uncle.

I had had enough." Do me a favor and don't make this icicle's shape into another disaster. Don't predict bad things. We've already had enough of every evil thing you can imagine."

"I just showed you what the icicles look like, that's all," said Rafat.

We returned toward the remains of Aram's house. People were still going through the rubble. We all sat on the stairs of Rafat's house, three houses up from Aram's, and watched everyone. I remembered that Aram's latest writing was kept in a small metal box. I decided to look for it and keep looking until I found it. I hoped it hadn't burned. I told that to my Uncle Sarwat.

"If he kept it in a metal box, it might've survived, said my Uncle Sarwat.

"I think you are right," I said.

"You know, I I'll help you to find it, I wonder what he last wrote" said Sarwat.

"They wouldn't let us near there for now. We'll have to wait until they are all gone," I said.

After lunch we went back to sit on the stairs of the house next to Rafat's. Rafat came out and more kids showed up later and we all sat together watching the people search the rubble. I couldn't wait for them to leave so that we could find Aram's writing in that little box. We waited and waited, and finally toward the middle of the afternoon they left and took the caskets to the mosque. It was cold and sunny. The streets were getting slippery and muddy and the snow was melting into a little stream along at the sides of the streets. People were coming and looking at Aram's house. It was gone, as well as half of the houses on either side, and all the houses in the neighborhood had shattered windows and most sustained good amount of damages.

I went to the rubble and started turning over all kind of garbage. There were pieces of cement, rocks and burned wood and everything was covered in mud. My Uncle Sarwat helped me to turn things. There was a cement block of the wall too heavy for me to move; my uncle and I tried to turn it over, but couldn't until Rafat and Essa came with a couple other kids. We all lifted the block and wasn't anything there.

As we searched, Rafat saw a thin finger with a beautiful ring. The finger was muddy with a light touch of blood. He showed it to us, and we all got scared.

"I think I know whose finger that is," said Essa.

"That is Aqdara's finger...the lady who just married Aram's brother."

"How do you know that?" I asked him.

"Because it's a wedding ring," said Essa.

"Yes, Essa, is right because Aqdara was coming with Aram's brother to visit," said Rafat.

We kept looking, turning everything over and searching beneath everything we could. We were all soon covered with mud. We put the finger and the ring on a peace of cloth and took it to the mosque. When we arrived at the mosque I saw grandpa, my father, and a crowd of more than two hundred people waiting to go to the graveyard. I went to my father.

"Dad, can I go to the funeral?" I asked.

"No, son I don't think you should," he said.

"Why not?"

"Son, if the army, Talabani and Barzani's men start shooting at each other you might not be able to make it home alive."

I left my dad to join my friends. Kids from the neighborhood were sitting quietly on a little hallway cement bench. I saw Aram's father quietly crying, his face wrinkled up and his eyes red. He looked weak like he was going to collapse any minutes. He wore the same clothes wearing the day before. My grandfather and the Mullah were talking to him.

We stayed until they got the caskets and headed to the graveyard. There were three caskets but just bundles of body parts.

As they left I talked to Aram quietly. "My good friend Aram, God be with you. I pray that you go to heaven. You had it difficult with your asthma attacks, yet you wanted to live. Good-bye my friend, I promise that I will never forget you. Should God let me live long enough, I will relate your story and the story of you family to others, and let everyone know what injustice has been done to you and your family. I promised you that I would write but so far haven't done much, but I promise that I will and I will try hard at it. I will miss you but they said that people can reunite in heaven, and if that is true then we will see each other again and toss snowballs again. There'll be no fighting in heaven, so we will one day all play soccer together. We will play and fear no curfews or bombs or machineguns or the Ba'th regime."

We were all in tears and left. Aram had always been nice to everyone, he was a peacemaker, and articulate, and the best student in his classes. We all looked up to him, as a strong and our role model.

I went back to the rubble searching for that little box which I thought fire nightmare blackened it, and made it hard to see. Still my Uncle Sarwat searched with me. My Uncle Omar came and got really mad at us, he thought that we were looking for valuables.

"How disgusting you are, looking for valuables," said my Uncle Omar as he shook his finger at us.

"No, what are you talking about? You think we are thieves?" I said.

"Okay, tell me what are you looking for, so that I can help you," said my Uncle Omar.

"We're not after anything to be sold for money, we are looking for something that belonged to Aram." I said.

"But what is it, this thing you are after. Why can't you tell me?" said my uncle.

"We can't tell," I said. I thought I had made a big mistake in opening myself up for further interrogation.

"Then you both go home. You two are not going to embarrass us. People passing by will think you are searching for something valuable," said my Uncle Omar.

"Okay, Sarwat, let's go," I said.

I kept walking and crossed the circle. The sun was still shining but it was late in the afternoon and had gotten really cold. I found that I had time to go back and go around by the main mosque. I don't really know why I did that I was cold and my head felt like a ball of ice. I put on my gloves and pulled my hat down to my eyebrows, put my hands into the pockets of my overcoat, and I passed by the mosque where Aram and I saw trucks full of dead bodies. I went around the mosque, crossed the street, and walked back to the same cement stairs, Shwan, Aram and I were chatting. I was freezing but I didn't care I just wanted to think of Aram and not to be bothered.

I knew that if Aram had survived he would've been a good writer. I already promised him when he was in his coffin that I would write and let many people know about his life, but I was afraid that the next bomb might hit my house. I hoped if I died that Aram would understand that I didn't have a chance write my stories and he'd know that I wasn't breaking my promise to him.

I felt a tap on my shoulder.

"Are you okay, Rauf?"

I turned around and saw Shwan.

I nodded. "Why are you crying Rauf?" said Shwan.

"I don't know, please don't ask," I said.

"I heard about Aram, and I can't believe it. What a good kid," said Shwan.

"He was my hero and I knew him since I was a little boy. He was like my older brother. He meant so much to me, you don't know," I said.

"It was just like a funeral in my house. Everybody was crying for Aram's family and praying for Aram's father. They were our good family friends you can understand they have been living in this town longer than most," said Shwan.

"I know your families were very close," I said.

"You know with all the tragedies that have hit this town, this one was closest to everyone's heart," said Shwan.

"It's hurt mine, I know that," I said.

I said goodbye to Shwan and walked home. On the way I passed by our old house yet another reminder of the past.

At home mom fixed me dinner, I ate it at no time for I was very hungry. Mom knew I felt bad for Aram's family, she tried in her words to ease my pain. As I was conversing with her, dad came back.

My father said, "every one of us at the funeral felt so bad for Mr. Aziz and his family. Poor Mr. Aziz was devastated and was very quiet. He used to be the best company and he always had good stories to tell. He read a lot and learned many things from books. He was like a teacher to all of us but today he was a student of the school of calamity. His back was curved as though he had aged twenty years in one day. "I tried to talk with him after the funeral was over but his mind was paralyzed, he looked demoralized. I don't blame him, It is way too much tragedy for any one person to burden."

I was fatigued physically and emotionally. I was so upset that I couldn't stand it anymore. I left to my room, and later when my father came to comfort me I was too upset to listen or talk, he understood and left me alone.

I went into another night of nightmares, tossing and rolling in bed. The next day was the holy Ramadan holiday. One month of fasting was over. As usual during the holy holiday, we had cooked dinner for breakfast. People dressed nicely, and I usually wore new clothes. My mom had new clothes and was cleaning the house to be ready to receive the guests. It was the time for people to reconcile and forgive, as people met each other, they asked each other for forgiveness. It was a beautiful tradition. There is a time for everything, and I am glad people took time twice a year during the two holy holidays to ask each other's forgiveness.

In the beginning I stayed home to see people who visited us during the holiday, and practically everyone came. Then I went with my father and it felt like we visited half the town. As we went to people's houses, they gave us candies, orange juice, homemade pastry, Baklava or whatever they could afford.

I still was thinking about Aram's writing and for some reason I knew that I would find it. Aram had told me that he had written few sentences, but I hoped that he had more. I hoped for at least a few pages.

There has been no freedom in my or my father's time. We've been left with nothing but stories which with time has lost much of their detail and essence. We have lost so much of our writing and our writer have suffered knowing that their work would never have a chance of seeing daylight.

Holy holidays went on for three days. By the third day it typically was business as usual. On the third day I went back to Aram's house with my Uncle Sarwat. We started searching again for that metal box, but this time we did it very discretely and tried not to be seen by anyone else. We went through the rubble with a shovel. We turned everything over and looked under all that mud and burned wood and found nothing.

Before we left, I told Sarwat, "could you please help me try to find Aram's room before we give up? I am confused and with this ruin I can't locate anything."

He was tired but nice enough to still try and help. He walked in the ruins and stopped. "I think this was Aram's room but I am not Sure."

We started looking. There was a big dark wooden object half-burned and was stuck in a mud between many burned objects. That took us about ten minutes to move. Once we moved it out of way we were both muddy and tired. As I walked, my foot hit something. It was dark like coal. I knocked to make sure it was metal, and it was. I wiped the thing with my hand and pulled it out of the mud.

"Here is what we are looking for, Sarwat," I said with excitement.

The fire had damaged it and the lock took no time to break. Then I opened the lock and saw some papers. The papers inside were all brown and brittle. I was afraid if I touched them it would fall into a hundred pieces.

"Can you go home and find a piece of plastic or some paper so that we can wrap up Aram's papers?" I asked Sarwat.

He rushed home and came back with a thick plastic wrapping. I laid the plastic on the snow and got the box next to it, gently holding the paper inside the box and putting it on the plastic. I wrapped the plastic around it, opened the buttons of my overcoat and put it inside.

"Sarwat, do you want to read it?" I asked

"Yes, I want to read it too," said Sarwat.

"Not here, please. I'll take it home and tomorrow you can come to our house and we can read it together. Now I need to go home, it's already late."

"I'll see you tomorrow," he said.

I ran home and couldn't wait to be in my room and read what Aram wrote. As soon as I got home I went to my room and took out the plastic bag. Thank God it was still in good shape. I put it under my math textbook among my school materials. I washed my face and hands several times. I was muddy and had been scrounging in rubble that still smelled from the dead bodies. Sure some body parts were left that they hadn't been able to take out. I changed my clothes and had my dinner. I ran to my room.

I put Aram's paper in front of me and placed it between the pages of my algebra textbook, I was immensely thankful that he'd put it in the metal box. It was painful to open it, for I knew I'd be reminded again of the friend I'd lost.

He wrote:

I write this piece about days of living hell. So far I've written a great deal since I learned to read and write, but I haven't been able to keep any of my writing. If I were to be caught with it I would be in prison along with my father. I wrote and destroyed my writing for that reason. That is the price for being a Kurd, and that is the evil of anarchy and dictatorship; all talent and good works are undermined. This time I write about days of my childhood that have been embedded in the tragedy of my family and the experiences of my town. I don't know if I will be able to write because I am in constant pain, and am ill without medicine. I am sick all the time and tired, making it difficult for me to focus. Yet while I am in pain, at least I can write about pain. I am bothered, and I can write about that. I know that I may not be able to finish what I want to write for I know that I may not have enough time to do so. However, I write and hide my writing, so it doesn't matter how much I write. What is important is that some little part of what I write will perhaps one day be found, a piece that mirrors the life of a Kurdish child in Halabja. If it is not found then let it be lost in a silent world toward our suffering, as it has been for so long. No one knows when our suffering will end.

My stories begin with the curfew and its aftermath. We were all confined in our houses and had to endure what was unthinkable. We experienced what was unexpected. We cried for days and days, and what transpired was worse than our most horrible nightmares, yet it came and we faced it, but not without consequence. I was confined in my room with a father who was sick before the curfew, and he grew sicker as his back pain intensified. It was the freezing cold winter. We had been left with little food and fuel. We prayed the curfew would be over, yet it went on and on. We counted every minute of it, and every day felt like a year. We consumed most of our food, and after a few days we were left with almost nothing. What little bit of food and fuel we had left, we had to ration so that it would last. We didn't know how long the curfew would last. It seemed like it would never end. At the beginning of every day we thought it would be over by the next day, yet after a while the end seemed to be nowhere near.

For almost a month we had one meal a day. I went to bed hungry every night. After a week the roof of our house started leaking and water was poured in, streaming down the wall and windows. Water on the walls and on the roof formed a layer of ice. We had no fuel and my room was just as cold as outside. I lived all that time in my room and it felt like living in a freezer. Our living room and my parent's room was the same.

I woke up in the middle of one night; and my blankets were all frozen, my body felt like ice, and I couldn't move my neck. Water had dripped onto my blanket and the water formed a layer of ice on my blanket. It felt like a blanket of ice. I got a stiff neck, my lungs were cold and my throat was sore. My nose was all stuffed, and my feet and hands were all numb from cold.

I don't know how I fell asleep that night while my blanket was all iced up. I thought I would die. I was crying every day and every night and praying for God's angel to save me. It was harsh and I thought that I would not survive. I was in pain and finally pain put me to sleep. I couldn't permit myself to complain so that my parents wouldn't be more upset than they were, in particular my father, who had already been in poor health even before these days. I knew that my parents were also going through the same difficult days. I was freezing every night and coughing throughout this unpleasant ordeal. Often I wished that I was dead for the pain and agony.

The curfew is over, but not its implications. I ended up sick. There hasn't been one single day since then when I've had a normal life, and this has gone on for years. I don't want to sound selfish and emphasize only myself while many others in this town faced equal tragedy. Many had it worse than I did. I am writing about myself as a child who survived harsh times but with a high price, I am writing about myself, ill, and I don't think that I will conquer the illness.

Every day things became more difficult for me. I now know that I am not here for long, yet I am not important. I am only one person in a town with thousands of people who are suffering and suffered so much. I am frustrated as I don't see a light on the horizon.

I am afraid that evil will dominant in this town for long time to come. It was difficult for us when we were united, and now with our division under two leaders, Barzani and Talabani, I see more pain on its way.

I know we will be free one day. When the spring of life starts and the flowers of freedom flourish, I doubt anyone of us will be there for our town has become a battlefield, and more and more of us will die. We live under a government that has denied God, it is worse than Communism, and that scares me. We may be free one day, but I have a feeling that very few of us will be here when that happens. Even if some happen to survive, they will be wounded and the suffering from their wounds will outweigh the joy of freedom. I must say it's still worth it, it's worth it even to sacrifice one generation for the well being of the next. I know it's not going to be for my generation, and I don't know how many generations will take to get there. Should my people be free one day, that will be the day when God's angels will all sing for us for God owes it to us and he shall grant us his mercy. True freedom is his blessing.

Now more than four decades after Aram wrote his piece, Kurds are still divided, we are still not free, and our future is as clear as mud. Our politicians and leaders all failed to see beyond their noses and they all failed the test of their time. They were more worried about themselves and their leadership than the well being of our people. It was amazing to me that a teenage kid could come to a true realization and see the world more clearly than the two power mongers and money lovers, Barzani and Talabani and their cronies.

I knew Aram. I grew up with him. There must be thousands of Arams all over my homeland. I wrote about one of them and the others will all leave this world in silence. Their stories were put into their coffins. This is the history of Kurds, a nation deprived of its natural rights. Every year has its own pioneers of talent, yet we have little to show for it because we were not allowed to write and are punished for any work, great or small.

When I finished reading what Aram wrote, I was in tears at his loss. He was just turning seventeen. I wondered how many kids could write like that at seventeen. I know he wanted no one to see his writing, so I would let no one read it. He was brave. I told myself I would not trash Aram's writing as he so often did. I'd keep this work of his in my heart. I told him, "my dear friend, your writing was great. I promise you I will try to be a writer, and when that happens, I will make sure I write a book to highlight this work of yours. I will write my best to show your suffering."

I kept his work and hand-copied it so that if I lost the original, I'd still have a copy. I valued it as a treasure and I thought it said so much about our time and the life, and people in that little town.

Chapter Thirteen

That was the year 1967, and when 1968 came it wasn't any better, destruction and imprisonment and the killing of civilians continued. The two Kurdish factions of Barzani and Talabani still were engaged in a bloody fight.

In 1966 I started as a freshman in junior high school. When I started in junior high school we were forced to study in Arabic. I hated every minute studying it. I was frustrated that I had to write, read, and study in someone else's language. I hated having it imposed on me, yet I must say that we were doing better than the Kurds of Turkey. Kurds in Turkey can't even speak their language and they couldn't even give their children Kurdish names. The same goes for Kurds in Syria and Iran. In Syria, Kurds are treated as second class citizens, in fact their citizenship is denied. Many had to register their property under someone's Arab name.

In elementary school we'd studied Kurdish, but from junior high school to the end of high school everything was in Arabic. That first year in junior high school studying everything in Arabic was the most difficult. I understood nothing. Imagine someone giving you an assignment in a different language and asking you to learn it and be prepared for the next day. That happened in all my classes.

On the second day of my history class, the teacher asked who wanted to recite what was on the first page of the homework. All the kids raised their hands. I knew if I didn't raise my hand he would know that I had not done the work. He usually went after those who didn't raise their hands.

I thought that if I were to hide under the table then he might not see me. I feared that if he found out, I would be deep in yogurt, and he would get the stick out and I'd be beaten in front of the class. I raised my hand and faked enthusiasm, saying, "Please teacher I know that page, please let me say it." the teacher was still looking around for someone who didn't raise hand so that he could get him.

No one left their hand down. The teacher pointed his finger at me and said, "Okay Rauf, you tell us about that page of history." I got up and I said didn't know it. The teacher got mad and said, "What are you doing, are you a poker player and trying to bluff?" I got embarrassed and was beaten three times on the hand with his stick.

I found it was not easy to learn another language in a few days or even in a year. I knew how to read that was easy, but understanding was not. I decided to memorize all subjects that were in Arabic including chemistry, history, biology, mathematics, and geography. I did really well and memorized everything. When I got up to speak about any subjects, the students all knew I memorized. They used to look at their textbooks to see if I had missed anything other than punctuation.

I went through three years of junior high school until, finally, it was over. Starting from the first year of high school we had to decide which way to go: either study the sciences or literature. After three years of high school, students majoring in science could go to college of engineers, medicine, pharmacy and other related sciences. Those who chose other than science could go to a college of art, history, law, languages, and other related collages.

It wasn't difficult to make my mind. I wanted to be a doctor or an engineer so I had to studying science for three years. I did that mostly because that is what my parents wanted me to be.

In 1970 I began my freshman year in high school. On March 11, 1970, the Ba'th party and Barzani had come to an agreement whereby an autonomous Kurdish region to be acknowledged within a federated Iraq. A ceasefire was declared and the negotiations between the government and Barzani began toward the implementation of such.

Under the leadership of Barzani, the Kurdish Democratic Party appointed governors, mayors, several cabinet ministry posts, and other government positions within the Kurdish regions. The declaration of a self-governing Kurdistan was announced on the radio and television by the President of Iraq, Ahmed Hassan Al Baker.

This ended the era of Talabani. Talabani himself went and settled in Beirut, Lebanon. Kurds, Arabs, and Assyrians welcomed the ceasefire and the end of bloodshed; they went into the streets and celebrated. There was dancing, music, chanted slogans, and singing in the streets throughout Kurdistan and the rest of the country.

Soon after the leaders of the Kurdish revolution became the government officials. At the same time Barzani and his armed men maintained the self-governing system pronounced by the Ba'th party. It was decided that Kurdish would be the official language of study in all schools and that Arabic, along with English, would be studied as a second language. A decision was made to translate all the Arabic textbooks into Kurdish—beginning with the first year of junior high school and updating one grade each year until all the high school grades had Kurdish texts.

My mother's cousin Hama Harseny was at that time a member of the executive and political committee of the Kurdish Democratic Party. Harseny was one of the prominent Kurdish nationalist social democrats known to be an extremist towards Arabs, Turks, and Persians. He was close friend to the Kurdish leader, Barzani. He was appointed the secretary of the KDP in Kirkuk, a state rich with oil fields that held a Turkish minority. Turkish minorities in Iraq have always been at odds with the Kurds.

Harseny came to Halabja and spent several days with us. During his visit he promised me that when I graduated from high school he would find me a scholarship through the KDP to study overseas. I was excited about this—I wanted to be a doctor and medicine was difficult to study in Iraq. One had to be straight-A student to be admitted to the school of medicine. In Halabja only one student was admitted to the school of medicine for the whole year and during many years no one was admitted.

The KDP was organizing and mobilizing Kurds on every level, including high school, and they dominated the student unions in every school in Kurdistan. I became active in the student union and soon we had a student union magazine, which was a huge paperboard carrying all kinds of political, social, and scientific articles. I took responsibility for the monthly publication of the magazine, handwriting and organizing the content and designing the layout. The students thought it was great, and the opinion columns I wrote produced many discussions—in particular about the Vietnam War and how it turned so many young Americans to drug addiction. I eventually discontinued writing for the paper—such involvement made me fall behind in my classes.

In my senior high school years, there were about fifteen boys and almost the same number of girls. The school board had decided to have a mixed class—probably the only one in the country. Girls would to sit on one side of the class and boys on the other side. The girls dressed in European rather than in traditional Kurdish clothing, they didn't wear veils or cover their hair or faces. During recess, the girls went to their own room and the boys went to the schoolyard or remained in the classroom. During most part of my high school years during recess I remained in the classroom with several others, all of us singing and drumming on the desks with our hands.

Although peace had been declared and negotiations were going on between Kurds and the Ba'th government, Ba'th secret agents remained as spies in town. I always thought that such spies were a waste—how could they collect any information if they didn't talk to people? Indeed people hated them and although there must have been nearly twenty of them in Halabja, none of them had any friends in the town.

The Communist Party retained their organization with members all over the country. There was a proposal that the Communist Party should participate in government and should share the freedoms of the Ba'th Socialist and Kurdish Democratic parties. This was not a popular proposal (except of course with the members of the Communist Party).

In high school some of my friends and teachers thought that I could write well. In my Arabic class my teacher asked us to write our opinion about the Communist Party's proposal. I read my opinion in front of the class, opposing the participation of the Communist Party in the government, citing their lack of respect for religious and personal beliefs. I offered as example how Communist-controlled countries were suppressing the freedom of their citizens, and that under Communist regimes the only freedom allowed was freedom to agree with what the party leaders said and did. I brought to attention the Kurdish struggle for freedom, and stated that Communism and freedom were mutually exclusive. The aim of our struggle for freedom was the well being of the nation, its economic prosperity and an individual's freedom, and as those were not permitted under Communism, the Communist Party, I opined, should not be given any power in the government. Furthermore, I considered the Communist Party an insult to God and to our way of life. I cited Karl Marx and Lenin's disbelief in God, and how it has been stated in Communist literature that they had caged God, and that he couldn't address questions regarding poverty, disease, and social injustice.

I went on to say that I admired every form of democracy so long as it didn't become absolute democracy—by that I meant that absolute freedom could bring about corruptions of our moral values. Having said that, communism offered no morality—for morality was defined in God's holy testaments, and communism denied this.

In my class was Qader, who was the head of the communist student union, as well as others from the KDP. The teacher said, "Now that we've heard Rauf opposing the freedom for communists to exercise their political rights, for all the reasons he so eloquently stated, now, ladies and gentlemen of the class, let us hear from Qader."

Qader started talking about the greatness of the Communist Party, using communist terminology—such as proletarian and imperialism. He spoke against religion and quoted Karl Marx, saying that "religion is the opiate of the masses." His speech was followed by a forum, where students were given chance to agree with either side of the argument. Only one student, Hussan, who was a member of the Communist Party, agreed with Qader. Everyone else complemented my essay.

The news of my essay got back to the regional leaders of the KDP, the Communist Party, and the conservative mullahs in town. The mullahs sent a message to me that I should not be afraid, that they would even provide me with security if I were to need it. The KDP also stood behind me. I found the entire situation to be outrageous and told the mullahs that I needed no protection, and that the situation needed to be considered for what it was—an opinion. In a free and democratic process everyone was entitled to his or her opinion. When I expressed that to all sides, things settled and I was relieved.

At school I was doing well. Towards the end of the year we had a final exam. An Arab teacher named Atya Kayse, who taught physics, used to come to my father's store every once in a while to have tea. He was a quiet person with a slightly curved back, so dark he looked like an African. He was very sharp and my first impression was that he was a decent man. Right before the final exam, Atya received a letter at home that, according to him, threatened him with death if he didn't include five questions in the final exam. The questions were listed in the letter. I couldn't imagine anyone writing such a letter, and was shocked when Atya claimed that the only person who could have written a letter with such perfect Arabic grammar was me.

It was early in the afternoon and I was in my father's store with my brother Abduel. A policeman came. He stood in a front of the store for a couple minutes and looked around, nervous and frowning. At first I thought that he may want to buy something, and as I was offering to help him he came forward and asked, "you are Rauf, aren't you?"

"Yes, I am," I said.

"An arrest warrant has been issued for you, and I have been sent here by the order of Adnan, the head of the Ba'th agency in town."

"Are you serious," I asked him. He nodded. "What is this for, can you tell me?" I asked.

"Honestly, I don't know. Come with me and you will find out for yourself," he said.

I told my brother that I was going with the policeman.

"I have been told to handcuff you, but I know your dad and I will not do that to you," he said.

I walked with him. At the beginning I thought it was a joke, but as I kept walking I grew worried. I thought of Adnan, the head of Ba'th intelligence office in the town, who could jail people for life with or without reason. We walked like we were just talking, I waved at people I knew. When we arrived at headquarters there were close to half-a-dozen policemen congregating in front of the jail's entrance gate. The guard opened the door and I entered the jail.

The jail was small and divided in half—one part for sleeping and the other part for going to the bathroom. It was unpleasantly dank and dark, and couldn't hold more than six people. I sat there worried about the order for my arrest. I understood that it could be serious, knowing that people were often sent away to firing squads or torture camps.

The jail housed three other people, all older than me. They all said hello.

"So, what brought you here, kid?" asked one of the prisoners as he smoked a cigarette.

"I have no idea, man," I said.

"Well, don't worry, you'll find out," he said.

After about an hour my father showed up looking very concerned and upset.

"Do you know why you're in jail?" he asked.

"I absolutely don't know of anything that I did to deserve this," I replied.

"I will be talking to the judge and the mayor," said my father as he left.

All of a sudden Qader, the head of Communist Party's student association, showed up. As they led him into the cell, I thought he had come to visit me.

"Qader, welcome. What the hell are you here for?" I asked.

"I don't know, man. A policeman came and told me to follow him. I didn't know that he was leading me here, otherwise I would have escaped."

"Good thing you didn't do that for I need a company."

All of the other prisoners were listening to us. The same prisoner who had asked me why I was brought in turned to me: "Now there are two of you, and you both don't know why you are here. I tell you, this is not a coincidence. I'm sure you are both involved in the same situation. Look kids, everyone here knows why they are here. But you both pretend that you are innocent and don't know why you are here. My feeling is that you both did something that you thought you'd get away with, but you didn't, and now you are here."

I frowned at him. "No, you're wrong, so please leave us alone." I was already frustrated and last thing I needed was this fellow's stupid comments.

A half an hour later Muhammed, who was a member of the KDP's student committee, showed up. Muhammed was an emotional and serious person. He wrote poetry and in his mind he thought that he was a great poet. We used to tease him about his poetry. He was sort of odd-looking and a bit overweight. Again, I thought he was coming to visit us. The police didn't open the door right away and Muhammed stood in front of the jail for a couple minutes. He looked upset and disoriented and I thought he must be feeling sorry for us, then they opened the gate and he entered the jail.

"Come on in, Muhammed, please feel at home," I said.

"You're crazy—what are you saying?" cried Muhammed.

"Muhammed, don't worry. It looks like we are going to have our entire class in jail. Just wait—they'll bring every one of our classmates here, including the girls," I said.

"Let's be serious," he said. "This is serious business. We've been rounded up by the intelligence agency and you know that could mean our lives."

"All right, let's get serious," I said with laugh.

Muhammed looked around warily. "I can't imagine what we could have done to deserve this."

I looked at both of them. "Well I don't know what you and Qader have done, but I have done nothing, so I will be out soon. I'm sure you two can manage, though."

"Come on, shut up, what are you joking about?" remonstrated Muhammed.

"You don't have to actually do anything—they end thousands of lives every year for no reason at all," said Qader.

I tried to calm them down. "Let's please not frighten ourselves, my dad is going to be talking to the mayor and if worse comes to worse, we can rely on my cousin Harseny. Believe me, he is not going to let them do anything to us. Just wait."

"Are you telling me that Harseny will let you out and leave us in jail?" protested Qader.

"No Qader, if he does anything, it will be for all of us," I assured him.

"That makes me feel better. But Rauf, I'm afraid of being on the Ba'th hit list."

Later in afternoon my dad came and asked the policeman for permission to talk with me. We were led to a separate area, where we sat next to each other on benches.

"I just spoke with the mayor and Judge," said my father. "I told them that you have been taken to jail just because your teacher Atya received a threatening letter. Atya has no proof that you or your friends wrote the letter, but he thinks that one of you must have."

"Okay, if one of us supposedly wrote this letter, then why have three of us been arrested?" I asked.

"The problem is these secret agents who are arresting people without any cause.

The mayor was upset and he will get all of you released—hopefully this evening," said Dad.

"That's good," I said.

"I will leave you for now. The mayor told me just before I came here that all three of you would be released today. Please say nothing as you get out and try not to complicate the matter any more," said Dad, and he left.

I went back to my cell and Qader and Muhammed looked worried.

"Rauf, what is going on, anything news?" inquired Qader in a rush.

Just to have them sweat it out, I remained silent.

"What is your problem? Did you forget how to talk? Answer the damn question, you donkey," demanded Qader.

"My dad saw you guys were having a good time; he figured you'd want to stay in here. He said he is glad that we are all getting along so well," I said.

"I think the only one who is unhappy is Muhammed. Let Muhammed go if he's so unhappy, and then we will have the jail for ourselves," said Qader.

"Yes, I am unhappy. You are the only ones who like this place. You guys deserve to be in jail," said Muhammed with a serious tone.

I nodded to Qadar. "We can turn this place into a little motel and charge people to stay and make a lot of money. How about that, Qader?"

"Yes, absolutely," assented Qader.

"This isn't school, you can't just gang up and make fun of people." Protested Muhammed, frowning.

"Rauf, for our motel we need to offer food too, so we'll remodel this cell and build in a little kitchen," suggested Qader.

"That's very clever, but instead we could turn this place into museum and bring in artwork to display."

Muhammed was not amused. "Rauf, please be serious. What did your dad say?"

"He said that we should be out in two hours. If you don't like that me and Qader will leave and you can stay here."

"Come on, be serious, man, this is not a joke," pleaded Muhammed, he continued. "Lay off man. You talk to me like I am five years old."

"You are eighteen years old but your brain stopped developing at age seven. You'll need to take a lot of vitamins to makeup for it," I said.

"You know Atya is a member of Ba'th Party and that is why the Ba'th intelligence is involved," said Qader.

A police officer came and told us to get ready to leave.

"Well Muhammed," said Qadar, "if you need a quiet place to write your poetry, this is the place."

"You shut up," said Muhammed, and he was the first out the door.

The policeman told us to return the next morning to the courthouse. We agreed, signed documents and left.

I was happy to be out, and proud of my father. "Muhammed, what did I tell you? Didn't I tell you that we would be released in two hours?"

"Yes, it's good that we got out. My parents don't know I was in jail," he said.

"So, just run fast and go tell your dad good news." I said.

"Why should I do that?"

"Just to make them happy," said Qader.

I laughed. "Man, don't worry. If your dad asks you about it, just tell him that you came to visit us. The door locked accidentally and you end up there for three hours till they unlock it."

We kept walking until we got close to my father's store, where we split up. I went into dad's store. As soon as he saw me, he said, "I'm glad you came back. I was worried about you."

"Yes, I am here, but I have to be in court tomorrow."

"I pray that this thing will be put behind us," said dad.

"I hope so. This is so unfair," I said.

"Forget about it, there is no such thing as fairness. You always look out for yourself in your life, and never let your guard down. You know there are enough evils out there, and at any time one of them could reach out for you."

I wanted Dad to end his lecture, so I cut my answers short to avoid further elaboration. "Yes, Dad, you are right. I am going to see my friends, and I may be a bit late for dinner."

"Don't be too late, and be sure to be back before dark," said dad.

It was getting to be late in afternoon. I went to the uptown café where Qader used to hang out. Sure enough I found Qader and Muhammed there. I joined them and ordered myself a Coke. I was upset and wanted to cool off. At least Muhammed was there and we could tease him and get some sort of a laugh out of it.

I arrived home before dark and held my stomach and pretended like I was going to throw up so that I would be left alone and could go to bed.

"What is wrong? Are you all right?" asked Mom.

"Yes, I'll be all right. I just need to rest and try to go sleep," I said.

"Do you want let me know what happened today?" asked Mom.

I knew she was well informed and there was nothing for me to add. "No, Mom, I just don't feel good," I said.

"Just go try and get some sleep," said Mom.

"Okay, Mom," I said and I jumped into bed.

The next day I went to court. I was the first to show up, and soon after Muhammed and Qader appeared. Soon we saw the policeman with a piece of paper in his hand, and when he called our names we stood before him.

"Upon the mayor's request, the judge has decided to dismiss your case, and now you may leave."

All three of us left, and relieved.

Atya failed all three of us on the final exam and we were to be held back one year if we didn't pass the makeup exam.

"I know what will be next—we'll go play backgammon. We'll play to see who pays for lunch, and I'll beat you both," I said.

"You always lose, but that is not what I meant," said Qader.

"No, stupid, we are afraid that Atya may pull another trick on us. Don't you understand?" shouted Muhammed.

"Good, shout louder so that I can hear you. I tell you I am not worried about a bastard like him. Let him go to hell," I said.

Qadar looked very serious. "Well he is not going to hell. Instead he will make our lives hell."

"Leave it alone and let us live our lives. I will not lose sleep over that idiot."

"Let's leave it there," agreed Muhammed.

That summer I had to spend most of it to study for the makeup exam. I hated every minute of it and throughout all that summer every time I opened my book, just before opening it I cursed Atya and I prayed that God to burn him in hell to give him back what he had done to me. Sometimes I had this imagination that Atya will be having an office in the hell. I could imagined have him placed in fire house and sitting on a fire chair with a fire desk in a front of him and fire pencil and evey other office equipment all made in fire, and I to tease him and laugh at him.

We all passed the makeup exam.

After my second year of high school during our three-month vacation I decided to do some work and earn some money. I had worked during summer vacation every year during my high school year, and I made enough money to pay for my school textbooks and for some of my clothes.

My father knew government health employees who were coming to town to recruit people to spray DDT in about fifty villages and several small towns around Halabja, and through his connections I was given a supervisor job.

During the first month we sprayed the villages around the town, being shuttled around in trucks. At lunch people in the villages fed us—we didn't have enough money to pay for our lodging and food, and very few of the villages had restaurants.

In every village there was one person designated to work with outsiders. When someone happened to stay in that village the designated person had to find that person a family to stay with. The outsider would stay with the family for free and share their food. This has been tradition in Kurdistan for as far back as anybody can remember. People in villages were usually very nice and treated their guests like their own family.

At the start of the second month we branched out further, and often we had to stop the truck and walk for a mile or two to get into a village. All of our equipment would be loaded on the backs of donkeys and carried in.

I stayed at night with different families and they fed me as if I was a member of their family. Most of the villagers were illiterate and thought highly of me being educated in high school. At every village I went to I would find someone who knew my father, because of our Naqishbendi family name, and because my father was the only one in our town selling both modern medicine and the herbs of traditional medicine. When I went to these villages, my brother and I were the youngest ones. Because I was a supervisor and because they knew my dad, I ended up staying with well-to-do families and eating good meals.

It was one of the best experiences of my life, to go to these remote villages and see the most beautiful people I ever encountered. I call these people original Kurds, for they were not like modern city people, fueled by greed and corruption. These people were honest and simple and seemed to be much happier than people in big towns and cities. They invited me to their houses and treated me well and offered what little food they had. They did that with everyone, and expected nothing in return. I often slept in the same room with the family members—and some families I stayed with had teenage girls about my age. These people were poor and most lived in small houses and didn't have a separate room for guests.

During my last day we went to the village of Hawar. People from this village were called Hawary. People in the village had fair skin. It is true that people in Kurdistan who live in the mountains have much lighter skin than those who live in the valleys and flatlands. There were some Hawaris in Halabja, all merchants and teachers. Hawar had about fifty houses. These people had no religious beliefs and they were considered atheist, yet I found them to be the most hospitable people I've ever met. They were a very proud people and they were proud of their way of life. Thanks to the harmony of their way of life, and their endless tolerance, they were able to survive in an area that was exclusively Muslim. A situation like this would not have lasted anywhere else in the Islamic world. These people were harmless and no one bothered them. As I interacted with these people I learned that people could be good even without being faithful to any religion. I found it comforting that my people hadn't forced these people to be converted against their will. I remember during my staying in Hawar, I had people with me who did their five time daily prayer. Yet people in Hawar was more than accommodating. Albeit they were atheist, they were tolerant and show respect for others faith. This is how tolerance can pacify people and make coexistence possible regardless of difference in faith.

We arrived Hawar about mid-morning and started working. After we put in eight hours of work, I went into a little café by the water spring, and the rest of the workers came with me. There were about a dozen villagers sitting around playing dominos and cards. The café had a grill. There were a few long wooden benches and about two dozen chairs and wooden tables.

I sat with couple of the people whom I supervised. We had a cup of tea and talked for an hour. Soon after the designated man arrived from the village. He was an old guy with a gray beard and moustache. He wore traditional Kurdish clothes just like the rest of the people in the village. He was holding a cane. He looked calm and spoke slowly.

"My name is Hawang," he said, unfastening his bag of loose tobacco. He took a piece of paper, wet one end across his lip, wrapped his cigarette and started smoking. "I will be taking care of you and assigning you families to stay with tonight. Who is your supervisor?"

"I am one of the supervisors," I said. "My name is Rauf."

"Are your men all here?" he asked.

"Yes," I answered.

"Do you want me take you first, Mr. Rauf?"

"Thank you, but if you wouldn't mind, let my men get settled first." I wanted to make sure first everyone's else would be taken care of."

"If you and your men would follow me, please," he said.

We followed him along a trail that curved around the houses. As we walked he dropped off the workers at houses along the way. He did that until everyone was settled and I was left alone.

"Okay, now all your men settled, and I kept the best for last," said Hawang.

"Thank you, you are a good man."

"Sure, everyone is good, you are a good young man yourself," said Hawang.

I was almost on the top of the hill. There was a little house. He went inside and yelled, "Ms. Goolshan!"

An old lady came out and welcomed me. She was short with only a few teeth left in her mouth. She had blue eyes and blonde and gray hair. She looked healthy and strong. It looked like she was just coming back from picking wood for cooking. It was customary in villages for women to collect firewood.

She lived in a small mud house surrounded by a small yard with two donkeys and a dog. The house had two rooms and there were little windows from each room looking outside. I looked into one of the windows and could see the floor was all bare and cemented with mud. In front of the house clothes hung from a clothesline.

This village, like almost all the villages, didn't have running water. The source of their water supply was a spring. Women went to the spring and brought back containers full of water for drinking, cooking and cleaning. Most of women took their dirty clothes to the spring and washed them there, then brought them back to dry in the sun during summer, or inside during winter.

Ms. Goolshan walked into the house and told me to follow her. She led me through stairs and ended up on the roof of the house. The sun was about to set and the sky as clear as could be. From the roof I could see the mountain and look over the entire village. Her granddaughter lived with her, and she came up to join us.

"Son what is your name?" asked Ms. Goolshan.

"Rauf," I said, standing a few feet away from them.

"Mr. Rauf, this is my granddaughter Nashmel."

"Pleasure to meet you both," I said.

"Nashmel, can you please set the places for dinner. I will be downstairs cooking.

As soon as you're done come down and help your grandmother," she said.

"Okay, Grandma," said Nashmel. She stepped down the ladder.

I saw about a dozen chickens and roosters in a little nest made of mud and stone with a little wooden gate, and I could hear the sound of chickens as she caught one of them. I knew there would be chicken for dinner. Chicken or turkey was considered the best, then lamb. Beef was okay but not very popular.

Nashmel asked me to sit down on a mattress with pillows on it. She was preparing tea on a Samovar. Ms. Goolshan returned with a chicken she had killed. She cleaned it, cut it into pieces and skewered it, and barbequed it over a small charcoal grill.

As the old lady cooked she spoke with me, and once in a while her daughter participated. Nashmel loved poetry. She had her radio tuned to the most popular Kurdish station, which was broadcasting a poetry program. Showkrla Baban, one of the most popular radio personalities in Kurdistan, was reciting poetry with music and every poem ended with a popular song

She set *sfra* and set out dishes and silverware for the three of us. We ate thin homemade bread with a plate of fresh vegetables, barbequed chicken, tomatoes, and onions. It was so delicious and tasted so good. I couldn't have asked for anything better. After dinner Ms. Goolshan picked up the dirty dishes and went downstairs, and I talked to her granddaughter and asked her where her parents were.

She told me, "My father went to Halabja about five years ago during the winter. We haven't heard from him since."

"Does your mother live with you here?" I asked.

"Yes, she is visiting her cousin in Khormal," she said. Khormal was a little town near Halabja.

194

"Did your father intend to come back?" I asked

"I don't really know, no one has heard from him and we don't know where he is." She was moving her shoulder near her head as she was talking, which I thought that was cute.

Her grandmother returned and said "forgive me, I didn't mean to leave you. You can't leave dishes with food around here because of animals."

We all had tea, then she and Nashmel sat down and started spinning. Nashmel spun and as she did she kept her head down. She had a traditional Kurdish dress on—a colorful red, pink and yellow v-neck dress. I could see her chest whenever she was bent, and as she moved I could see her breasts. A little kerosene lamp burned and the light was dim, but the full moon shone brightly. I kept looking at Nashmel. Her long hair was covering her face as she was spinning. I wanted her to stop spinning so that I could see her face. She had the most beautifully smooth skin.

I faced them both, but she was facing her grandmother. Then to get her attention I asked the old lady what she was spinning.

"I'm making a blanket," she replied.

Then Nashmel looked at me and smiled—a smile that stole my heart. As she was smiling her face was partially covered with her hair but her eyes were visible like stars shining on the horizon.

I wish she'd put that thing down so that she could sit straight and I could see her face, I thought. Every once in a while she'd turn to me and brush her hair out of her face. Nashmel means beautiful and slim in Kurdish—I found the justification for her name and felt pride in a language that had invented a way to describe her by her charms and beauty. The true meaning of the language was a picture of her. I had not had many romantic relationships in my life at that time, but I wrote romantic poetry and I wrote essays about romance. I started to see the garden of romance with its beautiful roses. I could feel the world of romance and understand how charm and beauty in their way can be so joyful and at the same to be so painful and grueling. As I watched Nashmel, her every glance was like a shooting ball of fire that blazed across my vision.

I found everything around me to be beautiful because of her. Every time I looked at her face in the moonlight, I found something to be thankful about—indeed I was thankful for everything. The whole universe was embedded in her charm and beauty.

When she talked to me, she spoke very briefly and shyly, but no matter what she said it imprinted in my mind and her voice was so comforting and soothing that I found peace and heaven in it.

When she was spinning, I watched her long fingers—though I had not touched them, I could tell they were soft. The sight and thought of her sent an electric feeling through my body, sprit, and soul.

As I was looking at her face, I could imagine the clear night sky with countless dancing stars that went on forever. Although my eyes could see only a handful of them, I could see in my mind that all of the stars were dressed like her, and they all whispered her beauty in my ear.

At that time I was confused about God and my faith was shaky. I knew according to my faith that it was wrong to have romantic feelings for her as I did. I questioned why it could be wrong and be such a big sin to notice and desire the charms, shyness, and body of such a wonderful creature that God himself had made. This thought was like a flash of light blazing through me. I decided not to let it bother me—in case there wasn't a heaven, I'd have my own right in this little village under the moonlight.

Finally, I had found some romantic feelings that I could relate to. I had found someone who I adored and her existence captured my imagination. That night I kept reciting poetry to them. I kept reciting, to keep them awake.

Lastly, it was time to go to sleep. They had set the beds so that both of theirs were parallel to each other and mine was perpendicular to theirs at their feet. It was a beautiful night, clear with millions of stars to count, yet I visualized only the sparkling stars of her eyes—it was the best of wine to fall asleep with. I fell asleep blessing God for his wonderful creation.

When we woke up I had to rush out to take care of business. As I said goodbye, Nashmel was standing by the door. I took my last look knowing I would not see her again, but I realized I'd seen and felt something that I could write about.

After we finished our job in Hawar, we moved on to other places and eventually my time on the job came to an end, and I returned home to begin my last year of high school.

Chapter Fourteen

My grades from my final year in high school would determine which college I would attend.

My mother was in the middle of a difficult and painful pregnancy. She would often cry, fearful that she would not survive her pregnancy, which was common.

I was bothered by my mother's condition—she'd had problems since she was five months pregnant, an in her fifth month she was as big as any woman might be after eight or nine months.

I used to stay up until one or two o'clock in the morning to study, which was common among my classmates in our struggle for good grades. The homework was overwhelming: we had five hundred page biology book that was used to study Darwin's theory of evolution, from the idea of a single cell through the full evolution of a human being. Almost every other page illustrated nasty drawings of the digestive, circulatory or nervous systems, all of which we had to memorize and to be able to draw. We studied nuclear physics, which was as dry as wood and very difficult to understand. Our math classes were all pre-calculus and calculus and our chemistry textbook had hundreds of formulas and chemical interactions. We were supposed to know everything from cover to cover for the final exam.

My mother would stay up with me until I went to bed. We usually drank tea, but occasionally we had coffee as thick as tomato juice. Often I'd invite other friends over and we'd study together. Sometimes my aunt

Lotfi, who was my classmate, used to come over or I went to Grandpa's house and we studied there.

Late one night as I studied, Mom was in pain and told me she couldn't get comfortable. At the time she was about eight months pregnant.

"I haven't been able to get comfortable for so many months," she said.

"Mom, try different positions until you get comfortable," I said.

She laughed to herself, through the pain. "Yes, yes, everyone is a doctor."

"Mom, you've only got a month to go, then you are going to have a beautiful baby. Just be patient," I said.

"I hope so, son," she said. She tried not to cry in front of me, yet sometimes she couldn't help herself. She continued with tears in her eyes. "Listen, my sweetheart, I'll tell you something I know you don't want to hear, but it's something I need to say."

"What is it Mom? Don't hold back, just spit it out," I said.

"Let me tell you son, there is no one who looks forward toward to the future more than a pregnant woman. They look forward to having their baby and nourishing it. It is something no one can understand but the mother-to-be," she said.

"But Mom, you are already a mother," I said.

"No matter how many children a woman has, still they feel like it is their first child. I must tell you this baby means a lot to me and I am not worried about myself but about this baby. I am afraid that I might leave this child as an orphan and have someone else take care of it. This is the fear that every mother faces.

This is something men don't understand. This may be natural and how God created us, and therefore I don't expect men to think like women do."

"Mom, I wish you wouldn't think that way," I said.

"There are times when you don't feel good and that is the time when one thinks about their mortality and that is why I said what I said. I have been pregnant before, but this is my most difficult experience."

"Mom, once it's over, it's going to be the best time of your life, given all these difficult days you have endured," I assured her.

"I am looking forward to the day that I can hold this baby and see him or her smiling at the face of heaven. I live for that moment—to see this baby smiling into my face."

She wanted to continue but I interrupted her. "Good, Mom, just dream of that day and don't let your fears overwhelm you. After all, good things can happen in life. Don't you think so?"

"Sure, it's easy for you to say. But being a mother means being fearful. No matter how healthy the child might be, still mothers are fearful. They love what they have so much, and for that same reason they fear that something might go wrong. When you have your own child, remember what I've said."

"But Mom, just think positive—think that everything will be all right. How difficult is that?"

"Yes, I know that, but if something happens to me and the baby survives, I would like you to be good to this baby. You will go to college and earn a decent living.

You will be able to support this little brother or sister of yours. I want him or her to go to school and to the university. You need to help because your father is getting old and by the time this child is ready to go college, your dad may not be here either. It may be you who will raise this child and help it through college.

That's all I have to say. It wasn't easy for me, but remember there are times one needs to say difficult things. Every day is not all sunshine—there are stormy days too."

I didn't blame her, for pregnancy was one of the major causes of death among women. I felt bad but didn't want to show it. She wiped the tears from her face and looked directly into my eyes.

"Well, I told you what I needed to tell you. Remember, if the baby happens to be a girl, I still want her to go to college. You know that you will always remember me as an illiterate mother, but I want her to go up as high as any man. I want her to be remembered as great writer or as highly intelligent and educated, unlike her mother who has to beg someone to read to her in order to satisfy her intellectual appetite." She said so passionately that it shook me up and opened my eyes.

"Mom, I'm sure you will be all right, but remember not many women will remain uneducated or illiterate—that was your generation, which is behind us now. Look my aunt Lotfi—she is my classmate, so don't worry about that."

Later my mother had twin baby boys. One of the babies was sick right from the beginning with a severe case of diarrhea. He must have been in pain, for he cried all the time. My mother stayed with the baby day and night, for about a month, and he fell sicker and sicker, losing so much weight that he looked like a skeleton. My poor mom had no time to rest. Since giving birth, her eyes were bloodshot and her face was swallowing from crying and luck of sleep.

I just didn't know what to make of it. I used to wonder why God would punish that little creature. Mom always tried to hold her feelings in so that we wouldn't be affected, but that didn't work when the baby's screams of pain tore at her heart.

Our house was anything but peaceful and I needed so badly to study for my final exam, which would determine my future. I often took my studying to a grade school nearby or to my grandparent's house.

A week before my final exam I was studying at the nearby school when my brother Abdul came by. The school gate was locked so he climbed up the wall.

"Rauf, I came to tell you that baby just died," he said, and climbed down and left.

I marked my place, closed my biology textbook, and stood up and didn't move for at least a half an hour. I just stood there as if I were asleep, or frozen. When I roused myself I didn't even know what I'd been doing.

I walked slowly, climbed the wall, jumped down and walked home. I wondered what else God had in store. I imagined flunking all of my exams, getting held back and being forced to join the army as a soldier. I felt there was no future.

I had to go home and see my mother and I didn't know how to comfort her. Mom had gone through so much in her life. This wasn't anything she needed to have happen, yet one never understands what God has in store for anyone of us at any place or any time.

I ran home right away and mom was crying over the dead baby and kissing him with tears pouring down her face. It was amazing to think that one baby had died and another would grow. When I saw the twins parting from one another, I was confused about how God's will work. I knew my dad would tell me to just pray—and I never knew whether he pretended or really meant that after every bad thing I should still thank God. I found the world full of nothing but injustice—for we had gone through so much and yet more of the same kept coming. Regardless, my poor dad always telling me that we should thank God for no matter how bad we had yet there would be worse. Well, I had seeing noting but tragedy, I wonder what could be worse, after all I thought may dad my have being right and I gave him the benefit of doubt but I left doubtful. I left in a world everything good happened was attributed to God which I so dearly faithful to him, but yet my problem was that everything bad happened they accused Evil for it. Then I had this theory of mine that perhaps everything I heard from believers was true except perhaps God himself didn't want to confess Devil is an escaped spirit from God's kingdom and he is even beyond God's control.

Then my father and my grandpa came and took the body to the mosque. Usually there is a person in the mosque who cleans the body and puts it in the coffin, but my father loved the baby so much for its suffering that he washed it himself, and that was his second time for he did the same with the previous dead baby. I stayed home with my mother and decided to be with her, and once they went to graveyard I joined them.

Thank God that my other brother Hemen survived.

During our last year of high school we had six subjects. It was the toughest year of all. If anyone flunked three or more subjects they were held back for one year. If the same happened the following year the student was expelled from school and had to join the military. However, if a student failed one or two subject, they offer makeup exam.

Because there were not many students in Halabja, we were asked to go to Sulaymanya and take our exams there. We were given a place to stay. By the end of the exams I knew that I might flunk at least one subject.

I returned home late in the evening and my parents, sensing that I was upset about the results, assured me that I'd do well on the makeup exam. I went to café and spent a long time playing cards and talking about the exam with friends. It got to be about 8:00 pm and I felt really tired. For the previous two months I had little sleep—studying until one or two in the morning and waking up early to study. It was a sigh of relief at last it was over with.

All throughout the summer I kept thinking about my grades. In the end it was as I had expected: I'd failed the math exam. I took the makeup exam and in early August my entire family listened to the announcement of the test results on the national radio. We all gathered at home that day, and stood by the radio. I was restless and nervous. They went on for long time reading a list of names, state by state. Every minute of that reading dragged on until they came to Sulaymanya. Finally I heard my name. I was thankful and happy for I wouldn't have to repeat my last year of high school. There was a sigh of relief from my parents who had worried as much as I had.

"Good Rauf, now you're done with your high school," said my father happily.

All of the stress left me. "I'll be able to leave home and live with Harseny."

"You mean that you're going to get your diploma translated into English, as Harseny suggested?" my father suggested.

"Yes, that's right. And I will be heading to Baghdad," I replied.

"But you must be careful," he said. "Things have changed. I heard today that there has been an assassination attempt on Barzani."

"Who did that?" I asked. I told myself "great that is all I need. And I will not be able to get my diploma translated and all my hopes for scholarship abroad will be erased".

"The Ba'th party. Who else could it be? This government and its Ba'th party can't be trusted."

Ba'th regime knew Barzani was a popular leader and his assassination would Leave the Kurdish revolution and the KDP in a state of chaos and disarray. When that happened they could easily end the Kurdish revolution.

As it happened, the Bath party sent a delegation of about half a dozen mullahs to visit Barzani pretending they were representing spiritual Islamic figures. They all dressed like mullahs and had long beards and mustaches. In reality they were all Saddam Hussein's secret agents. They drove to Barzani's headquarters in Haj Omran, which is in the mountains near the Iranian border. Their vehicles were all equipped with bombs and weapons. Their plan was to assassinate Barzani and run away. Barzani, however, kept very tight security and they killed the assassins. The KDP and Barzani both knew that the attempt was a plot by Saddam.

My father feared, "Harseny is okay and he is still Barzani's close friend. But be careful when you go to Baghdad. Try not to go out much. Just go do your business and the rest of time stay in your hotel. People know Harseny is our relative and the Ba'th don't like him, so they may well try to get you. After this assassination, the relationship between Barzani and the Ba'th government may deteriorate and make Baghdad a bad place for Kurds to be."

I went to Baghdad to have my high school diploma translated. My father's cousin, Najmadeen was a prominent Iraqi general. When I arrived Baghdad I telephoned him. He drove to my Hotel, and had me accompany him to his home. I stayed with him and his family for duration of my time in Baghdad. At the time Fasel and uncle Zaynadeen and his daughter Parween was living with Najmadeen. That was my last visit with them and haven't seen them since.

First I needed to get my Iraqi citizenship certificate. That was the most difficult and time consuming process. He send an army officer with me to get that taken care of, and he managed it very quickly. My diploma translation should have taken a day but they let it stretch for several days before it was stamped by the foreign ministry's office. I was grateful to Najmadeen for helping me manage and without him it could have taken over a month.

As I was coming back home, I was stopped by soldiers at the Kirkuk checkpoint. I didn't apply for college or any other institution to continue my education after high school. They therefore concluded that I needed to be drafted into the army for two years. I was arrested and taken straight to the army court.

In court, the judge, a tall man with mixed gray hair and a clean face, sat beneath an enormous Iraqi flag. "Do you know that you need to be drafted to the army?" He asked in a soft voice. He was very well mannered and quite respectful.

"Sir, I have just graduated from high school," I said.

"Did you apply for college?" asked the judge.

"Sir, I am in the process of doing that."

"I need you to bring your father or someone else to sign a paper and agree that you are going to join army unless documents are provided proving that you are enrolled in college or any other higher educational institution. If you do not go to college, or don't show up at the court to present the documents, then your father will be arrested."

"Sir, may I call someone in my town to let my father know that?" I asked.

"Yes you can, and you don't need to go to prison if your father gets here on time.

And remember that you'll need to return in two weeks from today. If you don't show up, your father will be arrested."

"Thank you sir, I will." I said.

"I will let you to use the telephone in my office. Once you are done, you'll stay here in court with a soldier's eye on you until your father arrives."

I agreed and followed the soldier down a long hallway and into an office. It was a sizable office with leather chairs, carpeted floor, and a big desk. There were photos of the judge's family, a big picture of Then Vice President Saddam Hussein, and another of Ahmed Hassan Al Baker, the Iraqi president.

It was about midday. I called my uncle, who was the mayor of Halabja at the time, and I let him know were I was and what was transpired. I went back to the courtroom with the soldier. My dad showed up at about 4:00 pm and we both went to see the judge. My dad signed some papers and they let us go.

I needed to have somebody else sign the papers to be responsible for my return to the army court—I couldn't let my dad be responsible for that and taken to prison. I talked to Harseny and he told me to go see Fatah, who was a general in the Kurdish revolutionary Army. I went to his office in Tawela, which was a small town near the border with Iran. I talked to his secretary, Ali, and his administrator, Dara, and told them that I was a cousin of Harseny. Dara went in and told him my story.

Fatah came out himself to receive me. He commanded at least one thousand *peshmargas*, and he was dressed in khaki clothing just like any other *peshmarga*. He was nearly six feet tall, well built, and perhaps a bit overweight. He had light skin and a very friendly voice. He called some people into his office, all very intelligent and polite college graduates. His office had several chairs and he had a very simple chair and desk. A few neatly hand-written Kurdish poems hung on the wall.

Fatah said, "We need to do something for Mr. Naqishbendi. He is going overseas to study and now they want him to go to court. If he goes he will be arrested because he didn't apply for college in Iraq. If he doesn't go, then his father will bearrested. What we need is to transfer the responsibility from Rauf's father to someone who the government can't find and can't touch—which is us. How about Tofek?"

"That will do," said Dara.

"Kamal, can you go get Tofek?" Kamal was one of Fatah's guard.

Kamal left the room and returned soon after with another man and Dara asked him to be seated.

"Rauf, this is the man who will be able to help you. He is one of my close guards and he is to be trusted. His name is Tofek," said Fatah pointed to Tofek.

I got up from my chair as is customary when someone introduced himself. I shook Tofek's hand. "Pleasure to meet you, Mr. Tofek," I said.

"Thank you," said Tofek.

He was an average tall and must have been about forty years old. He was dressed like a *peshmarga* in traditional Kurdish khaki clothes. He had a gun at his hip and carried a *kalashinkov* with several clips of bullets around his waist. He had a moustache and smelt strongly of tobacco.

Fatah moved his chair a bit, and stared at Tofek. "You go with Mr. Naqishbendi. Whatever paper they give you, sign it. If you have any problem or if anybody puts an obstacle in your way, let me know. I think you need to disarm yourself until you come back. Do you understand?"

"Yes, Sir," replied Tofek.

"Rauf, you are all taken care of. Say hello to Harseny for me, and I will see both of you soon." He nodded and smiled. "Tofek, come and see me upon your return."

"Thank you Mr. Fatah," I said.

"Of course, Sir," said Tofek.

I went out with Tofek and the others from the office. We all shook hands and said goodbye. I could tell Tofek was puzzled. We went to the taxi dispatcher and had to wait for a while. There was a café nearby so I sat with Tofek and told him the whole story. He didn't seem bothered. When I was done, he said, "Rauf, don't worry, I need to do this for my commander, Mr. Fatah."

"Thanks Tofek. I appreciate what you are going to do for me," I said.

We took a taxi, late in the evening we arrived at our house. Next day in a morning we went to the government's army recruiting office, which was inside the government's headquarters. The head of the army office was a Kurd named Akram. Most people avoided dealing with him, and considered him a royal pain in the neck. I went to the small bare office and Akram was at his desk shuffling through a big pile of paper. His desk was well organized, with at least a half-dozen neat piles of paperwork in Manila file holders. Akram was a slim, short guy dressed in an army uniform and a hat. He had brown hair and a tiny mustache and his face was sad, as though he'd being living on beans and was constantly constipated.

"Good morning Mr. Akram," I said.

"Good morning, Rauf. What I can do for you?"

I handed him the court paper. "Can you look at this document?"

"Give me a few minutes. I have other thing to do now. I'll go over your papers and I'll call for you. You can take a walk for about a half an hour, or just wait outside."

I stepped out and Tofek was outside the office.

"I heard it all," said Tofek.

"Let's go for a walk, have a cigarette, and come back," I said.

"That's fine, but I don't get it—you were the only one in his office. He could've helped you and then gone back to whatever he wanted to do," said Tofek.

"That makes sense, but some people act as though someone had gotten into their brain with a screwdriver and tangled the wires. After all not everyone is sensible. Do you understand what I am taking about?"

"Yes, I understand. This guy is just too stiff and he's a nervous wreck," said Tofek.

"I think this guy is going to take me for a journey around the world before we are done," I said.

"I wouldn't let him do that," laughed Tofek.

We went back to Akram's office. Tofek came inside with me this time.

"Mr. Akram, I am back. Did you have a chance to look at my file?"

He nodded. "You need to go back to court, and if you are enrolled in school, just get the document and present it to the clerks of court and you will be done with it," said Akram.

"It's not that, all I want is to transfer the custody from my father to this gentleman, Tofek," I said.

"Why? You don't want to appear in court and also you want to release your father as a custodian? This is a fraud, and I will not approve it," said Akram.

"I don't understand why you say that. I'm not doing anything illegal, so what is your problem?" He knew I was getting angry and my voice was carrying.

"Rauf, if you don't show up in court your father will be arrested. Sure I don't want your father to be in the military court, and if you are a good son you will not let your father serve any time in prison. You want to release your father? You can easily do that by appearing in court. If you go to college they'll let you go, otherwise just like anyone else you need to serve army for two years. But, if I am not mistaken, you want to release your father and then not to go to college and neither serve in the army, isn't that true?"

"You've brought someone into my office who may be a *peshmarga*. You know the government can't go out and arrest a *peshmarga* while we have a ceasefire with them, so you'll be free and no one will be arrested," said Akram.

"I'm leaving now, and I'll leave my file," I said. "I am not done with you. I'll be back for more...consultation."

I left the office. Tofek and I walked out into the street.

"What a bastard this guy. Why he is so difficult?" said Tofek.

"My family knows this ass. My dad told me before I came here watch out for him, that he can be very difficult and complicate matters for no reason. Imagine this idiot want me to serve in Iraqi army. Who want to do that?" I said.

"So what will you do?"

"Let's go to the mayor's office," I said.

Tofek and I went to the mayor, who knew me through Harseny. We got to the mayor's office and there were about four people in the waiting room. I knew his secretary, Rasol.

"Hello Rasol," I said.

"Hello Rauf, what are you here for?" he asked.

"I need to see the mayor," I said.

"He is on the phone," said Rasol.

Tofek and I sat. Another two people came and the place got crowded. I got concerned that if the mayor saw all these people before me, it could get late and we'd waste the whole day. Additionally I had Tofek to worry about, who I'd have to cater to.

After a few minutes Rasol entered the mayor's office. The mayor opened the door and invited us in. We entered and shook hands.

"What can I do for you?" he asked.

"I am planning to go and live with Harseny. He will be getting me a scholarship to study overseas through the KDP. Once I get my scholarship, I will be leaving the country," I said.

"Are you really going overseas to attend a university?" he asked.

"Yes sir, that is what my cousin Harseny said," I replied.

"Do you know where?" asked the mayor.

"No idea, perhaps Europe," I said.

"Well, congratulations. I know Harseny can do that," said the mayor.

"I didn't apply for college here and therefore they want to draft me. I have been ordered to go back to the military court in Kirkuk in two weeks. If I don't go my father will be arrested because he signed the paper to be my guardian. I went to

Mr. Fatah and he sent Tofek with me to take over as my guardian so that my Dad will be safe and released from responsibilities," I said.

"So what happened?" asked the mayor.

"Now Akram doesn't want to approve it," I said.

He picked up the phone and with a very serious look on his face he called Akram.

At the beginning of the conversation it sounded like that Akram didn't want to listen to him, and then the mayor call Akram to his office.

After a few minutes Akram came with the paperwork.

"What is the problem?" asked the mayor.

"I reviewed Mr. Rauf's case and I can't sign this," he said.

"Why not just sign it?" the mayor said.

"What about Adnan?" Akram asked. Adnan was the head of Ba'th secret agents in Halabja. "I am in charge of KDP and mayor, If that bastard says anything, just tell him I told you to do it. You better sign that right now!" he shouted.

"Fine, let me go bring the rest of the paperwork." Akram left the office and returned in a short while with a file full of documents and with a demeanor resembled defeat.

The mayor said, "Sit at my desk and do all your paperwork right here. I want everything to be complete, so make sure you review everything twice before you let these two gentlemen go. Remember, I don't want to revisit this case."

Akram sat down at the mayor's desk and said, "All right, Mr. Mayor."

Akram reviewed the documents, looked at the pages, and sorted them out. He took out about a half a dozen pages of documents and had Tofek sign them. Then he put everything in a file and dated and time-stamped all of them. He put a rubber band around the file, put it in an envelope and said, "This will be filed." Then he took three pages of documents, put them in an envelope, handed to me and said, "This is your copy." He then quickly left the office.

I shook the mayor's hand and thanked him, Tofek and I left.

"Thanks Tofek," I told him.

"You're welcome. Man what a tough case," said Tofek.

"Well it is done, thank God. That is all I can say. Now let us go have a good lunch on me, how about that?" I said.

"No Rauf, I really need to go."

I walked him to the taxi station and we said goodbye.

I was ready to join Harseny's family and go live with them until he could manage for me to go abroad. I was excited and couldn't wait to get out of Halabja. Although I had the court letter with me which allowed me to travel for another week without being drafted into the army, I was still afraid that Akram might report what I was doing and spoil my plan. A report like that could cause me serious problems, as I had to pass through at least a half a dozen army checkpoints before I got to Harseny.

It was about noon when I went to my father's store. He was busy with customers and I let him get his business done with them. Finally I told him the story of everything that had transpired and he looked happy.

"I am glad it's done," he said, smiling. "You know I haven't have heard people say many good things about Akram, and I pray he will not continue to be as difficult. Now, what is your plan?" my father asked.

"I will leave town tomorrow, spend the night in Sulaymanya, and head to Kawarte the day after to join Harseny and his family."

"Sounds like a good plan, son," my father said.

When I went home I told my mother what had happened and she was very happy. I smiled at her and said, "Mom I will be out here tomorrow, and that may be it." She started crying and looked at me with her eyes full of tears.

"Then I will not see you again—you will be out of the country. I'll have to wait years for you to come back," she said. "Don't worry mom, I don't think I will be gone right away. It will take some time and I am sure I'll see you before I leave the country," I said.

That night friends and relatives came by to say goodbye. The next day as I was about to leave, mom started crying, and we all hugged and kissed and said goodbye. I left the house and headed toward the taxi station. I took the taxi and left for Sulaymanya. Once I got to the checkpoint at Said sadiq, which was about forty kilometers from Sulaymanya, my heart started beating fast and I began to sweat. I was afraid that I would get drafted into the army or be put in jail. The taxi stopped near a couple of soldiers, but they waved for us to proceed. We drove until we arrived at the Sulaymanya checkpoint. One of the soldiers came forward. There were another four people in the taxi. Two of them were women, and they usually didn't bother women and children. The rest were all asked for their IDs. When it came to my turn,

I gave him the letter from court. He glanced at it and handed it back to me, then let us go.

We arrived at the station and I took my suitcase and walked for about five minutes to get to another taxi station where I could head toward Arbel. I quickly ordered and ate a kebob, boarded the taxi, and we left Sulaymanya heading towards Kirkuk. The plan was to take the taxi from Sulaymanya to Kirkuk and then switch at Kirkuk and head to Arbel. We stopped by the checkpoint at the outskirts of Sulaymanya on the highway exiting the city. The soldiers seemed to know the driver. Once the driver came to a full stop, the driver rolled down the window, and the soldier bent down and got his head close to the window. He glanced at the passengers.

"Go ahead," said the soldier. He waved to us.

"Thank you," said the driver in Arabic.

Once we left the checkpoint, the driver said, "Good, that was easy. They let us pass without being harassed. Sometimes some of these soldiers harass people just to make people's lives difficult."

There were five passengers in a taxi including myself, we kept talking and every passenger in the car complained about the ruling Ba'th party and their corrupted regime and leaders. Meanwhile, as they were complaining about the government and their discussion regarding Ba'th party grew heated, my mind was dwelling on the Kirkuk checkpoint ahead. I was still frightened that I'd be drafted or arrested. It was about an hour drive from Sulaymanya to Kirkuk and that hour felt more like a year.

We got to the Kirkuk checkpoint and our vehicle came to a full stop. All of the windows were rolled down as two soldiers, one on each side of the car, bent down to look inside. They asked everyone for identification. The soldiers checked each one and gave the IDs back. When came to my turn, I gave the soldier my paper. He looked at it and asked in Arabic, "What is this?"

"It's my passage through the checkpoints for another two weeks until I get admitted to a college," I said.

"What if you are not admitted to any collages?" asked the soldier. All the other passengers' eyes were on me.

"Then I will be a soldier just like you," I said.

"Wait here. I need to show this paperwork to my officer," said the soldier.

My blood pressure was up. *Perhaps instead of becoming a student with a scholarship abroad, I'll end up like this stupid soldier,* I thought.

The soldier left with my paper in hand, and then he came back after about five minutes. He handed me back my paper and said that we could go. I let out a sigh of relief and said my prayers and thanks. Yet I knew I'd still have to go through three more checkpoints.

We got to Kirkuk and stopped by the station. I was rushed to get out of Kirkuk. I checked in at the station and the taxi was ready. In just a few minutes we started moving towards Arbel.

We arrived at the checkpoint just outside of Kirkuk. I continued to pray and ask God for safe passage through the checkpoints. As we arrived at the next checkpoint there were two big trucks, several other civilian cars, and a couple of army trucks. One soldier came, looked inside our car, and let us go. I started praying we'd get the same treatment at the last checkpoints.

We arrived at the Arbel checkpoint and again there were loaded trucks and soldiers busy with truck drivers. It looked like the soldiers had more than they could handle. They waved for our driver to go without even looking inside the car.

As we arrived in Arbel I asked the driver to drop me by the Galala station. Galala was a small town near Kawarte where the Harseny family lived. The driver was kind enough to do that for me without any extra charges. I checked my suitcase and soon after we left Arbel in a Land Rover jeep. We passed through the final checkpoint without any problem, and I took a deep breath and said my thanks.

Chapter Fifteen

It was late in the evening when I got to Harseny's house. I got out of the car took my suitcase with me. Rafek, Abdullah, and Wahab came towards the car. They were all Harseny's bodyguards. Rafek was Harseny's brother-in-law, and Wahab was my mother's cousin and Harseny's cousin. Then Harseny's son Salah came and received me, as was the tradition we hugged each other and kissed on the cheek. Harseny and his wife were inside, and they called me to their bedroom.

When I went in Harseny got up and greeted me. Their bedroom was the biggest room in the house, they had their bed and two windows in their room, one window was facing the bare mountain and another overlooked the road. There were several photos on the wall. One of the portraits was Harseny's brother-in-law, Jamal who was a peshmarga and was killed in battle near Sulaymanya.

"Finally, you are here," said Harseny.

"Yes, thank God, I am here."

"Did you translate your diploma?" asked Harseny.

"Yes I did, it was stamped at the foreign ministry," I said.

"Make sure you give it to me tomorrow," said Harseny.

"I will."

"Then I'll see what I can do," said Harseny.

"Rauf, I am glad you here, Ary was excited when he knew you were coming," said Galawezh, Harseny's wife. Ary was Harseny's son, about five years old at the time.

"Now you may go stay with Salah and the rest of the guys, and you need to come with me to my office tomorrow," said Harseny.

"Sure, I will. Have a good night," I said and left to see the guys.

I stayed with the crew, talked and played cards and told jokes until sometime past midnight.

Harseny's family lived in a little valley, near the main road leading to Iran. There were four houses, one house for Harseny, one for his bodyguard Abdullah and his family, one for a photographer who had his studio nearby, another for a judge who was much like a Supreme Court judge. Another house was for an Iraqi communist army officer who was against the Ba'th party, and was given refuge in that area which was controlled by the Kurdish revolution. These houses had running water and electricity but no phones.

Harseny's house had five rooms. One was his own master bedroom, and two others were for the kids and his mother-in-law who lived with them. One room was sort of isolated, with Wahab and Salah and I, and there was another room for his brother-in-law Rafek and his family.

Where Harseny's family lived the houses were at the bottom of two bare mountains, littered with little rocks and gravel. Behind these four houses was a little village named Kawarte, which had about twenty houses. The people who lived in the village were all farmers; they farmed vegetables and had some fruit trees and raising cattle. The place was freezing in the winter and hot during the summer. Some of the mountains close by even had snow remaining all summer. Even in the summer the mountains were still cold and one could see the smoke of fires as shepherds burned wood late into the evening to warm themselves, cook or make tea.

In the winter we had to shovel the snow on the roof of the house because the house was cemented with mud. If the snow had melted, it would've leaked into the rooms. Usually summer was short. Harseny's son Salah was a few years older than I was. I'd known Salah since I was a little boy and used to visit them in Sulaymanya where they used to live with his father. Salah had two sisters. Later on Harseny divorced Salah's mother and married a younger woman, Galawezh. He had four young children, Ary, Ares Marywan and Hawraman from his new wife. The oldest when I arrived there was about five years old. Harseny also had another one of his brothers-in-law working for him, Awrahman, who was his chauffeur. Awrahman stayed with Harseny all day. Late in a day, he left home to stay with his family in the nearby town of Choman where he rented a house.

At the time Harseny was the secretary of the treasury, and he was one of the close friends of Musttafa Barzani, Kurdish leader. He used to visit Barzani more than once a month. In a couple occasions he offered me to visit Barzani with him, but declined.

The day after my arrival there, he got me registered as a peshmarga so that I could draw a salary. I went to his office, about a five minute drive from his home. His office was located in a flat area surrounded by mountains. His office was alongside the offices of other important Kurdish leaders such as the executive committee of the Kurdish revolution and the executive members of Kurdish Democratic Party. He had three people reporting to him, each with a very tiny office.

These offices were close to each other, separated with an open courtyard. These offices were all made from mud and wood, surrounded from two sides by mountains, and were close to the road leading to Haji Omaran where Barzani's family and his security people lived. The same road was connected to Iran. They had a big kitchen and a bakery to feed the people who worked there. Just across from these offices there was a grocery store and a fresh produce store. This area was called Nowperdan and it was very much like the headquarters of the KDP's political organization and their military.

During the day I stayed around Harseny's office. I had nothing else to do but talk to people, drink tea and, for the bulk of my time, read. Soon I was introduced to other peshmargas and clerks of the executive members of the KDP, and I started to hang out with them. It was sort of awkward situation but I had fun. I had no responsibilities. I stayed with Harseny, and I was well fed in his house. I was paid a salary, of which I spent little so that I could send the rest back to my parents. The salary was about thirty dollars a month, it wasn't great but wasn't bad either, given you could buy three good meals for a dollar.

It was peacetime and Kurdish leaders were negotiating with the Iraqi government to implement an autonomous Kurdish state within federated Iraq. One of the agreed upon articles was that the Iraqi government would pay the peshmargas and their leaders a monthly salary.

At the end of every month, one of those two-door Land Rovers used to come by Harseny's house, usually at night. Two *peshmargas* would come with a bag of Iraqi Dinar. After they left we'd count the money. It was close to a quarter million Iraqi Dinar, and that was then equivalent to three-quarters of a million US dollars at the time. After we counted it, the same night Aqdar, who was Harseny's accountant, took the money, and he was responsible for distributing the money as every brigade sent their representatives to claim their share to of the *peshmarga's* pay.

When Harseny was still the secretary of the treasury, he got permission from Barzani to have the revolution start trading so that he could raise some additional revenue for the revolution. Aside from that, he imposed tariffs on all goods coming from Iran, and that made him even more unpopular. He started importing all kinds of things such as auto parts and tobacco. He traded mostly with Kuwait because they had no taxes and he shipped all the goods to Kurdistan through Iran.

Harseny opened a small gift shop in Choman, a little town near Nowperdan. I was assigned to manage the gift shop. I did really well for them since I knew how to run a shop. I had experience working in both my grandpa's and my father's stores. One thing I learned was to be good to the customers and to be charming. I had a couple extra chairs in the shop. I had my customers sit down and I sweet talked them about anything they liked. My customers were all impressed that I spoke Arabic and that was exceedingly helpful as most of the customers were Arab tourist from south. I brought them soda or tea and then added it onto to the prices of the merchandise—I was able to do that because we had not tagged the prices. That was how anyone did the business, since lack of prices left room for bargaining. It is very much a custom in the Middle East.

The person who was in charge of doing inventory and accounting was an Assyrian Christian, Lazar. We all loved him for his good sense of humor and friendly attitude. Besides Kurdish and Arabic, Lazar spoke Assyrian. I couldn't speak or understand Assyrian so whenever he wanted to curse me he used to come to the shop storming and cursing me in Assyrian for a long time. When Lazar lied, he'd try make me believe him by swearing by the Qur'an, which meant nothing to him, since he was Christian.

One day I was in the shop and Lazar came in the morning.

"Rauf did you have breakfast?" asked Lazar.

"No, I was just thinking about it," I said.

"I want me buy you breakfast today," said Lazar.

"Why would you want to buy me breakfast? Since when are you so generous?" I asked jokingly.

"I am a generous person, you know that," said Lazar.

"So what do you want to order?" I asked.

"How is about a nice mixed grill, they'll deliver it to us and we can have our breakfast here while we talk."

"Hold on—you have something in mind, otherwise you wouldn't come this early in the morning just to buy me breakfast."

"I swear by every page of the Qur'an, I have nothing in mind," said Lazar with this evil look in his face just like he was trying to pull a trick on me.

"You idiot, every time you swear by the Qur'an, I know you are lying," I said.

"Let's order breakfast now. May I?"

"Yes, go ahead," I said.

He went out to the little grill place across the street from the shop, and he came back. He looked very motivated and I was darn sure that he was up to something no good.

"You see it takes a good Christian person like me to make you have a real breakfast," said Lazar with a big smile.

"Shut up Lazar, I can treat myself well," I said.

"Now listen, this is a serious talk, I want you to listen to me. I mean it, really," said Lazar and waving his hand.

"Before you go any further, Did you pay for the breakfast?" I asked.

"Yes, I did, why you asked such a stupid question. Don't you trust me?"

"I asked that because I don't want you leave me with the bill, okay now say your nonsense, and I will listen," I said.

"God talked to me last night," said Lazar with a very humble voice.

I covered my head with my hands and shook my head.

"Man, I'm trying to say something important to you," said Lazar.

"I doubt good things come from you, but I'll give you benefit of the doubt,"

"Rauf you know that you're going abroad to study, and most probably you'll go to Europe," said Lazar.

"I hope you are right," I said.

"Then, you will go to live in a country where everyone is a Christian, right?"

"So what?" I said.

"So what, if you keep saying to these Christians that you are Muslim, you'll get on their nerves and they'll stick it to your ass. So to be good, I want to prepare you for the new country and new people you'll be living with in the very near future," said Lazar.

"Good, go ahead, prepare me," I said.

"But you need to help me, I'm doing this for your benefit," said Lazar.

"I don't know where you're going with this; but continue," I said.

"Okay, I want to prepare you so you can be part of the new people that you'll be dealing with," said Lazar.

"You already said that, and that is what?" I said.

"First I want you to be a good Christian, and the first step is to be converted. I will do that for you free of charge," said Lazar.

The guy from restaurant came with our breakfast and put it on my desk.

"Good, Lazar let me eat and you keep talking," I said.

"This breakfast is for both of us. You only eat half, the other half is for me," said Lazar.

"You better eat now and talk later, you know that when I eat, I clean up. Don't blame me later. I want to eat, and I want to have breakfast paid by you more often," I said.

"No, I want to prepare you and convert you to be a good Christian person. I tell you that you'll make an excellent one, and I am talking about your salvation for all Moslems will end up in Hell." said Lazar.

"First Lazar, you are not a good Christian, and I must admit I am not a good Muslim either. In the end, you cannot make a good Christian out of a bad Muslim. I have been so bad, I assure you I will go to Hell. Having said that, you are, a bad Christian and will go to Hell too, so don't worry— we both see each other in Hell, so let's postpone this discussion until we get there. We're likely to be there for a long time, so we'll have a lot of time for these kinds of discussions," I said.

"I'm telling you, if you're not Christian, you will never see heaven," said Lazar.

"That's exactly what we Muslims tell others, that we have reserved the entirety of heaven and the tickets are all sold out," I said.

"Forget about it. You Muslims are full of it," Lazar said.

"Okay, isn't it true that to be a good Christian you need to believe in the Virgin Mary?" I asked.

"You're right."

"Isn't true that you have to believe in the old and new testaments?" I asked.

"Yes, you must," replied Lazar.

"Then you need to be a believer in God and he is the only God," I said.

"Yes, you're right," said Lazar.

"Good, so I believe in all those and every Muslim needs to believe the same, so making me Christian won't make me any different. Just don't bother, let people believe what they believe. As long as you believe in God, circumcised and do good for him, and you believe in any of the three main testaments, and you obideby the Ten Commandments, then you okay. To me that is the essence of been a good person and faithful to God, and I make it eleven commandments instead of ten, the eleventh is not listen to Lazar," I said.

"But you forgot if you believe in Christ, God will forgive your sins and you'll go to heaven," said Lazar.

"So what, my friend? That is exactly what Moses and Muhammed said to their followers," I said.

"Then which one is right?" said Lazar.

"They are all right and I personally weigh them equally. That is why I believe a good Muslim or a good Jew or a good Christian are equally right in their beliefs as long as they are true believers, and not nagging others," I said.

"Well I should delay my talk until you get ready, and for a stupid Muslim like you to get what I mean it takes a long time and many prayers," said Lazar.

"Good, leave it there," I said.

"I think you're right and we should wait until we get to Hell," said Lazar.

"You see man, this is your problem, you Christians all trying to convert people so that there will be more of you, but the point here is not the quantity but quality."

"So what we should do to help advance God's agenda?" asked Lazar.

"Just try not to be as much a smart ass as you have been and that will do it.

Another thing—you should buy more breakfasts for me and that will help too," I said.

"You should talk, you know, you are the biggest crook and I know that you'll always be a crook, but I thought if you became Christian you might be less of a crook and that would be good at least for the people in this area," said Lazar.

"Once we straighten ourselves out, then we can ask others to be good like us. Until then just tell everyone to stay put," I said.

"So I'll let you to be what you are for now, and I will come back to it later," said Lazar.

"So can we do the inventory and see the balancing?" I said.

"Well, why do that?" asked Lazar.

"Because everyone is short, and I don't want to be like them," I answered.

"Yes, I don't know what those guys are doing, if they keep coming short, they will be arrested or at least they will lose their jobs or they have to pay the money out of their pockets," said Lazar

"So, can we do that?" I asked.

"Sure, I have all I need in my briefcase," answered Lazar.

We started taking inventory and ended after a couple hours.

"How does it look?" I asked.

"You are okay. Indeed, you're the only one without any shortages. I congratulate you, Rauf. You must be overcharging your customers.

Didn't I tell you that you were a crook? You just proved to me," said Lazar.

"That shows how good and well organized I am," I replied.

"You don't know what the merchants in town say about you," said Lazar.

"I don't care what they say," I said.

"The merchants all think you are the most brilliant salesman in the area. Having said that, some think you're a con man, conning people into buying anything. In fact some believe you are a crook," said Lazar with laugh.

"Let them say what they want to say, I am here to do my job and that is to make money for the revolution," I said.

"How do you like your job?" asked Lazar.

"I like it, but I hope I am not going to get trapped here for too long. For the time being it's a good thing and saves me from boredom. If it wasn't for running this shop, I would have gone out of my mind. Day in and day out going to Nowperdan with Harseny, doing nothing but sit around, drink tea and talking," I said.

"Yes, you said that right and you really can talk, you can fool anyone with your smartness, even now you are turning this shop to a club," said Lazar with laugh.

"What club, Lazar? Are you nuts?" I answered.

"I mean a political club, having all your friends around and taking shots at our politicians, and bashing people," said Lazar.

As I wanted to reply to Lazar, a group of customers came in.

"I need to go," said Lazar.

"Thanks for breakfast," I said.

Harseny went abroad and when he returned from his trip abroad, I was excited that he might have seen some of the KDP officials abroad, and he might have some good news for me, but that didn't happen. I got frustrated and didn't want to stay at the gift shop for the rest of my life. I thought that my going abroad would not happen until Harseny's return. I was sometimes so disappointed that I thought it might not happen at all.

In December 1973, Harseny left on a business trip and some other political affair and told us that he wouldn't be back for two more months.

That got me upset, as it meant I had to wait another two months longer. I didn't ask Harseny the status of my scholarship and he said nothing to me about it all that time. I knew that he was cognizant how eager I was to attain scholarship, therefore I didn't mention to him or remind him about it.

One evening on January 1974, it was snowing heavily. I was in the boy's room with the rest of the guys. It was one of those moments we were as loud as we could be. We were playing cards and drinking and I was singing. They were all losing to me; it was my lucky day. I really cleaned them all out, winning like never before. We were in the midst of this joy when someone came with one of those land rovers from Barzani's center with three *peshmargas* inside. They parked the car and one of them walked toward the house. Harseny's wife knocked on our door and asked us to go out and see what they wanted.

Okay, Rafek got up and put his shoe on and I went with him.

I went toward the car and there were three *peshmargas* inside the car. One of them stepped out. "Is Mr. Harseny home?" asked the *peshmarga*.

"No he is out, but his wife is here. Do you want to talk to her instead?" I asked.

"Yes."

"Let me go and tell Mrs. Harseny."

I went and told Mrs. Harseny someone wanted to see her.

"Let him in Rauf," said Harseny's wife.

I let the *peshmarga* in. About five minutes later, he came out, said goodbye and left.

"Rauf, come here now!" yelled Harseny's wife. I was confused and couldn't make out exactly what was going on. I had probably had one too many drinks and couldn't quite keep my balance.

Her face was flushed and she had a big smile on her face.

"What's going on?" I asked.

"I have good news for you," she said, "Come on, let's go to the boys' room."

We went to the room which shared with Salah, Rafek, Awrahman and Wahab. They were all there and playing card.

"So, the *peshmargas* came from Barzani's office to let you know to be prepared to leave the country," she pointed to me, "You need to go tonight to Haji

Homaran. Awrahman, you need to get ready too, to give him a ride. Rauf, you've been granted a scholarship from Tehran University. I am so glad you got what you hoped for. Now I'll cook dinner and we can all celebrate. You'll need to leave right after that for the hotel and get to bed about eight o'clock. You'll need to be up before five in the morning so that you'll be ready to be picked up before six. You are not to worry about hotel expenses—it will be paid by Barzani's office."

"Rauf, this is even better than Europe. Tehran University is a well recognized university and it's close to home. You could even take a bus in the morning and be in Halabja the next day," said Salah.

"I know that, it is really good," I said.

"So, I'll leave you for now, I have to prepare dinner, please let Rauf get prepared, and no more playing cards." said Mrs. Harseny looking at the boys.

"All right, but he got all our money, he cleaned up." said Salah.

"I just told you get that deck of cards out there—no more playing until Rauf leaves," she said, and left.

We had our dinner all together, and afterward Awrahman gave me a ride to Haji Homaran. He was drunk, I wasn't sure that I could make it to Haji Homaran safe. Even though I was uneasy about him being drunk, yet I loved every minute of it because he was drunk and talked like stupid, and that was the moments I could laugh at him, tell him off and make fun of him.

Finally we arrived at the hotel. I checked into the hotel and said goodbye to Awrahman and told him to drive carefully, I was worried about his safe return to Harseny's house. As I got in the hotel, they already had my name. They told me that I was Barzani's Guest and the hotel personal would knock on my door in the morning to wake me up.

I went to the hotel room and wanted to sleep early so that I could wake up early in the morning. It was still snowing and freezing outside. The hotel room has a queen-size bed and the little table stand, there was little else, not even a carpet. The hotel was a two-story building; next to it was a café and a restaurant. The town was small. At the time its population other than that of the Barzani family and their *peshmargas* was around a thousand people or possibly a bit more. The town was located on the high rocky mountains that extended to Iranian Kurdistan, and that area used to be the headquarters and home of Kurdish leader, Mustafa Barzani. The hotel had no heat and was freezing. I had to ask the help desk in the hotel for two extra blankets. There was a shared bathroom in the hallway, and there wasn't hot water. That was the only Hotel in the town.

That night I went to sleep and I was excited that I was going abroad to study. I had been waiting over a year for that moment. I was afraid that it might never happen and I'd be stuck in that shop for as long as the revolution lasted or until the next war with Iraq. It was peacetime, and negotiation was underway between the revolution's leaders and the Iraqi government to implement what government had committed to, an autonomous Kurdistan within Iraq. I didn't believe from the outset of the negotiations that a lasting peace would be achieved. I believed, as I do now, three decades later, that the only solution to end the Kurdish problem would be a sovereign Kurdish state.

I'd heard all kinds of talk about Tehran, what a big city and how beautiful it was. I'd heard that universities in Tehran weren't rated as highly as their counterparts in Iraq. Iraqi students studying in Iran who graduated in the school of engineering or medicine had to take exam to be certified when they returned to Iraq. I thought the real problem with the school of medicine in Tehran was that they studied in Persian rather than in English as in Iraq, and it wasn't the school of medicine that I was interested in but I had no choice.

I got up in the morning and had tea, bread and yogurt for breakfast. Short after my breakfast, a *peshmarga* came and introduced me to the man who would take me to Tehran. The man's name was Amer. The *peshmarga* left and Amer asked me to bring my suitcase. He put it in the back of his jeep and I got in. There was another passenger in the car.

It was snowing heavily, and Amer was driving through mountains covered in snow for as far as eye could see. We could barely see the road and Amer was driving very slowly. Several times he couldn't see the road at all when the windshield wiper got caught up in the snow, and he had to stop to clean it off. I thought if the car broke down and we stayed there over night, we'd all freeze to death. As we were traveling I saw very few cars in the road. We were supposed to be in Tehran the same day but it took us twice as long because of the snow.

The other person with us was a student heading for Sweden. He couldn't travel through Iraq because he'd gotten his scholarship through revolution as well, and he traveled abroad with a Swedish passport. His name was Sardasht.

Finally we passed through the mountains and the snow slowed down. We stopped for lunch in Razaya, a Kurdish city. As we headed on, it got to be late in the evening and every one of us was exhausted when we finally arrived at Tabriz, one of the big industrial cities in Iran. We stopped that night at a hotel and they served us dinner. I ate the Iranian favorite, Chlu Kebab—barbequed ground lamb served with rice, raw onion, and a thin bread called Lavash. Sardasht had the same.

When we got to the hotel, I saw two men come over and start talking to our driver. I knew right away they were from Iranian intelligence, Savak. The driver and the two intelligence officer ushered us to our rooms. Later on I found out that Amer was also an officer of Savak.

The next day we got up and got into a jeep and headed to Tehran. We arrived in Tehran about 8:00 P.M. The city was alive. The stores were still open and the streets were crowded with people. It was cold and the city was covered with snow. Amer took us to the Middletown and we checked into the hotel.

We went to the hotel reception in the ground floor, which was nice and clean. The walls on the ground floor had large scenic pictures hung on the wall. They had couches and tables so that people could sit, drink and talk. We got the keys to our rooms and they had someone to take our suitcase to the room. Before we separated and went to our room, Sardasht told me that he would stop by within half an hour.

I checked into my room and a minute later the front desk called and said the waiter would be up to take my order for dinner. The bellhop came. He spoke in Persian and I didn't know what the hell he was talking about. I just said. "Okay." Then a waiter came and gave me the menu. At least many things had the same names as they did in Kurdish, for example rice and kebobs. I had my dinner. I went to bed just to woke up with what the great city of Tehran is about and how my life is destined to be in this city for the duration of my time in Iran.

Chapter Sixteen

I was in Tehran, and I must say I didn't care for it at all. I didn't have any enthusiasm about Tehran otherwise I'd probably have been impatiently waiting to get out and see the city.

I woke up and had breakfast. I heard a knock on my door.

"Please come in," I said. He was dressed in a three-piece blue navy suit with a colorful tie. He had a salt and pepper kind of hair combed toward back with clean face and huge eyebrows. He had a long face and a bit overweight about 5.8 inches tall. He came in and introduced himself in Kurdish, "Mr. Naqishbendi, my name is Kesachy." I knew that was a made-up name, in Kurdish, *kesa* means bag or pocket. His name meant the man with the bag. I thought immediately that *Kesachy* was a crook.

"Pleasure to meet you, Mr. *Kesachy*, please be seated." I pointed to the chair in my room and I sat on the bed.

"I will be your point of contact until you settle in and register at the university," *Kesachy* said.

"Very good, sir," I said.

"If you have any questions or concern, please let me know," *Kesachy* said. It was obvious from his heavy accent that he was not Kurdish, but he still spoke well.

"Sure, I have many questions, but if you tell me where we go from here, that will answer some of my questions," I asked.

"You'll stay in this hotel for another day before you're taken to the house uptown. You will have cooks and a housekeeper. You will be very well taken care of. Also, you will be given a scholarship of 400 Tomans*. Next week you will Register in Tehran university. You will be studying Farsi, the official Iranian language, for six months. Next fall you will attend the college of your own choice."

"I prefer the College of Medicine if possible," I said.

"That will be taken care of. You will be enrolled in the school of medicine in Tehran University," Kesachy said.

"Thank you, Mr. Kesachy."

"Before I leave, I need a translated copy of your diploma," Kesachy asked.

I reached for my suitcase, I got the original copy of my diploma and handed to him. In fact that was the only copy. He took my diploma and placed in his briefcase.

"Thank you, and I will be in touch with you. Let me give you my number and call me whenever you need me or if you may have any questions," Kesachy said.

He wrote down his telephone number on a piece of paper and handed it to me.

I stayed for another day in the hotel as planned and then I was transferred to a house located uptown in one of the most exclusive areas of Tehran. The Iranian government owned the house and they had cooks and housekeepers who were members of Savak. There were four other students in the house and other people sent by Barzani to go to Europe or other countries, who stayed there while waiting for their visa. Others who stayed there were sent by Barzani for a vacation or to see doctors.

After a week my admission to the school of medicine was arranged and I was told to start studying Farsi. I found the whole process moved very quick.

After a couple weeks I was introduced to a student named Shoresh. He studied liberal arts and he was one of the best tennis players in the university. He was well-known in the university. Shoresh's father used to be an employee of Iranian embassy in Iraq. He was a good Kurd, and someone I could trust and talk to.

---

* At the time, the equivalent of about $60

Shoresh later introduced me to Khalil, who was one of the Iranians who had lived in Iraq, but were kicked out by Saddam when the relationship between Iraq and Iran went sour.

I asked Shoresh to help me out. I related to him I don't know Tehran, and asked him if he could find a place where I could buy an Arabic-Farsi dictionary. I didn't know any Farsi, and had no dictionary and that made it very difficult for me. He told me he'd help.

One day Shoresh came and with him was Khalil.

"Rauf do you want to buy Arabic-Persian dictionary?" asked Shoresh.

"Yes please, did you find a place?" I asked.

"Yes, I found one, at a good price too. You can get a good discount just by showing your student ID and telling them you are a foreign student," said Shoresh with a smile. I could tell that he was hiding something behind his sly smile.

"Shoresh knows everything, Mr. Naqishbendi," said Khalil with a smile.

"Where is this place?" I asked.

"Just follow me, it's downtown, and we need to get a taxi," said Shoresh.

The three of us walked a couple blocks and took a taxi from there supposedly to go to a bookstore to get my dictionary.

We came to a stop.

"Rauf, talk to nobody. This area is strange. Just follow me," said Shoresh.

We walked through a street that didn't look like any place a bookstore would be found. Every store I saw on the block had a huge display of condoms. There were stores of all kinds, very loud music everywhere. It was just like a town by itself. I knew that I was on the wrong side of the tracks, but I didn't want to say anything because I didn't know the place, and I didn't know what that little district was about.

"Now we'll go in. This is the bookstore. Please don't be too friendly with these people, just tell them you need dictionary, and show them your student ID and let them know you are a foreign student so that you get your discount," said Shoresh with a straight face.

"Okay," I said.

I followed him into the building, it was a two-story building.

When we got in, I saw naked women in the front, about a half dozen of them lined up and sitting on chairs displaying their naked bodies. They were all colors, sizes and heights. On the opposite side they had about three rows of seats and more than two dozen men were sitting. Shoresh and Khalil sat with them and asked me to sit. I sat with them.

"You see those six women sitting down? Go to the fifth one, the slim one with that red thing in her hair, and tell her you are here to buy an Arabic-Persian dictionary," said Shoresh.

Khalil couldn't help himself and started laughing. I said nothing. I wanted to know where this was going to take me.

"Why are you laughing, idiot?" said Shoresh to Khalil.

"Nothing, just Rauf doesn't want to make a move," said Khalil.

"Come on, get up off your ass and tell her—the fifth one—tell her you want a dictionary," said Shoresh.

"You know that this is a brothel. You want me to treat a prostitute like a bookseller?" I said.

"You had no brothels in Kurdistan, so you must have been here before. Otherwise how could you tell what this place is?" said Shoresh.

"It doesn't take much to figure out, Shoresh. Come on, move your ass and let's get out here. I asked for a bookstore and I end up in a whorehouse," I said.

"Well, you are so stupid, you have to go their room...that is were all the books are. You're such a coward you couldn't do that. Are you afraid of women?" asked Shoresh with a big laugh as we were in our way out.

"It'd be horrible if someone who knows me spotted me here. What would I tell them?" I asked.

"Well, just tell them how about them and what brought them here." Answered Shoresh.

After that we took a taxi back to the university.

I wasn't very serious about learning Farsi. Shortly after I settled in Tehran, I realized my resentment toward the Shah's regime. It was a country of injustice and brutality. Anyone who was close to the Shah of Iran had it made, they had money, big houses and big cars. One's ability didn't matter, what mattered most was who you knew.

Teheran was a huge city with millions of people. The city was divided into north and south by a street called Shahraza. Every thing on the north was European, exclusive and expensive. The standard of living was decent. Every thing south of Shahraza was dilapidated, dirty and poor. Poor people lived there and some times six or seven people lived in one little room, while some people in the north part of the city had houses worth millions of dollars occupying an entire city block.

In the north they had huge, gorgeous houses, so large that you could only rarely find their equivalents in European cities. The south part of the city housed one of the biggest prostitution industries in the entire Middle East. There were elegant restaurants; cafés and nightclubs built to resemble pieces of Europe in the north, while poverty and substandard living conditions were the facts of life in the south. The portrait of the Shah of Iran was everywhere and many streets were named after the Shah's family.

What bothered me the most was that I felt like I was a secret agent myself. Every official I dealt with was a secret agent. Whenever I needed to get some bureaucratic thing done at the university, they had a designated official in the university take care of it for me. They would inevitably be a secret agent too.

I knew that the secret agents were following me and all the other Kurdish students as well. I had to be very careful what I said to anyone, including my Kurdish friends.

Savak engaged in a nasty campaign of threat and intimidation. They created a society of mistrust whereby people feared each other as everyone thought that everyone else was a member of Savak. The problem in Iran was people couldn't get together as a group without being watched by Savak. Savak was like Big Brother, monitoring every word and every movement people made.

In Farsi class language they started us with Persian poetry and ended with it as well. That was supposed to be teaching Farsi to foreign students. I thought they'd start with something simple, but instead they started with Persian poetry from prominent poets, the classical poets. It would be like trying to teach English by having students study Shakespeare. I found that

231

the teachers were all nationalistic, chauvinistic and some were extremist and anti-western.

I learned about modern Iranian history and the role of the west in particular the United States in shaping Iran. After the Second World War, the father of the Shah of Iran, Muhammed Raza Pahlavi, had been sent into exile for he was a pro-Nazi. After the departure of Shah Raza, a popular government with Prime Minister Dr. Mosadiq was formed as a result of national election. Dr. Mosadiq was against the confiscation of Iranian natural resources by Great Britain and he was determined to nationalize the oil industry in Iran.

The United States didn't like Doctor Mosadiq and they wanted their own man there. They financed a military coup to get rid of Dr. Mosadiq and imposed the Shah of Iran on the Iranian people as a king. Many Iranians considered that an act of evil, to impose a king on a country against the people's will. Many Iranians, in particular those on the left wing started to fight the Shah's regime.

Turks are the majority of the population in Iran, but they call themselves Azary and they don't speak the same dialect as Turks in Turkey. The Persians are second after the Turks. Kurds are the minority in Iran with about five million people by the best estimates and they live in the west of Iran near the border of Iraq and Turkey.

Iran was a polarized nation and without any harmony among the different groups. The Persians overshadowed the Turks' majority in Iran. Even though the Turks make up a majority of Iranian population, the Persians has been in control of the country and the Turks' political clout was very insignificant.

The Shah's regime was at its time one of the most totalitarian known to the world. So often Shah of Iran talked about freedom and tried to paint himself as a statesman, but the reality was that one had freedom in Iran to agree with what the Shah of Iran said and did. Any criticism of the Shah was replied to with torture, death or imprisonment.

Shah had two well-funded intelligence organizations, and the primary one was Savak. Savak had imprisoned and executed tens of thousands of Iranians for not agreeing with the Shah. With four to five million Kurds living in Iran, Iranian authorities, just like their counterparts in Turkey banned Kurdish publications, organization, speeches and lectures.

Once the Kurds in Iraq revolted against the Iraqi regime and demanded their national rights to be recognized, the Shah of Iran eased the restrictions somewhat for the Kurds in Iran. In many cases this was just a trap to get rid of the outspoken Kurds and put them behind bars.

Kurdish revolutionaries under Barzani were considered by Iranian left wing Marxists as evil and pro-American, the puppets of the Shah of Iran and the US. For that same reason, the people in Iran who were against the Shah didn't like Kurdish revolutionaries which I was a part of.

I knew my father had many relatives in Iran whom I was about to meet. Most of these lived in Iraq. After the Iraqi revolution of 1958 they fled the Communist Party's persecution and settled in Iran.

One of my Iranian Kurdish student friends at Tehran University informed me that there was a Kurdish Language class on campus. That caught me by surprise; Kurdish publications were forbidden yet they taught Kurdish language. I got curious and decided to see that for myself. I asked my Kurdish student friend for the class schedule and he gave it to me.

In my Persian class there were students from all over the world, including the US and Japan. There were about twenty of us. One day after class I asked my Farsi language classmates if they wanted to attend Kurdish language class. They seemed interested and some came with me to the class before the teacher showed up. There were two Hungarian ladies, an Italian, a couple of Indians, three of my Kurdish friends and myself.

There were normally fewer than ten students in the Kurdish language class. When the teacher came and looked around, he seemed puzzled and didn't know why the number of students in his class had almost doubled. He said nothing about it and conducted the class as usual. Once the class was over the teacher was very happy about the sudden popularity of his class, and he expressed his admiration for those who sought knowledge of Kurdish language and culture.

At the end of the session he introduced himself as Dr. Sadiq Moftizade. I hadn't met him before. His name was familiar to me but I wasn't sure if he was the same Dr. Moftizade that I knew. He was probably in his late forties or early fifties, tall and slim with a moustache. He was dressed in three-piece suit and his hair was getting gray and thin. He was very gentle, well mannered, well tempered and a good communicator.

"Who invited these students to my class?" asked Dr. Moftizade with a big smile and joy.

"I did," I replied.

"Where you from?" he asked.

"I am from Halabja?"

"What is your name?" he asked.

"My name is Rauf Naqishbendi," I replied.

"Who is your father?"

"My father is Gareeb, grandson of Shaykh Najmadeen," I replied.

"We are cousins! Do you know we are relatives, Rauf?" he said as he hugged me.

"I know I have many relatives here but I haven't met any yet. You are the first one," I said.

"Do you have time to walk with me to my car?"

"Of course, I'd be delighted," I said.

We started walking toward the faculty parking lot, which was at the other side of the building.

"Rauf, have you met Dr. Abed Serajaddeni?" he asked.

"Not really, I remember my dad mentioned him many times and he was very fond of him. I actually know him through the radio," I said.

"Yes, he is a Member of Parliament now. He is very outspoken and well regarded member of the Iranian parliament. I am sure he will be pleased to meet you," he said.

"Thanks, I'd love to meet him," I said.

"Mr. Naqishbendi I'd like to invite you to my house for lunch so that we can share a meal. You can meet my family and spend the afternoon with us," he said.

"That would be an honor," I said.

"How about tomorrow? My last class will be about one o'clock. Will you meet me by my classroom?" he asked.

"Surely, I will,"

When I was a little boy I used to listen to Dr. Moftizade's radio broadcasts about Kurdish language grammar. That program went on for over a year. He and his brother Dr. Abdulrahman Mofty were the first ones to outline Kurdish grammar, and they published that in the only Iranian Kurdish newspaper, *Kurdistan*, which he and his brother co-founded. The newspaper operated from 1960 to 1964. Once the newspaper got some publicity, the government of Iran decided to close down the newspaper.

After I left Dr. Moftizade, I was afraid that I might cause him trouble because I knew Savak was watching me and for some reason they really didn't want me, as an Iraqi Kurd, to get close to the Iranian Kurds. They might have been afraid that the Iraqi Kurds would talk more about Kurdish freedom and encourage Iranian Kurds to demand the same things as their counterparts in Iraq.

The next day, after my classes were over, I met Dr. Moftizade and went to his house. On our way to his house, while he was driving, he said, "Mr. Naqishbendi do you know you have many relatives in the city here?" He said.

"My father told me about them and my cousin Rauf, the son of Shaykh Otman, who was the leader of the Naqishbendi. He told me that Rauf's brothers Shaykh Naseh and Dr. Madeh are here and asked me to visit them," I said.

"I already told you about Dr. Serajaddeni, and the rest of your relatives will be happy to meet you. Once they all find out you are here, you are going to have a hard time making time for them all because there are so many of them," he said.

"I heard about Dr. Serajaddeni, he was the head of the Kurdish radio and TV, and he is a good writer and poet," I said.

"That's true but he left radio and TV. He's now one of the very prominent members of the Iranian Parliament," he said.

"That is good to know," I said.

"He is a very good man. I talked to him last night and he wants to see you as soon as he can. He told me that he will make arrangements to come take you to his house for dinner," said Dr. Moftizade.

"That might be difficult for him with his busy schedule. It will be easier for me to go to his house than for him to come to the university," I said.

"Don't worry about it. I'll give you his number."

At that point I was living at the government house. There was only one phone for almost fifteen people. I knew it was difficult for people to call, because there was always someone on the phone. For this reason, I generally just told people I had no phone.

Dr. Moftizade's residence was in what looked like an upper-middle class area. His house had immaculate landscaping in both front and back. They had a huge living room carpeted with gorgeous Persian rugs, and they had beautiful paintings all done on Persian rugs hung on the wall. In their living room, they had a nice china cabinet and what looked liked a walnut dining table with more than half a dozen chairs around it.

He introduced me to both of his daughters and to his nephew, Abed and his wife. They all had red hair and blue eyes, beautiful and handsome people. He had a beautiful family. His daughter, who was around my age at the time, was the picture of beauty and charm. We sat and had some tea and they had prepared an elaborate and delicious lunch. It was beans, rice and lamb with salad and vegetables.

After lunch we sat and had tea and baklava and fruit, which is a usual Iranian desert. He got his collection of the entire *Kurdistan* newspaper, which he'd organized in five volumes, neatly put together. The majority of writing in the newspaper had been done by Dr. Moftizade, his brother Dr. Abdulrahman Mofty and some by Dr. Abed Serajaddeni. He talked about his work with pride and I was surprised that he talked to me freely at a time when in Iran most people were so fearful, hesitant and suspicious of one another to say anything political. I went over the newspaper and read as much as I could. I read the poetry, commentaries and the Kurdish grammar section. He didn't want me to miss some of his masterpieces, he knew exactly where they were in his collection. He went on and read them to me.

"Doctor, why did they close the newspaper?" I asked.

"They let us print that newspaper for one reason."

"Why is that?" I asked.

"Because the Kurdish movement for freedom and liberty intensified in Iraqi Kurdistan, and the Iranian government didn't know how to react to such a new development," he said.

"How did that change anything?" I asked

"They allowed that and opened a powerful radio station to broadcast Kurdish cultural program. They thought that it would be a good message for the Iranian Kurds that the Shah of Iran had already given Iranian Kurds their cultural freedom, since they didn't want another armed movement like their counterparts in Iraq," he said.

"But we all know Shah of Iran is the enemy of freedom. He is fearful that freedom may mark the end of his royal authority," I said.

He continued, "That is absolutely correct, and for that same reason Savak was afraid that our newspaper might lead to something else and eventually get out of their control. In Turkey, the Turks deny the existence of one third of their population, the Kurds. You know Kurds in Turkey with support of the United States' policies, are deprived from every human rights including the most natural one, talking in their language. There are tens of thousands of Kurds in Turkish prisons as we speak and these Kurds are imprisoned for one reason, for being Kurds."

"Yes, I know, Turkey has committed genocide against Armenians and Assyrians and killed almost a million of them, killed them because they were Christians. They are still not willing to admit to, let alone apologize for their crimes. To Turks it was all right because they were not Muslims. On the other hand they kill Kurds even though Kurds are Muslims but their rationale is that Kurds need to think of themselves Turks and give up their identity," I said.

"Then, Mr. Naqishbendi, what you think the Iranian nationalists and Chauvinists think?" He asked.

"We all are one race and there is no difference," I said.

"Yes, they try to tell us that Kurds are Persian. They try to fool themselves and us by saying that Kurdish language is a dialect of Persian, and Kurds are Persian. They fooling no one but themselves," he said, "Let me tell you what happened to me."

This was Dr. sadiq Moftizade's story:

A Savak agent called me down to his office one morning. At the same time they called my brother, Dr. Abdulrahman Mofty. They took us to different rooms and different people briefed us at the same time. They asked me to write an article in the paper stating that Kurds were Persian and Kurdish language was a dialect of the Persian language.

I asked the Savak agent, "How I can do that?"

"You just need to write a well-written article, and you need to support it with a few facts," the agent said.

"But my friend, I don't have any historic or linguistic evidence or proof to support that," I said.

"No, you just don't want to do it, otherwise you could find the arguments you need. We can find people help you if you want, but I think with your knowledge you need no one. You can do that, can't you?"

"No I can't do anything like that. If I did, it would be lies and history would not forgive me. I've done a lot of good work for my people. Doing what you ask me to do will without any doubt destroy my past work," I replied.

"I have hard time understanding this. I don't know why it should be so difficult," said the agent.

"I think I made myself very clear, I think you don't want to understand that what you're asking is immoral and unethical. It would be like a physician killing his patient."

"All right, you make up your mind whether you want to write the article, or have us close down your newspaper."

"You do whatever you wish, you have the power but I have a will. You have your boss to satisfy, I have my people to serve. I must tell you that myself and others like me are not willing to compromise their integrity and cover truth with false even for a minute no matter what the personal gain or loss may be."

"You could write the article and continue to have the prestige of running an influential newspaper."

"The only reason I have been influential and our newspaper is respected is because we didn't do things like what you are asking. Respect is not given but gained. I must tell you in the world of academics, you can't maintain prestige through the fabrication of lies and illusion," I said.

"What illusion are you talking about?"

"You want me to fabricate a false history and intellectual materials to say Kurds are Persians? For heaven's sake, Kurds are Kurds and Persians are Persians just like apples are apples and oranges are oranges."

He looked me and continued, "Mr. Naqishbendi, that was how they closed down the newspaper," he said.

"What about your brother?" I asked.

"I saw him an hour later and he responded very much like I did," he said.

"That must have been painful."

"Sure it was, I will never forget that, that took away so many years of my life. I can't express it. I thought that at last I was able to do something for my people and my language. The newspaper got to be popular. Just as it was getting more readers locally and abroad, they closed it down," he said.

Years later I met Ms. Thuraya Mufti, daughter of Dr. Abdulrahman Mofty in the US and we started talking about her father and her uncle. She told me,

"You don't know how painful the closure of the Kurdistan newspaper was to my father. I was a little girl when Savak called my father in. When my father came home that day, he was very distressed. I asked him what happened? He took my hand and we walked together to the building where they printed the newspaper.

They had posted a sign written on a thin cloth around the building saying, 'Closed Forever.'"

She added, "My father was proud of his work. Before he passed away he told me, 'I have no money or property for you to inherit, but I will leave you with my best work. I want you to be the custodian of it.' I must tell you my father was never the same after that. My dad's purpose was publishing that newspaper. He wanted it to be the beginning of cultural freedom for Kurds in Iran. He was an advocate of free speech which he understood not only Kurds but the Iranian overall were deprived from it. He strived for cultural and literary freedom. He did his best but sometimes the hands of evil overpowers benevolent deeds of good people.

My dad understood the repression we Kurds were subjected to, and he attempted to ease that repression. Sadly that didn't happen. My dad used to tell me that although you can have simple demands, sometimes they don't seem so simple in the eyes of the authorities."

"My dear, the best of my lifetime was four years during which with my brother humbly managed the Kurdistan Newspaper. My able pen allowed me elucidate our true identity and history. In awake of enthusiastic public reception our newspaper has attained, authorities engaged in unfair campaign of falsifying facts

After visiting with Dr. Moftizade, I went and saw Dr. Abed Serajaddeni. The night I went there it was only him, his servant and his maid. The rest of his family had left for their vacation in Iranian Kurdistan. Dr. Abed at the time must have been near fifty years old, his hair had turned gray. He wore eyeglasses and he was in a good physical shape. I had dinner with him and then after dinner we started talking. Even though it was the first time we had met, I felt very comfortable talking with him and he was very charming. He started telling me about his work in the Iranian Parliament and we talked about the Naqishbendis in Iraq. Dr. Abed was very strong opinionated and assertive about his ideas. He was a kind of man who had no reservation to tell people off when they were wrong or when he was contradicted. He was well read and often quoted a great thinker to support his assertion.

Dr. Serajaddeni was a good writer, and he had been one of the main contributors to the *Kurdistan* newspaper. When he was the head of Kermansha radio, he produced and directed many radio plays, and wrote commentaries. He and his brother Asad were very well known throughout both Iraqi and Iranian Kurdistan through the Kurdish radio in Kermansha. I ended up visiting Dr. Serajaddeni at least once a month. I got to be friends with his children as well and we hung out together occasionally. I also met Amjad Serajaddeni who was about my age, and we got to be very close friend up to this day.

I met other family members who were close friends to Shah of Iran's family including Dr. Mazhar Naqishbendi, who used to be the Shah's personal Arabic translator. I also met Mr. Shaykh Naseh Naqishbendi, who used to work in Shah's royal palace as a director of one of the agricultural affairs departments. I spent practically all my time outside of school with these relatives I'd just discovered. Soon after I attended school of medicine, I met another Naqishbendi, Omar the son of Shaykh Masom whose father was another prominent Naqishbendi's member in Iran and he was well respected. Shaykh Masom was an adviser and confident of Qasi Mohammed, the head of The Kurdish Republic of Mahabad. For the rest of my life in Tehran Omar remained one of the most close friend of mine and we were roommates in dorm. After my first year in Tehran Shaykh Masom invited me to join his son Omar in a visit to Mahabad, in Kurdistan where he resided. I joined Omar and visited Shaykh and his family. They were one of the most respectable traditional Kurdish family I have met, and I indebted to their kindness and their sincerity toward me. Then later I met Mr. Latef Islamy whom later become the member of Iranian Parliament and we become friend and I used to give him and his family frequent visit with my cousin Omar.

Even though Naqishbendis had close association with the Shah of Iran, they were not necessarily in unison with Shah's policy toward Kurds and they resented Shah's moral corruption.

One day I met my father's second cousin, Ahsan. At the time I was about twenty-two and he must have been a couple years older than I was. That day we went with a couple more of my relatives to midtown Tehran. We spend the whole day together before heading to the house of Shaykh Amen for dinner. We took the bus. Ahsan loved to sing. We got onto one of the double-decker buses and we went and sat upstairs. Ahsan started singing Kurdish songs at the top of his voice, and four of us were singing the chorus. We could be heard a mile away. As the bus drove on, the windows were open and people on the street could hear us. As people were looking at the bus they were all laughing, and some people in the street were applauding as we sang happy songs. Some people probably thought that we must have been a wedding party. The bus kept driving and the bus driver started yelling, "Hey, Chief, if you don't stop singing, I will drive straight to the police station!"

Ahsan said, "Let the *Haramzad** take us wherever he wants, we only have one stop to go!" With that, he resumed singing. We got off the bus,

---

* Kurdish/Persian for an illegitimate child

laughing. Ahsan didn't stop singing until we got to Mr. Amen Naqishbendi's house. Ahsan was singing and we sang with him, as we passed by houses, some people didn't know what was going on, they opened their windows and watched us. Some thought it was a demonstration.

Shaykh Amen must have been in his fifties. He managed several radio programs. He was very well respected among the Naqishbendi family and among the Kurds. He was the most well mannered man I have encountered. He was a man of integrity and a true believer in God. I always remember him as never wanting to hold a grudge or think ill of others. His wife Nageba was sweet and good natured. She was a good Muslim and very loving person, always concerned for others. She knew that I was alone in Tehran and used to treat me well, and for her treatment I am indebted to her kind generosity. Mr. Amen had four children and I've been very close to them up to this day.

Chapter Seventeen

March 11, 1970 had brought the promise of implementation of self-government for the Kurds in Iraq within a four year period. Kurdish leader and Iraqi authorities commenced negotiating the terms of an agreement, and the negotiations lasted for four years. At the end of the four years it collapsed, for neither Kurds nor Iraqi Ba'th were serious about the negotiations succeeding. Barzani and Iraqi President, Bakar both started to beat their war drums, and disaster wasn't long in coming after the failure to implement that agreement.

In March, 1974 I was on my way to school on the bus and reading the Iranian official paper *Kayhan*. I read that Halabja and Kaladeza had been bombed and the two towns had been destroyed, their population devastated.

I got totally disoriented and didn't know what to do. At the next bus stop I got off. I sat down at the bus station and read the story again. Then I went back to the dorm and I made a phone call to the office of the KDP in Tehran. I talked to the chief administrator, Muhmood. He told me that six Iraqi planes have bombed Halabja and Kaladeza with a variety of bombs, including Napalm. He indicated that was all he knew at the time and would call me should he heard further news.

I went to the bus stop and took the bus to go back to the dorm. I sat on the last seat in the back of the bus. I was depressed, angry and frustrated and keep thinking about Halabja. I kept thinking, *Oh, my God my parents must be dead, and everyone else. How horrible it will be all of a sudden if someone calls me with a long list of dead and wounded friends and relatives.* I knew that I would hear the list eventually.

I arrived at the dorm and went right to bed, but after a few minutes I got up. I made myself tea, and still it was light outside. I stood there drinking tea and looking out the windows of my room for more than an hour with the bombing of my hometown in mind with that I felt asleep. About 3:00 A.M. I was in my bed soaking wet from sweat, my pillow looked like someone poured water on it. I found blood on my bed, and when I felt my forehead, dried blood flaked off. I ran to the bathroom and looked in the mirror. I saw a cut on my forehead.

I knew I must have fainted and fallen against the metal edge of the bed. I went back to the room and looked the edge of the bed, which was covered with the sheet; I saw it was also red from blood.

I looked at the bed again and saw blood on both sides of the pillow. Early in the morning around 6:30, the student next door came and asked how I was doing. He asked, "Mr. Naqishbendi your door was open last night, I knocked several times, but you must have been in a deep sleep."

"Yes, I wasn't feeling well," I said.

"I closed the door so that you wouldn't be bothered," he said.

"Thank you sir. I appreciate it."

I went back to my room took another look at the cut on my forehead. I was concerned about what I would tell people…not that I cared about them seeing the cut itself, but that people might get curious and want to know what had happened. I didn't feel like answering the questions of a bunch of people who only wanted to hear a story they could pass on and who didn't care anything about me.

I didn't like what I saw in the mirror. I told myself that the tragedy had marked itself right on my forehead, just as I was sure it would leave its imprint on my heart and mind. I had a bad headache and it felt like a mountain was resting on my head. I lay on my bed and cried for hours. When I got up my headache got so bad I barely could see.

I thought when people saw me, they'd probably perceive that I'd gotten into a fight on the street with someone and they think of me as a drunken idiot. Some might think that I was into drugs and fallen down the stairs or on the street in a stupor. I felt ashamed even to go out of the dorm. I knew the wound would not heal for a few weeks, and I would have to face the outside world. I thought that I'd have to accept the mark as a small token of a larger tragedy. I knew that when the tragedy happened, its implications last a long time and sometimes it leaves its scars for others to see.

I took myself to the medical center in the dorm. The dorm was like a small town; it had about ten huge multi-story buildings, with two main cafeterias, and a medical center near the entrance. The medical center was like a small unit with several rooms, a little pharmacy, nurses and a doctor. I checked in and the nurse took me to a room and asked me to wait for the doctor. I waited and the doctor came. He was an older man in his late sixties. We introduced ourselves, thereafter:

"Son, what brought you here?" the doctor asked.

"I must have been unconscious because I don't remember how it happened. I assume that I have fallen on my bed, the bed's sharp metal edge might have cut my forehead. All I know when I woke up from a deep sleep, I detected blood on my bed and I was soaked in sweat," I said.

"Has a similar incident such as this occurred before?" he asked.

"No" I replied with confidence.

"Were you drunk or on drug?"

"No." I answered.

"So that can't be it. What else then did happen?"

"Dr., I wasn't drunk. It was a personal tragedy," I said.

"Then what happened?" he persisted.

"I told you, it was a tragedy. It overwhelmed me to the point that I fainted in the late afternoon, woke up early this morning and saw myself as you see me now,"

"I'm sorry, I have seen that happen."

He got some ointment put on my forehead and bandaged the wound.

"You should be all right. You are lucky, you could have had a concussion, but you need to keep this bandage on your forehead for two days. After that you can take it off. You can take this tube of ointment and apply it to the wound afterward. I'll give you a prescription and that is to relieve pain, take as needed," he said.

I wondered why these doctors always say, take as needed. I didn't know what is in their mind, they think one will take medicine even if they don't need it. I mean this is not a candy or a chocolate to say I don't need it but yet it taste good. Why in the world people take medicine if they don't need it, are these doctors stupid or they think their patients are naïve. After all it's a painkiller, once the pain gone away, there would be no need for it.

"Thank you doctor," I said.

"You're welcome. Remember if you need my help, just come by and knock on my door. You said it had nothing with narcotics or alcohol?" he said suspiciously.

"Yes sir, you heard me right," I said.

"I don't want to annoy you, was that a family tragedy?"

"Yes, sir."

"You have an accent, Mr. Naqishbendi, is your family the famous Naqishbendis?"

"Yes."

"You know I am a Kurd. I know a few members of Naqishbendi family."

"Where are you from?" he asked.

"I am from Halabja."

He guided me with his hand pointing to chair in a front of me "Please have a seat.

You are an Iraqi Kurd...I heard about the bombing of Halabja. You have my sympathy. Is your family okay?" he asked sympathetically.

"I don't know, and that is all about this visit to your office," I said.

"We Kurds will keep being victims until we are free. We are a people without a country and our tragedy will remain until we are free of occupations. I know your family, and my prayers goes to you and people of Halabja. I'll give you my home and office number. Call me when you need me, anytime, day or night. After all, I am a Kurd and your tragedy is mine, we all share the same tragedy no matter if it's in Iran, Syria, Turkey or Iraq," he said.

"Thanks Doctor, I appreciate your solidarity, but to be frank with you I am frustrated with this mark on my forehead," I said.

"Son, the occupation will leave its bruises for as long as it goes on.

Take it and pray for the *peshmargas*, they are the ones who can get us out of this mess, if they don't make it any worse. I must tell you as an Iranian Kurd Barzani will regret his reliance on this serpent, the Shah."

"I have the same feeling, but what can I do? Thanks doctor Parwez," I said.

"Good luck, and let me know if I can be of any help. You have my number," he said.

"Yes I do, thanks."

We shook hands and said goodbye.

I left the medical center to go back to my room. My roommate, Omar was spending a week with his uncle's family in Tehran, and at least I could be alone and not be bothered.

I turned the radio on but there wasn't any news. I decided to visit Shaykh Naseh's house and hoped that they might've heard something. I felt uncomfortable walking outside with my head bandaged, but I left the dorm and took a taxi to Shaykh Naseh's house. I knocked on the door and Khatoon, their maid let me in.

Shaykh Naseh's was at work. Dada Tala, Naseh's wife was at home with Naseh's cousin Adham and Khatoon. Dada Tala came right away, welcomed me.

"Rauf, what happened? You look like a mullah with that white turban. Did you decide to become a mullah instead of a doctor?" she laughed.

I didn't want to go much into detail. "I just fell on my bed, that's an easy way to become a mullah," I said.

"I think you'll make a good mullah. Mullah Shaykh Rauf?"

"That will be very elegant, dada Tala. Do you know what has happened in Halabja and Kaladeza?"

She took a deep breath. "When you showed up, I didn't want to hurt your feelings and pretended as nothing has transpired, well now you know, yes, we all know. It is ugly and evil what has happened to Halabja. We have been on the phone with the Shaykh's house and they are supposed let us know everything today."

"Any news so far?" I asked.

"It's too early, and we will know today, just stay here."

"Are you sure they will call?" I asked.

"They will, and Shaykh Naseh called your dorm several times last night, he wanted you to come here and stay with us until we hear the news. We were all worried about you," she said.

"Thanks Dada Tala, I was at dorm but I slept early," I said.

I loved this lady, she was like my older sister. She was always worried about me and I treated her house just like my own parent's house. I showed up at her house all the time and without any notice, and I was always welcomed. Her husband Shaykh Naseh was the same. During my years in Tehran, I made their house just like mine, and never felt anything less than earnest welcome.

Shaykh Naseh came back about 1:30 P.M. We all had lunch. As usual in Shaykh Naseh's house there was fried chicken, white Basmati rice or Basmati Spanish rice. It was always delicious fried chicken. But no matter how often I had it, it was so delicious it always felt like I was tasting it for the first time.

After lunch I played backgammon with Shaykh Naseh—I wanted something to keep my mind away from Halabja. I finished the game, and still I heard nothing. I was getting impatient with everything. The phone rang several times and every time the phone rang, I prayed that it would be a call from the Shaykh's house.

"Shaykh Naseh I am going out of my mind," I said.

"I didn't know you had a mind, Rauf," said Shaykh Naseh.

"Come on, I'm serious," I said.

"I know that, you little *terkan*. What do you think I'm feeling? I am feeling the same way," he said.

The phone rung again. Shaykh Naseh picked it up and listened, he kept knotting his forehead. The phone call went on and on, and all I heard was Shaykh Naseh saying, "Okay. Oh no! My God!" Every minute he was on the phone was my excruciating torture. As he talked, Dr. Abed Serajaddeni knocked the door and I greeted him and let him in. I was too anxious to hear Shaykh Naseh's conversation, so I went back and sat watching Shaykh Naseh. After almost fifteen minutes Shaykh Naseh hung up and greeted Dr. Abed. We all sat down while tea was served.

"Rauf, your parents and grandparents had left Halabja the day before the bombing. They all are in Byra, and the rest of the Naqishbendis are all

248

fine but at least a thousand people are dead and the town is in ruins." said Shaykh Naseh.

That night I left Shaykh Naseh's house still demoralized and the news of my family being safe didn't help my feelings for the people of Halabja. I left his house as disheartened as I was before I went there.

Chapter Eighteen

The summer of that same year I went back to Kurdistan. I had nothing else to do in Tehran so I went to see my family. My parents were living in the town of Byra near the Iranian border. At that time the Sulaymanya University was closed and many of its students were in that area as they had joined the Kurdish revolution, so I had many of my old friends there.

I saw my parents. They were staying in Shaykh Rauf's house, the son of Shaykh Osman, the elder and leader of the family. My father had opened a a small grocery store in Byra's little shopping center, which had about a dozen stores.

I was broke and didn't have much money to spend. I went to the KDP center in Tawela, which was about twenty minutes from Byra, another town on the border with Iran. Tawela had a population of several thousand people. It was a beautiful little town built between two tall rocky mountains. The center of the town was built in the little narrow valley between the two mountains. Houses were built on sides of the mountains and some of the houses were built on top of each other, just as they were in most of the villages and towns in mountain area in Kurdistan.

There was a little shopping center with about fifty stores, cafés and restaurants as well as a small hotel. Because Tawela was a border town, it was a commercial town with immense business activities. Tawela was a part of what is called Hawraman, which started from Byra and stretched to the west of Iran.

Fatah was the head of a division of about two thousand *peshmarga* and his headquarter was in Tawela. Administrators in Fatah's office were the same as those l had dealt with just a few years ago, and they all knew me.

Ali still was there and he was of Fatah's main administrators. He shook my hand, "Then let me know what any thing we can do for you,"

"That is indeed what I am here for, it's my summer vacation, and I wanted to see if there was anything I can do to help," I said.

"We can always use a wise young man like yourself. How is your Farsi?" he asked.

"It isn't great. I've been in Iran about a year but I can translate if you need me to," I said.

"That is good enough, I'll enroll you on the payroll as of today. Just come by for an hour or two a day, and we may have you write a few letters in Farsi," he said.

"Thanks Ali, you are very kind and I must confess I needed that," I said.

"Sure, man I have been student myself, and I know every little bit helps," he said, "Rauf, I'm going to let Fatah know you're here, just give me a minute," he said.

He left and talked to Fatah for about five minutes.

Fatah came out and shook my hand and put his hands on my shoulders.

"Glad to see you again young man," said he.

"Thank you sir, I appreciate Mr. Ali's arrangements and I will be glad to help."

I went back to Byra and spent that night with my parents and they brought me up to date. As usual my dad wasn't good company at night. He would wake up at five in the morning to do his first daily prayer and read the Qur'an, so he would get tired at night and usually went to sleep before nine o'clock. I stayed up with my mother until midnight and she told me about Halabja and our family. She told me that just a day before the bombing they left the town, but there were others who left earlier. Our house was bombed and destroyed.

I saw my good friend, Osman Khalifa who was my close friend through high school. He was one of my best friends.

I found he'd settled in Tawela. I had a lot to catch up on with my old friends. Osman had been a student in the civil engineering college in Sulaymanya University, and after the closure of the university he had joined the revolution.

Osman and one of his friends from Sulaymanya named Barywan, a former engineering student, lived in a little tent. Barywan seemed to be a shy person. They invited me to have dinner with them and stay overnight. Their tent was on the mountainside, among several huge trees. They had a little kerosene stove they used to cook food and make tea. There was a little *bara** lying on the ground, a portable radio and a small alarm clock. They had a ceramic container for water. On top of the *bara* they had a couple mattresses. It was dusty and they kept dusting off the *bara* and their blankets. There were other people in tents nearby them and they were a short walking distance from the town. There was a bathroom a couple minutes walking distance from them, or walk to the nearby mosque, which was about five minutes away. Osman had also made a little grill outside of their tent just a few feet away from the tent. The grill was only a few stones laid on the ground about a foot high. He had bought lamb, he cut it and skewed it, and we cooked it on fire. We put the *sfra* on the ground and had dinner.

We had tea and afterward I had brought half a bottle Arak. Then Osman's friend Barywan and I drunk and kept talking, I was hoping to find out exactly what had happened in Halabja, and learn some detailed account of bombing and human casualties. I had heard many versions of it but none from people who were there at the time of the bombing.

I asked Osman if he'd go back to Halabja with me. He was silent for a long while and looked me right in the eyes just like I'd lost my mind.

"You don't want to do that Rauf," he said.

"How do you know that?" I asked.

"Do you want to hear what happened first?" he asked

"Yes," I said.

"Did you hear all about the bombing?" he asked.

"I just heard a bit of it, and very little was written about it," I said.

"Man, forget about it. Who writes about Kurds? Even we ourselves

---

* A small hand-made rug

are too lazy to write about our experiences. You may have read an Iranian newspaper, and you know it was about their own people more than about us," said Osman. "Do you want to know in detail and have your heart broken?"

"I want you tell me in detail as much as you can recall. My heart already broken and the same with my dream, which happened to be Halabja," I said.

This was Osman's story:

Before the bombing we were warned that the Ba'th might bomb the town. Some people left but most stayed. People didn't think the bombing would be so devastating. People were told the bombing would be very heavy, but the *peshmargas* said they had a weapon that could be used as an anti-aircraft weapon. And people thought that they might be able to bring down the planes. In the end, they found out these were just heavy machineguns like those mounted on a tank, they weren't effective at all. As a result we were defenseless in the bombing. *Peshmargas* organized a group of volunteers, among them a doctor, nurses and other volunteers from the town, and they were trained to help out in case of emergency.

It was March 16th. Five jet fighters flew by the town. Soon we flea to the basement franticly. They circled around the town twice and then one of the planes dropped the first bomb. The noise of that first explosion was so loud that it nearly deafened everyone. Then the second bomb came, and a third, and so on. They kept bombing for almost half an hour and left. Imagine for half an hour bombing such a small town with those big bombs. The planes each dropped one bomb at a time, circling in the sky and then coming back in nosedives. They did that more than ten times. Sometimes two or three planes were bombing at once and you could hear the bombs exploding one right after another.

With every bomb that exploded we all jumped. My brother, Wahab was sitting next to his daughters, Sharmen and Golzar, three and five years old. They were both holding their mother tightly and crying their eyes out. My brother Rahem was there as well. My God, it wasn't only the bombs because these planes were flying low and they sounded like they would deafen everyone. That was the longest half-hour in my life.

We were all terrified and all we did was pray to God. None of us believed that we would make it through the bombing. My heart was beating so fast as my blood pressure shot up. I thought that even if I didn't get hit with a bomb, a heart attack would kill me. We all covered our ears, yet the noise was so devastating, it was shaking us like electric shocks. Our house was shaking just like an earthquake had hit.

Once the noise quieted down, Wahab said that we should all stay there for another ten minutes since the planes might came back for another round. We waited and tried to comfort the children as they were both shaking and screaming.

When ten minutes had passed and we knew the planes were gone, we got out of the basement. I saw the glasses of doors and the windows of our house had all been shattered. We had a metal door cemented to the stone, it was heavy metal and cemented in about four inches deep, but it was bent right in the middle. I went back to our living room, and checked the rooms. It was like a heavy earthquake had hit, leaving nothing in its place. Almost everything had fallen to the floor and pieces of shattered window glasses cascaded allover. After everyone came out of the basement, we congregated in the living room. Every one of us was pale and shaking and damp from sweat, just like waking up from a long nightmare.

"Thank God we are all alive. I'll stay with the family, we don't both need to be here. I'm sure many will be screaming for help. Osman, you and Wahab go and try to help whoever you can," said my brother Rahem.

I left with my brother Wahab.

When I went out you could see dust, smoke and fire everywhere. The dust and smoke from the fire formed a thick layer of cloud over the town. You could smell the smoke miles away. I could hear from close and far crying women and children. After I got a little closer to midtown, I could hear more screaming and crying. I saw people running out into the street and leaving their houses.

I was still deaf from bombing boisterous noise and fidget. Soon I found my brother Wahab wasn't with me; he'd gone off on his own. I got closer to the middle of town and there were no doors or windows left in any of the houses, they were all down and houses were all open.

I went into the first house I heard crying, from. That was the house of

Haji Nagi. My God, I saw a little kid about three years old crying, he'd stand and then fall down right on his face. He was covered with dust and his mother was lying next to him dead all covered in mud and blood. I started crying but soon I realized that I needed to control myself or I wouldn't be able to help.

I stepped a bit further into the house and the roof was slowly coming down. I took the kid's hand and wanted to take him aside and look for more survivors. The kid couldn't stand up on his feet, so I carried him out of the house. I found myself all covered in blood. I put the child down and looked his face with big tears and crying from pain. I got so disheartened that I can't express it in words, but it all came to my mind as I looked at that child, *God this poor child should have a life to live, this child should have enjoyed his childhood and not left wounded and having lost his mother.*

One of the emergency teams came. I wanted to set the kid down, but the poor kid couldn't sit, he lay down, and one of the emergency workers took the kid's jacket off and found a huge piece of a metal right in his back. They wanted to take him to the hospital, but I heard the nurse say just a minute later that he was dead. I thought the nurse was mistaken, I'd taken the child out, and he hadn't looked like he would've died in those few minutes. I went and checked the kid's heart, which was stopped.

I'd just seen a women and a little child in the house. I am sure the husband must have been out of town and I imagined him coming back to Halabja and getting the news. I was so disappointed in everything that I wished that I'd never been born. I just felt that life with all these tragedies was not worth living, I had to force myself forward knowing for a fact that was the first of God knows how many more horrors I would encounter that day.

Two of the emergency crew and I left and went to the next house. We saw several bodies all chopped up by the bomb and the house was in ruins. God, you just don't know how many places like that I saw that day, how many places I went to rescue someone and found that everyone was already dead. If I live to be a father these are the stories that need to be passed to my children so that the genocide committed against us and these desolated days will be remembered.

We kept on walking, and I was wet from the blood of that child I held.

His tragedy and his innocence were clinging to me. I smelled of blood, and my clothes were all dusty and the blood mixed with the dust to form mud.

Each time I went inside a house with one of the volunteers, we were fearful that the roofs of the houses might collapse over our heads.

In one house we saw a crack in the floor we thought might lead to a basement. We started clearing our way, it was all dirt and dust sitting on the rubble of the house, and soon we found out that we were walking on dead bodies. We cleared the way but we couldn't tell how many bodies there were. We found three dead bodies, two of young women and one of an older man, but we could not recognize who was who as bodies all chopped in destroyed house. We felt guilty leaving those dead bodies lying there, but then we had to keep moving so that we could try and save some lives.

We moved to the next house, and two other emergency workers joined us. The house was almost flat; it looked like the bomb must have hit the house directly. I could hear crying and it sounded like it was coming under the wreckage of the house.

"Do you hear the crying?" I said.

"Yes, do you know where it's coming from?" one of the volunteers asked.

The poor guy was shaking and confused. He was one of the young volunteers; his face was covered with dust and looked sad and frustrated. He looked like he was drained out of energy and might fall on the floor himself.

I pointed to the spot where I thought the crying was coming from. There were blocks of cement, rocks and wood covering the area. We started to clear it. We dug down as fast as we could and came across a metal object.

"Let's take out this thing, it looks like a metal door," I said.

"Okay. My name is Naryman, let's call each other by name," said the volunteer.

"I am Osman. Thank you, my friend," I said.

"I am Mukhtar," said the other volunteer as he was trying to move a big rock out of the way.

"This may lead to the basement. Let's hurry."

We cleared the way, and sure enough, it was leading to the basement.

He looked at me and said, "Rauf in just three minutes we did more than one day of work."

When I saw how much we'd cleaned up, I thought it was miracle, but by the time we'd cleared the way to the basement, the crying had already faded away. We looked around and saw a young mother had been killed as she was breast-feeding her baby. You could see still the baby was lying on her mother's chest and another little girl just about two years old was lying right next to the mother. We lifted the women's body and her face was all bloody, and the children were all dead and bloody from debris. They were all covered with dirt and a pool of blood was forming next to the three of them. I felt so useless. All we wanted was to save some lives, but we hadn't managed to rescue anyone.

I rejoined the emergency crew and we went uptown.

It was horrible, every house was virtually destroyed and people were walking over dead bodies everywhere. I continued with the emergency crew, and when we went a few houses up, we heard crying again. The house was coming down, the roof of the house had collapsed and the walls were all about to go down, and I knew that from the direction of the crying that someone was trapped in the wreckage.

Those emergency crew volunteers really worked their hearts out and kept moving tirelessly from one place to another. We had no tools or equipment and done everything manually. We thought we made progress toward the crying person, but we found collapsed walls in our way, and we just kept digging.

We got in and finally there was a room where the walls were bending down just like it was going to collapse any second, more than half of the house was gone, we were all scared and thought we'd be under the wall any moment.

We finally got to the crying person, it was a pregnant women. She'd been wounded and she may have given a birth to a child or may have had a miscarriage, I am not sure which. The woman was wounded in the leg, and a baby was lying next to her, dead. The poor lady was in excruciating pain and was screaming her lungs out. We saw a man and a young boy about twelve years old. Both were wounded and bloody and they looked like that they were waiting for help.

We picked the mother up gently and took her out of the rubble, she was crying, "I lost my baby, I wish I was dead with her!" We cleaned a small area and put her down alongside her husband and a little boy. Another three volunteers came by, and one of them stopped, recognizing one of the victims.

We stayed there and tried to help, but we were so helpless, unequipped not even having a bandage. Soon a nurse came to take care of them. The good news we heard next day that all three survived. The volunteers I worked with was the bright part of all our work. Thank God we could help someone.

Not a single house was left undamaged. Even the houses that stood had cracks on the walls. Windows and doors were all popped out and most had major structural damages including our house.

The next block we looked at it was almost flattened, I got scared and I knew it would be very bloody and ugly. We went house-to-house, looking under the rubble to find survivors. We went to more than a dozen houses and there weren't any who'd survived. We looked under the rubble, turning over every piece of cement, wood and rocks to rescue someone, but all we saw was blood and body parts. They were so violently blown apart that no one could put these parts together and tell the identity of these victims.

Osman stopped his story and turned to me. He reached for his pack a cigarette, he offered me one, and got one for himself. He lit my cigarette and then his and started smoking.

"You know, it was a good thing your parents and your grandparents were out, I swear nothing was left of your house, it got hit with a bomb and flattened."

He continued:

I told you, I started from my house and was going uptown, toward late afternoon I got close to the hospital, and I wanted to know what was going on there, by then the volunteers from emergency crew and I had already divided up.

I was just a few minutes away walking to the hospital. So many people were in the street, I saw people coming in and out of the hospital. One couldn't see a dry eye among all those people. I went inside the hospital to see who else had gotten hit. I knew I would find more people. As soon as I went inside the outpatient area Ibrahem was in the first bed. I didn't know it was him but I saw Abas, Ibrahem's uncle and his parents. Abas told me it was Ibrahem. He said he'd been hit in the spinal cord. He was holding Ibrahem's hand and crying.

I placed my hands on his heart because still he was breathing, unconscious. I must tell you that broke my heart as I was holding my former classmate and felt his heartbeat slowing down. All I hoped was that he could open his eyes and stay conscious long enough for me to have a word with him, or at least to say goodbye. Next to his bed was his poor father, he was crying like a child and so did his mother.

The nurse came and checked his temperature and his blood pressure. The nurse looked at Abas and said, "I hate to tell you, but his heart is beating too slow, let us pray that he will make it. The nurse stayed around, and I knew that Ibrahem's life was fading away. I stayed by his bed and watched him die. You know what a lively person was he, also, handsome tall with a blue eyes, just a couple days before that we'd been sitting in the café, and he told us jokes and his blue eyes was sparkling like shinning star. I gave him a kiss on his cheek and said goodbye to him but I couldn't believe he was dead. Here was a person so close to me and his friendship meant so much to me, at that young age I witnessed how his heart stopped, and, how he left this world of injustice. When I was in a hospital, I couldn't take my eyes and my heart away from him. That day was one of the worst days in my life and he even made it worst. I must tell you that his picture laying in a bed as he was dieing will remain with me for the rest of my life. You don't believe how many nights since then my sleep was disturbed by that scene wakeup at night wet in sweat with the same scene in mind. My God how heartless these barbaric authorities are. I stayed there until they took his body and the next day I went to his funeral.

The day turned to night, and the town looked like a graveyard. People were walking on the street just like the living dead. The town was in ruins, the destruction was everywhere and you could smell blood everywhere you went.

I got home, and I had blood all over me, even my ears were full of blood.

You could see people outside who had no place to go, no one's house was fit to live in. *Peshmargas* came with trucks and took people away from the town to nearby villages, they took some people to Iran and placed them in the refugee camp. People were confused and couldn't make any sense out of what had happened.

The next day the planes came again and bombed some more, but by then most people had left. For days afterward many volunteers went back to bury the dead. There were very few bodies, most were just body parts that they bagged and took to the funerals. No one knew the identity of those who were bagged. You could smell the dead bodies way before you get to the town. The smell of dead people, and those cut into pieces and found under the rubble had become an attraction for wild dogs and wolves.

"That's why I don't want you to go back, it's tragic and ugly to see that. No one wants to witness that. Now months have gone by and the story is still the same, the town smells of the death of its victims," said Osman.

"Is there anyone living there now?" I asked.

"Yes, there are few people, and every day someone goes back to try to rebuild whatever they can," he said.

"That is the story of our lives. We need to continue to rebuild and survive for as long as we can. Most people would be surprised to see how anyone could have a life after so many calamities, but the fact is we are determined to live and be free. We keep on going," said Barywan, "but I wonder if the town will ever be a town again."

"Yes it will be, and people have already started rebuilding. It may not come as fast as we like but it will gradually become a town again," said Osman.

"It won't be easy and it will take them a long time to rebuild. My fear is that when they rebuild Halabja, there will just be another bombing attack," I said.

"Rauf, you know the two sisters in our high school class, the really quiet girls?" Osman asked.

"You mean Haji Kafoor's daughters?"

"Yes, they both got killed in the bombing," said Osman.

"I don't really know who's left," I said.

"More than a thousand people were killed, and that is a lot for a small town like ours, almost one out of every ten people perished or wounded," said Osman.

"I feel just like I've been on another planet for a century and now I'm coming back to a world fallen into disaster. I'm furious and I'm not sure why no one written to me or talked to me about all this," I said.

"You've been in a different country and you were alone, if you'd heard all this without anyone around to talk to about it, you would have lost your mind. That is why no one bothered to inform you besides, we all knew you'd hear it all eventually," said Osman.

It got late and I could see that the lights were off in the nearby tents.

"I think we've covered all that happened in Halabja. When we talk again, we'll speak about the other things that happened since you left," said Osman. He was tired, rubbing his eyes, and I could tell Barywan was ready to go sleep. We all drifted off to sleep.

I spent that summer in Tawela and Byra. I went home about three days a week to stay with my parents and the rest I stayed at my cousin Aziz's house or with Osman.

I went to the office and stayed for a few hours everyday. I wrote letters in Persian to the official Iranian Savak, arranging for people go for treatment, to do business, and so on.

Osman had invited me and an older man about sixty year old, Fayzollah. Osman had bought some Arak and made all kind of food to go with it. He had found a fresh sea bass and some lamb. It was my last day with him and he wanted to see me off properly.

A few minutes after my arrival Fayzollah showed up. He wasn't that old but I thought he was way old for our occasion as we were all in our early twenties. He dressed and resembled a traditional Mullah with long robe and turban. He had one of those long worry beans on his hand. He had a short beard and his rob was so puffy that one couldn't tell if he was really big or his robe made him look that way. First I countered him, I thought that he might be a quite and calm kind a guy. He had a thin eyeglass on. Osman told me Fayzollah was very knowledgeable about

Islam and he knows more than any mullah's he ever known; and to an extend he performs marriage ceremony, and funeral ritual. He added that he was religiously very conservative but socially liberal. That I couldn't digest and told Osman so, but he told me not to rush to judgment, wait and see.

We were introduced and we all conversed while Osman was putting his finishing touch on his prepared food. Osman seemed to have managed food all right, food was very much ready to be cooked. Osman served as tea. We were having a good time, and Fayzollah started with a joke, "there was a man who lived in

Sulaymanya named Baram, and his doctor told him that he would only have a few weeks to live. So he was in bed and waiting to die. One of his neighbors, Yaseen, came to visit him "'You know Mr. Baram, my dad passed away when I was on a business trip to Baghdad, it's been difficult for me not to have been around my dad when he passed away. I really wanted to give him a message and let him know that, would you be kind enough to give him my message,' said Yaseen.

"Baram said, 'Sorry, I'm not going to hell.'"

"In line with heaven and hell and marriage he told us another joke:

There was this guy who lived in Sulaymania and he married to a women who happened to be any body's nightmare. She was a witch. Her poor husband a nice guy, and this woman tortured him form the first day they married until he died. This women was well known in a city as a royal pain you know where?

Anyhow the guy passed away. After a while the women saw her husband in her dream, then the women asked her husband:

"Honey how are you doing sweetheart."

"I am doing really good, replied the husband in her dream."

"Are you happy there honey," asked the wife?

"Oh, yes very happy," said the husband.

"You mean you are happier now than when you were with me," asked the wife.

"Oh, yes and much happier," said the husband.

"So darling tell me about heaven and its glory," said the wife.

"No, I am not in heaven." said the husband.

I didn't know Fayzollah yet. I was worried that Osman and I had Arak there. "Man, what are you doing, are you nuts inviting Fayzollah such a conservative fellow and having this big bottle of Arak?" I said when we stepped away to collect wood for the barbeque. "He is real person and an ass, not your real Kurdish mullah. Just watch and listen to him, he is very understanding and yet faithful and enlightening," he said.

"So if he is faithful, how can we drink around him? He'll take that bottle and break it on our heads or least he can do is to leave and thus we will be Embarrassed and he will be offended. He will be offended, and it's not nice to offend someone's faith. Osman, sometimes you make no sense man, you just told me this guy is an ass and also you said he is faithful. The two don't go together," I said.

"Rauf, I invited him so that we can laugh. We cried together so much when I told you what had happened to our town, and you can't be serious or crying all the time. There is a time for prayer, there is time for crying and tonight is ours. We talk, drink and laugh with Fayzollah—just relax man you are going to like him," said Osman.

I had hard time to imagine Fayzollah to be anything but mullah, as he was dressed just like a usual mullah with his robe, beard and turban, and we were sitting around fire with our feast. It didn't look right and things didn't add up quite right. The fish was so delicious and had these little tiny bones. Osman made it with *somak* and a lot of salt and some turmeric.

"Osman pour me a shot." We toasted our glasses and said, *salute.*

"What about me, you ass?" said Fayzollah.

"I thought God said no alcohol, period, and if you drink you'll go to hell," said Osman with a serious look.

"Period your ass. God didn't say 'No drinking, period'. Where did this period come from? He said no drinking and driving, so I am sitting on the ground, I am not driving, it is okay therefore for me to drink. Come on, pour me one before I declare Jihad on your ass and your period,". We were all cracking up and rolling on the ground.

Osman poured everyone a drink. We toasted each other and tossed back the glasses.

"You owe me one, this is your second and it's my first, so let us keep democracy and equality alive, for God's sake. You know my favorite religious figure was Christ who turned water into wine, what a godly man. We Muslims are supposed to believe in Christ, and I adore him. Then Muhammed came and said no drinking and driving," said Fayzollah with a big smile and I could see he was full of joy.

"Then, what about women? You know God is serious about that," I said.

"What about women?" He replied.

"I mean womanizing," I said quietly and sort concern for what I said, I thought I went too far. I wanted to take back what I said, but then it was already too late.

"That is nuisance, my friend, let me tell you the same people who told you that you should not womanize, they turned around and do exactly what they tell others not do. Harona Al Rashed, he was the Islamic Emperor during Islam's golden age. He had a garden of his own women. He had a big palace with ladders leading to the upper floors, his stairs were not made of planks or stone, instead he had one young beautiful woman as each rung. As he climbed, he held each woman's breast. Imagine that. He was the head of the Islamic Empire in his time. If you read the Torah, that is the holy God's book, you come across many prophets who had several wives. Even the prophet Muhammed himself had more than one wife but we don't know for sure how many he had," Said Fayzollah, waving his drink around, and you could tell he was really enjoying himself.

"So what is wrong with that?" I asked.

"There are many things wrong with that, its immoral to use any religion for your own pleasure or your own personal interests. God just doesn't with that."

"Let us talk about the forty virgin women for every man in heaven. That is one of the reasons I want to go to heaven. Just imagine what fun that will be," said Osman.

"It's the most stupid thing people ever talked about, it makes heaven look like a brothel for a rich man. When I preach and tell people the truth, they think I am an atheist. Man, where in the Qur'an did God say that? I challenge anyone to find that in the Qur'an. It's the word of politicians who misuse Islam for their own purposes." He continued, "they talk about all these virgins, where can you find them? Even in heaven. I tell you that there are only forty virgins altogether in heaven. Not forty per person but forty all together, period." He put his glass down and clapped his hands once,' then continued, "then you may do your work here kids, if you wait to have it in heaven, I promise you there will be a drought of virgins there. Are you people stupid? You think God will have the stomach for orgies and having forty virgins for every man? First, where are all these virgins coming from? I must tell you that you will be kicked in the ass by forty giants but not kissed by forty virgins. I want to make it clear to you and all those idiots who have such a fantasy," Fayzollah said.

"Please don't disappoint me, I have been praying to go heaven everyday not because of food or wine but because of the forty virgins and now you say that's not true," said Barywan.

"Tell us about prayers," I asked just to get some laugh out of it.

"We contradict ourselves all the time, here you have a Kurdish proverb saying, 'If it was for the prayer, all goat droppings would turned to dates,' yet in the Qur'an God says, 'call me, I am close to you, and I will answer your prayer."

"My friend, God has a weird sense of humor. On one hand he wants you to pray and tells you he'll respond. Sure he always does, but almost always the answer is no. Let me tell you one more thing, boys. They tell you when a little kid or baby dies, they will became the birds in heaven. Where did that come from? From some man with a good imagination but yet people say that's just like something coming from God."

"I have two kids and they are constantly crying. Imagine having these kids as the birds of heaven, then you will have crying babies just like mine, and enough to take your head off. That will make you plead for vacation in hell. So what I am telling you is that people have been for centuries putting words in God's mouth. They tell you things on behalf of God and his prophets, which has no truth."

"You gave us enough examples of that. Do you think we'll go to heaven?" asked Osman.

"Well I have given you enough, already, so reciprocate and give me another drink," said Fayzollah as he stared at the bottle Osman was holding.

"Mullah, now you've drunk more than everyone else," said Barywan.

"Just one more, please."

Barywan took the bottle from Osman and poured him another drink.

"Here you go," said Barywan.

"I forgot your question," said Fayzollah.

"Do you think we all go to heaven?" asked Osman.

"Hell no, God made it so difficult to get there, and sometimes I think he will have it all for himself."

We kept laughing. We kept talking and we all fell asleep, one after another.

Osman got up and said, "Rauf, let's have another shot."

I got up and rubbed my eyes. "You woke me up.... God, the air smells so good.

Look at the beauty of the full moon. Yes, let us have another one," I said.

He reached for the bottle and it was empty.

"You bastard Fayzollah, how could you drink all that Arak? He was drinking from the bottle not the glass," said Osman.

I laughed so hard, I don't think I ever laughed so hard in my life, as I thought about this conservative idiot drinking that much and also the expression on Osman's furious face.

Most mullahs in Kurdistan are poor. Mullahs used to live on what people gave them. In villages, people paid a portion of their tithe to the mullah and that came down to a very little. People in villages also offered them grain and other food to live on. There were no seminaries or other official collage to enroll in order to be a Mullah, therefore, people who decided to be Mullah had to go to the big masques and get their education from the mullah's in those mosques. In the big mosques there were always students who wanted to be mullahs and these students went to see several mullahs and went to different towns in the course of their studies. Students used to come every evening to the houses, and every house gave him a piece of bread or two, they collected their bread and usually cooked a very meager meal for themselves. Every once in a while people who wanted to give to charity would cook a meal and took it to them.

Mullahs in Kurdistan offered many services to the people and they were not into politics. Mullahs used to give services, teach faith, offer service in weddings and funerals, and preach on Fridays, Muslim's holy day. That was short and barely exceeded half an hour. During their preaching they talked about the importance of prayer and most of the time and almost in every session they talked about helping the poor and needy. In Islam, supporting those who are widows and orphans is considered high on the list of giving.

People in non-Kurdish area in Iran are Shiites and mullahs had a lot of power. People offer their tithe, a fair amount to mullahs; and they grew wealthy and powerful. By contrast, in Kurdistan people give to the mullahs voluntarily, and they were by no means rich or powerful. Mullahs in Iran lived a good life and they were wealthy, and for that matter what comes naturally with wealth is power. Iranian mullahs also talked politics and they bashed the authorities if they didn't like them. By contrast Kurds wanted mullahs to take care of God's work and, it's not for the mullahs to declare revolution or promote or disgrace leaders unless the principles of their politics were atheistic or ungodly.

The Shah of Iran wasn't popular among most of the Iranian, and that spoke for the poor and unprivileged, but what the Shah of Iran had was money, and he tried to buy all the prominent religious people and mullahs, most of whom wound up on the Shah's payroll. That is to be said of contrasting Kurdish Mullah's with their counter part in Iran.

My brother Hemen and my sister Ronak were still both living with my parents, my brother Abdul was at the time in Sulaymanya and he was in his last year of study at the Agricultural Institute. My brother Hemen was the baby of the house, and when he was just about two years old, he spent a lot of his time playing with some cats. He'd attempting to sit on a cat, thinking he could ride it like a horse. He'd get close to the cat, and as the cat stopped, he'd try to sit on back of the cat. He didn't notice the cat had slipped away, so his butt would hit the brick and rock floor. Then he'd cry and curse the cats. He kept doing that over and over until his butt was all red from falling on the floor.

I saw the university of Sulaymanya was closed and all the university faculties and students had joined the Kurdish revolution. These students and faculties were given a salary by the Kurdish revolution, but it was meager and just enough to survive on. The revolution had little revenue.

It survived on aid provided by the US intelligence and the Shah of Iran. I saw corruption amongst Kurdish leaders most of whom has gotten wealthy on expense of people's misery while their leader Barzany has made no attempt to cleanse his ranking file from prevailing corruptions, indeed his own cronies were the most corrupt. I noticed the revolution had over-extended itself to the point that the revolution couldn't pay to support all the people it had attracted.

Meanwhile, I wasn't convinced that the revolution could protect people in areas they controlled. We dealt with a powerful and rich enemy, an enemy that was cruel, barbaric and could get any weapon it needed to crush the Kurdish revolution. The government was able give concessions to make a deal with its adversaries, the US as well Iran if it desired. I knew that one day the Kurdish revolution was going to end and I might be handed over to the Iraqi regime. Given the weakness of the Kurdish leaders, the corruption and the source of their backup, it was inevitable that would end tragically.

My summer was coming close to an end. That visit happened to be my last time in Kurdistan. At the end of my trip, I was very much convinced that was going to be my last trip to Kurdistan so I tried to see as many of my friends and relatives that I could.

It was my last night I was sitting with my parents, we had dinner and had a couple kerosene lamps burning. It was a beautiful night except for some mosquitoes around. My mother was sad that I was leaving. She took nothing for granted and was apprehensive about the future as many people did. I agreed with her fear given what happened to us and our town.

"So, you will leave us tomorrow," Mom said.

"Yes, that's it for this trip mom," I said.

"I want you to write us and there are always people coming and going who can bring us your letters," she said.

"I will be doing just that, Mom," I said.

"I don't want you to go on like you have been so far, writing us once every six months. That is not fair to us. I am always worried about you," said my mother.

"I want you to focus on your studies, and come back as a doctor," said my father.

"That's why I left, to study," I replied.

"So, what is your plan after you finish school?" my dad asked.

"First, it's a seven-year program, I haven't even entered my first year. God knows what is going to happen in seven years. Let's take one day at a time," I said.

"Rauf, I'm growing old. All I want is for you to finish your schooling and be in a comfortable enough position to help your brother Hemen, your sister and your mom."

"Don't worry," I said.

"Do you want more tea?" Mom asked my father.

"No, that is enough. Can you cut the watermelon?" my father asked.

"I have it already cut, let me get it" she went and came back with a tray of sliced watermelon.

"Rauf, Son, what if things get bad and we can't see each other?" asked my mother.

"No, Mom, don't bother yourself with those kind of thoughts, just take one day at a time and that is what our life has come down to," I said

"I am worried, that's all. When there is war, there is always fear. I am fearful. I hope that this war is over soon and this government will seek peace rather than war and bloodshed," she said.

"Mom, this is getting too complicated, and it's far out of our control. Just leave it there and let's have some of that watermelon," I said. I reached over and had some.

"It's good Mom, really sweet," I said.

"It's getting late for me, I should be going to bed. I'll see you tomorrow," my father said as he got up to go to bed.

My mother was still sitting by the *samovar* and Hemen was lying asleep in her arms. I went to sleep.

Next day I woke and had our breakfast. Then Osman and his friend Sarbast showed up to say goodbye. I told my mother I wanted to go for a short walk with Osman and Sarbast. We all took a cup of tea with us. We arrived at the little stream that was at the border dividing Iraq and Iran.

"Let's sit here for a minute," I told Osman and Sarbast.

Osman got his cigarettes out and he passed, we all lit up our cigarettes.

"You know the reason I brought you here?" I asked.

"I thought you just liked the early morning as you used to when we were in high school. Also, I think you wanted to stop by this little water stream that divides Kurdistan and separates Iraqi Kurds from Iranian Kurds said Osman.

"Yes but if I happen not to see you again, this water stream resembles our suffering," I said.

"Look at the stream and see how clear the water is. See how sands and gravels are dancing! But I see something else about us as Kurds," said Osman.

"Yes, I see the faces and see the crying of so many of Kurds who gave their lives for our freedom, I see so many faces struggled to have this stream just to be a stream not a border," said Sarbast.

"Yes my friends, there are the faces of unknown soldiers who tried to unify people from both side of this stream, now one nation and two countries. When we go to the border of Syria and Turkey we see the same injustice," I said.

"We are fighting as are the Kurds in Turkey, Syria and Iran, as our forefathers fought, and we will overcome," said Sarbast.

We sat in silence smoking cigarettes and drinking our tea, and stared deep into that little water stream. I knew if that stream could talk, it would have stories of generations whose lives were as difficult as ours. It could tell the story of struggle and battlefields where we didn't succeed to unite our land. I wondered our dream for the day when we would be a sovereign nation will ever become a reality.

Afterward we left and walked back home to see my parents and to get ready to leave. We got back home and had our breakfast. After break fast I got my suitcase out and got ready to leave.

That was my farewell, since I haven't been back. That was my last trip to my homeland and the beginning of my isolation from the land and its people which both meant so much to me.

Chapter Nineteen

In 1976 for an extended period, the US State Department worked overtime pressuring Saddam Hussein and the Shah of Iran to agree on resolving their border disputes. The only bargaining token Iran could use to get concession from Saddam was abandoning the Kurdish revolution. In March of 1976, the Shah of Iran and Saddam Hussein were brought together in Algeria by Henry Kissinger to shake hands and agree to resolve their territorial disputes. Iran and the US would stop aiding the Kurdish revolution so that the armed struggle would end.

The Kurdish revolution was obviously in trouble. Mustafa Barzani had to decide the fate of his armed men and the fate of tens of thousands of Kurdish refugees in Iran.

When we, the Kurds in Tehran, heard that news, our gatherings became like funerals. We didn't know what to expect. The Kurdish leaders mostly came to Tehran. At the time I spent a great deal of time with Harseny. I was eager to follow any new developments and Harseny knew everything. At the time Barzani was in Teheran and Harseny used to see him every day and spend a great deal of time with him. People were still hopeful that Barzani would not stop and keep on fighting.

At the same time Harseny had an office in Teheran. I used to go there and sit down in his office and listen to what his friends had to say. Most of the people who came to his office were prominent members of the KDP and others were poets and writers.

We knew that Barzani was in town, and all the Iraqi Kurds in Tehran wanted to know what his decision would be. Barzani was the only leader, even though we had a political organization, the KDP, but the Kurdish revolution was very much a dictatorial revolution with only one man's decision, Mustafa Barzani's. There wasn't any such thing as a democratic process to help us through that difficult time. All decisions regarding the future of the Kurdish revolution was going to be decided by Barzani.

That was the longest and most powerful revolution in Kurdish history, and unlike the others, it had the support of the great majority of Kurds, not only in Iraq but also in Turkey, Iran and Syria. It was every Kurd's dream. It was a hope for freedom, we thought of it as a dawn of a new age and the time that struggle could bring our dreams of freedom and independence to reality.

So many lives were invested in that revolution yet it was struck down by one handshake with the United States' influence playing as a referee to bring the Shah of Iran and Saddam Hussein together. That bargain was the funeral of the Kurdish revolution.

No one imagined that a revolution of almost one hundred thousand armed men could be ended so fast. It happened the day after Barzani decided not to fight. No one imagined a revolution with backing by such a powerful political organization and so much internal support could end as it did.

At the end, when the dust settled and Barzani asked people to lay down their weapon, there were still scattered groups who fought like heroes. They knew their resistance would get them nowhere but they didn't trust Saddam's regime. They fought and they wanted to die with dignity on the battlefield rather than live under Saddam's regime with torture. We kept hearing more and more about these heroes while our leaders were given asylum and as some enjoyed life with accommodations provided for by the Shah of Iran, in particular Barzany's family and their close circle. One could not say for sure how much money Kurdish revolution had at the time, but Harseny informed me there was about 150 million dollars. It was all in Barzani's name and they kept it secret from people.

I knew the revolution was ended, and if I stayed in Iran I would not be able to go home. I didn't feel comfortable living in Iran, in particular Iranian Savak with their machinations, imprisonments and torture.

I thought it was my last chance to go home, visit my parents and see my hometown. I got myself prepared. One early morning I took a bus to Sanandaj, a major Kurdish city in Iran. From there I took bus and taxi to get to Shaykh Osman's house in Dorwa, which was located near Iraq's border with Iran. My plan was to have a trip to Halabja be arranged for me by Shaykh's family.

I arrived at Dowrwa late in the afternoon. I met Shaykh for the first time. That night I had dinner with Shaykh himself, and they had cooked deer meat with rice and fried chicken. Deer meat is a special treat and served to someone very special. Deer were not sold and had to be hunted. The Shaykh was about eighty years old at the time, but still looked strong and healthy. I met his brother Shaykh Mawlana who was a year younger than Shaykh, the father of Dr. Serajaddeni.

In the Shaykh's house, regardless of circumstances, people were coming from and going to Iraq, and I was told that Saddam was already back in most of Kurdistan. That was when I knew I might never be able to go back home. I was troubled, disappointed and felt the purpose of my trip was defeated.

As usual Shaykh's house was crowded with Naqishbendi's and their followers. I met many more new relatives for the first time. I enjoyed the crowd and stayed there for a few days and then went back to Tehran.

That was my first year in the school of medicine. After the demise of the Kurdish revolution, I felt vulnerable and insecure and, as a result, I had no motivation to go forward and I flunked some of my classes, yet I didn't really care. I was telling myself what even I failed all my classes, still I could get a job writing for a radio station through my relatives' connection or do something like that.

I saw more scrutiny by Savak, I knew I was being watched closely. In my dormitory room I saw one janitor over and over, cleaning outside my room with his mop. As he mopped the tiled floor, he'd eavesdrop on what I was saying. The hallway by my room always shone and was the cleanest spot in the entire dorm, probably in the entire city of Tehran. One day as I came out in my room, I saw the janitor was mopping the floor and obviously he was eavesdropping on me again. When I opened the door I crashed into him.

"Sorry mister, pardon me. I hope you're okay," I said angrily.

"I'm okay, are you all right?" he said

"Why spend so much energy on one little spot? How about the rest of the dorm?

Or how about anywhere else in Tehran for God's sake? What is your obsession with cleaning this one place?" I said.

The janitor still kept doing what he was doing and entirely ignored me, pretending like nothing happened, and said nothing, took his mop and left.

The person next door heard the conversation, I knew him but in Iran you couldn't trust anyone in particular with my situation. He was a Kurd and seemed like a nice fellow. I had talked to him every once in a while. His name was Amer.

"Mr. Naqishbendi, what's going on?" he asked.

"I don't know, forgive me for being so loud, things just got on my nerves."

"Sorry, I wasn't really trying to be nosy, but I'd seen that guy eavesdropping on you many times. I didn't want to tell you and worry you," said Amer.

We were both talking in the very low tones so that no one could hear us, at the same time looking around to make sure that no one was around.

"Mr. Amer, this is not about feelings, this goes much beyond that," I said.

"Mr. Naqishbendi I must tell you, you are a target but I don't know what is going on. Please be aware that you are watched," said Amer.

"Thank you sir, I need to go I will see you later," I said.

"Goodbye, Mr. Naqishbendi," said Amer.

This went on for a long time. I saw my privacy was violated, and my peace of mind was stolen from me. I could go nowhere without thinking Savak agents were following me.

One early morning I was called to the dorm's administrations office. I asked for the subject matter and was told it would be discussed in person. I went to the administration's building. I feared it wasn't going to be good and couldn't think of anything that might have triggered that.

I entered the building. There was an armed policeman and an administrator there.

"I am Rauf Naqishbendi, you called me about half an hour ago," I told the dorm administrator.

"Oh, yes. Mr. Naqishbendi, please have a seat, my name is Ali."

I sat down.

"Mr. Naqishbendi, the reason I called you, you have been reported as a drug addict. You know we can't allow that in the dorm. If you want to protest it, you'll need to go to the health lab and have your blood tested. I'll give you the name of the lab," said Ali. He pulled out some files and took a document and handed to me.

"You need to go to the lab today, and you have one week to settle this matter. If you can't get your name cleared, you will be expelled from the university and for sure the dorm," said Ali.

"Okay, Mr. Ali. Thank you and I'll try to get back to you soon," I said and left the office back to my room.

I hadn't touched any drugs; I didn't even know what drugs might look like. I have never been a user of any drugs.

I went to take the blood test and it comes back positive. I knew right away that was nothing more than a setup.

I called Dr. Madeh Naqishbendi and told him that I needed to see him. He was the best to come to my rescue and get me out of that mess. I didn't want to tell him the story on the phone because I was afraid that the telephone might be wiretapped, and if I were to tell him anything that would cause myself even more trouble. We decided to see each other in his brother Shaykh Naseh's house that night. I left the dorm and went to Shaykh Naseh's house.

Madeh showed up an hour after I arrived Naseh's house.

"So, Rauf, what is bothering you?" asked Dr. Madeh.

I handed him the letter I got from school indicating that I was a drug addict.

"Would you read this letter?" I said. He took the letter and read it.

"This is so stupid and ridiculous," Dr. Madeh said.

"If that is not enough, please read this," I said. I handed him the lab test results.

"This is even more ridiculous. You should not gone to this lab, instead you should have let me handle it," said Dr. Madeh.

"Sorry, I thought this might've been a case of mistaken identity or just an error, I didn't know it was a setup."

"Yes it's a setup. They knew what lab to send you to for the blood test. They sent you to the lab of a hospital that is run by Savak," said Dr. Madeh.

"So what do I do now?" I asked.

"I know you are not involved with drugs, not you or any member of the Naqishbendi family. They sent you to this hospital and they wrote the result even before they took your blood test. Tomorrow we will be going to a reputable lab and get the results from them," said Dr. Madeh.

"Thanks, hopefully I can clear my name," I said.

"This will be taken care of. Don't dwell on it or get yourself upset," said Dr. Madeh.

"My God how I can not get upset? What else could they have done more insulting than this? This is psychological warfare," I said.

"Yes it is, what you think they are doing? This is the intelligence agency's practice. They exist to harass people. They are not there to help people. Once they don't like someone, this is the kind of the dirty trick they'll do against them. Do me a favor don't talk politics to anyone you don't know," said Dr. Madeh.

Shaykh Naseh was sitting all that time having said nothing, going through the letters and getting angry, he seemed angry. I could see that through his facial expression. "Rauf we can't afford any more than what's already happened to this family and our followers. Look at what's happened in Halabja recently, and Saddam is back in power. The imprisonments, executions and torture of the members of our family and of others. My brother, this is not the right time to be Kurd anywhere, whether in Iran or Iraq or Turkey or Syria. Things have always been bad and now all four countries are united to suppress the voice of freedom with help of the superpowers, the United States and the Soviet Union," said Shaykh Naseh.

"I know that, but I don't know what to do. I can't go back to Iraq," I said.

"Not Iraq. You have close family ties to Harseny. You were granted a scholarship in Iran through the Kurdish revolution. If the Iraqi government gets a hold of you, you will be send in front of a firing squad. You stay here in Tehran and see how things develop," said Shaykh Naseh.

"I know that I can't go back home, but what do I do if I can't clear my name? I can't even get a job in this country, and I will be expelled from college," I said.

We kept talking for a while and that night I stayed in Shaykh Naseh's house.

The next day after breakfast Dr. Madeh showed up to take me to the hospital for the blood test. We arrived at the hospital and we were directed to the lab. I was given forms to be filled out. I filled out the paperwork and Madeh left for a bit.

I sat there, waiting for about fifteen minutes for my blood to be drawn, but my name wasn't called. I asked the clerk, "Ma'am, sorry to bother you, I wanted to remind you I am here in case you've missed my name," I said.

"Sure, Mr. Naqishbendi. I took your form. Just be seated, and I'll call your name soon," she said.

I sat down and was so nervous, I couldn't wait to have this thing over with. I was afraid with some twist of bad luck the result would confirm that I was a drug addict. If that happened, I'd embarrass my family and they wouldn't forgive me. I feared anything or everything could go wrong.

It got to be half an hour, and Dr. Madeh had disappeared and my name wasn't called. I must say it was a nasty and an anxious trial. It was unfair and totally out of my hands, and all I knew was that I had to defend myself and not to allow being labeled as a drug addict.

After almost an hour had passed, Dr. Madeh came back, and I was still waiting for my blood test to be taken. He talked to the clerk. The clerk called me and took me to a room where a nurse drew my blood. When my blood drawn, I got out and back to the hospital lobby short after I saw Dr. Madeh. He approached me with a big smile, "So, now they drew your blood Just came back an hour and they should have the result."

Dr Madeh left to work. I hang out for another hour and went back to the lab to see if they have blood test result. I went to the clerk and she had the result form me. She handed to me.

The result was negative.

That was a sigh of relief and felt lucky having such a caring relatives and I thanked God for them. I rushed back to the university and I had the paper work to reinstate my status and clear my name.

At the end of April 1976, most of the Kurdish refugees had returned to Iraq but hundreds of the high-ranking Kurdish Democratic Party members and thousands of others stayed in Iran. The United States and European countries gave asylum to those who wanted to leave Iran. A month later I heard the news that political asylum would be granted to selected people.

When I heard about it, I went to Harseny's office. I arrived at his office and sat with him. His reception as usual brought served tea. We sat down and he talked about his business with me for a while. I waited until he was done. "Did you hear about the application for political asylum in the United States and Europe?" I asked.

"Yes, Muhmood upstairs has been working on that," said Harseny.

The floor above was the Kurdish consulate and they had a staff of three or four employees.

"I thought about it and want to consult you. How you feel about having me apply for it?" I asked Harseny hesitantly for I wasn't sure he would like that idea.

"It's up to you. I brought you here through the revolution and got you a scholarship. You were admitted in school of medicine, and do you really want to give that all up?" He asked.

"I wish I was happy here and could stay near you and your family and have graduated from college. In fat, it's not even a matter of being happy...I'm afraid and I think that anything bad can happen to me here. With the recent false accusation by Savak and their monitoring my every move, I'm concerned. It's also been a drag on my studies," I said.

"Explain," he said.

"I have a hard time focusing on my studies and I am behind," I said.

"So you want to go to America or Europe, or perhaps more simply, you want to leave Iran."

"I've been considering it," I said.

"So, that is easy, at the Kurdish Consulate office upstairs they all know you, and I will tell Dr. Shafeq you are seeking asylum abroad." He said.

"Can I go and talk to them about it now," I asked eagerly.

"You may go now but come back afterward,".

I left his office, walked upstairs to Dr. Shafeq's office.

That made me happy because I couldn't do something like that without his approval. He was like the elder of my family who have been with me every step of my life since I graduated from high school, and he meant to me as much as my father. With all my father's relatives around in Tehran, he was the one I could count on the most, and he was willing to help me as much as he could.

Dr. Shafeq's office represented Kurdish democratic party in Teharan. Even though the Kurdish revolution ended, but that office left to operate for a while. I entered the office, Muhmood who was an administrator, and friend of mine had me to have a tea with him and we talked for about half an hour. Then he let me to Dr. Shafeq's office. He was talking on the phone and pointed to a seat to be seated. Soon he got off the phone and we shook hand.

"Well, Rauf I was just with Mr. Harseny on the phone before you showed up. He mentioned that you are seeking asylum. You are lucky because I can manage that for you. You have a choice between going to America or Europe. Let me know which one do you prefer," he said confidently.

"I think America is a better choice, which do you suggest?" I asked humbly.

"I got my PHD in the U.S, and if you are ambitious, I think America will do you good," he said.

"Then let us leave it there," I said.

"Good, so I will have Muhmood to file your application, and that will take about two weeks. Just start getting ready. Muhmood will contact you and he will manage your trip and let you know in detail," he said.

I thanked him and went back to Muhmood. We talked about my asylum. He told me he would call me the day before my departure, and at that day I should check into a designated hotel and the next day Savak vehicle will take me to the airport, and will be handed a temporary visa to West Germany. He told me that the cost of the trip is covered by the US government.

I was completely taken by surprise as how this can be managed so easily. Just one visit to Dr. Shafeq's office and let it be known that I will leave Iran to America in two weeks. I went back to Harseny's office and he told me he had just hanged up the phone with Dr. Shafeq and that I will be out of Iran in two weeks.

The following two weeks I visited all my relatives in Tehran, and for most part of it Omar accompanied me. It wasn't an easy occasion to say goodbye to all those near and dear friends and relatives. Omar was my roommate for more than a year, we were almost together at all time except when I spend my time with Harsey's. Not only a roommate, Omar also was my classmate in most of my classes.

Just about two weeks, early in the morning, I received a phone call from Harseny informing me that my asylum to America has been granted, and should go to see him immediately. I went to Harseny's office that same morning. He told me I should be getting ready to travel next day. He invited me to spend dinner with them and to spend my last night with him and his family. Then after dinner, I should be going to Hotel Vanak and in the morning I will be taken to the airport.

I had dinner with Harseny's family. Harseny's children were young and I felt bad leaving them. I used to take them to movies, parks and entertain them.We had dinner and we talked all about the prospects of my journey. I gathered that they were happy for me to leave Iran as it had become a trap for me, but they were still sorry to see me go. After all those years that we were so close together, we'd soon have an ocean and thousands of miles of lands separating us. In a meanwhile I worried about them in particular Harseny and his safety.

After dinner I said good night and took the bus to the dorm. It was about 8:00 P.M. and I couldn't wait to get to the dorm and get my suitcase. I was fearful that Savak might mess up everything for me and jeopardize my political asylum in US. I had a feeling that they might come up with some setup. I got to dorm and Omar was there. I sat with him and we chat for a while. I got my suitcase and walked out of the dorm accompanied by

Omar. Then we said goodnight knowing I would meet him in airport next day.

The night before I left Iran, I was in the hotel, and about a half dozen other Kurds were all in the hotel to leave Iran the next day. I sat with the Kurds in the hotel and had a couple drinks. That was enough to get me ready for bed. I left to my hotel room and went to bed. Still I was afraid that something might go wrong and the whole thing would be canceled. I knew that if I were to remain in Iran, at some point all the Iraqi Kurds including myself would be turned over to Saddam in exchange for another concession to the Shah, or if that didn't happen, I would be sent to prison. In any case, my staying in Iran would have been regrettable.

The next day I received a wakeup call from the lobby, got my things together, and one of Savak's Land Rovers picked us up to take us to Tehran airport.

Harseny, his children and his wife. came to say goodbye to me at the airport. When I saw them I was in tears. I held the children, my God, what a painful moment. I'd lived with them for almost two years back in Kurdistan and for the two years they were in Tehran, I was with them most of the time, and if it wasn't for him I would never had a chance to be granted scholarship in Tehran University. When the time came to leave them behind, I wasn't sure if I would ever see them again.

"You have been like my father. You have done so much for me that I can never forget. I wish that one day I could pay you back or at least to your children," I said to Harseny as I was crying.

Harseny replied, "Whatever I've done for you I did as a matter of duty and love. If you feel the need to owe anyone anything, that will be the Kurds. Do well for them, for they are your people and you are a part of them. I want to tell you that I will always be there when you need me, but I hope you will not. I hope you will prove that you are the one Kurd who can help others rather than asking for help yourself," He continued. "I spent most of my life pursuing the struggle for the freedom of my people, and I mean my people no matter whether they are in Iraq, Iran, Turkey or Syria. We all are disappointed with the collapse of our revolution as we were sold out. Remember the end of our revolution doesn't mean the end of our struggle. It's just the beginning of our struggle, as we will see the next revolution on the horizon. I assure you that we will be free and independent one day. I may or I may not be here to see it, but if I am here, we will celebrate together. If I am not, you celebrate when my dream of an independent and free Kurdistan at last sees the sunlight."

He continued, "you leave behind your people and their country, prisoners of the biggest jail in the world. Do what you can do for their freedom. When you arrive in the US and get settled, you can tell American people all about the Kurds and let our cause to be known," Harseny said.

We held each other, and I held his children and I kissed every one of them more than once. Then I left. I left them and looked behind me and saw Harseny and his family. They stood out right in my heart and I could remember their kindness to me, and how all those years Harseny worried so much about me and wanted to do everything he could for me and my family.

I found it so strange, often life itself seems to be strange and foreign to us. Where I came from and where I was going to both seemed like a puzzle. I knew why I'd left home, why I'd gone to Tehran and why I was leaving Tehran, but where I was going was uncharted territory. I realized the uncertainty of my life, uncertain about everything and certain about nothing.

I started thinking about the new life that I would start in America. I would be going to a country where it would be me and only me, not knowing even one person, and not having even a single member of my immediate family. If I get sick it would be none of my beloved around me, and when I die perhaps no one even may know.

Later on, after I settled in the US and was living in New York, one of my fellow Kurdish friends, Dr. Jalal, who obtained his PhD in physics at UC Berkey, at the time he was a researcher for the United technology told me the story of Professor Marywani, one of the early Kurdish immigrants who came to the US. There wasn't many Kurds in the United States then. In fact, when I arrived in New York there were less than half a dozen Kurds in the whole state. Professor Marywani got sick and my friend had heard his story. During his last days, professor Marywani was crying like a child and begging to find someone who he could speak his last words to in Kurdish. He died in a foreign land away from his own people.

If one day I die, I'll be on my hospital bed all alone and not even one of my near relatives or immediate family will be there to say goodbye. When I hear the news of someone dying, I have to go off by myself to cry all alone. If I make great achievements in this life I will have to celebrate with others who may mean not much to me or celebrate alone. I realized was going to the United States as a political refugee and all that meant was that I'd come from a nation devastated and I'd escaped death and prosecutions. If that was the case, how selfish I felt—I'd let myself out and left others to suffer.

I got on a plane and we were to go to West Germany. I was given a temporary visa, one way from Iran to West Germany. As soon I got to Frankfurt, Germany, the temporary visa expired. The US officials picked me up at the Frankfurt airport. As I got to the airport the immigration officers from West Germany were there, and they came to help me and other Kurds. I went to get my suitcase and it wasn't there. I found out that it had been stolen, so I left the airport empty handed. The next day I went back with a Kurdish gentleman who'd been designated by the Kurdish Democratic Party to help us in Germany. My suitcase was stolen and really the only thing I had there and meant anything to me were the few photos of my family, a few Kurdish books and my friend Aram's writing.

I was taken with about a half a dozen or so other Kurds to a village near Frankfurt. The name of the village if my memory serve me right was Buding, and they had a house for us. The house was big and had at least six rooms, a large living room and a dining room. The house was neatly landscaped and it had a swimming pool and ping pong table. There was a cook and couple ladies to help us and they guided us when we wanted to go out of the house.

We stayed there for about three weeks while they had all our paperwork done, and at the end they got us plane tickets on board a Pan American flight to New York City. It was the summer of 1976. At last I arrived at America and I end up to be a proud adopted son of America, and America added to my hopes and my security, yet as to be seen the tragedy in my native land subtracted so much from my life.

Chapter Twenty

I arrived at New York Kennedy Airport late in the evening. There were a couple of Kurdish gentlemen there who lived in New York area along with a few Kurdish refugees who'd been in the New York area for a couple of months. They came to receive us along with an officer from the International Rescue Committee.

That night they dropped us at Hotel Latham in the lower part of Manhattan. At that time there were two Kurdish men by name Ahmed and Najar staying at Hotel Latham as well. They were informed that I was coming to N.Y.C. Shortly after I arrived at the hotel they came to see me. We introduced ourselves. Ahmed was from Mosel, and Najar was from Sulaymanya. Ahmed had introduced me to his Armenian friend named Nino. We chatted for a while and they appeared to be too eager to show me around. I thought they undermined how far I came from and how tired I was. An important point I considered was that I had less than a hundred dollar. I wasn't sure how long that would last, therefore, I was afraid if I go with them and spend from a little money I had. I was eager to see what America looked like and I went out with them. I thought that I heard a lot about America and I should see it all for myself. I went out with them. We walked for more than twenty city blocks to Times Square. I felt that I was in a different world than they were, I still much influenced by the traveling and change of time. I was disappointed. All I saw were the drug dealers, prostitutes and strange people hanging on the street who looked like they were ready to commit some crime. At the same time amongst the same crowd, I saw well dressed people, ladies and gentlemen alike. I was confounded as how these all can be possible at the same place and the same time. It was noisy and streets were crowded with people and cars, nonstop police sirens, and fire trucks, cars honking their horns, drivers yelling at each other. Some where flipping their fingers and I thought they might be waving to each other. Then the way they screamed I knew that wasn't greeting, and, I didn't know exactly what that meant until sometimes later. Panhandlers were in every corner. The streets were nothing but dirty, pornographic places flashing naked women and selling every imaginable dirty sex toys which I never seen before and neither I wanted to see, magazines and movies. It wasn't to say one magazine but hundreds of them. One could see homeless people, drug addicts, drunks, and alcoholics with growling and screaming hangovers. I had never seen a place like that in my life with so many corrupted people all in one place at the same time. It was a reflection of moral disgrace and a system of people that has gone so far in pursuing immorality against their own faith. As we walked, we got stopped by people on the street handing away leaflets with pictures of naked women. Then the contradicting and clashing scene as I saw a gracious soul with a Bible preaching and trying to get crowd's attention. I saw no one listening to him but he kept on preaching. People stopped us trying to sell us things. I didn't really know at the time what these people were trying to sell. I didn't see these people carrying any merchandise to sell. Then I was told that they were selling drugs.

It was a place where you could find almost everything God had forbidden and devil demanded. I just couldn't make anything good out of what I saw. I asked Ahmed and Nino to go back to the Hotel with me and I was really tired.

Najar was an odd character. He had his head shaved and wore a baseball hat. I didn't exactly know why he had shaved his hair but sure he looked odd. Quickly I realized that he wasn't terribly smart. What surprised me, was when we were walking, we crossed the street on red traffic lights constantly and so did the other pedestrians.

"Najar you know, we could be hit by a car. Can we wait for the green light next time?" I asked.

"No Rauf, people in America have no time to wait for green lights. People are too busy. Just wait and you'll learn all about America."

That sounded stupid even though a bunch of others did what we did, I thought those must have been from foreign countries just as we were. I let it pass.

I felt foolish. After twenty hours on a plane, I should have been resting. I felt that these guys were morons. I thought that they'd taken me to the worst place in the city, but I wasn't sure so I told myself that I'd need some more time to sort things out.

I came back to my hotel room. It was simple with a couple chairs, a bed and a bath and nothing else. Najar came and sat on a chair. I really wanted him to leave so that I could go to sleep not to say I was already tired from his nuisances. He kept talking nonsense. He started telling jokes but only he laughed at his jokes and I kept quite except at the end of his jokes I looked at him saying really is that true. After a while I felt asleep and he must have left.

The next day I woke up and had breakfast in a little coffee shop on the ground floor. It was the usual coffee shop with booths that could seat about twenty to thirty people. I had scrambled eggs and toast with a glass of orange juice. I sat for breakfast and there were two couples sitting one across from me and other facing me. I looked at the couple facing me in a front, it was a young lady about my age. She was blond with a blue eyes, sort of good looking. She steered at me for less than a minute, I don't know if that triggered her boy friend or husband to look back and give me a sour look. Soon I realized the man must be jealous and I stopped looking. Then came a man sit by himself with a newspaper in his hand. Soon he sat he started reading the paper. I thought that is the way in America. If one goes to the restaurants by himself he would take a newspaper or a magazine and when he sits he starts reading so that he wouldn't look at other men's wife or girlfriend and cause trouble. Then I looked down at my plate so that I would not provoke someone and getting beaten up. So I thought from that point on when I go to restaurant by myself I would take with me a newspaper to read even though I couldn't read well or understand much. I thought of that to be a good idea in particular if I carried with me the New York Times that may impress others.

Once I was done with my breakfast I attempted to call Professor Ahmed, who taught at dentistry colleage. When I was in Tehran Harseny had given me the Professor's number and got a letter from his brother so that he could assist me with my schooling. I went to a pay phone in a lobby. I talked to Professor Bahzad for about ten minutes. I introduced myself to him and he was very gentle and kind to me. He asked me first to get settled in and then decide what I wanted to do. If anything that he could do for me he would. When I hung up the phone, coins started pouring out by the hundreds. I caught most of it in my long shirt so that it wouldn't drop on the ground. It was like a jackpot. To make sure I got the full benefit I checked around to be sure I left no coins on a floor. I knew if some left would be picked up by others but I thought I needed it the most and for the time being forget others, they are Americans and they can speak English and hence they can help themselves. I quietly took it to my room and counted it. It was a bit over seventy dollars. I told myself what a good country…I hoped that would keep happening. I had a huge mirror in my room and I stood before it and told myself: "You are well taken care of. You are in this great country and watch more of the same will happen". It came to my mind that was probably why they called America land of opportunity. I had read about the gold rush and the 49ers and thought perhaps people made their fortune in America by mere luck, just as the pay phone became a slot machine for me. I got out of the hotel and rushed to hit another jackpot.

This gave me a fresh optimistic prospect regarding my life in America than the fearful doom and gloom I perceived before.

I didn't know anyone else to call other than the few people I met at the airport the night before, and I had no good reason to call them. Then I thought of going to the pay phone to call myself.

I walked a few blocks away from my hotel and found a pay phone. A big, young guy was on the phone. I waited for him to get done with his call, but the guy kept talking and talking as loudly as he could. I wondered if it was a custom in America for people to talk so loud. Well, I thought that Americans are smart and when they say things it has to be very important and wise, so I didn't blame them to be loud so that their important words wouldn't be missed. Sure, the guys in the hotel were loud. I was also reminded of Najar. He said people in America had no time to wait for green light and they cross on red light, so that made a perfect sense to me. They talked loudly so that they could be heard the first time and wouldn't have to waste time repeating themselves. I waited and the man kept talking. After a few minutes I got really uneasy about him and thought he might pick a fight with me, and if I were to fight with him, I might get deported. I had no country to go to, and I thought that if I got deported they might send me to a country of their own choice like Mozambique. I asked myself, who wants to live in Mozambique? They all want come to America. I thought I'd better leave him alone and cancel my one ticket to Mozambique.

I walked another couple blocks toward midtown and saw another pay phone, but this time one person was on the phone and another was waiting in line. I went and stood next to the lady waiting to get on the phone. Soon the lady saw me she told me that she is going to have very long phone call. She warned me but I didn't care at all for I had nothing else to do.

While I was waiting for the phone, a young girl passed by with a dollar bill in her hand, asking for change. She'd come to the right person. I had over seventy dollars of coins in my pockets and it was sort of heavy. She approached me with her dollar bill. I took a handful of change from my pocket and extended my hand. She gave me her dollar bill and took five quarters. I said nothing, but I knew that four quarters was a dollar, not five. I said to myself that wasn't a good business deal but she was pretty and when they are they can even get away from murder.

The man was still on the phone and again, he was really loud. One hand was on the phone and the other was waving nonstop just like a traffic cop. He was about fifty years old, smoking a huge cigar with a smell that could make people sick. He was very well dressed in suit and tie, shiny shoes and a handsome hat. He was spitting on the floor frequently, every time the man was spat I could see the lady next to me turning her head the other way and saying something which I didn't understand but I knew as upset as she looked, what she said wasn't anything nice. I looked the lady and she looked disgusted. I had a feeling the lady might throw up. If that wasn't enough, the lady had a big bag of sunflower seeds. As she ate the seeds, she too spat the shells right on the street. I felt like I was back home with people spitting on the street and spitting sunflower shells everywhere in a street as the streets turns to an ashtray.

The man and the lady both got done with their phone calls. I deposited a coin and dialed my hotel. The hotel operator answered the phone and I asked her to ring my room. The operator asked nastily, "What room do you want?" I barely could speak English. She got nastier and nastier and then hung up the phone. I hung up and looked for the change to pour out and nothing happened. I learned that was just beginner's luck and my welcome to America. I needed to try something else, and life can't be that easy and jackpots is not too often, and it may be only once in life time if fortune to permit.

I returned to the hotel and I had to go and meet Barbara from the International Rescue Committee, the organization who had sponsored me. The IRC's headquarters were in Manhattan and I walked there with Ahmed. I went in and Ahmed was supposed to help translate for me because he'd been in US for about three months and could speak better broken English than I did.

We went to Barbara's office, a small room with three chairs and she was sitting behind her desk with a typewriter in front of her. She was blond, blue eyes, slim with little wrinkles in her face triggered most by her smiles and she looked good. She looked sweet and acted so too with her frequent smiles.

"Welcome to America, Rauf," Barbara said.

"Thank you."

"How do you like your hotel?" she asked.

"It's good," I said.

"You can stay in your hotel and we can send you to school to learn English. At the same time we'll pay for your living expenses. Once you learn English, we'll find you a job," she said. She was constantly smiling. She had a beautiful natural smile.

"No, I don't want that," I said.

"Why not?"

"I want to go to work and learn English as I work," I said.

She paused for a moment "the only job I could get you would be a dishwashing job. Would you want that?" she asked. She looked me in the eye and I had a feeling that she thought that I would reject it.

"That's very good. I'd like that," I said to her surprise.

"All right, I will make all necessary arrangement, and I'll telephone you and you can come back and see me to discuss," she said.

"Thank you," I said.

We shook hands and said goodbye to each other.

I left and walked back to hotel with Ahmed. After a few blocks Ahmed left to go to work and I walked back to the hotel by myself. On the way I saw a grocery store, I went and checked in to see what they had to offer. The night before Najar had told me that he goes to store and buys food and eats it in his hotel room. He said that was more affordable because eating out was very expensive. It was a small store just like any typical grocery store. I looked around the store, and found cans of chicken liver pilled on the top of each other. Chicken liver was my favorite food. I was sort of surprised and wondered where in the world they'd found so many chicken livers. Back home my mother used to cook the whole chicken and there was only one chicken liver. We had to take turns having that. I picked two cans of chicken liver and I found it for less than a dollar, I couldn't wait to open two cans of chicken liver and I rushed back to my hotel room. I thought it was a great meal with a frugal price. I thought if I were to go out for a meal like that, I might have to pay ten dollars or even more.

I liked my food hot, in Kurdistan we don't eat cold meat or cold sandwiches. My hotel room didn't have grill, so I turned the hot water and let it ran until got really hot. Then I placed the can food one at a time on a small bowl filled with hot water. I let it stay for a while impatiently waiting for it to get hot. I opened the can and started eating, but I found that it didn't taste anything like the chicken liver my mother used to cook. At first, I thought that American chickens must have different liver than those in Kurdistan then contradicted myself. I forced myself to eat one full can and had started on the second when there was a knock at the door. It was Najar.

"What are you doing?" he asked.

"I'm eating my lunch," I said.

"Good thing you've learned to cook for yourself. Isn't that cheaper?" he asked.

"Yes, it is," I replied.

"What are you eating?" he asked.

"Chicken liver," I said. My face must've looked like I was going to throw up. I'd had it with that damn chicken liver. I wanted to throw it away.

"That's good," said Najar.

"Yes, would you like to finish it? I ate too much."

"Yes, let me have it," said Najar.

I handed to him. I was happy to let him have it.

Najar stopped and looked at it and for a minute.

"How does it taste?" asked Najar.

"Just eat it and you'll find out. It's okay," I said.

"You know, I can see by your face it's no good," said Najar.

"No, that isn't true at all, I love it. Come on, finish it, or I will," I said.

"Did you look at the label on the can?" he asked.

"Yes, can't you read? Doesn't that say chicken liver?" I said.

"Yes, that's right. See the cat picture?"

"What does that mean?"

"It means this is cat food. Did you really eat it?" he asked.

"Meow, meow," I said.

"That is damn right, you will be meowing for a long time. I think I should take you to see veterinarian," said Najar.

"Shut up Najar," I said.

Late in the evening the housekeeper showed up to cleanup. She looked at the garbage can.

"Sir, do you have a cat?" she asked.

I kept quite. I knew exactly what she was asking but thought I'd better be silent. If I told her the truth she would've thought that I was nuts. I must admit that in Kurdistan there wasn't such a thing as cat food or dog food. People fed their leftovers to the cats and dogs. I was really caught by surprise when I found that there were such things as pet food and pet stores.

She held up the empty can and pointed to the cat's picture on a can, "listen fellow, this is cat food. You know young man pets are not allowed in the hotel." she said.

Again I didn't reply.

"I am just telling you if they find cat in your room, you will be kicked out," she paused for a moment and resumed "this is a hotel for people not for pets. Next time you need to leave your pet home. Imagine if everyone bring their pets with them to the hotel, then it will be no hotel but zoo with pets running around everywhere. By the way how did you came here."

"I am a refugee." I said she stood in a front of me looking at me "not that I mean how you traveled to NYC." She asked.

"Oh that, yes by airplane." I replied.

"How did they let you bring the damn cat with you, well now the cat is refugee too."

I didn't know what she meant. "No cats here," I said.

"Where are you from?" She asked.

"I am from Kurdistan."

"I never heard of such. That is not a country. I heard of New Jersey, California but not Turstan." she said.

"Not Turstan I said Kurdistan." I replied.

"I meant that. You just made it up." she said that and left.

Several years later I was in Oakland, California. I knew a lady from work named Linda. I really wanted to befriend her, so no matter what she said, I agreed with her. One day I was sitting with Linda at work for coffee.

"Rauf, do you like cats?" she asked.

"Do you like cats?" I asked. I asked so that my answer would be the same as hers.

"Yes, I like cats," she replied.

"Me too," I said.

"I have a cat and I'll give it to you," she said.

"Good," I said.

"I'll drop it by your apartment this evening, just give me your address," she said.

I gave her my address and she said she'd bring the cat by that evening. Late in the evening Linda showed up with a cat and all the cat's stuff.

I wasn't allowed to have pet in my apartment. When the apartment manager saw me with the cat she had a fit, and she gave me one month's notice to leave.

My apartment was on the first floor and the door of my kitchen opened up to a small lawn. I let the cat out there, and it came back with fleas and my apartment became like flea's nest. When my friends came to my apartment they all complained of itching.

I wanted to keep the cat clean, and I gave bath almost everyday. Then the cat became like a tiger, jumping up the cabinet and scratching everywhere. Then, I clipped his fingernails.

One day I went to get the cat food, I came across that same nasty chicken liver, cat food. It was identical to the one I'd had before. I thought that I knew how it tasted and no cat should have to eat that damn thing.

The cat became a burden and I didn't know what to do with him. One day I was sitting in a café in Berkley, a young man introduced himself. His name was Jim, and we started talking.

"Do you like cats?" I asked.

"I love cats," he replied.

"I have a lovely and friendly cat. Do you want to have it?"

"Yes, please, me and my girl friend been looking for one," he said.

"You just wait here, I will be back in less than half an hour," I said.

"If you want I can come with you," he said.

"No that's okay, just stay here and I will be back," I said.

I didn't want Jim to know where I lived because I was afraid he might return the cat. I also didn't want to have to pay for whatever damages the cat might cause. I knew my cat wasn't an average cat. It acted more like a tiger. I drove home, got the cat and went back to the café. Sure enough, Jim was still waiting there. I told myself "poor guy is all excited, he doesn't know what is he about to Get."

"Jim here is the cat. This is his food and his things," I told him.

"Thank you," he said with a big smile.

"I have to run. Good luck with the cat," I said.

I left and got rid of that burden.

After I'd had such a horrible gourmet chicken liver, I decided not to eat anything in my hotel room other than fruit since I knew tomatoes and cucumbers couldn't be pet food. Whenever I ate out they gave so much food in the restaurants that barely I could even finish half of it. Then one day I asked the waitress in the restaurant, "Can you get me only half of a steak for half the money?"

"No, we don't do that in America," replied the waitress.

"How about if I bring my friend? We'll both order one meal and split it."

"No, we don't do that in America either," she replied.

It was a disappointment, since I thought I might bring Najar or Ahmed to share the meal and its cost. I thought about the waitress realizing she talked on behalf of all Americans as she said with her nasty answer: "we don't do this or that in America". I wonder if every American were talking on behalf of all Americans and that may be how things go and, wonder that kind of delegation can be a birth right or to be licensed.

One day I passed by a nice restaurant and they had their menu posted outside in a frame with glass. I read the menu but I didn't know what kind of food they were serving. I went in and asked and was told it was French food. I came back and looked the menu again. To my delight I found something that I wanted to see and that was the Chateau Brian for two. I went in again and talked to one of the waiters.

"Sir, what is 'Chateau Brian for two?'" I asked.

"It's a huge tender piece of meat gently broiled, served with potatoes and vegetables," he said.

"What is 'for two,'" I asked.

"That means we cut the steak on half, it's a meal for two people," he said.

I thought that was great. How sensible the French people were toward people with less money. Suppose two people had money to buy only one meal, then one would have to eat but not the other. I thought that was a good idea and perhaps French people couldn't afford to buy full meals and they doubled up together to have their meals in the restaurant for half price. I told myself that I should keep this in mind when I had guests, I could take them to a French restaurant where they charged one price for two people.

Then I started thinking about the waiter's description of Chateau Brian. He told me it was 'broiled gently'. I started wondering what he meant by 'gently'. Did that mean people were quiet and nice when they cooked the meat? I didn't get it. Well, I thought French people might think others were fighting and roughhouse while they cooked their meals, so to distinguish themselves from others they reminded people how gentle they are. Then I thought that may not be the case, and decided when I pass by the restaurant again I'd go back and ask exactly what the waiter meant by 'gently broiled'. When I went back and looked at the price, it was $60.00. That was ten times what I had paid for my meal. I realized then why it is for two, because that was too much money for one person. You needed two rich people to share the price. If I dined in a French restaurant, I couldn't have more than one meal a week, and for that meal I had to find someone else to split the bill. It wasn't only the $60.00 for the meal, you had to buy a bottle of wine. When I looked at the price, wine was between $30.00 to $100.00. If I went to the French restaurant and didn't have wine with the meal, they would think there got to be something wrong with me.

I gave up on the French. I thought they might not be as compassionate as I first thought.

On my third day in New York City, I received a call to go and see Ms. Barbara. I went to her office.

"Congratulations, you got a job in one of the nicest restaurants in Long Island at Montauk point," Barbara said.

"Thank you, where is that?" I asked.

"It's a few hours from here, Montauk is a resort area. You'll be working there as a dishwasher and you can stay at Journey's Inn. It's a hotel and restaurant," she said.

"Good, when do I start?"

"You go today and they'll put you to work immediately. If you don't like the place you can call me and I'll get you another job," she said.

"Thank you, Ms. Barbara," I said.

"Now this is a package with complete instructions on how to get to Montauk, and there is a telephone number for you to call once you get to Montauk. Someone will be there to take you to the Journey's Inn," she said.

"Thank you Ms. Barbara."

"You welcome and good luck and if you need anything, feel free to call me."

I went to Grand Central Station and took the train. It was a very nice Amtrak train. After about an hour I changed trains. The next train was awful. It looked even worse than those trains one saw in the old movies. It was as slow as a sick donkey; in fact I could have run faster than that train. It took hours to arrive at Montauk. Once I got to the train station I called the telephone number Ms. Barbara gave me. I waited about half an hour before I was picked up at the station by a limousine. My God, why'd they have such a huge car for only one person? I was amazed. I realized how wasteful Americans are; you went to a restaurant and they served you enough food for three people, you needed a car and they sent a limousine.

When I got to the resort, they gave me a room I shared with two other person. The next day I started working as a dishwasher and I was paid minimum wage.

I worked six full days a week. Notably, one of the great benefit about the job was getting free meal. At the Journey's Inn they had a small restaurant only for the employees, they had a chef employed full time to cook for employees. For breakfast they had eggs, toast, fresh orange juice and sausages. For lunch and dinner they always served us more than one entree and one could eat as much as desired. In addition, every once in a while I went to the kitchen and got a nice piece of steak or fish. I didn't have to pay rent because I was given a room, which I shared with others. I got along with everyone and people were friendly. Some were college students who'd come to spend their summer there and make some money.

I worked really hard. I washed the huge dishes that didn't fit or weren't suitable for the dishwasher. Some of the dishes were bigger than myself. I really didn't know much about the work habits and everything to me was strange. I thought that I had to be busy during my full eight hours, then when I didn't have dishes to wash, I went to my boss and told him I had nothing to do. Every time I told him that, he laughed and found me something else to do like mopping the floor or taking out the garbage. I didn't even know that there was such a thing as a coffee break. I must admit for all fairness employees as well as management they were very kind to me.

My roommate was Azy. He was from the Midwest and he was a student in one of the colleges in the Midwest. He was also a dishwasher. Azy drunk a lot of beer and he smoked marijuana and on his day off he went to the Montauk bars. I was wondering why the kid had to drink so much and make such a mess out of himself. Then he told me everything about himself. An alcoholic father beating his mother. He told me that he persisted that his mother to divorce his father but his mother declined his proposition. Well, I thought that his mother was happy with the beating otherwise she would have left her husband or she might have been desperate. I was amazed how open people were about their family affairs. Back home no one would tell their family affairs to others, they thought family affairs is not outsiders business. If people had good things to say about their family they said it to others and the rest they kept it to themselves. Azy was a big mess, I had to clean up after him. Later my friend Ahmed joined me and I got him a job as a dishwasher. Ahmed became my roommate and three of us shared a room. Ahmed was as messy as Azy and I had to get after them to clean up their mess. These guys were mess machines, generating messes as they went along. Azy used tell me I was like his mother, constantly asking him to clean up otherwise our room would have been a pit hole.

Journey's Inn was about a five-minute drive from Montauk, and Azy and the rest of the kids used to hitchhike. Most of the people who worked there were young students and they all smoked marijuana or any other drugs they could get. One day they were all smoking Hashish and they had no pipe so they made one from a carrot. I realized how creative Americans were. Then they used to get hungry and they asked me to bring them milk because I worked until midnight and sometimes until 2:00 A.M. I remember there were three of those kids smoking marijuana one night they came and asked me to go to the kitchen and get them milk. I must have given them more than ten pitches full of milk. When those kids smoked up they could've easily dried up a cow.

Once I arrived in the US, my primary objective was to learn English, and to learn about Americans before going out and meeting others. There were less than half a dozen Kurds living in New York City at the time. I really had no one to guide me. In that sense I was very much on my own.

I found one way to learn English and also learn about America's economic, political and government systems was through newspapers and magazines. I used to pick up any magazine people threw away and read it. I knew some English from my schooling. We studied English from the fifth grade through high school. We had at least three hours of English class a week on average. It's amazing how little English we learned given so many years of studying. Even at the last year of high school we couldn't write a letter in English or even a simple essay.

During my work at the Journey's Inn, all I did in my spare time was study English. I only went to Montauk a few times. I saved practically every dollar I made.

After a couple of month Azy went to work at the Montauk Yacht Club. After a week Azy came by and told me about a job for me in his new workplace. I went to see the manager at the Montauk Yacht Club and he offered me job as a dishwasher with about fifty cents more an hour than that I earned at Journey's Inn, with the same accommodations. I accepted his offer started working there as a dishwasher on the graveyard shift. I washed dishes for a couple hours and after that I had to cleanup the kitchen. The manager in the club liked me so I approached him for another part time job. The day after he called me and gave a part time job cleaning and mopping the hotel floor. Once I was done with my job in the kitchen at 8:00 A.M, I commenced my part-time job and continued until noon. After a while they had me supervise another person who was supposed to help me out cleaning the kitchen and washing dishes and so on.

I got frustrated by the guy who supposed to help me. He used to show up and work for half an hour, make himself the biggest sandwich stuffed with everything he found in the kitchen and then take off. He'd come back in the morning and punch his timecard. He wasn't any help so I ended up doing his job too.

Then winter came and it got really cold. There were not many customers, but still a few used to come there and rent boats for fishing. Just before the Thanksgiving holiday I returned back to New York and stayed with my friend, Tareq. He let me stay with him until I got my own apartment. Tareq Nouri was from Sulaymania, he was electric engineer but couldn't find job in his field, and he was working on repairing sewing machines. He was my helper and he assisted me in every way he could, and we became each others close friend. He was a great man and one of the most honest people I encountered.

I went and saw Ms. Barbara from the IRC.

"Good, you're back Rauf. How are you doing?"

"I'm doing fine. I am back to the city," I said.

"Your English is much better," she said.

"Thanks," I said.

"Now that you're here, you need to rent an apartment. You go ahead and find an apartment. IRC will pay the first and last month for you. We will also find you a job and you can pay your rent," she said.

"Thanks, I have money and I can pay for myself. All I need is a job," I replied.

"Good, so you did save some money. It's good to have savings," she said.

"Well, I saved practically all my money, I have saved $3,600," I said.

"That's very good. You were gone for less than five months. $3,600 is more than what you have earned. How did you manage that?"

"I worked two jobs, and most of the time I worked seven days a week," I said.

"That explain your incredible saving. I am really pleased," she said.

"Are you sure you can find an apartment?" she asked.

"Yes, for now I am staying with my friend Tareq, and there are vacant furnished apartments in his apartment complex. I will see the building manager tonight," I said.

"Very good. I will be looking for a job for you. Just call me around 10:00 A.M. every day until I place you at your new job," she said.

I thanked her and left. That same day I got myself a furnished apartment for $90.00 a month in the Astoria Queen. The apartment wasn't a dream apartment but given my situation it was good enough.

My friend Tareq told me about LaGuardia Community College in Long Island City, which was close to where I lived. I went there and got an application from admission office.

Tareq advised me that I should be reading the *New York Times* because it was a well-written paper with a good English.

When I was in Manhattan I picked up a copy of the *New York Times*. I took it home and started reading. Strangely, I couldn't find any of the vocabulary used in my dictionary. I got really frustrated. I thought the *Times'* English must be really high class English. Later on Tareq came to my apartment and saw the New York Times on my desk. "Good, you're reading the *Times*. Smart man," said Tareq.

"Not smart enough. Let me ask you man, what kind of English is this? I can't find any of the vocabulary used here in my dictionary," I said.

He looked the paper and started laughing.

"Why are you laughing? What is so funny?" I said.

"No wonder, Rauf. You picked up the Spanish version,"

"How do you know that? Do you speak Spanish?" I asked.

"No."

"Then how do you know that?" I asked.

"It tells you right there," he replied. He pointed to the top right corner of the newspaper.

"Okay, I will buy the English version from now on," I said. I felt so stupid after spending more than an hour reading that paper and going nuts with dictionary that wasn't even English. To cheer myself up, I thought after all I didn't do too bad, at least I didn't buy the Chinese version.

I wasn't doing too badly. The second day after my return to New York City I had my own apartment. As soon as I got my apartment got a telephone and I had to go to Con Edison to fill out paperwork to get electricity. It was freezing cold outside. I checked yellow pages and found two offices in Manhattan for Con Edison. One of them was around 136th street, but I don't recall the exact location. I took the subway there and managed to do whatever was needed to have the electricity turned on. After I left Con Edison office I got confused and couldn't find the subway. I decided to take a taxi. I kept walking and the taxis kept passing by. I waved to them and yell, "Taxi!" but none stopped even though most were without passengers. I walked for almost thirty city blocks in the freezing cold before I got a taxi. I was very disappointed and feared no one want my business or I might looked weird. I didn't know why after all I would pay just like anyone else.

When I went back to my apartment, Tareq stopped by after work. My apartment and Tareq's apartment both were in the same floor.

"Good, now you are all set. You just need to find a job. I am sure the IRC will get you one," said Tareq.

"You know I got frozen to the bone today," I said.

"What happened?"

"I went to Con Edison around 136th street, but after I left the office I walked for almost an hour before I got a hold of a taxi. I tell you I saw more than a hundred taxis passed by and none wanted my business," I said.

"You know, you're a lucky man. Nothing happened to you. Just don't go there any more," he said.

"Why is that?" I asked.

"That's Harlem. It's not a safe neighborhood," he said.

Less than a week after my return to the city, Barbara called me. She found me a job as a busboy at the Tavern On The Green, one of the famous restaurants in the city.

Once I started working as a busboy and knew my schedule, I went to LaGuardia Community College and got admitted. A month later I found a better apartment, a furnished one-bedroom apartment for $160.00 a month. It was a one-bedroom apartment with a small living room. Again it wasn't a dream home but I was thankful for it was by far much better than my previous apartment and I was happy with it.

While I'd been at Montauk, two more Kurds came to New York, Karem and Majeed. Karem was relatively young, about eighteen years old. Majeed was about my age. They both stayed in Manhattan at the same hotel I used to stay in.

One day I invited Karem to my place, I gave him instructions on how to get to my place. Karim was an odd person much like an absent-minded professor. Karem took a subway and he got off at a wrong station. He called me to let me know he'd gotten lost.

"Karem do you know where you are?" I asked.

"Wait, let me ask this lady," said Karem and I could hear him talking to a women.

"Never mind, I asked the lady where I am, she said she can't speak English," said Karem.

He couldn't speak more than twenty English words. All he knew were 'hi', 'bye' and a few more.

"Karem, now get out of the subway station, go to the street and call me from there," I said.

"Okay, I'll do that," he said and left the subway.

My phone rang again.

"Karem, can you tell me the street name?" I asked.

"Hold on. Let me go see the sign," said Karem.

A minute later he came back. "Yes, I got the street name," said Karem.

"What is the street name?" I asked.

"The street name is 'One Way,'" he said.

Somehow we finally managed to meet.

Later on Majeed and Karem got an apartment near where I lived. Majeed used to call me whenever he knew I was off work.

"Rauf, how are you doing?" He asked. That is how he always started his conversations.

"I am cooking," I said.

"Good thing. Get it ready. I'll join you for dinner," he said. That was the usual pattern of our conversations.

He was fussy, though. One day he came for dinner.

"What is for dinner?" he asked.

"Fried chicken liver," I said.

He said nothing. I put chicken liver on the plate and put on the dinner table.

"Come on Majeed, eat," I said.

"No, that's okay, I'll wait for the chicken breast."

"There is no chicken breast, I told you, its chicken livers," I said.

"Wait a minute…you have more than twenty chicken livers on both plates, so what happened to the rest of the chickens? It's okay, you sit down and eat. I'll cook the chicken breast," he said.

"You're so stupid, why in the world would I need to by twenty chickens? You think it's like back home you by the whole chicken? In America you can buy chicken legs, breast, liver, or any part," I said.

"I didn't know that. When I saw twenty chicken livers, I thought you'd bought twenty chickens. I was surprised and I thought you may be giving a wedding party or something like that," said Majeed.

"Well, nothing like that and eat what's on your plate,'

I had another Kurdish friend, Hussan. Sometimes I invited all my Kurdish friends to have a meal in my apartment. Hussan always asked, "What's to eat?" Whenever I told him chicken, he used to say, "No thanks. I don't eat chicken, only steak or leg of lamb."

Well I found myself with tough customers.

I got stuck with Karem and Majeed. They were roommates but they fought all the time. Karem wanted to burden Majeed and score his point and make it to a story to tell others about. One day I was home and Karem called me.

"Rauf, please come here right now," he said.

"What's wrong, Karem?" I asked.

"I'm not feeling well," he said.

They lived nearby I went to his apartment and Majeed was there too.

"You know what happened Rauf?" said Majeed as he was laughing.

"What?"

Majeed was laughing hysterically, "Seems this idiot was holding this…." He showed me an empty olive oil bottle.

"So what?" I said.

"Karem thought it was whiskey. He told me he closed his nose and drank the whole damn thing. He wanted to waste my money because it was mine. He drank all that damn olive oil and now he's complaining his stomach doesn't feel good. Are you surprise?"

"Karem, forget about yourself. Now you owe Majeed a full bottle of olive oil," I said.

A few months later both Karem and Majeed left for south California. I sort of missed them.

I felt bad for Karem. The kid was really too young to be on his own in the US. He wasn't educated and I don't think he even had the high school diploma. He was a good kid and was handsome too. He was very much willing to listen to others…except Majeed. Later on I found out that Karem's father and his brother had both been killed. His parents were in the refugee camp in Iran, but after the Kurdish revolution ended they went back to Kurdistan. Kurdistan was then under Saddam's occupation. Once the Kurdish revolution ended, hundreds of thousands of Kurds who were living in refugee camps in Iran returned to Kurdistan. Saddam slaughtered so many people for their affiliations with the failed Kurdish revolution or for running away and taking refuge in Iran.

No one told Karem what happened to his father and his brother and he didn't find out about it. He used to talk to me about his father and his brother, and every time he mentioned their names to me, I felt sad. I didn't want to tell the poor kid what happened to his father and brother for I knew telling him wouldn't do him any good. But what I struggle with was that at some point this kid needed to know.

At that time I was very disconnected with my family and there wasn't much communication, either through letters or telephone calls. That was the time the Iranian revolution started and Iran had turned into a chaotic state under the rule of the formerly deposed Shah of Iran.

The only way for me to get the news was through Harseny in Tehran. I used to call him every now and then. One day early in the morning I received a phone call from Harseny's older son Salah.

"Rauf, I don't have good news for you," he said.

"I don't expect much good news, Salah. Tell me, what's happening?" I asked.

"You know that Mustafa Barzani is dead?" he asked.

"Yes I know that, is that it for the bad news?" I asked.

"No, my father has disappeared. No one knows where he is," he said.

"How did that happen? He was in Tehran, wasn't he?" I asked.

"No, my father went to Kurdistan for Barzani's funeral. We were all there. He had his camcorder and was making a video. He was among the crowd. A couple hours later we couldn't find him. It's been three days and we don't know where he is," he said.

"Salah are you telling me he may have been kidnapped?" I asked.

"Yes, that is exactly what we think happened." he said.

"Do you think you know who might have done it?" I asked.

"Oh yes. Barzani's sons, Masaud and Idress," he said.

"How could that happen? Masaud and Idress…they are nobodies and they have no armed men," I said.

"That's not true. They still have some armed men in Iranian Kurdistan," he said.

"But how could this happen? Masaud and Idress must be mourning. I don't think they'd attempt an assassination or a kidnapping at their father's funeral," I said.

"We'll find out, Rauf," he said.

"So what's being done to get your father back?" I asked.

"My stepmother, Galawezh has gone to see Idress and Masaud," he said.

"Please keep me updated. I'll pray for your father's safe return home," I said.

I kept close touch with Harseny's family. I was all confused, I couldn't believe the sons of Barzani would ever try to harm Harseny. Harseny was one of the most loyal to their father, if loyalty to meant anything to them.

About one month had passed when Salah called again and told me Harseny had been killed. His body was never located. Harseny was the closest members of my family and he meant so much to me. I always looked up to him. Even after I left Tehran, we used to call and talk to each other once a month and sometimes more. I knew that I could not go back home, but I was hopeful that once I got an American passport at least I could go to Tehran and spend some time with him and his family. He was very much like my father. From the time I left home, he was the only one who took care of me and tried to do the best he could for me. His death left me feeling like I was wandering in the world all alone.

I was disenchanted with everything in particular my being in the US without any members of my family, but in case things at home one day got better, I needed to prepare myself to go home. I had to enroll in college so I could go back home with some kind of a degree. I got serious about my schooling. I attended school while working full at a restaurant.

I went to school and didn't know what I was majoring in. First I took English as a second language and pre-calculus and introduction to data processing courses. I attended English as a second language class, What the teacher taught us was, to the point, ridiculous. The first day in class he came in and introduced himself. He stood at the front of the class and smiled.

"This is English as a second language. That means you've all come to America. And you are all foreigners. Some perhaps make it through four years of college and get a good job, some others will end up in jail, and the rest will be crooks ripping of American citizens."

"Is that right?" he pointed to me.

I got all confused and didn't understand what a crook meant, and he talked too fast for me to understand what he was talking about. I said nothing and kept staring at him.

"Do you want to answer me?" he said. Then a student who was from South America nudged me with his elbow and said, "Just say yes."

I looked the teacher and pointed to the student next to me and said, "Professor, he said yes."

"That's good."

I looked in my dictionary for the word crook, and I found it meant a hooked or curved staff. That didn't mean anything to me, how I could be a curved staff in America and what was that supposed to mean? I looked the dictionary again and I found another meaning, and that was 'thief.' I told myself to forget it and I'd see where he was going with this. Anyhow, it wasn't bad so far. I learned one new word, 'crook.' He might yet be a good teacher. "No matter what you become, I know you will be reminded of me. Let me tell you all, you need to learn English and speak it just like ordinary people in the street. You are not going to talk to a moron in the street in Shakespearean language. You talk to a moron just like a moron. Does that makes sense?" He looked at us.

Again, this was another word I didn't know, 'moron.' I thought about it…what is a moron in the street? I couldn't figure that out because I hadn't seen anything labeled 'moron' and I'd been walking in many streets in New York City. Again, I took out my dictionary and looked for the word moron. I didn't know how it was spelled out, but I landed on the word, 'Mormon' and I thought that may be it. It meant, 'a member of the church of Jesus Christ.' I asked myself, why he is talking about Jesus in the street?

The teacher was still waiting for response and looking at us.

I raised my hand. "Professor, what is a Mormon in the street?"

"God, listen to me. I didn't say 'Mormon,' I said 'moron.'"

I had my finger on the page of my dictionary, so I opened the same page and found the word 'moron,' it meant a very stupid person. Again I told myself, good, I learned another word, moron. Actually I liked the way it sounded and I thought that was really good. I should use it a lot because there are too many morons in this world and in fact the way this professor was talking, he sounded just like one.

"I will help you, suppose someone is very difficult person, what you call that person?" asked the professor.

The class was silent, and no one answered.

"Well, you call such a person a pain in the ass, and you hear this expression a lot.

Why is that? Because there are too many morons in this world and they all are pains in the ass."

Then professor went on to say the 'F' word wasn't dirty, that words can't be dirty but only minds can be dirty. He went on and cited examples how one professor in one of the colleges in New York used the 'F' word and discovered that students were more tuned to his lectures and even learned more than classes without it.

Back then 1977, swearing wasn't as common on the TV as it is now. I thought those words were inappropriate. Even now as swearing is so common in movies and TV shows, I think that every comedian who uses the 'F' word really had nothing funny to say. Good comedy doesn't need swearing like that.

In New York I was amazed at the cultural diversity. I met people from almost every ethnic, national and religious background. Later I found that the US had the biggest telescope in a world stationed in Puerto Rico, those multimillion-dollar telescopes were used to locate life in other galaxies. I thought that was stupid, after all we had every nationality one can imagine, so why bother still looking for more people? If you wanted to study other cultures, there they were, all in one place, in America and one didn't have to go too far. So I was puzzled by locating life in other galaxies and wonder the purpose. I thought that to be ridiculous not knowing what did American want? Find populated galaxy and bring its people to US and enroll them in our welfare program. Or simply give them generous foreign aid as we do to so many other countries.

When I first came to the US, I had no passport, not even a driver's license. They gave me what was called an 'Alien Registration Card' that I had to carry with me as my only piece of identification.

Once I got my card, I looked at it and saw word 'alien'. I went home and looked in the dictionary to see what it meant, I looked it up and read alien means repugnant. I didn't know what repugnant meant. I looked that up and found it meant distasteful, offensive, contradictory or opposed. I paused and thought about it, I said to myself this card must be a joke. Let me substitute the name 'alien' for 'repugnant', then my ID card would read, 'repugnant registration card'. I thought that wasn't right so I looked in the dictionary again and found another meaning for word alien, the word 'strange'. I substituted the word strange for alien to see how it sounded, 'strange registration card.' I thought that wasn't right either, so I found another meaning, 'foreign born,' well that was it. I decided I shouldn't care whether I am repugnant or strange because that was the American way to name people. Then why in the hell would they choose the word alien to describe someone born outside the US? How could people tell which one of the meanings to use, repugnant, strange or foreign born?

I had difficulty with the way they used the English language. When I became a citizen, I was called a 'Naturalized Citizen'. I thought about it, and it didn't make any sense. It meant that I was not natural. What did that imply? Perhaps I was manufactured by some factory, but when they gave me a piece of paper I was all naturalized. I thought that was totally wrong. Mankind can't naturalize anything. For things to be natural they have to come from nature. Since we cannot create or modify nature, use of the word 'naturalize' by humans is a fallacy. I let it pass and I said to myself, if that's what it takes for Americans to be happy, let them have it.

In my second year at college I was sent to Chemical Bank as an intern for three months. At the end of my three-month internship I was hired as a computer programmer. After a year at Chemical Bank I left and worked for Paine Webber. I was also hired part-time as a computer programmer teacher at Albert Merrill Institute in the city. After about a year at Paine Webber, I found a job at another brokerage firm around Wall Street.

After a month in my new job things didn't work out and I resigned and decided to leave New York. I left for California. I thought that I would go to the San Francisco Bay area, where I knew I'd have no problem finding a job. I settled with my landlord and I sold whatever furniture I had. I got myself a one-way plane ticket to San Francisco Bay Area.

Chapter Twenty-One

After a couple weeks on the West Coast I found myself a job in Oakland. I found it very difficult to get around without a car, since it wasn't like the New York area. I didn't have a driver's license, but I'd taken some driving courses when I was in New York. When I'd taken the driving test in New York, a policeman came in the car with me. At first I didn't feel good about the policeman, but I couldn't refuse him and get another tester. He was just too stiff and he looked like someone who had a severe case of hemorrhoids. What I could have done for such a miserable person who looked like he really enjoyed his own misery? He seemed like he'd find Kafka funny. It was early in the morning and I must have been his first victim.

"Good morning, officer," I said.

"What is so good about it?" he replied. I just knew he wasn't going to say anything nice.

"Officer, cheer up and think that something good will happen today," I said.

"I don't know, my life is the same everyday, taking people like you for driving test. Most of them can't pass," he said with a very serious.

He looked around, checked the mirrors and looked at me to see I had my seatbelt on. He started telling me what to do, and I drove until we got to a street with a steep slope with cars all parked on both side of the street. He found a small space between two cars and asked me to Parallel Park. I knew that my car wouldn't fit but I didn't want to argue with him. I tried to park, I advanced then tried to back into the space, indeed I did a perfect park but there just wasn't enough room.

"Officer there isn't enough room to park, what do you want me to do?" I asked.

"Let's drive back to the office," he said.

"How I have I done so far?" I asked.

"Just drive please. You couldn't do the parallel parking. You need more practice, and that is what I tell almost everyone," he said.

"Can we try that again? You know there wasn't room, my car couldn't even fit," I said.

"What do you need? Maybe you need fifty car lengths to parallel park?"

Anyhow I went back to the office and found that I'd flunked the test.

I didn't try that again until I came to the San Francisco Bay area. After I settled in the Bay area I went to take the driving test again. I went to the Department of Motor Vehicles and I rented a car from the driving school. The officer who gave me the test was a young lady, she looked like that she had been dying her hair, her eyelashes and her eyebrows, she was an absolute mess. She got in the car.

"Do you have your mirrors all set? And you're buckled up?" she asked with a smile so big that the corners of her lips looked like they were merging with her ears.

"Yes, I'm ready to go," I said.

Again, she gave me one of those big nonsense smiles of hers.

She took me around for a few blocks and then came back to the DMV.

"How did I do?" I asked.

With another disturbing smile, she said, "I am not supposed to tell you, you will receive a note in a mail."

"Thank you," I said.

I left DMV very happy, I thought, thank God she didn't ask me to do the parallel parking like in New York. What an easy test, she let me drive three quiet blocks and all she asked me to do was make left turns and right turns. In the meanwhile I was a little concerned that if the test was that easy, then the freeways must be a big mess with so many people who didn't even know how to drive.

In a couple weeks I got my driver's license. I still didn't buy a car and indeed I didn't need one at the time. I lived about a five-minute walk away from work. I remained there without a car for over a year.

My second cousin Barzan was living in Santa Maria, which was about 250 miles from where I lived. Barzan used to go to car auctions so I gave him money to buy me a car. He bought me a Honda Civic station wagon, manual transmission. I took the bus and went to Santa Maria to bring my car back.

I arrived at Santa Maria and spent a night with Barzan who was living with his girlfriend. The day after I left Santa Maria, I talked to Barzan about the car.

"Barzan this is a stick shift, I can barely drive an automatic transmission, and now this," I said pointing to the car.

"Rauf don't worry about it, I'll teach you how to drive a stick shift car in just a minute or two, It's easy," he said.

I took his word for granted and thought he might be right. Right before I left asked Barzan to take me on a tour of the town.

"Let us go for a tour around the town and show me how to use a stick shift," I said.

"No, here's how you do it, just move the gear to '4', and that will take you back home," he said.

"That's all?" I said.

"Yes, what else?" he said.

I told him goodbye and drove away. I stopped by a place in Santa Maria, bought a bag of pomegranates and placed in the back seat of my car. In fact I didn't know the word for pomegranate. That reminded me of my friend Peter. One day I was in Astoria Queens in New York with Peter. We went to a store to get change for the subway. The storeowner was a tall blond guy with blue eyes and a balding head.

We asked him for the change, I don't recall exactly how the exchange went, all I remember the guy gave us a sour look and he got really nasty and started cursing at us in Greek. I didn't understand Greek but Peter was Greek.

"Peter, what is he saying?" I asked.

"He called us SOB punks," said Peter. He was laughing.

"What did we do to him to make him say that?" I asked.

"What do you expect? He's Greek," he said.

"You're Greek too," I said.

"Forget about it, the guy is a bastard," he said.

The storeowner came out stretching, he had fruits in the front of his store and some of them were pomegranates. I wanted to learn the word for pomegranate, so I pointed to it and asked Peter what is the name for this.

"It's called a Chinese apple," said Peter.

The storeowner got even nastier, "If you don't buy things don't touch them, what do you think this is? You want make my store into an English class?" he said with a heavy accent.

"I don't know what you mean," I said.

"I mean I don't want you go around my store touching everything and asking your Friend what you call this and what you call that." Anyway we left the guy's store, and I thought that a pomegranate was called a Chinese apple.

Anyhow, I drove and right before I got to the freeway there were a couple hitchhikers. I stopped my car and they ran toward me.

"Where are you going?" I asked.

"San Jose," they said.

"Come on in, I'm going to Oakland, so you're on my way," I said.

They got in the back of the car and both thanked me at the same time.

"Its about 200 miles from here," I said.

"Yes that's about right," he said.

"Do you have enough money to share the gas with me?" I asked.

"Not really, we are broke," she said.

I drove for about ten miles.

"Can we have some pomegranates?" she asked. They were on the back seat and they didn't have to look hard to see them.

"What was that you said? What's a pomegranate?" I asked.

She took one from the bag and held it in her hand and lifted up so that I could see it from the mirror, "This is a pomegranate," she said.

"Not ma'am, it's called a Chinese apple," I said.

"No it's called a pomegranate," she said.

"In New York that is called a Chinese apple," I said. "Please use the bag to throw away the peel," I said.

"Sure, we aren't going to make a mess in your car," she said.

I set the gear on four as Barzan had told me. The car was driving really nicely and I was pleased with its performance. When I got about fifty miles to San Jose the traffic slew down and got worse when I got about twenty miles from San Jose. When I drove fast it was okay, but when I slowed down the damn car wasn't moving easily and I got on every driver's nerves. I got embarrassed around stoplights where I could not pick up speed and people were looking at me and thinking that I must have been stupid.

Once we got to San Jose, I dropped off the hitchhikers and drove to Oakland. And once I got home I found out that I had two flat tires. I looked at the wheels and there was very little tread left. Who knows how long I'd been driving on flat tires? I didn't care much about it. The next day I towed my car to a nearby gas station and they put new tires. That happened just going into my second year in California. By then, I got laid off at work but with almost six month's pay.

When I came back to Oakland, that was just the beginning of my driving. I had problems with the stick shift and asked other people about how to drive with one. I got good tips that I tried, but I was still nervous. After a month the car wasn't driving too well and I was a nervous driver. One day I was driving in Oakland and a policeman stopped me. He gave me two citations at once. I looked at the paper before signing and asked, "Officer, what is this?"

"You know the stop sign behind you?" he asked.

"Yes, I do."

"You didn't stop there. You understand that?"

"Yes."

"And you know the stop sign before this one, you see that?" He pointed to the stop sign blocks away.

"Yes."

"You didn't stop there either. I was just following you to see where you were heading to," he said.

I said nothing. He asked for the driver's license and I gave it to him. As usual before they wrote the citation, they asked if your address was current, just like they really wanted to know where to deliver your birthday gift.

The next day I was walking in the street and the street was quiet; I crossed the street on a red traffic light. Right in the middle of the street I saw a policeman next to me.

"Sir, can I see your driver's license?" he asked.

"Sure officer, why do you need my driver's license?" I said.

"You see, you just crossed the street on a red light and that's jaywalking," he said.

I reached my pocket, got my driver's license out and gave it to him.

"By the way, did I give a ticket yesterday?" he asked.

"No, Officer. Why? Am I supposed to get a ticket everyday?"

I had enough trouble when I started driving. My biggest problem was that I drove about forty miles an hour everywhere. I got pulled aside on the freeway for driving too slowly, and I was cited for driving too fast in the city.

When I learned to drive better and my fear diminished, I drove my car like it was an ambulance. At the time the speed limit was 55 mph. I thought that was the most stupid law and indeed I thought it was made to generate revenue through citations, I thought if they really didn't want people to drive more than 55 mph, then they should have passed that law for the automakers rather than the drivers. The government should have forced the automakers not to make their cars able to drive faster than the speed limit. I blamed the government for that. They made the cars capable of driving 100 mph and yet they told people they weren't allowed to go more than 55 mph. If the cars weren't supposed to speed more than 55, were these automakers sick to make the cars capable of 100 mph? I really thought that was a setup just to give away more citations. And I got more than my own share.

When I came to San Francisco, I didn't know any Kurds in the area. About a month after I settled, I sort of felt lonely and I wanted to know someone I could speak Kurdish with, and through them to learn the news and new developments in Kurdistan. At least with the few Kurds in New York, we managed to learn a little about what was going back home. To this end, I called Ms. Barbara in New York and got from her the name of the director of the IRC in San Francisco. I made a point to go to the IRC office in San Francisco and Leslie was the officer.

"Rauf, welcome to San Francisco." said Leslie and we shook hands. She was a young blonde and a very attractive lady.

"Thank you," I said.

"I talked to Barbara and she told me how successful you are, and she told me you are very hardworking and all sorts of good things about you," she said with a smile.

"Thanks you."

"Just let me know if you need anything, I'll be more than happy to help you," she said.

"Sure, you can help me through your organization. I was wondering if you know any Kurds here?" I asked.

"Not really, I don't even know one, in fact you are the first Kurd I've seen in my

life, but I know many Chinese," she said with a laugh.

"That's really good, what am I suppose to do with Chinese other than breaking egg rolls or fighting with chopsticks," I said.

She laughed and laughed. "You must be homesick," she said.

"Yes, I have been for years," I said.

"I'll be making some contacts and if I find any Kurds, I'll let you know," she said.

The next day Leslie called me.

"Rauf, I found two Kurdish gentlemen. They've come to this area recently through American Lutheran charges, and just like you they've been trying to locate other Kurds in the area," she said.

"That is great, where are they from?" I asked.

"They are Kurds from Turkey. They are refugees and they've been sponsored by a

Lutheran organization as I mentioned to you earlier. They've been told about you and they'll call you," she said.

316

"Thanks, Leslie," I said.

Just a couple hours after I talked with Leslie, I received a phone call from Madad and Darwesh. That same day I went to San Francisco and we introduced ourselves. We became friends and met frequently.

After I got laid off at work, I decided to leave Oakland and move to the city. I wanted to go back to school. I was admitted to San Francisco State University. I enrolled in school and moved in with Madad and Darwesh, who were renting a house in Daly City a few miles away from San Francisco.

Both Madad and Darwesh worked in a restaurant in 'San Francisco. They left for work about 3:00 P.M. and they made it home after midnight, in a morning. I left home early in the morning to go to school and got back about 5:00 P.M. It was a good arrangement. Later Darwesh left and moved in with his girlfriend. The house was two stories, it had two rooms upstairs with a nice living room and a kitchen, that where we lived. The ground floor was where the landlord, Isac lived. He was an army officer and friend of Madad. He was an Assyrian from Kirkuk, in Iraqi Kurdistan. Isac was a gentleman and a good man. Isac used to come up and pick fight with Darwesh and they fought in Turkish, Isacs poke broken Turkish he learned in Kirkuk, which was a bastardized version of the Turkish language.

Darwesh didn't have a car. The supermarket, Patrini, was about five minutes walk away from the house. Darwesh used to go there to purchase produce and other things. Every time he brought a shopping cart back and he didn't bother to return any of them, he just parked them in front of the house. After a while, the front of the house looked like a supermarket with so many shopping carts. On the weekend, Isac, Madad and I used to return those carts. Once as we were returning the carts, Isac was coming back and fighting with Darwesh and cursing him in Turkish.

Just before I'd moved in with Madad and Darwesh, Darwesh had brought his girlfriend who was a jewelry maker to live with them. She used to stay up until the early morning, pounding on metal. That made Isac frustrated enough to force Darwesh's girlfriend to move out.

It was odd that I had to talk English with Madad and Darwesh because they spoke very little Kurdish. Speaking, reading or writing in Kurdish language was forbidden in Turkey, so they hadn't learned much of the language. Darwesh and Madad usually spoke to each other in Turkish.

During the 80s, war broke out between Iraq and Iran. Kurdish soldiers who were drafted into the Iraqi army fled the military and joined the Kurdish revolution, which sided with Iran and the US in fighting Saddam Hussein.

My brother, Abduel escaped and went to Iran. From Iran he made his way to Denmark. When I went to San Francisco State I met my wife. We used to see each other occasionally, then she disappeared for a year. Then one day she came back to school, auditioning for a play. We talked and we went on dating, and we got married shortly after.

Chapter Twenty-Two

In March of 1988 I was working for a semiconductor firm in Silicon Valley as a computer programmer analyst. At the time my son Vincent was about one year old and my wife was pregnant. We rented a place in the town of Pacifica, near San Francisco.

It was a difficult time for my family and me. I'd gotten into an auto accident about three years before and had injured my neck. I had chronic pain in my neck and shoulders every once in a while. What aggravated my condition was long working hours. My job was demanding. I was on call as a primary support person for several systems for a firm in Santa Clara County, near San Jose, about forty miles from where I used to live. I was working nearly ten hours a day and had a two hours commute.

I was listed for primary support on an accounts payable system. One day there were discrepancies of over a million dollars, which I had to reconcile. It took me twenty-six hours of straight work, which I passed with coffee and cigarettes. That was during the time when I could smoke at my desk. In the end I found that the missing money had been accounted for in one of the reports—one which the accounts payable employees didn't know about. Those same long hours of working had triggered my neck problem and the full symptoms and pain surfaced. It was frustrating, as all of my bosses were watching and waiting for my findings.

Doctors prescribed all kinds of medicines for me. I was on anti-inflammatory medicine, a muscle relaxant, and heavy painkillers. Their combined side effects made me tired and drowsy.

The pain and exhaustion forced me to cut my hours in half and remove myself from the call list. I went on half-time disability and thought that, because of my insurance, I'd still collect close to my normal wages.

One of the employee benefits was to sign up for long-term disability. Long-term disability, if it was granted, would pay nearly the same as my salary. One of the questions they asked during the application was if I'd had a history of cervical disk problems. I answered no. The next day I realized that my answer wasn't right. I went back to the person from the human resources department and told her that I needed to correct my answer. She told me that she had already submitted my application, and that I shouldn't worry about it. The insurance companies received their premiums and they didn't argue.

When it came time to collect disability, the insurance company checked my medical history and I was disqualified for the long-term disability due to a pre-existing condition. I had to collect part-time state disability insurance and half of my normal paycheck. Even with my full paycheck I could barely keep up with my bills. State disability pays practically nothing, and I lived in the San Francisco Bay area—one of the most expensive places to live in the world.

I was demoralized by the pain in my shoulder and neck. I was devastated and worried that I'd became a burden to myself. I went with my wife Teresa to see my neurosurgeon, and signed up to have surgery on March 19, 1988.

It was a difficult time financially. We had no savings, and all I received for income was half of my paycheck. Going into surgery meant that I had to go on short-term disability. What came in from state disability wasn't even enough to pay for our groceries. I feared that I might be disabled for the rest of my life if the surgery didn't go well. The surgeon warned me that surgery didn't guarantee complete recovery, and that some people didn't see any improvement at all.

On March 17, 1988, a couple of days before my surgery, I was at work. I went to have a cup coffee in the café—my usual morning routine—and

I picked up the local newspaper, *the San Francisco Chronicle*, and returned to my desk.

The front page story was about Saddam bombing the town of Halabja. I read in horror that the town had been gassed, that thousands were killed, and children were found lying dead like rag dolls in the streets. I went to the page where they had the news in detail and saw a picture of a father holding his child, both lying dead in the street. Behind them other kids lay dead in their colorful Kurdish clothes.

The article said the town was hit with a chemical bomb. I couldn't help, I started crying. I didn't want anyone to see me so I went to the restroom, still holding the newspaper in my hand. I kept looking at the picture of the father holding his child. It was obvious from the picture that the father had tried to save his child's life. It was a heartbreaking scene. I thought "Why my people? What had they done wrong to deserve this catastrophe? Oh, my God, how could people be so heartless and do things like this to others?"

I couldn't stand being at work. I needed to hide and let my emotions out. I rushed back to my desk. I didn't want to let others know about my feelings. I took a deep breath and wrote down my user ID and the passwords associated with it, and went to see my manager.

That was my last day before leaving on LTD, so I had to do a quick turnover. I went to my manager, who was reading from a binder with a tall cup of coffee in his hand.

"Good morning, Scott," I said.

"Good morning, Rauf," he said. He looked at me as though he knew that I had to tell him something.

"I am not feeling well. I know I was scheduled to stay until noon, but I have to leave."

"You have turned over everything to Tina, haven't you," he asked.

"Yes, I did. All I have is my user ID and the passwords for my accounts. I have them written down here." I handed him the paper. And he took it and placed on his desk on a top of a pile of paper.

"That will do it. I think you should go home—you don't look too good," he said.

"Okay, boss, I'll see you after my surgery."

"I hope so. Good luck. I'll talk to you soon. Keep in touch and let us know how things go."

I left work. On my way home I stopped and picked up *The Los Angeles Times* as well as *The New York Times* from the newsstand and anxiously searched for some more detail about what had happened, but neither paper contained any more news than what I read in San Francisco Chronicle. The radio was also void of any information. There wasn't anyone I could call to get the news about my parents, my grandparents, or any of my relatives and friends. It was a devastating event, and I imagined that it might take a long time to be sorted out and publicized.

I was angry and frustrated. I didn't know who should I be angry at— but thought of the US and Europe for helping Saddam make and use these kinds of weapons on a mass scale against defenseless populations. I was sure that Saddam must have used weapons against other towns and villages—and later my fears were confirmed.

I wondered if I should write to members of the congress and senate and voice my frustration—as an American citizen for what had happened to my hometown, courtesy of US aid to Saddam. Then I told myself *leave those idiots alone. They raise their voices to cry for human rights but when they are needed to do something right they always do wrong. They sided with a wrongdoer and blamed the victims.*

To add insult to injury, right after the chemical bombing of Halabja, then president of the United States, Ronald Reagan, stood before the United Nations and condemned Saddam for using chemical weapons against civilians. The next day I read in *The New York Times* that the United States had given billions of dollars in low-interest loans to Saddam to finance his war against the Iranian regime—while turning a blind eye to what Saddam has done to my people.

What bothered me the most was that not even one Arabian or Islamic government seriously raised their voice against Saddam or stood up against what he'd done to the Kurds, who were also Muslims. The only Islamic country that protested Saddam's chemical bombing of Halabja was Iran, but that was part of their public propaganda campaign for their war with Iraq. I hadn't heard any protest from Saudi Arabia, despite the fact that they claimed to be the custodian of the prophet Mohammed.

And none of the Arab countries, with all their money, had come forward to offer any kind of humanitarian assistance to the devastated people in Halabja.

I felt that we Kurds were living in the world all alone. The only people who helped us, I found out later on, was Iran. Most of the Iranian help came from Iran's Kurdish population, which I admire deeply from my heart.

All of my friends and family flashed through my mind and I was afraid that at any minute I would get a phone call or receive a letter with a long list of the dead. I wished that I could travel back home—but not only had I arranged for surgery, I couldn't travel through Iran because of the Iran-Iraq war.

I was angry and uneasy and found I was too upset to go home. I went to a café to sit and have a cup of coffee, but I could not sit still or think clearly. I took a coffee to go and drove to the ocean near our house. I parked the car facing the ocean. It was about 10:00 A.M. and the area was quiet. I stared at the waves, but the view of the ocean turned into my hometown. I cried hopelessly, both for those who died and for those who survived.

I cried for my parents. I started thinking about my father and of all of the days of destruction in my hometown, the suffering he went through, and the financial difficulties he endured. Dad never got a break. I prayed *please, God, I hope nothing happened to him. Could you please save him? You took away both his parents when he was an infant, and he didn't even know what his parents looked like. You created this orphan and he deserves a break in life.*

I cried for my little brother who was just a couple years old when I left him. He was the baby of the house and my parents loved him so much. It has been so long since I left home, perhaps if I saw him, I wouldn't even have recognized him.

My poor mother, she told me over and over after years of separation that she'd been praying to live so that she could see me again. I wonder if that would happen.

I was emotionally overwhelmed. I cried and shouted as loudly as I could, "Please, God, I want your answer—where are you in all of this?"

Someone knocked on the window of my car. I turned and saw a policeman.

"Sir, are you okay?" he asked.

"Yes, I'm perfectly all right, thank you for asking," I said while the tears were still coming.

"I don't want to bother you, but if you're not feeling well I can call an ambulance," he said.

"No, sir, I live up the hill. I'm about to drive home," I said. He left me alone as he saw I started the car.

As I drove, I looked the mirror and saw that the policeman was following me. I kept driving and once I arrived home and parked in my driveway the policeman disappeared.

What a royal pain in the neck these policemen are—they come to help you when you don't need them, otherwise all they want to do is write tickets and generate revenue. All I wanted was to stay near the ocean in quiet and cry and think, but then an ass comes and distracts me. They come to help you when you don't need them, and when you need them they are hard to find, I thought.

I went inside and saw my wife playing with my little son, Vincent.

"What are you doing home so early?" my wife asked.

I gave her a kiss. "Honey, I decided to come back early," I said.

"Are you in pain?" she asked.

"Yes, I'm in pain, but it isn't that. I read something in the paper about Halabja that made me feel sick."

"What happened?"

"Here's the newspaper. Read it." I handed her the newspaper.

As she read she started crying. She finished reading and gave me a hug. "Oh my God, what kind of evil person can do that? I can't believe he is doing this to those poor people."

"He does it because he knows he can get away with it. And our government is helping him," I said.

"All I know is that whoever helps evil is evil. I can't understand why we should be a part of this, I just can't understand it," she said.

"I wish that someone had told that to our president, Ronald Regan."

"All we can do is pray for your parents and relatives," she said.

"I guess that is the only option we have. What else can we do?"

"Can you call anyone and find out about your family?"

"I called Arian and she told me that she'd call the Shaykhs' house. Hopefully they'll know something. I don't know of anybody else. I'm afraid even to think about it. I'm not sure how I'll take the news when I hear it," I said.

"Don't say that, dear, and don't assume it'll be bad news beforehand. I am sure that God will save your parents."

"I don't know that, but I fear that I may get a long list of beloved ones and be told that they all are dead or disabled," I said.

"No, don't think that way, please. Just pray."

"Tomorrow I'll have my surgery. At least they'll put me out for one day and I won't have to worry about it for a little while."

I had my surgery and was thankful that it went well.

After two days I was out of the hospital. I started making contacts and searching to find out where my parents were. I kept thinking about everyone and had this nightmare that there were no survivors amongst my family.

I was very disappointed that I couldn't get any news and was convinced that the news was so bad that no one was willing to announce it. During all of the time that I waited to hear the news I didn't talk to anyone about it. I cried quietly and waited impatiently. What aggravated me the most were horror stories I read in a media and also what people to told me. Nothing is worse than uncertainty, and that consumed me badly and stole my peace of mind. This was one of the most difficult time I encountered in my life. I was lucky enough to have a wonderful and caring wife who was fully supporting me, and without her I would have been emotionally devastated.

What led to the gassing of Halabja was the Iraq/Iran war. The Iraqi government couldn't conclusively defeat the Iranian regime. Another headache for the Ba'th regime was the rebirth of the Kurdish revolution under its old failing leadership, the Barzani family and the Talabani. The revolution was sponsored and backed by the Iranian regime.

After the collapse of the Shah's regime and the takeover by the Islamic Shiite extremists in Iran, Ayatollah Khomani, the head of the state, was eager to ruin Saddam's regime.

Khomani was an outspoken mullah who declared that the former Shah of Iran and its sponsor the United States were evil. He was asked to leave Iran by the former Shah. Khomani left Iran and was given asylum in Iraq. Saddam Hussein's regime soon asked the Ayatollah to leave Iraq. He left Iraq and was given asylum in France, where he remained in exile until the Shah's regime was toppled. He then came back as a spiritual leader, and became head of state.

Khomani declared that Saddam Hussein was an evil man. His provocative actions and talk soon led to war between the two countries.

When the Iraq/Iran war started, the Iranian regime influenced the Kurdish leaders—the Barzani and Talabani—to initiate another Kurdish revolution aimed at freedom for the Kurds. The Iranian regime backed the leaders with military and monetary support. The Kurds sided with Iran and fought Saddam's regime.

In an orchestrated political and military organization, with arms provided by the Iranian Islamic regime, Kurdish leaders quickly consolidated their power and fought beside the Iranian army in Kurdistan, recruiting enough personnel and old loyalists to form a formidable armed revolution.

Halabja was in a strategic place between Iran and Iraq. Until March 1988, Halabja was under the control of Iraq. There was a sizable Iraqi armed force and intelligence staff led by an officer, Khalid.

The Iraqi regime was now facing threats from the Kurds in the north and the Iranians in the south. The war wasn't going well for Iraq. Iraq at that time possessed a stockpile of fatal chemical and biological weapons and used them to display their devastating power so the Iranians would be discouraged and give up the war.

In 1988, a few months after the bombing of Halabja, I talked to my brother Abduel who lived in Denmark. He informed me that prior to the bombing my entire family, except for my father, had fled the town. It was not until years later that I heard the true story—that my entire family was in town during the bombing. I talked to my younger brother who found his way to Germany in 1996. He told me what had transpired.

Chapter Twenty-Three

March is the beginning of spring and Kurdistan is beautiful—the surrounding mountains, valleys, and lands are all green and colored with flowers and full of people picnicking, dancing, singing, and enjoying the beauty of nature.

The Kurdish and Persian New Year, Newroz, is celebrated on the twenty-first of March. It is a day when people celebrate victory of right over wrong, and their freedom from tyrants.

Centuries before the birth of Christ there was a king, Zohak of the land of Med, the land of Kurds and Persians. Some believed Zohak to be descended from Arab ancestry and others believe he was an Assyrian. His residence was in the capital of his kingdom, and some believed it was the town of Khormal, which is about a half an hour's drive from Halabja.

Legend has it that the king had a wound in his chest, and from each side of that wound rose two snakes. Evil visited the king as a doctor and prescribed a young person's head for each one of the snakes. The king accepted evil's prescription. Every day two young children were sacrificed to feed the snakes. The nation was terrified and the citizens hid their children. The king had no consideration for anyone's life or property, and the more he tortured, abused, and stole from his people, the more they prayed for the end of king Zohak.

A Kurdish blacksmith named Kawa lost nearly a dozen of his children as food for the snakes. Left with only one daughter, who was about to be taken, Kawa killed a lamb and prepared its head for the king instead of killing his own daughter.

Kawa was afraid hiding his daughter, and sent her out to the wild. When others found what Kawa had done, they too turned their doomed children out to the wild. After many many years these wild children became an army, skilled in the art of hunting and adapted to a wild life.

One day the army of children came back to civilization, into Zohak's kingdom. With Kawa and a crowd of disenchanted people, they raced to the king's palace. Kawa killed the king and crowned a new king, Faraydoon, in his place.

A tyrant did exist, as did a Kurdish blacksmith, by the name of Kawa, who killed the king. These are all historical facts—the rest might be fact or fiction. Perhaps as the story passed from generation to generation, the story of the king's wound and the snakes were added for drama.

Kurds and Persians share this holy day, Newroz, every year they celebrate the victory of Kawa over the tyrant. In Iran it's an official holiday. Persians have specific dishes and menus for the New Year. In Iraq after the peace treaty with the Iraqi government, the Kurds also declared this day as a holiday. Turkish and Syrian Kurds, who were and are still not allowed to celebrate it, called it a celebration of plants and trees.

Kurds in particular light bonfires in the mountains and hills, and they dance and sing in schools, in the streets, and everywhere. Theater groups make special plays, and musical bands prepare their best music. It's a day of celebration for Kurdish nationalists, who want to reclaim their land and be freed from the hands of tyrants and occupiers.

Lighting fires as a means of celebration goes back thousands of years to when Kurds were Zoroastrians. In the Zoroastrian religion it is believed that there exists a god of good and a god of evil. Anything light was associated with the god of good; Zoroastrians believed that god was light and therefore light was sacred to them.

This year the preparation for Newroz was different: people sought hiding places. The New Year usually brings hope and a sense of optimism, as it marks the end of the cold winter and the beginning of natural growth, when the flowers and plants will flourish and outdoor activity will begin.

This year there was a sense of pessimism and sadness. The prospect of impending calamity loomed. People feared for their lives. Just a week earlier the town and its surroundings had been bombed by planes and many people had left to seek refugee in nearby villages and mountains.

This spring was a reminder of the spring of 1974, when Halabja had been hit with bombs and napalm. Instead of picnics, people dealt with bombing and bloodshed. March 1974 and its tragedy was still fresh in the town's memory.

The Iran-Iraq war was in progress—a war that devastated both countries. More than a million Iraqi and Iranian soldiers and civilians perished. The ruin and death from the war—by far the most horrifying in the entire Middle East's modern history—haunted every major city in Iraq and Iran.

The head of the Iraqi army command in Halabja was an Arab Shiite. Mullah Ali headed the Islamic movement in Halabja and had ties with the Iranian regime of Ayatollah Khomaini. Mullah Ali had managed to connect with the Iraqi general who was in command of both the Iraqi army and the local armed men loyal to Saddam Hussein. There were about fifty thousand Iraqi soldiers and local Saddam loyalists stationed in Halabja; they were supported by heavy war machines, tanks, long and short range missiles, and other air defense.

The Iraqi general made arrangements with the Iranians to give up Halabja. At the same time the Iraqi army was pressured and Saddam was suspicious of the situation. Twenty-four hours before Halabja was taken over by the Iranians, Saddam came to Sulaymania and from there he contacted his general in Halabja—who cursed Saddam in a language not to be repeated here. Saddam returned to Baghdad, knowing that he would lose his army in Halabja.

The people of Halabja didn't like the idea of having Khomani's troops in their town. Just like any religious extremist group, Khomani's regime wasn't popular, and their atrocities against the Kurds were known: the regime had their bloody hands in Iranian Kurdistan, rounding up thousands and burying them alive in public executions. People had already experienced enough destruction and tragedy at the hands of the Ba'th Party under the leadership of Saddam Hussein. They believed that if the Iranian army would take over the town, with the *peshmargas* siding with them, the town would become a battlefield, and they would suffer the casualties of their bloody confrontations.

The commander of the Iraqi army gave himself up and left fifty thousand armed Iraqi's in a leaderless state of confusion. At that point the Iranian army, backed by *peshmarga,* poured into the town. Units of the Iraqi army engaged in battle with Iranian troops, Iranian militias, and *peshmarga,* and were easily defeated.

Zalem bridge, about fifteen miles away from Halabja, was destroyed, blocking transportation between Halabja to Sulaymanya. Thousands of Iraqi soldiers attempted to escape, even trying to swim to the other side of the river. Most were caught by Iranian troops and very few Iraqi soldiers escaped alive.

Once the bridge was blown up, Halabja was isolated and many people couldn't get back to Sulaymanya. The destruction of the bridge was part of a strategy to trap Iraqi officials and soldiers who had left Halabja and to make it difficult for Saddam's army to reach Halabja.

The destruction of the bridge affected many in my family. Mahabad, Harseny's daughter, had graduated from education institute and for her first job she was employed as a teacher in Halabja. My grandfather and step grandmother Amena, along with her son, Ali, and two daughters Sabeh and Shereen, were living in Halabja, and the rest lived in Sulaymania. My aunt Mahsoom was living in Sulaymania. Aunt Mahsoom was a worrier—she worried about everyone in the family. Right before Zalem Bridge was blown up, aunt Mahsoom came to Halabja. Here what she has to say:

It was March 13,1988. I went to the shopping center in Sulaymania for groceries. I saw one of my friends, dada ("older sister") Shamsa, in a butcher shop. Usually butchers sell a mix of every thing—a good chunk of meat as well as some bones. Dada Shamsa let her presence to be known. She was telling the butcher that he'd given her more bone than meat, while the butcher tried to persuade her that she received a fair deal. In a middle of this I tapped her in her shoulder, she turned toward me, and we greeted each other. She then took the meat from the butcher, placed it her little basket, and paid without further complaint. I saw a sigh of relief from the butcher, and he quietly thanked me.

Shamsa was an older lady about sixty who wore black vale. She was a loud, curious who knew all news and gossip of the town. She was perfectionist, picky and nosy, but very kind. She put down her basket and placed her hand on her chin. There was concern on her face. She knew some of my immediate family lived in Halabja, and asked me if I had heard any recent news from there. I told her that I had heard of the ongoing skirmish between the Iranian militia and the Iraqi troops. Her face showed still more concern, and I asked her to tell me all that she knew.

"From what I heard," she said, "Iranian troops and militias are pouring into Halabja by the thousands. I was told that bloody fighting is underway as we speak."

I couldn't believe it. "Are you sure things are so bad?" I asked Shamsa. "Indeed, I haven't heard any such a thing."

She was grim, but comforting. "My sister, things change very fast. Its wartime, and these times are anything but usual."

We said good-bye to each other and split. I purchased all my groceries and rushed home, thinking all the way about everyone, worried especially about my father's family and my sister and her family. Imagining that civilians would get caught in the crossfire, I thought that the best I could do would be to travel to Halabja and bring my sister, her family, and my father's family back with me to Sulaymania, and have them to stay with me until quieter times. My husband Hama was a decent man and I knew that he wouldn't object to my plans.

When I arrived at home, Hama was sitting in the living room listening to the news. I put away the groceries, quickly packed my suitcase, and went to the living room.

He looked at me. "Mahsoom, sit down. What you up to?"

I told him "I was going to Halabja immediately, before it was too late."

He sat up, alarmed. "What brought about this urgency?"

I stood before him. "I heard that bloody fighting is under way in Halabja. Before they flatten the town, I need to go and get my sister's and father's families out of town, and have them stay with us until things are safe."

"You know, if things are as bad as you claim, then you are risking your life. I am afraid not only that you won't be able get them out of town, but also that you may not be able to make it back yourself."

I stood up and picked up my suitcase. "Don't you worry about me. I should be able to manage. I better get going."

Hama looked disoriented. "You must be kidding me."

"No, I am not. Say prayer for me." I said, and walked toward the door.

"Make sure you have enough money with you. Take some extra money just in case."

"I have enough with me." I replied, and picked up my suitcase and left for the taxi station. There were no taxis—instead close to a hundred people stood waiting for taxis. Some of these people, like me, wanted to travel into town and bring back their relatives; others, from the town, were trying to return.

Soon a huge bus arrived, headed toward Halabja. In a few minutes the bus was packed with passengers. The driver climbed in. He was a large man with a soft voice. His face was troubled. He stood up and spoke to us: "Ladies and gentlemen, I must tell you all that the road to Halabja is very dangerous, and I beg you all not to risk your lives."

An old woman stood up. "Son, if it's as dangerous as you claim, then why you risk your own life?"

"Mother, I am from Halabja and my family is there. I have no choice but to return home. I will give you all five minutes to decide, and then we will be going."

We stood for five minutes and no one left. The driver started the engine, and we all said our prayers for a safe trip. Once we started moving, I grew concerned that we might be caught in crossfire between the Iranian and the Iraqi troops.

We finally arrived at the edge of town. The driver stopped the bus and asked us to leave. He told us that he lived nearby and that he would go no further.

Nearby, tanks had lined up for at least a quarter of a mile and their cannons roared continuously. I didn't know what they fired at.

In order not to be seen, we all lined up and walked close to the roofs of the houses. The empty streets felt haunted. One could hear nothing other than the sound of heavy artillery. I walked along with two ladies and a young man. After we walked a few blocks the young man turned in a different direction. I was frightened to walk all by myself, so I continued along with the other two ladies until I arrived at the home of one of our old neighbors, Mr. Khalaf. Once we arrived there I split and went into Mr. Khalaf's house. They welcomed me and I told them that I needed to go to my father's house. Mr. Kalaf saw a man in a street who said he was going toward my father's house. The man agreed to help me get to my father's, and as I accompanied him, with every artillery explosion we moved closer to the walls of the houses.

I arrived at my father's house. All of their doors were locked and windows all closed. I thought they might be with one of their neighbors. I went to Haji Farag's house a few houses from them. The door to their house was open. I entered Haji Farag's house and saw nobody but I could hear people from the basement. I went to their basement through the stairs by the door. The basement, two adjacent rooms carpeted with rugs and small mattresses, was full of people. I saw my father, my step-mother, both my stepsisters, and my stepbrother.

My dad was taken by surprise. "Mahsoom what are you doing here?"

"I came here to take you all, along with Ghareeb's family, to Sulaymania."

He looked skeptical and frightened. "Mahsoom you know there is no taxi. No one can travel now. Don't you see we are all confined in the basement?"

"Dad, I just came from Sulaymania. How do you think I got here?"

"That must be the only driver who was willing to travel," he said.

I told him that he was right.

"Listen, Mahsoom," he continued, "you shouldn't have left your family. We should wait until this bombing quiets down."

I stayed with them. I knew most of the people in a crowd. In about an hour the bombing slowed down. We left Haji Farag's basement and went to my father's house.

At the time Mahabad, my cousin Harseny's daughter, was living with my parents. After her graduation she was sent to Halabja to teach grammar school, and my father had offered her a room in his house.

Mahabad was a beautiful girl, light skinned with big brown eyes and long dark brown hair. As we walked she gave me a troubled look. "Dada I wished that you didn't make this trip. You came her to rescue us, but now you got stuck with us."

Amena my stepmother cooked a lunch of scrambled eggs, then served tea.

As I took a cup I turned to my father. "Dad, I came all the way to take all of you back with me. I am going to Mahboob's house. If I can find a taxi I will return for all of you."

My father spoke calmly. "We are going to be fine. You see, there has been bombing here for a long time and we are still alive. Don't you worry about us. But I don't want you to go anywhere in this fire."

"Dad it's okay. I will go to visit Mahboob and do what I told you."

He gave me a worried look. "Let me escort you to Mahboob's house."

I stood up, shaking my head. "Dad I don't want an escort. If you came with me, then I would be bothered with your safe return home."

I said good-bye and left. I was disappointed that my father didn't agree with my plan and feared that there would be no transportation into or out of the town.

I walked toward Mahboob's house. Except for sporadic artillery shelling, the streets were quiet. I was very cautious and stayed near the houses. The streets were empty. The shops and stores were all closed. Tanks and armored vehicles roamed everywhere. I realized my father was right—no one in their right mind would go out traveling.

I made it to Mahboob's house. When I knocked, she opened the door. We hugged and kissed each other and walked to the living room. Shaykh Gareeb greeted me, beaming.

"You are an amazing lady. How in the world did you make it here with all this bombing going on? You must have found a brave or ambitious driver."

Mahboob hugged me again. "You must have known how bad the situation is here. I don't know why you would come here at this time. Mahsoom you have truly chosen the worst of times."

"The reason I came here was to take you and your family, as well my father's family with me back to Sulaymania. I knew about the situation, but not as bad as it actually is. Anyway, I may be able to find a bus or a taxi, and I hope you all come with me."

Shaykh Gareeb grew serious. "I really doubt that you will find transportation, Mahsoom, but I hope you do. But we will stay here. We can't come to you every time something happens—this kind of chaos has been a part of our lives for years. No one can ever know when it might end."

I couldn't believe what I was hearing, and what trouble I had caused myself. I had come all the way from Sulaymania to Halabja to rescue the members of my family and they had all refused. And it looked like that I might be stuck without transportation back to Sulaymania.

I had no choice. I had to stay. I wasn't comfortable with the situation and I knew things could get worse. If Iraqi troops to returned to Halabja while Iranian militia, *peshmarga,* and Iranian troops were in control, Halabja would turn into a battlefield and no life would be spared.

Halabja was disconnected from the rest of the world and I couldn't get in touch with my family in Sulaymania. I knew my poor husband must have gone through hell. My son Soran was about fourteen and my daughter Joan was about thirteen and both were attending middle school at the time. From where we lived, in a nice section of the city, enjoying an upper-middle-class lifestyle, I knew they would be overwhelmed with worry.

My first day had been very disappointing. For days we packed food and other supplies and then left to the house of Shaykh Gareeb's nephew, Jamal, where we hid in the basement until late in the evening before returning to Mahboob's. In this manner we planned to stay out of harm's way and wait for more peaceful times to return.

That is the story of my aunt Mahsoom and how she arrived Halabja.

I was told the rest of the story by my brother Hemen. At the time he was about sixteen years old. This is what he had to say:

For weeks the fighting around Halabja intensified. People went into hiding every day from early morning until dusk. We were told that Halabja would be chemical bombed after its takeover by the Iranian army. The *peshmargas,* however, insisted that these reports were false and tried to stop people from leaving town.

It was early morning on March 16ᵗʰ 1988. Aunt Mahsoom stood by the freezer looking at my mom, "Mahbob there is no electricity, and all the food will soon spoil. We better use as much as we can now otherwise you have to throw most of this food away." After a brief exchange between the two, they decided to take as much as possible for lunch at Jamal's house. All the Naqishbendi families in the neighborhood would be there. They packed all of the chicken and lamb, and left well before eight o'clock, when the airplanes would usually show up.

There were close to fifty people in Jamal's living room. They sat on the couch and on floor, having tea. The women congregated in the kitchen, preparing food. Badaw, Jamal's wife, helped with the food we had brought while Aunt Mahsoom and mom got to work washing and cutting the meat.

It was a typical gathering for us. The men were all sitting and talking, the children were running all over and playing, making noise, and the women were working together and conversing with one another—eight of them carrying on five different conversations.

Mom interrupted their conversation and pointed at Badaw. "Badaw, I've asked you over and over to remove a few of those concrete blocks from the wall separating our houses, to clear a path from my house to yours. Look, my dear, every time an airplane comes I have to run a round the house to reach your basement. What if I don't make it on time and get killed? If we have a little path through the wall, I can easily get into your basement."

Badaw nodded. "My dear, I have no objections to that. I told Jamal but he doesn't want to be bothered. Just go tell him what you told me."

"I told Jamal and he told me no. I even told him that I will pay the cost," Aunt Mahsoom replied, standing up to stretch. She pointed to mom. "If that is the case Mahboob, just ask him later."

By ten o'clock in the morning mom, Badaw, and Aunt Mahsoom begun sautéing chicken and meat. Badaw's daughter, Lana, came into the kitchen crying, her hair all tangled. She was about six years old, a little tiny quiet thing. Her hair was wet and her clothes soaked.

"Come here," demanded Badaw, taking her hand. "Where the hell have you been?

"Dana did it," Lana said between sobs. "He poured a big container of water all over me and Sharmeen."

Badaw looked furious. "Mahsoom, let her stay here. I'll have to change her clothes, and find this little terror Dana and spank his butt for troubles he has caused."

"This isn't fair, Badaw," said Atya. "This brat Dana has been terrifying the kids. Let his father know and have him beat him up."

Badaw shook her head. "I will spank him, and then let his father know. But first he needs a good spanking."

Sabraya opened her mouth to speak, but was interrupted by Jamal's loud announcement from the other room: "come on, everyone, the airplane is here."

I held Sharmeen's hand and ran through the backyard toward the metal door that covered the stairs to the basement. The basement was slightly bigger than a standard living room and was cemented from the roof to the floor. The floor was clean and covered with inexpensive rugs, mattresses placed against the walls, and pillows set on top of the mattresses.

Everyone packed into the basement until there was no room to move around. The planes sounded as if they were flying right above our heads.

We all sat and everyone began to pray. Terrified children sat next to their parents. After a few minutes we heard the first explosion, so loud we thought it had been dropped in the backyard. With the sound of the explosion all of the children started screaming and crying. Everyone was shaking and pale, praying as loud as they could.

A couple minutes after the first explosion we heard two more explosions simultaneously. The loud noise of the explosions as well the sound of the supersonics could make one deaf. I imagined that none of us would make it through the bombing.

The bombing intensified, and with every bomb explosion the children's screaming and the women's crying got louder. The explosions rocked the foundation of the house. I don't remember exactly how long the bombing continued, but felt like years.

After a while the bombing stopped. Most were afraid to leave, but some of us went upstairs. Not a single window remained in the house and the doors had all blown out. The same was true for every house in town.

A while later the cautious crowd in the basement came upstairs. My brother Noradeen was shaking like a tree. "Now, I am going to leave the town," he said to dad in front of everyone. "I tell you, the bombing is not going to stop and we should all leave." He looked around at everyone, stood up, and said in a loud voice for everyone to follow him. Noradeen's call went unanswered. He wrapped up a few pieces of chicken with a big piece of bread and placed it in his pocket, and left the house. The brief interruption in the bombing made few people leave the town as he did, but most of the people stayed where they were.

A while later a man came by and told us that there had been chemical bombing and that we should all go to Muhmood Haji Enayat's basement. We were all frightened and decided to leave for Muhmood's house.

As walked we saw entire families heading toward Muhmood's house. We entered the concrete basement from the front yard. The basement had two levels deep in the ground and with several hundreds people were already inside. Most were their relatives and neighbors. We wanted to be as deep underground as possible but there were no room in the lower level, so we had no choice but to stay in a first layer. My dad and my aunt sat by the entrance with mom facing them.

It was still chilly and some people had brought blankets and sweaters. Some had bags of bread and food, but most, in their rush and fear, had left their houses empty-handed. People shared their fears with each other, they voiced disenchantment about the war that had consumed their lives and robbed their peace of mind. They all seemed to expect the worst. So many people in one place sharing their fears with one another was good therapy, at least for the time being.

Yosef, one of our neighbors, suddenly shouted to the crowd that he heard planes. The noise grew louder. People stampeded down the basement stairs and the explosions began. The basement was packed wall-to-wall with people. Many young children and babies were terrified and crying. They couldn't understand what was going on.

The explosions continued. We felt bombs dropped nearby close to us. The whole ground and the basement was shaking. No one could tolerate the noise, most of which came from the planes themselves as their supersonic booms hit the town. They were flying low—there was no air defense. They were bombing defenseless civilians.

Children were crying, women were screaming, and mothers were holding their babies and children as tightly as they could. Women with more than one child had children clinging to them.

I had a small blanket with me that I used in vain to cover my head to ease the sound of the explosions. Sitting next to me was Majeed, another one of our neighbors, with his wife and three children. Majeed was holding his four-year-old son Rozh, and his six-year-old daughter Naza was lying flat on the floor with head was in her mother's lap. Majeed's wife, Soham, lay against the cement wall holding her nine-month old baby and prayed, "Please, God, be kind to this baby, to all these children, and don't let us die here."

Her daughter Naza looked up at her. "Mommy, are we all going to die?"

"I pray to God we won't, sweetheart," Soham said as she cried. "Please pray. That is all we can do in our defense."

I pushed my blanket under Naza.

Everyone was shaking, terrified and pale. Almost everyone thought that we would all die and that the basement would be a mass graveyard. Nearly everyone raised their hands in the air as they prayed to God. A few older ladies cried loud as they were praying, asking for their lives to be spared.

I saw Majeed's mother, Talat, lying next to him, saying, "Please, I can't breathe, son."

"Mom, please try to be strong. Please, mom, I don't want anything happen to you," he said to her.

"Oh, with my heart condition, I don't know if I can handle this evil day. I can't breathe. I smell something strange," said Talat.

Another bomb exploded and rattled the foundation of the house. The sound was so powerful that everyone jumped. I saw Majeed's mother jump and fall into Majeed's arms as he was holding his son Rozh.

"Mom, are you okay?" Majeed cried out. "Please talk to me."

She could barely move. She opened her eyes for a moment but didn't move. "Son, I love you, and I love my grandchildren. God wants me. Please take care of the family, darling." She breathed rapidly for a moment, and closed her eyes.

"Mom, please talk to me!" cried Majeed.

To start with the poor lady wasn't well before the bombing. I felt bad for Majeed. And that was the day all you felt was pain and sorrow and to make the matter worse being helpless. His children were horrified—they cried and called to their grandmother and Majeed's little daughter was cried, "grandma, please open your eyes."

Several older people among us had fainted. Some had fallen against the cement walls, others had fallen onto the floor and their faces were bruised. A few young men in their late twenties and thirties were bravely walking around trying to help.

My aunt Mahsoom, my mother, and me were sitting closely together across from my father. "God, I think Noradeen was right. We should have left," said my mother.

Mahsoom stood up. "We can't change the course of events. Forget about what we should have done, that was a few hours ago and now is now. You can't turn the clock back. Let's deal with now and not dwell on what we did or we didn't do."

In the middle of the basement a woman had gotten sick and lying on the ground, was vomiting. She had three young children who were all crying. My aunt went and held the baby and poured water on a towel and rubbed the women's face to comfort her.

I was holding my father's hand and he was frozen. He looked at me twice, like he wanted to tell me something. His voice was fading away and he knew he had to talk loudly to be heard. At last there came a moment of silence, without explosions. He looked at us and said, "I want you to leave my body here if something happens to me. I want you all to get out of town and save your lives rather than worrying about my dead body." My father turned to me and put his right hand on my shoulder. "Please do one thing for me. "Write your brother in America and tell him that all I wanted was to see him one more time before my redemption. Tell him, on my behalf, that the fifteen years of his exile have been my burden, but I am happy he is in a safer place and with us. Thank God for that and God willing, I will see him in heaven. Just tell him. I haven't seen his family, but every day I have prayed for them." With every sentence he paused to wipe his eyes.

"Dad, please don't say things like that," I said.He continued. "Also, I want you to tell your brother Abdul how much I love him, and your sister Ronak."

My mother nodded to me. "I want you to say the same thing for me to your brother Rauf and Abdul. Just as your dad said, I want you write them and tell them how much we all love them."

"I don't know what you are saying. if you both die, how will I survive? So forget about the messages," I said.

"I smelled poison in the air," said my father.

"Dad, what do you smell? I don't smell anything," I said.

"I hope you're right," he said. "My eyes are watering."

My mother looked around the room. "I see many people with tears pouring from their eyes. You must be crying and you don't know you are crying."

"If many others in the basement are like me, then it's a poison and many others probably feel it. We'll find out later," said my father.

"Dad give it time. Your eyes will be healed," I said.

"Son I already have blurry vision."

Then I kissed my father and told him, "Dad, God willing, we'll all be safe and leave this place alive."

There was nothing that day but crying. People felt bad just for being alive and having to live through so much horror. I looked around and saw people lying on top of each other. With every explosion people would shut their eyes and cover their heads. The crying of women and children filled up the air of the basement—and the elderly, who could not stand on their feet, lay in terror, short of breath.

I started thinking about my dad. Tears kept running from his eyes, for a moment I thought he might be right. I said a prayer for him.

A moment of silence came and it appeared that the planes had left. It had been about a half an hour of intensive bombing, but every minute of it felt like a year.

It was time to see if the planes had gone. We were thankful for all those who helped inside, but I tell you that no one wanted to go up. Finally Jalal, Jamel's brother, made an announcement. "Please stay here and don't rush out. We are not sure if the planes have left yet. I should be back in just a minute." He climbed the stairs and disappeared.

While he was gone everyone prayed in silence, their hands raised. They all prayed to God that this would be the end of it.

Soon Jamal descended back into the basement. "The planes are gone. I looked all over the sky and saw none. Let's get out of here, but please stay calm so that no one gets hurt."

Some people rushed to get out of the basement. People weren't stampeding to get out, instead they lined up and climbed out one at a time. We and all Naqishbendi families and more than half of the people in a basement remained inside fearing that the planes would return and resume bombing.

My father looked tired. His eyes were watering and his face was pale. My aunt Mahsoom was helping someone, but she soon rejoined us.

"God forgive me," said Mahsoom as she joined us, pale and shaking. "I had to leave that lady alone. She needs help, and I feel so bad leaving her."

My mother sat close to her. "Don't feel bad. You helped the lady and now, believe me, almost everyone needs help. Let's get out there and see what the bombing has done to the town."

Aunt Mahsoom shook her head. "No, let's stay here. The planes may come back at any minute.

Mom stood up, shaking and disoriented. "Well, we can't stay here forever, or we will be the only ones here."

In the middle of this decision making, Muhmood came in and told us that we should all leave the basement. He warned that the bombs were powerful enough to flatten the whole house and collapse the basement.

We had no choice but leave. As we found our way out, I saw that people were crying, and I heard several people saying the same thing that my dad had complained about—poison in the air.

In the street a cloud of black smoke hung over the sky. People rushed and walked as fast as they could, trucks roared by loaded with people panicking to leave. Families ran in two directions—either toward Anab or

Ababayle, the two villages nearby. People were hoping that once they got to either of those villages they could manage to get to the mountains near the Iranian border, which they thought would be safer. People walked in the street and passed by dead bodies and sick people uncaring for them as they rushed to exit the town. The bombing had been so devastating that people would do anything to avoid facing it again.

The saddest thing—which will echo in my memory for as long as I live—was the crying of the babies and children. They were jumped at the sound of every explosion, at every pass of the planes. They cried their lungs out. Mothers were dying while their children cried next to them.

The people who had the most difficult walk were those who had children. I heard parents begging their kids to walk faster, and saw parents carrying their children. Everyone was running for their lives. No one dared to stop to help anyone, for it might delay their own escape from the town. Everyone was left on their own, and everyone was helpless and terrified. Everyone believed that the planes would be back and whatever was left of the town would be consumed. People left their houses and their property behind and nothing mattered to them but their survival. It was a race for life, for survival.

After we got out of the basement, my mother was still holding my father's hand. He was walking very slowly. We passed by our house. An explosion had demolished the front, and the entire structure was shaky enough that we were afraid to enter.

Dad stood in front of the house. He looked defeated. "That was the only house I ever had. Your brothers Abdul and Rauf bought it for us, gave us all the furniture and all the beautiful things that I couldn't have ever afforded. Many people in town couldn't afford what we had." He couldn't help himself from crying. The house looked like it could fall at any minute.

Mom lifted her hand up and said, "God, please don't accept this, this is not right. What have we done to deserve this day? They made us homeless. I loved my house and now it's destroyed."

My aunt Mahsoom took my mother's hand. "Please, let's save our lives. Don't worry about your house now. You are going to have a lot of time to think about it later." They walked away.

"Dad, let me hold your hand please," I said.

"Yes, son, please do," said my father. He barely had the strength to walk. "I'd feel horrible if the planes came back and something happened to any of you. I don't care about myself. I am old. If it wasn't for me you would probably have gotten to the edge of the town by now, or all the way to Ababyle. I think you should leave me alone and save your life." He seemed to be in pain and was short of breath.

Aunt Mahsoom, walking next to him, said, "we will all be together and this is our journey. I can't leave you alone. We will make our way out of town together, or we will die together."

As we left our house we joined Jamal and his family. My aunt Mahsoom and I started talking with Jamal and his wife Badaw. She was crying about losing everything they had, and complaining about pain in her chest.

We turned to my mom and my dad, but they were nowhere to be seen. We'd lost them in the movement of people. My aunt told all of us to keep on walking straight ahead, and she ran to find my parents.

Soon after, Jamal's wife felt ill and we stopped walking and sat in the street. Badaw had her hands on her stomach and was complaining about the pain. We saw people passing by, most of whom we knew, but no one want to be slowed down. People hurried like they were racing with time. Indeed they did and it was a race for life.

After about five minutes my aunt returned with my parents. As we continued walking other Naqishbendi families joined us. Soon Yosef and his family joined us. Yosef, told us that his mother had died. He looked at my father with tears in his eyes. The poor guy looked like a wrecked ship, completely physically and emotionally broken. Speaking through a wrinkled tired face he said, "I can't believe this day. Even if it had been a dream, it would have driven me totally insane. But it is not a dream, it is a real day of our lives." said Yosef.

"I am really sorry for your mother," my father said to him. "You have my condolences, but let me remind you that the game is not over. We still have to run for our lives."

Yosef was staring down the street. "I can not believe that I had to leave my mother's dead body behind in my house. By the time I come back, her body may have decomposed. I feel disgusting for not even burying her."

"She is gone," said my cousin Jamal, quietly. "She has it good. I wouldn't really mind having a quick death instead of this violent life. Look at us—what we are doing in this horror? At least she is dead and with God. As far as your mom's dead body is concerned, she'll be left like thousands of others. Don't beat yourself up. You are doing the right thing in saving your and your family's lives."

"I don't want you think that I am a coward for leaving behind my mother's dead body. I really had to do that so that my young children and my wife wouldn't be killed in the next round of bombing."

My father nodded to him. "I'm glad you've come to your senses. I am sure God will help you."

"I don't know where God is in all this injustice, Shaykh."

"Yosef, you must believe in him. This is not God's doing. This is evil working against innocent people. Let us leave God out of this evil business and not to blame him."

Nobody wanted to have anything to do with Halabja any longer. It resembled hell. The sidewalks and streets that used to be like playgrounds for children were crowded with wounded and with dead bodies, many of them children. I saw a woman holding her child and both she and the child were lying dead on the ground. Poisoned people on the street coughed, cried, vomited and screamed in pain and often there were no apparent wounds. Wounded, bleeding people were trying to run, to flee from the town.

As we walked through the streets, we saw hundreds of dead bodies laying on a streets. The streets and sidewalks were full of dead bodies. They were people from all ages, man and women, young and old. It was a deadly poison and in most cases didn't killed people violently. However many people were complaining and they died with excruciating pains.

We walked in the direction of Ababyle and others were headed toward Anab. I'd never seen such a crowd of people in the two main streets. People walked in caravans, empty-handed, carrying only their little children and occasionally a bag of bread. They walked out of town without knowing where they'd end up or where they would stay. None of them could look back toward the town. The destruction was unbearable and unbelievable. We passed the last house in uptown and still more people joined us. Once outside of the town we started feeling a bit more secure but were still terrified that the planes would return.

"My vision is getting blurry," my father said to me.

I didn't know what to tell him. I said, "dad, once we get out of here and arrive at Ababayle, you may feel better."

I could see hundreds of people like my father whose vision was affected. They rubbed their eyes with a wet towel rubbed in charcoal, which, we had been told, would supposedly help prevent blindness associated with the chemical poisoning.

Both my mother and aunt were crying, and my mother slowed her pace, complaining of fatigue. We kept on walking, further and further from town. Thousands of people marched along the wet and muddy dirt road.

My father turned his head toward me. "I can't see anything. I am blind."

"Dad, you mean you can't see me?" I asked.

"No, I can't see anything. I mean it."

"Dad, just hold my hand, and let's walk."

I was in denial refusing to accept what my father had told me. I had to convince myself that his blindness was just temporary and that as soon as we'd rested he'd regain his sight. My mom was stunned and devastated—she cried and appeared to be out of words. Sometimes people are unable to find words to comfort each other. I couldn't think of anything to say that could comfort dad.

I felt sort of fatigue fearing I must have inhaled the same poison gas and that its effect might be not blindness but some other disease. I kept that fear out of mind knowing I had to survive in order to help. We kept walking and were just about halfway to Ababyle when we heard a noise and looked up into the sky. The planes were returning toward town. The crowd around us scattered and tried to hide, but we knew there were still people trying to leave Halabja.

"Let me hold your dad's hand," my mother said to me.

My aunt stepped closer to her. "No, leave him, Mahboob. You are already sick.

346

You need to take care of yourself."

I searched around and found a small dry spot on the ground where my father could rest. "Please don't move, just sit. I am going to hold your hand."

My aunt Mahsoom and my mom sat on the ground near my dad. All around us people took cover, and told their kids to lie flat.

I sat up and I saw four planes dive down two at a time over the town. I could see the bombs exploding. More planes were bombing the road from Halabja to Anab. The planes came toward us and dropped bombs nearby, shaking the ground and throwing tons of rock and dirt over our heads. I was afraid that someone among us might have been wounded or killed by the flying debris.

I saw a plane carpet-bomb the road to Anab road. I feared for people who had chosen that direction. I was fairly sure that no one survived. From every direction smoke and fire rose from the ground. We found out later that many of those who had fled for Anab had been all killed—at least one thousand people were killed along the mile-long stretch of that dirt road.

And then the planes were gone and the sky was silent. People stayed on the ground for a long time, and finally began to stand up, all covered in mud.

I reached for my father. He was tired and moving with difficulty. I went back and held my father's hand. My aunt Mahsoom came to us and her right arm was bleeding. "Its never ending day," she said.

"All I know is that I am wounded. Right after the explosion I felt something hit my arm."

"Please let me use my t-shirt to bind your arm so that the bleeding stops," I said.

"No, don't worry about me," she said. "I can wait until we arrive at the village."

"No," I insisted, and took off my undershirt and cut it into pieces with a shard of rock. My mother took the shreds of t-shirt and bound her arm, and the bleeding slowed.

By late in the afternoon we were all still on the run, attempting to arrive the village, and then continue on to the Iranian border. In our way to the village many died or left in their own for they couldn't walk. We had no choice but leave behind the bodies of our friends and keep on walking. We felt guilty leaving but we couldn't carry them. Everyone of us had more than could handle. There were so many amongst us who needed care and help. Most of adults were carrying children, and so many of us were sick. We had to push on to the village and hope that the people from the village would find the bodies of our people and bury them.

I must tell you that that day, every minute of it, will be with me, in memory and heart, until I die. Nobody in their right mind could imagine that people could be as savage to other people as our attackers were to us. If we had been offered a peaceful death, every one of us would have accepted it to avoid the pain and horror of such painful death. This is a story of helpless and defenseless people trapped between the most brutal regimes in the world—Saddam's Ba'th party and the Iranian Ayatollahs.

We didn't know what to expect in Ababayle, but we were all determined to cross over into Iran. I feared that my dad wouldn't make it. I'd hoped his blindness would be temporary but soon I felt that my poor father might be blind for the rest of his life. I could see my mother having difficulty holding herself together, and sorrow poured from her as she walked with my father. She was fallen into despair, I feared she might not be able survive.

A year ago Dad had become prosperous with his business. We'd had a nice house in a good section of the town. The future was full of hope. And suddenly, as we walked, I understood that our house was destroyed, the business was gone, my dad was blind, and both my dad and my mother were sick. It was horrible to imagine, in the middle of nowhere on a desolate road to Iran that my parents might die, we would be left with their dead bodies, and I would end up as an orphaned teenager.

Surrounded by such sudden destruction and bloodshed, none of us could imagine that there would be better days ahead. I tried to concentrate on taking care of my parents and not focus on the overwhelming tragedy. If it wasn't for my parents, and my aunt, who needed me, I would have given up.

As we got closer to the village, dad grew weaker and weaker. We had a long way to go, and I knew that night would bring the cold. We would be walking in the mountains, which would be covered with snow. We were not prepared for the cold.

Near Ababyle the road to the village grew steep. We had to stop now and then so that my parents could get a few minutes rest before they resumed walking. Others around us were suffering, but as we were on the run, I had to hold Dad's hand and there was no time to check with or help anyone else. While some were getting sick and going blind, others went insane as a result of the nerve gas, running around, crying, and holding their heads, and often falling and hurting themselves.

We arrived at the village. One could see hundreds of people climbing the hill like ants. We followed the trail to the mosque, which was almost full of people from Halabja. The mullah of the mosque was there along with a few people from the village. The rest of the villagers had remained in their homes or fled for the Iranian border.

We went inside the mosque and sat down for a short time to rest and think about our next move. I took Dad to the bathroom, which, like those in most mosques, had water running along the ground with a large drain hole in every stall. I had to go with Dad inside the stall so that he would not fall into the hole. He was despairing and yet kept it all to himself, occasionally taking a deep breath and saying, "thank you God, please don't make it worse than it is." We left the bathroom and I took him to the pool and helped him wash his face, hands, and feet, afraid he might fall into the pool. After a short rest we went and sat in the mosque's spacious main room where the prayer services took place. The stone floor was cemented with mud and covered with cheap carpets. In the middle of the room sat a conical metal fireplace, typical in mosques.

Some men prayed. Women and children congregated on the other side of the room. When the prayer was over I took Dad's hand and we sat down. People started talking to each other—almost half were blind or had some respiratory or nerve disorder. Some were seriously ill and vomiting violently, and most everyone was coughing and complaining of shortness of breath. There were no doctors or nurses and no one knew what to do. Our only hope we had was that we would survive the journey into Iran and find doctors and hospitals.

My brother Noradeen found us. During the walk from Muhmood's basement we were separated from most of the Naqishbendi families, but after an hour in the mosque we were all reunited. We Naqishbendis had all decided to stick together, and we did.

In the mosque people were sitting in groups, and individuals were asking people if they knew the whereabouts of this person or that person. Many people had lost each other as they'd tried to exit the town in the panic and rush. I saw parents looking for their children, and children looking for their parents. When I looked around and saw the children it broke my heart. They were quiet and scared, still holding their parents, looking like the pictures of victims of concentration camps.

That day in the mosque more than twenty people died from illnesses attributed to the chemicals and nerve gas. Dozens of children and babies had gone blind. Some people were paralyzed—their entire muscle systems were ruined—and they couldn't move at all.

My dad turned to my mother and said, "I wish your father and his family were with us. Have you heard anyone talk about him?" She answered that she didn't, and aunt Mahsoom left and went to ask the various groups. She returned with news that their house seemed to be okay and that was all she could gather.

As we were talking, Sofi Hayder, who was one of the followers of the Naqishbendis and who loved uncle Sayfadeen, came to us crying. He held my father's hand and looked like he was going to say something, but he was emotionally overwhelmed. We all kept looking at him and knew he didn't bring good news.

My father grew impatient. "What is going on? I thought you were going to tell me something."

"Shaykh," said Sofi Hayder, finally, "I am sorry for your uncle and his family."

I am sure the first thing that came to my father's mind was my Grandpa. Both my mom and my aunt opened their eyes wide and stared at Sofi Hayder.

"Which uncle, dear Sofi? Please let me know," demanded my father.

"Your uncle Sayfadeen," said Sofi.

"What happened to them, Sofi?"

350

Sofi was crying like a baby. "Oh, my dear Shaykh, I don't know how I can cope with what I've seen. He was my saint, and now he is gone."

"What about his family?" asked my father. Dad's eyes were still tearing and it was hard for me to tell whether he was crying or suffering from the chemicals.

"I was running to get out of town and crossed the road nearby the sewer stream. I saw Shaykh there, so I said to myself that he was trying to get out of the town and it would be a blessing to go along with him. He would be my savior for he is my saint. I ran toward him but fell down on the ground, short of breath. I could see him disappearing, sinking into the stream, and I saw his wife reaching for him, trying to hold his hand and get him out of the stream. But she disappeared too.

Then I saw his son Akram trying to save them, but he disappeared too. I thought they might all have fallen on the ground just like I did, and I rushed toward the stream. My God, what I saw is unforgettable and heartbreaking.

"What did you see Sofi?" My dad was disheartened and in shock.

"I saw all three of them dead, along with a half-dozen others. Oh my God, what a calamity this is. Shaykh, please, we need to pray for an end to this horror."

"Sofi, did you really see them as you said?" asked Jamal.

"Oh, yes, my dear friend. I wish I was dead instead of them. I am not making it up. I saw their bodies, and I have been crying since then. How I can stop crying?

My holy man and spiritual guide, Shaykh Sayfadeen, is dead. I saw the person I valued more than anything in my life, including myself, lying beside his son and wife in a sewer stream with human waste running over his body."

My mother was frantic. "What can we do? I think we know nothing about the casualties. We are going to hear more as we go along, and we will find that thousands are dead."

The *peshmargas,* concerned that the bombing would continue. They ordered families with wounded and sick stay inside the masque and the rest to spread around. We stayed in the mosque and had some bread and water. Friends of my parents, Hama Nawroly, and his wife and son and grandsons, came closer to us.

"Shaykh Gareeb, is your family okay?" he asked.

"I don't know anyone to be okay. I think I have gone blind, Mr. Hama."

"I can't see either," said Mr. Hama.

"There are too many people like us. I don't know what kind of poison these devils used."

Mr. Hama nodded. "They are after us to kill us. This is war, and this is the kind of tragedy war brings."

"I think you are right," said my father. "Back in 1961 we started the revolution and since we endured hardship, bloodshed, and destruction. We thought that revolution would bring us freedom. Yet one handshake brought our revolution to an end and decades of revolution brought us nothing but disaster. Now we started another revolution, led by the same old leadership proven to be nothing but a failure. I hope this revolution will be more fruitful than before."

"Fruitful…I don't know of any fruit coming out of this chaos and these leaders. I hope its fruit is not going to be what we are harvesting now." Mr. Hama paused and breathed deeply. "This revolution will be a long struggle. God knows how long it will take, or if it'll ever end. This revolution is about our leaders—who are putting themselves in power and making their families and their friends wealthy."

"Let us forget about that and see what we are going to do today," said my father.

"I don't know," continued Mr. Hama. "All I know is that I can't see and can't go anywhere without someone holding my hand."

"Mahsoom, how is your arm?" asked my dad.

"I think there is a piece of a metal inside, but I'm not letting that bother me. I cleaned it up and found a good piece of cloth to tie the wound with."

"That's painful, Mahsoom," said my dad.

"Forget about it, Shaykh. Once we get to a hospital I'll have it taken care of. It is not going to kill me."

Mr. Hama left. When Sabre and Atya returned, dad told them what he heard about their uncle Sayfadeen and his family. They both cried and dad warned them, "We should realize that we don't know much about anyone. There will be more bad news as we go along."

The day declined into the evening and there was no food. People were sick and hungry. Late at night Iranian soldiers entered the village and called people to come to receive bread. Thousands of people flooded down to the village's main road. The soldiers threw the bread from their trucks and the people ran after them. People were hungry and the trucks couldn't reach everyone at the same time, and a few fights broke out.

Soon after, the *peshmargas* came and asked everyone to leave the mosque. They reported that planes were still pounding the surrounding area, and they were worried about overcrowded masque with people. We were directed to a house and directed into the basement, where the odor of animal waste and the moist floor was disgusting. We had no blankets to put on a floor, so we all sat in the dirt, talking about our fears and our misfortune. We stayed at that disgusting place until early morning.

In the morning we were brought out and directed toward the Iranian border. The Iranians were using the road to transport their army and ammunition to their camps around Halabja, and it was getting bombed daily. The walk to Iranian aimed destination would take a number of days, and though many were too sick to walk that far, but we all began the journey. It was dark and cold and we had to climb the mountains. I was holding my father's hand—he and my mother both felt fatigue and barely could walk. While climbing my father fell down and bruised his arms and legs, and my mother hit her head on a rock and started bleeding. My aunt had cloth that she had used to tie her wounded arm. She took it off to bind the wound on my mother's head with.

We walked for days through muddy lands and across rocky mountains. We had decided not to leave anyone behind. We topped frequently to rest. We saw women giving birth and screaming in pain. We saw people in the road who were dead and left behind.

After two days walking, we were all exhausted. We found a small spring by a cave and stopped to drink and wash our faces. We looked like wild animals and were afraid to look at each other.

We rested and talking about what to eat but it produced nothing more than despair. We were all starving, forlorn in a wild and couldn't even imagine where food could come from. We almost gave up and looking at one another with a feeling that hours of our lives are counted. We were all despair and desolate, but none expressed our gloomy condition for we were striving to walk and arrive at some community.

We almost gave up when I saw, far away, an approaching caravan. I yelled, "look, there is a caravan coming this way!"

Atya, Sabre, my aunt and I rushed toward the caravan. When we got close to them all three ladies went and told the men that we were refugees and that we hadn't eaten for days. A very old man with a big tobacco-stained beard approached my aunt and they talked for more than ten minutes. Now I think about it, I realize that she did an incredible job of begging. She almost made the old fellow to cry for us. Before he left he prayed for us and said, "I pray, lady, that God will bring justice to you all'. He said a little poem by the Kurdish poet Mawlawy—which I now cannot remember—regarding his feelings. The caravan was on its way to Iraq with smuggled goods from Iran, left us with two huge bags of canned fish.

Soon after I spotted another caravan and we waited for them. My aunt repeated to them the story of our hardship and they gave us a big bag of cheese and nuts. My aunt looked at me with a sigh of relief and said, "God is not going to lock every door on us."

Back at the cave we passed around the nuts and collected wood to barbeque the fish. We stayed in that cave for almost more than a day, while the Iraqi planes pounded away at the surrounding area.

Next day we prepared to move toward one of the nearby towns. We walked into the cold dark night and finally saw Iranian army vehicles on the road. We were instructed by the Iranian soldiers to follow the road. Near the mountains Iranian soldiers directed us toward a huge cave used by their military personnel. We were told to stay there and rest until evening, and warned not to walk in the day because of the Iraqi planes. Iranian soldiers brought us blankets and gave us bread and water and some rice soup. The cave could have fit hundreds of people—in several places narrow passages lead to larger caverns. It was clean and looked like a natural cave but the army had extended it for use as a hiding place for troops.

Late in the evening an army officer told us that we all needed to leave.

We packed into a huge bus and were driven to a small town, Sahtla. In Sahtla they housed us in several schools and a mosque until they could get us to a refugee camp. Army officers went around the town announcing to the people in the village that civilians from Halabja had escaped their town for fear of more chemical bombing and nerve gas by the government of Iraq. The announcer asked the people in the town to help us. The people, God bless their souls, shared with us the little that they had. They were Iranian Kurds. They gave us whatever food and clothes they could spare. I'll never forget those people's generosity and kindness toward us. They tried to help us in every way they could. They knew of our tragedy, and some cried for us. They came and talked to us and wanted to know in detail what had happened.

We stayed in this town nearly a month, sleeping in the mosque. Every night people from the village came to visit us, bringing much needed prayers and emotional support.

The mosque had a small kitchen, which we used for cooking and bathing. My parents and aunt Mahsoom had brought some money with them, which they used to buy food. We met a few people who let us use their kitchen, and mom and aunt Mahsoom cooked the food there and brought it back to share with the others.

In the town there was a very big and well-equipped hospital, but no good doctors. Aunt Mahsoom went for treatment for her arm. She was in a lot of pain, and the doctor told her that her wound was infected and that the only treatment was to cut her hand off. My aunt refused, thank God, and in less than a month her arm was almost healed.

Soon after we arrived in town an Iranian helicopter arrived. We were told that anyone affected with chemical substances would be taken to Teharan where they had volunteered French doctors to treat them. My mother and aunt asked my father to go for treatment but he refused. Later on we discovered that there wasn't much treatment available. Many of the people who were blind and seriously sick came back as they'd left, uncured. The illnesses they suffered from were severe and there wasn't much of anything that could be done.

The government of Iran put up tents outside of town and gradually moved us to this refugee camp. In the camp they had a medical center, a police station, and they cooked three meals a day for us, the food they gave us was meager and most of the time it was vegetable soup. My aunt Mahsoom, however, still went to the nearby town twice a week food shopping and cooked it in the camp.

My parents, my aunt, and I were in one tent, my cousin Jamal's family was next to us. All Naqishbendi were together. Anywhere safe from the bombing seemed to be a blessing, but after a few days we grew tired of the camp and hoped that the Iran-Iraq war would end so that we could return home.

Badaw, my cousin Jamal's wife, was still coughing day and night. Like many other infected people with nerve and chemicals agents, she was taken to see many doctors. She lost so much weight that she became unrecognizable. After almost two months of pain she passed away.

After a month in a camp, Aunt Mahsoom wanted to go back to Sulaymania. She missed her family. Traveling back to Iraq was not allowed without permission from the Iranian authorities. She visited the authorities and begged them to let her return to Sulaymania, but was told that people from Sulaymania would eventually come to the camp and that she shouldn't bother going back.

Harseny's ex-wife Rahma was searching for her daughter Mahabad, who lived with grandpa's family in Halabja. She had searched in vain all around Halabja. We still didn't know what had happened to Grandpa and his family, and we went around asking if anyone knew about them. My aunt Mahsoom and my mom started talking to many people, and aunt went asking at several other camps, but nothing surfaced.

Rahma stayed with us for a few days and then prepared to return to Iraq. Aunt Mahsoom decided to go back with her. They went together to one of the *peshmarga* leaders, an old friend of Harsenys, who managed to help them reach Penjeween, an Iraqi border town. At the border they went to the Iraqi army checkpoint and were questioned and had to fill out forms. After hours of interrogation an Iraqi officer agreed to transfer them onto an army truck that was leaving for another army location near Sulaymania. When they climbed into the back of the truck, they saw that it was loaded with cases of bullets. They returned to the officer and expressed concern, knowing that if the truck was hit they would be blown up. Their concerns were understood and they boarded a different vehicle.

They were transferred to an army location near the village of Chwarqrna. Upon arrival they were taken to a prison, a dirty small room full of people. Hours later they were called in for interrogation by an army officer from Mokhabarat, a secret agency. They were asked questioned for hours—why they went to Iran, whom they contacted there, why they came back, and whom they had seen. The officer, worried of Iranian spies, often rephrased and asked the same questions several times.

After three days without food and water they were set free, and my aunt made it back home. A few months after her return her young husband Hama died of a heart attack.

The Iraqi war ended a few months after the bombing of Halabja. The Iranians told us that Saddam had issued amnesty and we need to leave. By then we were tired of being in the refugee camp and were eager to return home. We were told that after the chemical bombing the Iraqi planes had pounded Halabja for days and the town was flattened. We realized that we had no home left to return to.

We were frightened and we didn't know how we would survive and make a living. Our store in Halabja was gone, dad was blind, and mother was sick. We were destitute by all mean and couldn't do much on our own, in all matters we relied on family.

Finally we got together with the rest of the Naqishbendi families and decided to return home. A bus dumped us near the Iraqi border, and the Iraqi Army transferred us all to an area near Bynjan, a village close to Sulaymania. In Bynjan we were put in a refugee camp without sanitation or running water, and with tents made of thin clear plastic which couldn't withstand even mildest wind. I must tell you that the refugee camp in Iran looked like a castle compared with what the Iraqi army had to offer. It was scary to think about staying in that camp through the winter—and when winter came thousands of people died in similar camps throughout Iraq.

We managed to let aunt Mahsoom know where we were, and the next day she came with her stepson Falah. Initially our camp was fenced in and no one was allowed in or out. I don't know how, but Falah snuck into the camp and smuggled us out and drove us to Sulaymania where we stayed in my aunt' house for the next two months. We then went and stayed for a month with Aunt Kalthoom and uncle Omar, and then rented a house. We had no furniture and no money, but on the day that we moved to the new house, aunt Mahsoom showed up with a truck full of every necessity.

Due to the chemical poisoning my father had an excruciating headache. We took him to several doctors in Iran but they could not help. After we settled in Sulaymania we took him to doctors who attributed his headaches to the pressure in his eyes. To release the pressure they had to inject a needle, and he ended up losing his eyeballs permanently.

My mother had been suffering from back problem, but doctors could not help her. The nerve gas and chemical agents used in the bombing created many diseases that are beyond any doctor's diagnosis. Now my mother's back is curved so badly that when she walks one is afraid that her head may touch the ground.

Aunt Mahsoom continued to search for my grandpa and his family, and it was not until a month after our return that we heard, from Roshna, the story of what happened to them.

Chapter Twenty-Four
Roshna's Story

Rumor had it that Saddam was planning to bomb Halabja with chemicals. We didn't know exactly what kind of chemical substance would be used but we could guess that the result would be devastating. At school they told of the dangers of chemical weapons, and there were some published materials describing self-protection methods in chemical warfare, but it was different now, when the threat was real. We knew Saddam would take revenge for the takeover of Halabja—which had been his biggest defeat in his war with Iran up to that point.

For many days prior to the chemical bombing we were confined to the basement. Bombing and fighting around Halabja had raged without pause. It was difficult time and we were uncertain about the outcome of Iraq-Iran war. The fear made us hide together in a large number. Our basement had been a place of refuge for many of our neighbors and some of our relatives. We were fearful and frightened by the prospect of bombing but we enjoyed being together. The women were all together cooking, the kids were playing and everyone shared fascinating stories. If it hadn't been for the closeness of our families, the fear of war could have been emotionally devastating.

My sister Kazhal had two daughters, six-month-old, Chra and five-year-old Razawa. About a week prior to the bombing Kazhal went with Chra to Sulaymania to see a doctor and left Razawa with us.

The day before chemical bombing, my father woke up early and we all sat for breakfast. The skies were quite that morning. Fearful of bombing, people started pouring in right after breakfast, and by noon there were at least seventy people in our house, and the number kept on growing. Some stayed in the living room, others crowded down into the basement. The Kids as usual, were sneaking out into the backyard playing. People had brought food and other necessary children staff with them. Mom started preparing for dinner, and other women helped with cleaning, and cooking.

During those days town had basically shut down. People didn't go anywhere unless they had to. Stores and shops were all closed, except for a few grocery and butcher shops. Iranian tanks and armored vehicles lined up to guard the road leading to Sulaymania.

We had relatively a large house, with spacious living room. The house was surrounded by a five-foot wall of stone. The entrance to the basement descended down several stairs from our living room. The basement, which had previously been used for storage, was now cleaned out, the floor was carpeted, and mattresses placed along the wall.

My mom was an extremely neat and clean person, very creative in making the house look nice and presentable. With a few minor details, such as pictures and an old couch she turned the basement into another living room.

A couple months earlier I had gotten married and planned to move out of the house by summer, eager to move to Sulaymania and establish my own family.

That day Mahabad, Harseny's daughter, who lived with Haji Ezat's family, arrived at our house. We were close friends. She came as usual with a huge bag fastened with a thin string. She looked beautiful and relaxed with a natural smooth face as if she had a goodnight sleep. She loved clothes and always dressed beautifully and immaculate, whether in Kurdish or Western style.

"Mahabad, why are you bringing this huge bag with you?" I asked.

"It has some of my clothes," she said. "If Haji Ezat's house is bombed I will have enough clothes to wear."

"What are you planning to do as Halabja is taken over by Iranians?" I asked her.

"With my luck, anything can go wrong," she said with a smile, "well, if that to occurs, I may have to go back to the city and live with mother. But that may not help me finding another job,"

Mahabad recently employed as a school teacher. This teaching job was her first, and she was excited with the prospect of earning salary and helping her mother. Her mother lived with her sister, Bayan, in Sulaymania, and Mahabad was eager to help them out financially.

Mahabad's parents were divorced when she was a few years old. Her father had been kidnapped and rumor had it that he was assassinated by Masoud and Idres Barzani's men. His body was never recovered.

In those days our basement was often crowded, and though we were hiding fear of bombing, we all enjoyed the food and company. The sixteenth of March was a similar day, our neighbors and relatives poured in. By late morning the crowd grew to more than eighty people stood around, and as kids ran everywhere playing. Most of the time people congregated in a scattered small groups and holding conversation while the main gathering took place in the living room. Mom made tea and we shared it with the crowd.

At 11:20 a.m. we heard the sound of airplanes. Everyone rushed into the basement. The first explosion was terrifying, and was followed by more until all of the glass in the house above us shattered. We feared that a bomb would hit us at any minute, and imagined that Halabja, being such a small town, would soon be demolished should the bombings with that intensity were to continue.

As a bombing was in progress, one of our neighbors came and told us the town has been hit with chemical bombs. We had all felt something abnormal but hadn't known what it was. We all felt it would be safer to leave the basement and go upstairs, for chemical agents are heavy and settle along the lowest levels. The sonic boom of the planes along with the bombing had blown out every door and windows in every house. That was done on purpose so that nothing could block the flow of the chemical and biological agents. We found the living room floor covered with shattered glass.

It was a pause in bombing, I began cleaning up with my brother Ako, my sister Nask, and Mahabad came to help. I told the crowd to put on sandals to avoid being cut.

Just as we finished cleaning the planes returned and resumed bombing. Some people returned to the basement and some remained upstairs. The crowd felt environment was contaminated with chemicals from bombing, and they searched for water to clean chemicals off their faces and bodies.

My brother and I soaked towels and blankets in water and passed them around. I saw my father leaning against the living-room wall with his eyes closed. I handed him a wet towel and he opened his eyes, and said to me, "my sweat daughter, I am gone. Good-bye."

I couldn't believe what I had heard, and thought he must have been upset or just wanted to be left alone. He stood for a few moments longer and then collapse on the ground. I fell to my knees and held his face with my hands, asking him to wake up. I put my ear against his heart and heard nothing. I put my hands against his heart and couldn't fell his heartbeats. I placed my ear to his lips but I heard no breathing. "Oh my God," I screamed, "dad is dead."

Salah Sharazori and his wife were sitting nearby, their son laying in a front of them. All three of them were dead. I realized that we were all trapped and that everyone's turn would come. I realized that the chemical bombing was real. My mind was in a weird state, I couldn't cry, scream, yell or get angry, my entire faculties were numb.

I didn't want to stand up or look around for I knew there would be more death around me. Fearing for my life and for what I would see, I stood up and looked around the room. My brother Ako was laying on a floor with the towels spread around him. I looked at him for a moment, but I knew that he was already perished. My sister Nask was lying dead next to him. The chemicals were consuming us at an incredible rate.

It was a moment of silence, the bombing stopped. I heard no crying babies or children. No voices came from the basement or from upstairs. I knew that I must be the only survivor. It was dreadful to see how fast the crowd disappearing. I wondered was it by incident or by design the way chemical worked on human as I observed painless and silent death.

I went lying next to my dead brother. "Is this true or, maybe a dream? I think I am dreaming. It can't be that everyone is dead. Then if so, how I could be alive? Yes, I am dreaming and should go back to sleep and finish this nightmare."

I closed my eyes, but the voice of reality opened my eyes and told me that this was real. I opened my eyes, and ran to the front yard. My Mother lay face down on the cemented pathway with her face in the grass. "Mom get up," I said," I screamed knowing that she was dead like everyone else.

I went back into the living room and saw my sister Ashna lying on the ground. Gradually I could hear people wailing throughout neighborhood. I descended into the basement and saw my sister Jowan with her back against the wall leaning to one side with a pillow clenched in her arms. I truly was the only one who survived.

I returned to the living room and lay next to my sister Ashna. Ashna had been in her early twenties, two years older than me. She used to call me "little sister". She loved children and all she hoped for was to get married and have her own family.

I felt strange and didn't know why everyone else dead while I remained alive. I knew that the same poison that had killed them would kill me too, but I was puzzled as to why it worked so slowly on me. I frazzled and my vision grew blurry. I said a prayer to God pleading silent death rather than be blind or crippled. I languished and couldn't stand up, I breathed a sigh of relief knowing my end was near.

I heard a noise thought that someone else may have survived. I checked around in the hallway and went down into the basement, but everyone was dead. I returned to my sister Ashna and fell a sleep. When I woke it was morning. I had no idea how long I had slept. It was a sunny day and sort of warm for that time of the year.

I was wondering about the rest of the town, I didn't know what was going on outside our house until I opened the door, I saw several dead bodies on the street. I visited my mother, I was worried that she might have it rough in her last minutes, I checked her face and her hands. I was comforted when I didn't see bruises, scars or blood. The street was silent. I pulled Kochar's body behind the door inside and placed it against the door so that it would be difficult for anyone to enter. With a towel I wiped foam from Kochar's mouth. She was twenty years old and had planned to attend the university. She loved to sing and have picnics. I said to her, "we all go to heaven and she can have picnic there." Her brother, Soara, on the other side of the living room. He was a year older then my brother Ako. When I had passed wet towels around to the crowd he had walked around with a big container of water and a bowl and poured water on the crowd, enjoyed what he did, with everyone laughing at him. Imagine among all the horrors and fears surrounding us, still there was some humor. He had continued to fill the container with water, and pour it over everyone until he dropped dead.

I was still convinced that at any minute I would drop dead. I saw my nephew Razawa laying by the coach with a towel over her face. "It was so strange that just yesterday at the same time all these people had been alive. Poor Razawa had been following mom everywhere with mom hugging and kissing her every chance she had "Oh, my God, I asked, the such a little innocent creature. She was just a little girl. She was full of joy, playful and as happy as any little girl could be around her age."

I wonder what would my poor sister Kazhal would do when she heard Razawa was dead. I knew she would cry for all the dead, and I could imagine that once she heard the news, she would be much happier to be dead than alive. Kazhal loved her little daughter, when she had left for Sulaymania she kissed her countless time and told us she would be worried about her until she came back. When she had left, Razawa was sleeping next to my mom. I looked at Razawa and said, "you know, your mom will go insane when she hears what happened to you."

The family room, living room, and basement were full of bodies—it was difficult to walk through the house. I checked the family room and spotted my Uncle Hewa, my mother's youngest brother. He and his four children and wife all lay dead next to each other. I wonder if they had known that they would die and had moved next to one another. Hewa's older daughter was in Sulaymania attending the university. I held my uncle, "dear uncle you left but your daughter's life will be a living nightmare for the rest of her life. She is left with enough pain to overwhelm her for the rest of her life."

I saw my uncle's wife with her three-year-old daughter between her arms and her five-year-old son with his head on her lap. That reminded me of those nights we stayed up late and the kids felt a sleep on her. Just a few feet from them, lay my Uncle Nouri's wife and her four children.

When we were in hide, we all enjoyed our togetherness, families and friends alike. Even though we had no peace of mind and we were inundated with uncertainty about our lives, yet one thing was for sure we had and that was our togetherness as a society caring for one another. Now when I looked around me it seems they all gone together. Right in this house were I was eager to feel my last heartbeat to join the caravan of their eternal journey scattered the dearest people in my life and almost most of the world which I count on. I cared not for myself for I knew I will join them but those who survived us and have them to be reminded of our stories.

My poor uncle Nouri was away on a business trip to Sulaymania. When he would hear what had become of his family, he would be bereaved for the rest of his life. I knew that I was going to join the crowd in our house, but I wondered what life meant to those who left behind? Perhaps—

Hanging on the hallway wall was a picture of my brother Ako gardening with my dad. I went to Ako's body. He was lying with his mouth on the floor. I turned his face, and he looked as he had the day before when I had tried to wake him up, and he had fought, grabbing the blanket and covering his face. Ako was dad's favorite, for he was the youngest, and they went everywhere together. He had been about twelve years old, was smart and extremely good at school. He was a tall, slim, handsome and friendly kid who had many friends. I kissed him many time and told him how much I loved him. I am sure he heard me.

I could see a large photo of my brother Awat. He was dad's hero besides being father and son, they were best friends. Whenever anything happened dad used to call him, solicit his opinion and besides he was his oldest child. I wondered how Awat would weather this. I looked at his picture and said to him, "Oh, my dear brother, we really didn't want to leave you, we wanted to be with you, but evil tore us apart. As I approach my destiny I will leave you with my prayer, praying that you have the strength to weather this calamity. My dear brother, I wish I could write you and my sister Ashna a letter, but for now my sweet brother goodbye, and may God be with you both."

I got close to dad and looked at him. Just a few weeks prior to the bombing he was going through my engagement and wedding pictures. During my wedding dad took so many photo's that it got on my nerves, but he continued, saying that it would be such a beautiful memory. Before leaving dad I said to him, "You have been always optimistic and told us that the chaos would end and we enjoy picnics and Rashbalack (a Kurdish group dance where all people hold each others hands, all dressed in traditional Kurdish clothes, often forming a circle with a singer in the middle) Dad, while you are asleep, I can see everyone, instead of dancing and singing, all dead and silent. Perhaps there will be a Rashbalak, but for sure we will not be there. Poor dad, you always try to see the sunny side of everything in life. The world didn't live up to your optimism. I have always been fond of you and I always loved you. Dad, did you hear me?" I bend down and kissed him on his cheeks.

I went to the little window and saw my mom laying dead. I wished that I could brought her inside but I wasn't strong enough to do that. I said to her, "dear mom, I have to have a talk with you. Oh, sweet mom. You promised me that when I go to my home in Sulaymania to join my husband, you would escort me and stay with me to decorate the house. I know that I have always been in your mind; you always tried to do your best for me. I love you mom, God knows how much I love you. Oh, my beloved mom I love you. You all had quick death, but my journey seems to be taking a little longer. Mom, I tell you, I know you are with God now, and, please, I want my end, I can no longer endure this horrible life. You know where I am. I want to join you, please, and stop this suffering. Mom I love you, and I have to go now, and visit others."

I went to my sister Nask. She was at fourteen, and absolutely amiable. She was a quiet teenager, she loved to read, and wanted to be a doctor. She had planned to buy a big house and have my parents live with her. As she lay dead she was still beautiful. Poor thing had a plan for everything in her life from early age. She was ambitious and used to tell me that she will climb as high as her potential can take her. She perhaps thought of many good things in life, now all her hopes are blighted and her dreams are thundered. "My dear sister, you are gone too," I said to her. "Don't feel bad; being dead is better than living with the memory of this day."

By that point my vision was impeded. I saw my surroundings as shadows and felt extremely weak, tardy and dizzy. I was discombobulated, and afraid that I was going to suffer and die slowly for I prayed for a quick end. I wished that I was dead. The only thing I didn't pray for was to escape death. I couldn't eat because I knew the food was contaminated, and though I drank the water I knew it was also contaminated. I knew if nothing else would kill me, starvation would.

I laid down on the hallway floor and fell asleep, waking sometimes to the voice of a mother crying for her child. The voice was real and overwhelming. I got up and followed the voice into the living room, walking around until the crying stopped. I thought it might have been a dream, or my mind playing tricks on me.

Soon after I heard several voices outside. I thought I heard Persian and thought they must be Iranian Pasdar (militias). They pushed against the door. I ignored them and went back to sleep. I really didn't want to see people. I wanted to be left alone and die amongst my family and friends.

I fell asleep and woke once into the black night and then slept until morning. I was too weak to move. All that I could perceive were the dark shadows of objects, and I knew that I had lost my vision.

After three days had passed I couldn't move to get water. I was happy and thought that I would soon be out of misery. In those days I visited with everyone and talked to them all as if though they were alive. There was a small window looking into

the front yard. I would look out at my mom and talk to her. The bodies were all turning dark, except Mahabad Harseny, whose body turned pinkish. I wondered why she was different than the rest. I visited mostly with the children, and felt disheartened for them. Things could have been even worse if these children were die with pain and suffering. It was unbelievable how everyone died so silently and painlessly.

I laid down on a floor growing sleepy, knowing that this finally would be the end of me. I wished to crawl and say last good-bye to everyone, but I couldn't make it. I closed my eyes to go to my final resting place, and immediately heard a noise outside—voices speaking in Kurdish. They pushed the door and I ignored them. "Is anyone here"? Came a man's voice. Please, open the door. I didn't respond. I was annoyed and thought if they knew what I was going through they would leave me alone. They continued to push the door and I knew they wouldn't give up. Finally I responded, "yes I am here."

They rushed in and said they were *peshmargas*. A few people entered and I could hear more of them outside. I could see shadows and hear their footsteps. They were noisy and cursed in rage.

"Where are you?" someone asked, "can you hear me, lady?"

"Yes, I can hear you. I am here."

He got closer and stood by me, and asked me if I could stand. I told him that I could not, and that I was blind. Another man said "Oh my God, what had happened here?"

Another man interrupted him. "This is the worst I have seen so far, oh my dear God."

They called another *peshmarga* into the house. They asked me my name.

"My name is Roshna," I said.

"You must have been here for three days," someone said.

"I don't exactly know how many days I have been here."

"Do you know if there is anybody else alive in this house?"

I said that everyone were dead.

"Is there a basement?"

I pointed them toward the stairs and heard them descended and start to yell.

They called the others down into the basement. "This is unbelievable, get a vehicle ready, we need to take care of this young lady. Her name is Roshna. We need to get her somewhere for treatment. She can't walk and she can't see." Said the head of *Peshmarga* to his men.

"No, please, take me nowhere. I want to stay with my parents with my sisters. I want to stay with everyone here I don't want to leave them. Please leave me alone." I said and I really meant what I said for the only thing that didn't cross my mind during all that time was help.

"We are not going to hurt you, we are here to help you," I was told.

I shook my head. "I don't know you and I don't know who you are.

Please leave me here. I need no help. If you want to help me, just leave me where I am and go about your own business."

A new voice spoke to me. "Roshna, do you know me?"

"No, who are you?" I asked.

"I am Falah. Falh Hama Bore."

I knew Falah. Our families had been friends. I went silent but still I didn't want to be taken anywhere. I knew I was going to die, and wanted to die next to my parents, my sisters, and my brother.

"Come here and help me to carry this lady to the car. Be very gentle," said one of the *peshmarga*'s to another.

Two *peshmarga* held me and placed me inside a vehicle heading to Ababayle, a nearby village. In Ababayle, we stopped at a house. They offered me soup and bread. After a brief rest, I realized they were all men. I felt uncomfortable and crying to be taken somewhere with women. I didn't feel comfortable with all those men around me, and I could not see. They dressed me in boy's clothes, handing me the clothes in sequence so that I could dress correctly.

They drove me in an Iranian military vehicle to Sazan, nearby village with a military hospital. I was in a front of a pickup truck and could not sit up straight. After I hit my head against the window, the driver asked a soldier to come in a front and hold me. The soldier jumped through the back window, into the front, and sat next to me.

I stayed in the hospital for about two weeks. I was treated and my vision gradually begun to return. My mind and vision was dominated by the horror of the bombing, the scene of the house crowded with dead. I kept thinking about everyone in our house, my family, relatives and neighbors. I had clear pictures of every one of them, what they looked like and how I found them dead. They were with me every minute.

I thought about my husband. I had a bad feeling that he might not be interested in me anymore. I wouldn't have blamed him. I knew that if he was to want me again, it would prove his tremendous love and affection. I feared that no one would be willing to partner with me with such tragic memories nested in my mind. I loved my husband, even if he would deny me as his wife. Terrible things had happened to me, and I would bear the burden.

I couldn't believe I had survived, and felt guilty for all those who had died. Death would have been painless; being a live was now painful. I wondered in melancholy what made me different than them. I had no special clothes or mask. I thought that my rescue was a mistake. I wondered how my life would be beyond that point. Perhaps I would live in my memories of past calamities, careless about the future and, the world that had treated me, my family, and neighbors so brutally. I wasn't sure if I would ever live a normal, peaceful day for the rest of my life.

I lost my parents, my sisters Ashna, Jewan, and Nask, and my younger brother Ako, and most members of my close relatives. I kept recalling beautiful memories of my brother and my sisters. My poor brother Awat and my sister Kazhal wouldn't know what had happened to our family, but who would have the courage to give them the news? I wondered if I would ever reunite with them. I didn't trust my health. Even though I was treated and regaining my sight. I was very sure that the same poison that had killed so many would take me to my coffin too, its just a matter of time.

The doctor who treated me said that I had developed high blood pressure, much too high for my age. Indeed I didn't care and didn't even bother to ask the reading. I really didn't care whether I would live or die.

Peshmarga were in touch with me on a daily basis. They asked me if I had left any money or jewelry at home. I remember that on the day of the bombing my sister Ashna and my mom had attached a wallet full of money and jewelry to their backs when they asked me to do the same, I had refused.

I gave the *peshmarga* descriptions of my mother and sister. They left, and returned with a golden nickel, a golden belt, some jewelry, and the equivalent of one thousand U.S. dollars. I knew my parents had carried much more than that, but there wasn't anything that I could do.

After two weeks in Sazan they arranged for me to move to Kamyaran, a refugee camp in Iran. My father's uncle, Mustafa, lived in Marywan, a Kurdish town close to the Iraqi border. I had seen him only once, when I was a little girl when he visited us. He knew what had happened in Halabja and knew that my family had been affected, but he didn't know the horrible details.

I arrived at the refugee camp late in the evening. I recognized several people from Halabja. A few days after my arrival at camp, I was taken to the office of camp manager. The office contained a few chairs, a desk, and a telephone. I saw a young armed man about twenty years old with a short beard, who looked like *Pasddar* extended his hand to me. The camp manger stood up and pointed to the young man, "this gentleman is Jafr. He is here to see you." I shook Jafr's hand and we sat down. Jafr took a deep breath. He turned to me and said nerviously, "I am here to have you accompany me to your uncle Mustafa's house."

I shook my head. "I don't know you, and I can't go with you."

"I am your husband's cosine. Your uncle has sent me here."

"Forgive me," I repeated "but I don't know you."

He reached for his packet, got out a small bag from which he removed a plastic cover that covered a stock of portraits. They were photographs taken of me and my husband at our engagement and wedding party. I was convinced, and felt comfortable with him. I went with him to Marywan.

We arrived at Marywan in the evening just before sunset. No one was home. The town was quiet. We were told that all throughout Iraq-Iran war people had been leaving their houses in the morning, for fear of bombing, and returning late in the evening.

We waited and an hour later uncle's family returned. They gave me a very warm welcome. My uncle had a very big house was full of children. Their entire block was made up of his sons and daughters. He was financially successful and very prominent in his community.

Soon after my uncle returned home and came into the living room. He rushed to me and held me in his arms. He was in his late sixties, a bit taller than average with a strong chest, a mustache, and a clean face. He looked handsome and healthy for his age.

He sat down next to his wife, Soyba, and asked me what had happened.

"It's a long story, and I don't know were to start," I said.

"I see you alone here. What about everyone else?" he asked.

"My sister Kazhal, a week before the bombing, took Chra and went to Sulaymania to see a doctor, and my brother Awat is in Mosul, as you know he is a student." I broke into tears, and my uncle held me. "And the rest are dead."

"I had feared something like that had happened, but I prayed I would hear differently," cried my uncle, tears raining from his shiny eyes.

We sat in silence for a moment, and then they reclined the sfra and we ate dinner. They served *Khoresht*, an Iranian dish of lamb and green vegetables. We were sad and quiet. I felt bad for ruining their time, thinking that on my first visit to my uncle's house I had brought them only mourning and grief.

After dinner my uncle's son Rostam showed up with his family and his two daughters with their family and other cousins. The living room was full of people, who all came and greeted me.

A housekeeper brought a huge *samovar* and served tea. My uncle asked me gently to tell everyone what had happened. I paused for a moment, not wanting to talk, not wanting to remember the calamity, and I prayed to God that I would not break down. Looking around, I realized that it would be better for me to tell it all at once instead of being asked by everyone.

As I told them the story, the entire audience sat quietly, looking disheartened and angry. I cried, afraid that I would break down, and everyone else cried with me. I told them the story as briefly as I could, and I felt I was sitting in a movie, watching the memory play out as I spoke it aloud.

"My dear," said my uncle when I had finished "you will always have a place in my house and you will stay with us. Be comforted, you would be taken care of. I wish I could bring your brother, your sister and your husband here and have them live with us."

"Thank you," I said quietly as my tears were raining.

"But tell me, how did my nephew die? What were the last words he spoke to you?"

"Uncle, after the bombing, I went around with wet towels. When I gave one to my dad, he told me that he was finished, and he told me that he loved me.". he was the first one to die.

"Oh, my God, I loved my nephew, I still have a memory of him as a child with my sister, Raena. We need divine intervention, or the same tragedy that occurred in Halabja will occur everywhere in Iran and Iraq."

We sat and talked until late into the night. My aunt showed me to my room and I went to bed. The next day we woke up early in a morning, and drove to the mountain. Whenever the Iraqi planes passed overhead we went up and hid in cave. We did that every day until the truce was declared and the fighting had stopped.

I stayed with my uncle's family. They were exceedingly compassionate and kind to me and they did everything to ease my pain. I knew they felt sorry for me, and I didn't want that, yet I could do nothing but feeling bad for what I had become.

The bombing and its evil consequences were stuck in my mind. I cried every night thinking about my sister Kazhal and my brother Awat and everyone else. I kept thinking of my cosine Shadan and wondered if she knew everyone in her family were dead, and how she would react to the news! I wondered if my sister and brother and my Uncle Nouri had been told what had happened. Who would have the courage to tell, who could go to my uncle and tell him that his wife and all of his four children were dead? Who could tell my cousin Shadan that her parents, brother, and sister were dead?

Two months later the Iraq-Iran war ended. The Iraqi government declared amnesty for all Kurds who took refuge in Iran to return. My husband showed up to see me traveling illegally from Iraq to Iran.

When he arrived, my uncle threw us a wedding party. I told my uncle that we were already married, but he told me that that was fine, and just do it again. My husband stayed for two weeks and then returned to Sulaymania. He had just graduated from collage, and accepted a job as a civil engineer.

September of 1988 I returned back to Sulaymania. Saddam's amnesty became a trap for many people. Thousands of families were sent to refugee camps allover the country, and thousands died from cold, malnutrition, and diseases. I was lucky and returned to Sulaymania safely.

I joined my sister Kazhal and my brother Awat. Mean while Iraqi intelligence learned of my husband's trip to Iran, and put him in jail. Later, when they released him, we were sent to Tikrit, Saddam's hometown, as a penalty for his illegal trip. After all that had happened to us under Saddam's rule, we were forced to go to his hometown, where people idealized and worshipped him, and where we were considered traitors and treated pariah like for not siding with him in his war against Iran.

My brother and sister didn't hear the news until two months after the fact. The bombing had continued and people were afraid to go to Halabja. There were more than five thousand dead bodies, and the Iranian army and the *peshmarga* used bulldozers to cover them in mass graves.

When I returned from Tikrit people were still trying to locate their loved-ones. I found those families whose loved-ones had been in our house during the bombing, and I told them what had happened. I told dada Rahma, Mahabad's mother, that her daughter had died in our house. She was in denial and believed her daughter was alive and well in Iran. It is a difficult reality, and her loss was too great, and she wanted to believe what she believes.

That was Roshna's story.

Roshna after her return to Sulaymania told my family that my grandfather, step grandmother, uncle, aunt and Harseny's daughter, Mahabad—had all been in her house during the bombing. Her news brought closure to the search for my grandfather's family.

Chapter Twenty-Five

At the time of the bombing of Halabja, my father's second cousin, Chnoor and her family experienced the bombing first hand. I collected her story through her sister, and this is what I gathered from her:

We knew that Halabja would be bombed as revengeful Saddam was determined to crush Iranian Ayatollahs and their allies. Exiting town was thought of but we were tricked by *peshmargas* as they told us that chemical bombing is just rumor and we sort of believed.

I'd studied physics for four years in a collage also chemistry and I studied biological warfare on my own after I graduated from college with a degree in physics. I dreaded to think about chemical and biological warfare for I realized what calamity that would bring to people as well to the environment. What bothered me the most was both Iraq and Iran had capable scientific community to produce such. While the two country were at war, I was much sure each one would produce whatever they could to win the war, after all war is about winning and one of them had to bow to the other to end the war. To me chemical and biological warfare was real. That frightened me, feared its consequences, and the worst part about it was not knowing what to do and there wasn't anything one can do to prepare for it or avoid its impact. I knew that gas mask can help but even that has its duration and couldn't completely prevent impacts.

I knew unlike nuclear war with chemical and biological warfare people can escape death and yet live painful and disabling life for years. That worried me every time I thought about it and imagining what that do to my children. It was war and all that bring people is fear of the impending tragedies. Yet I tried not to be overwhelmed with negative thinking, I imagined one day Saddam's regime will be toppled and I could see my children living in a more peaceful world. Even when I fantasize peace on a horizon I was so often destructed with horror feeling embodied in our reality.

The day of the bombing we were home and went through the horror of conventional bombing and thought that easily we could all be killed and the town could be flatten. That day toward early afternoon we sensed chemical agent in the air. Our eyes started tearing. I knew that was the chemical bombing right after our eyes started watering, I got all the towels and blankets wet and blocked off anywhere with exposure to outside such as windows and doors. Having said that our windows were all popped with the sound of the first few bombs hit the town. I and my children used wet towels to rub our faces constantly. That really saved us, but still our vision was blurred and we thought that we would all go blind. After the first bomb explosion we thought of getting out of the town, but I feared that we might be caught out in the open on our way out of the town when the planes would come back for the next round. I was afraid that the second round would be a more intensive bombing, and we wouldn't be able to make it out of the town.

That exactly what happened to many people when they tried to escape. The planes caught up with them and they were all killed, there were hundreds and hundreds of them.

The reality had hit me and woke me up. "You lady see what is happening, you all are sick and watch as you could see with your own eyes your children will die slowly and so your husband and you will be the last to go. This is going to be a tragic story with miserable ending."

I didn't want to sound defeated in a front of my children and my husband. I went to the bathroom cried "please dear God don't you let that happen. I don't want to watch my children die. Please God help us. I don't want watch my husband die."

The bombing quiet down. It was late in the evening.

Since a first round of the bombing I could hear people outside walking and crying. I thought that I had covered windows and doors and I had no strength to put them back. In a mean while I thought that I knew what was going on. People died or in pain crying and others trying to leave the town. I decided not to bother.

I looked my three years old Parwana her long blond hair was all tangled and her shiny blue eyes looked teary, tired and sleepy. Her little beautiful face was all pale, her lips all dry and walked like an old lady. I could see how this little beauty turned to a picture of sorrow to be told later if we could make it through that nasty ordeal. I knew what was wrong with her but not much I could do for her. Oh, my God how difficult is to be a mother and see the suffering of your child, I must tell you I was more than happy to give my own life just to stop her suffering, This is only for mothers to know. It was the only time in my life I regretted to be a mother. I felt bad to have given a birth to this little creature and see her going through all that. I remember when she was born, still Iraq and Iran war was under way. I was so happy when she was born as I held her between my arms and kissed her. But then I wished she wasn't born for it wasn't so easy to watch what she was going through. That is what war can do, and that was the worse scenario next to nuclear holocaust. It's a chemical and biological warfare.

Came night. It was dark and sort of quite. We had no electricity. I lighted up a couple candles. Up to that minute I didn't tell my daughters about chemical bombing and I didn't want to scare them. I knew they were sick and all I did comfort them. I saw them sick, pale and fatigue. I put them to bed and when I put Parwana in a bed she looked me with her sleepy eyes: "mom are planes coming back tomorrow?"

"Sweetheart just go sleep."

As she was laying flat on her back "but mom I am scared, planes are too loud. I hate them."

"You know mom and dad are here with you. Just say your prayer and God will make you strong not to be scared."

She rolled over "mom bombs kills people. Kill us too."

I knew she was in pain and perhaps was trying to find a comfortable position "yes it kills people but we said our prayer and God didn't let that happen."

"Mom where God lives."

"I think you are tired and you need to go sleep."

She put her right hand on her stomach "mom my tummy hearts."

"Just give it sometime, you will feel better."

I put Parwana in a bed, I thought God had made it easy for me. I was afraid if she asked some question to be related to the heart of the matter, knowing what had transpired. I mean if she knew about chemical bombing. Oh poor children they are and always the victims of adult's doing. To that end, I wondered why we had to go through all that hell. War among nations are the doing of adults not children and if adults were to care for children war would never had happened. Its so contradictory that men always want the best for their children yet they engage in war and they know for fact the children are the primary victim of such.

Then I dealt with my older daughter Pary and she was more frightened and I needed to calm her down. She was sick and knew what was going on. She ripped my heart and never forget the expression from her pale face when she told me "mom are we going to die.". "No my sweaty I pray God would not let that to happen.". It was difficult and painful to deal with the children in a situation like that.

I kept one feet with the children and another with my husband. I was sick, my stomach was killing me and had a bad headache. My vision was getting worse with the passage of every hour and couldn't see things as clear as I should. At the same time my husband's eyes was affected and complained of every symptoms that I had and plus. He was laying in bed and rolling over.

Thank God at least children felt asleep. I was worried about them and I went to check them often to see if they were alive. It was my fear that when I woke up and see them dead. At the same time I tried to comfort my husband. That was for the first day.

Then the next day we had the same fear. We couldn't go anywhere. I knew many people might have gotten hurt yet we were confined at home and too afraid to step out of the house.

We all started vomiting right after we ate anything. The food we had had been sitting in the house since before the bombing. I knew that the food had been exposed to the air and that chemicals must have gotten into the food and the food was all contaminated.

Then, after that I decided not to give my children any food, they still got sick drinking water. They got all dizzy and vomited violently. We got to the point that we thought we would all die, at some point after my husband Hamza got really sick. He was lying in bed, and I laid next to him. I had a headache that felt like a mountain was piled on my head.

"Dear, I don't think I'll make it," said my husband shakily. He was short of breath and despaired.

"Oh, no darling, we will make it, you need to hung in tough," I replied.

"I am telling you that I'm really sick. I hope you can make it to save our two children, I mean it I don't know how long I last." said Hamza.

I touched his forehead, which was as hot as fire. He was sweating and the mattress and the bed sheet had gotten soaked with sweat. During all that time I pretended to be okay even though I was sick. He got me all scared and frightened for as sick as I was I didn't know how I could handle two sick child while I wasn't well myself.

"Please get well. I know it's not easy to fight, but I am not feeling well either, but we need each other, I beg you not to give up," I said.

In middle of this conversation my daughter Pary, the six-year old came in screaming.

"What's bothering you, sweetheart?" I asked.

She put her hand on her stomach.

"Mom, it hurts here," said Pary.

I didn't know what to tell her or what to do for her. It was the poison in the air and the water. I knew that was going to happen for as long as we ate or drunk.

"So sweetie, lay next to mom, let me hold you."

She held me, and I kept her between my arms. "Tomorrow we will go out of town and see a doctor. Just be patient until tomorrow," I said.

Then Parwana, my three-year old came in and she had the same problem. That was the second day. The horrible thought came to me "what if my husband and I both died, who would take care of our children? What kind of life would they have even if they survived?"

I was sort of selfish and hopeless praying if my husband and I both died, so too would the children. I didn't want my children to be orphaned and taken care of by somebody else. I knew that was terrible thing to wish but sometimes terrible things bring out terrible wishes. I forgot all about my own suffering as I got so weak that every move was painful effort. I couldn't give up for the sake of my two children and my sick husband.

I loved my two children and I couldn't afford to lose either of them. I prayed that if anything were to happen, I wanted to die first. I just didn't want to leave with the memory of losing my children to that fatal bombing.

When the moment that I had to talk to God, I read the Qur'an and lifted my hands up, crying aloud saying, "my God, we don't deserve this, we have been a peace loving people. Why should we carry this burden? What have we done to the people who are doing this to us? What wrong the Kurds have done to these Arabs?"

I got so sick and tired that I was just about to give up. My children and Hamza fell asleep. I didn't think they were asleep; I thought that they were all dead. I got very frightened and afraid to check on them. I got braver and went check everyone and they all seemed to be alive and breathing. I woke up a couple hours later. I am not sure if I fell asleep or if I fainted.

We didn't know exactly what was going on. At last we heard people coming and going on a street. I opened the door and went out. I saw Iranian militias. One of them came to me and he spoke to me in Persian. I didn't know how to speak Farsi besides I was sick of the Iranian fanatics. I turned my back on him and went back to the house. We heard crying and screaming all around us.

It was the morning of the third day. I guessed that we could go without food and water for three days and after would be the end. I decided to do some things. I went outside and looked around and saw empty streets. I saw dead bodies in a street. I could hear army vehicles passing by the street. I stayed in a street for about fifteen minutes hoping that I would spot some one who could help. Finally I spotted several *Peshmarga.*

They got close to me and I told them we need help to get out of the town. I told them to get us a car and I would pay for it. One of them asked me to stay and he would be back with help. I went back in a house and told my husband.

No later than half an hour I heard someone knocked on the door. I went outside and saw a man with a truck. We made arrangements to be driven to Nawso an Iranian border town. I got the kids into the truck and left the house. Still I was concerned that the planes would come back and hit us and never make it. We were all sick, pale and all looked awful.

It was spring and the ground was wet; we got in the truck to drive toward the Iranian border. We went two blocks and the truck got stuck. We saw relief aid workers were coming into town, most of them volunteers. We saw dead bodies everywhere and volunteers were trying to identify dead people.

The truck got stuck in the mud, and the driver used a shovel to try to clean up around the tires and get the truck going. In the meanwhile my family and me were all coughing and our eyes were weeping. In the middle of that, I saw a little boy around five years old ran toward our truck and jump on the truck.

The child was shaking, his feet were shaking and crying like I'd never seen. He looked pale, eyes swollen, seemingly from crying and sleep depravation. I asked the little boy, "What is your name?" I asked.

His lips started trembling as he was crying "My name is Barham."

He had difficulty pronouncing his name. As sick as I was, I ignored myself and decided to take care of that child. I said to myself that although I was so worried about my children, this child once belonged to a parent and he must have no one now. Mother's fear run through me telling myself if I was not to care for this child, God would take it out on me and my children. I held Bahman and tried to comfort him. After a few minutes released him and he stood silently stirring at me.

"What happened?" I asked. My children and my husband all laid in the seats of the truck.

"My house is right there." He pointed as he was crying.

"How long do you think it will take to get the truck going?" I asked the driver.

"It will probably take about fifteen to twenty minutes. All the tires are stuck in the mud, I am trying as hard as I can to get you out of town as quick as possible," said the driver as he stopped shoveling.

I felt bad for little Barham and wanted to know why this boy had come to me. I wanted to know his story so that I could help him out.

"I'll be gone with this little boy to the house right there. I should be back soon," I said looking at Hamza and the driver. Hamza was holding the children.

"Can we go to your house?" I asked the little boy.

He nodded his head downward but he seemed not to be able to talk. I held his hand and we walked toward his house.

We arrived at the house. The house looked all right except for the windows and doors that had all popped out, just like those of every other house in Halabja.

I stepped at the house. My God, what a tragedy I saw. The entire family was dead from poison or gas. More than ten dead bodies all lay dead close to each other in their living room. Barham went over all the dead bodies, crying, "This is my mom."

That tore my heart. He walked a couple step and stood pointing with his finger.

"This is my father."

"This is my little sister Sarah."

"This is my older brother Mazen. He was in the fourth grade and he did a good painting. He wanted to draw a picture of me and mom standing next to each other."

"This is my grandfather."

"This is my grandmother. She helped my mom to make our house look good with flowers and plants."

He found another body under the collapsed windows all covered with dirt.

"This is my uncle."

Another body was next to him.

My heart was broken and I was crying. I looked the wall and saw the family photos, and some were in a floor. I thought to myself "this family was here in this house just a few days ago and now see what evil had done to them". I saw the little boy and girl laying dead next to each other.

The little boy's eyes were all red from crying and still he was crying and shaking. As I turn back the clock, even now, I can't do anything about that little boy and how he introduced me the member of his family. What a little boy...my God, and how he started those introductions. *That same boy should tell the story of Halabja. I held onto his story to describe the calamity.*

How did this kid survive, and why did God leave him all alone and separated from his family? God must have his own purpose, so what had that little boy done so wrong to earn that punishment? I thought my family had it bad, but you can always find someone to feel sorry for, no matter how bad one has it. Seeing all those dead bodies in Barham's house made me feel like I could handle no more but I knew there were many more just like that in the ruins of the town. I thought that might not be the worse, it rather just one of many.

I held Barham's hand and ran toward the truck. I was terrified and scared, and wanted out of the town as quickly as I could. Still the truck driver was working when I came back, but he thought he had it all managed. He went back into the truck and tried to drive the truck. This time he made matters even worse. The tires of the truck kept rotating and made the muddy holes even deeper. He stopped the engine and got back with the shovel and tried to cleanup and clear the way.

This is the mystery as I found later on: in so many families who were affected with the chemical bombing, like Barham's, you could find the whole family all dead except one who survived or everyone in family was all right except one who was blinded or killed.

I didn't know what to tell little Barham to comfort him, my family and I were all sick and I was crying and overwhelmed with what I had seen. Once we got the truck out of the mud, I told the truck driver, "Please, I've had enough, I can take no more. We need to get to a hospital in Iran. Please keep on going no matter what."

I watched my kids—they were all shaking and coughing so badly that I thought that their lungs would come out. My husband was lying flat in the truck. He seemed to be having hard time breathing. In the meanwhile I was holding my little daughter Pary and had Parwana lay her head on my lap. The little boy was sitting next to me. I was in pain but decided to fight it, and not let my nausea and fatigue to make me give in when I'd struggled so hard up to that minute. I promised myself that I wouldn't let my family down.

I felt like fainting, but during the harshest moments, I kept giving myself reasons to hope and it helped me survive and keep me going on.

Once we got out of the town and got near the next village, Anab, I had some containers with me. I asked the truck driver to fill them up with water. We drove until we got near the border town of Byra and still fearful that the planes may come back, and my mind still was in Barham's house.

I could have raised that little boy and taken care of him for the rest of my life, and I knew it would be a good thing to do, but I wasn't sure what would happened to me and my family. We were all sick and I wasn't sure that we would be able to get healthy again. Little Bahram told me that the day after bombing he'd stayed around his house. The poor little kid still spent the night in that same house where all the dead were lying on the floor. That same day everyone had been running out of the town and there wasn't help for anyone. I gave it some thought and I finally said to myself that while my family's health and mine were all in jeopardy, I shouldn't let this kid stay with us. I couldn't take care of myself and my family, so how I could take care of him?

It was a heartbreaking decision to make. My heart dropped when we stopped at the town of Byra and I handed him over to the *peshmargas* there. They were taking displaced and missing children. God, I cried and felt guilty.

So as I tell you this story, years later, I must admit that I fear something bad may happen to me because I let that little boy go for my uncertain destiny. Now and then still the picture of Bahram flashes in my memory and I regret not taking him with us and raising him. It's sad, but when calamity hits, it's not only its immediate impact, but its implications and its consequences that stay with us. The feelings of anger and guilt haunt so many as long as we live. I have framed the picture of that little boy and his misery in my heart, the picture of him when first I saw him shaking and crying. My God, how could I do any less unless I was a heartless being?

We left Byra after we left Bahram there. Before I left, I'd kissed him and hugged him, and told him that we needed to leave him in Byra, and he would be taken care of. I told him that if I happened to be well when I came back, I would have him come live with us. Barham looked disappointed and cried. I cried with him and it broke my heart see that little boy left uncared for. I have seen so many tragedies in my life but this little boy's event was the most tragic.

We got to Nawsor, an Iranian town about an hour away from Iraq-Iran border. We went to the hospital and they admitted all of us. I told the hospital that we hadn't eaten for days, and the first thing they did was feed us. Then they took us to the hospital beds. Our beds were all near each other. A doctor came and examined each one of us.

Once we checked into the hospital, we found that most of the patients in the hospital were from Halabja. It was packed with patients. Most of these patients were blind and some others had illnesses that the doctors had difficulties diagnosing.

We were all treated and got much better after a few days, but still had symptoms of nerve damage and respiratory disease.

So many people were unconscious at the time they were taken from Halabja, and these people didn't know what had happened to their immediate families. I had my little daughter in the bed, and a lady nearby woke up and didn't know where she was. She came to me, crying for her daughter.

"This girl lying on that bed is my daughter," she said.

"No ma'am, she is my daughter," I said.

"Can I check her because she is my daughter," she persisted.

My daughter had the covers over half of her face. I took the covers off her face, and she looked at her and knew it wasn't her daughter. She cried and asked about her daughter. She wasn't the only one. People kept coming and asking me about their son, or their husband or their daughter.... Many of these people had woken as if from a nightmare and didn't know what happened to anyone they knew.

After we got treated and felt better, we let out of the hospital and send to the refugee camp nearby. We lived in a tent there for about two month. Once the Iraq-Iran war ended we returned to Iraq.

In Iraq they send us to the refugee camp. They forced us to stay there for months and after that they send us to Basra. Our story didn't end with the bombing of Halabja. We lost everything and left destitute.

During the bombing I was confined at home, and when I went out of the house, I rushed to leave the town. I knew horrible things had happened there, but I didn't learn the full extent of it until later.

Epilogue

I have taken you on a journey to my hometown, opening a window onto the Kurdistan of the past. I've described the rhythm of life prior to the Kurdish revolution in 1961 as peaceful, where harmony and tranquility flourished in that little town, Halabja. The revolution was our struggle for freedom. But the ideals of freedom and democracy meant nothing to the evil occupying forces in the Middle East, who savagely fought against us Kurds to ensure that we would continue to be deprived of our freedom.

This resulted in one tragedy after another, until the tragedies became calamities. My hometown did not suffer alone, as significant portions of Kurdistan endured similar atrocities committed by the Turks, the Arabs, and the Persians throughout centuries of occupation.

Saddam wasn't the only barbarian in power; in fact, all the ruling authorities, from Saddam's predecessors to Iranian and Syrian rulers, marginalized and demonized the Kurds, and stood by watching as Saddam and Turkish authorities committed genocide against us.

I've shared heartbreaking stories and first-hand accounts of tragic events from my personal history as a little child growing up in Halabja. When I left my hometown as a teenager, things only worsened and the tragedies continued to multiply.

Interestingly enough, these calamitous events occurred in the same time period that our occupiers were cutting deals with several world superpowers, including the United States. The atrocities kept intensifying until torture escalated into genocide, yet our cries for help and justice were ignored by a world where corporate interest supplanted human rights.

Today, two decades after the gassing and chemical bombing of Halabja, the town has become a common place for incurable diseases, unknown in the scientific community, and claims the title of world capital for birth defects.

About a week before the bombing of Halabja, I prepared a parcel to send home, with some pictures of my family in the United States. I managed to send the parcel to an acquaintance in Europe to hand deliver to my parents, which was less risky than delivering by mail. Knowing how precious that parcel would be to my family filled me with pride and happiness. I imagined how my father would react and how joyous my grandparents would be to see my little ones for the first time.

I loved my little town, and it was my dream that I could visit it again and see my old friends, with whom I had attended school all the way from grade school through my high school years. I wanted my children to see that little town and get a feeling for Kurdish culture as it flourished in the Garden of the Poets. I wanted my hometown to provide my children with an awareness of their forefathers and a new sense of the man their father had become in the place where he was at his best, in the heart of the country and people of Kurdistan.

Years after the day of the bombing, I received a letter from my brother, who'd ended up in Germany. He sent me a long list of the people who had been killed, and informed me that my Aunt Mahsoom had finally been able to verify the death of my grandparents. At the time, I already knew that my dad had been blinded.

I thought of the timing of the bombing. It had occurred just a few days before my parents would receive my parcel if it wasn't for the bombing. The bombing left my father blind, ensuring that he will never know what his grandchildren look like. My grandparents are both dead, and my children will never get to see them. As for my hometown, it has become a ghost town with ruins standing as towers of tragedy, its people fearful and saddened. They have not seen any redress for the tragedies they've endured. In that same town where I knew almost everyone as a child, I would now forever be a stranger when I visited.

I'm still hopeful that one day my people will be free, and that my family can travel to a new Kurdistan: a free and sovereign country with a dawn of freedom to mark the beginning of a new age and the end of the dark days of occupation. When that day comes, I will rejoice in such freedom, knowing that all the sacrifices and suffering of my generation and our forefathers paved the way for the freedom and well-being of our children and the generations to come. That is the testament of my people and the proclamation of truth so deeply rooted in our hearts and so indelibly imprinted on our minds. .